"Larson makes clear how inseparable were the concepts of freedom and bondage in these early years, and thereby makes understandable why the contradictions they created have so long vexed us."

—H. W. Brands, author of *Our First Civil War*

"Larson has brought a true historian's sensibility to the fierce new debate over slavery at the founding. *American Inheritance* unearths a legacy of unexpected ironies, terrible tragedies, and fateful opportunities—a legacy with which Americans still struggle today."

—John Fabian Witt, author of *Lincoln's Code*

"A master storyteller and meticulous analyst, Larson offers a wise and balanced account of the founding era's thorniest themes: liberty, equality, slavery, and race. Larson's trademark blend of deep erudition and easygoing prose animates every page of this instant classic."

—Akhil Reed Amar, author of *The Words That Made Us*

American Inheritance

ALSO BY EDWARD J. LARSON

Franklin & Washington: The Founding Partnership

To the Edges of the Earth: 1909, the Race for the Three Poles, and the Climax of the Age of Exploration

The Return of George Washington: Uniting the States, 1783–1789

An Empire of Ice: Scott, Shackleton, and the Heroic Age of Antarctic Science

A Magnificent Catastrophe: The Tumultuous Election of 1800, America's First Presidential Campaign

Summer for the Gods: The Scopes Trial and America's Continuing Debate over Science and Religion

Evolution: The Remarkable History of a Scientific Theory

Trial and Error: The American Controversy over Creation and Evolution

Evolution's Workshop: God and Science on the Galapagos Islands

Sex, Race, and Science: Eugenics in the Deep South

George Washington, Nationalist

The Constitutional Convention: A Narrative History from the Notes of James Madison (with Michael Winship)

On Faith and Science (with Michael Ruse)

American Inheritance

LIBERTY AND SLAVERY IN THE BIRTH OF A NATION, 1765–1795

EDWARD J. LARSON

W. W. NORTON & COMPANY
Celebrating a Century of Independent Publishing

For information about permission to reproduce selections from this book, write to
Permissions, W. W. Norton & Company, Inc., 500 Fifth Avenue, New York, NY 10110

For information about special discounts for bulk purchases, please contact
W. W. Norton Special Sales at specialsales@wwnorton.com or 800-233-4830

Manufacturing by Lakeside Book Company
Book design by Chris Welch
Production manager: Lauren Abbate

ISBN 978-1-324-07521-9 pbk.

W. W. Norton & Company, Inc., 500 Fifth Avenue, New York, N.Y. 10110
www.wwnorton.com

W. W. Norton & Company Ltd., 15 Carlisle Street, London W1D 3BS

1 2 3 4 5 6 7 8 9 0

CONTENTS

The role of liberty and slavery in the American Revolution is a partisan minefield. Drawing on a popular narrative presenting the expansion of liberty as a driving force in American history, some on the right dismiss the role of slavery in the founding of the republic. Appealing to a progressive narrative of economic self-interest, and racial and gender bias in American history, some on the left see the defense of state-sanctioned slavery as a cause of the Revolution and an effect of the Constitution. Public debate over the place of liberty and slavery in the Revolutionary era has opened the way for rigorous historical scholarship to examine the subject in the tradition of such time-tested classics as Edmund Morgan's 1975 *American Slavery American Freedom* and Benjamin Quarles's 1961 *The Negro in the American Revolution*.

Where Morgan focused on seventeenth-century Virginia and Quarles concentrated on Blacks in the military, this book centers on the thirty core years of the Revolutionary era, 1765 to 1795, and broadens the lens to include Blacks and whites, patriots and loyalists, politics and warfare, and all the states from New England to the lower South. Women play a central part, from the enslaved Boston poet Phillis Wheatley to Martha

Washington's runaway maid, Ona Judge. This book includes a close study of two measures related to the controversy over slavery and the Revolution: the 1772 *Somerset* legal decision and Lord Dunmore's Proclamation of 1775. *Somerset*, which held slavery to be "so odious, that nothing can be suffered to support it, but positive law," found no such law in England. Slaveholders in the American colonies, where such laws did exist, considered *Somerset* derisive and unsettling.[1] During the war, British promises of freedom for enslaved Blacks who turned against their patriot owners, which began with Dunmore, added to the outrage against imperial rule. Black Americans took their chances however they could find them— fleeing or fighting for their liberty in an era turned upside down by revolution. We can gather their thinking through the voices, among others, of Wheatley, Judge, and Benjamin Banneker, and through the actions of Crispus Attucks, the first to die in the Boston Massacre, and Harry Washington, who fled from Mount Vernon to Dunmore's banner.

The Revolutionary era changed the American understanding of liberty and slavery. Combining their rights-respecting English legal heritage with a New World sense of opportunity, political and economic liberty became the justification for independence and the founding ideal of the republic. In this context, perhaps because of their experience with race-based bondage, American patriots adopted and adapted the established metaphor of slavery used by English opponents of absolutism to express all that they abhorred about imperial rule. A lack of political agency, as the original metaphor implied to its English users, gave way in American usage to images of British bondage and brutality. "We won't be their negroes," John Adams shouted against the British during the Stamp Act crisis of 1765.[2]

Along with a sense of white liberty, Black slavery in a form unlike anything in England had emerged in Britain's North American colonies and become central to the economic, political, and social life of the southern ones from Maryland to Georgia. "Where is the difference between the British Senator who attempts to enslave his fellow subjects in America . . . and the American patriot who reduces his African Brethren to Slavery," the Philadelphia patriot and signer of the Declaration of Independence Benjamin Rush could ask, without the drafter of that document, Thomas Jefferson, ever offering a clear answer.[3] Especially in northern states, a Revolutionary era embrace of liberty fired many revivalist Protestants, principled Quakers (who had long opposed slavery on egalitarian religious grounds), and reform-minded rationalists to reject race-based slavery. More so in southern states, for slaveholders and those who did not see Blacks as sufficiently American or even fully human, the Revolutionary era emphasis on individual rights could lead to a defense of property rights in enslaved Africans.

Countless Black Americans heard the cries for liberty and acted on them. In the North, enslaved Blacks such as Felix Holbrook and freed ones like Cæsar Sarter pushed their states to live up to the promise of liberty for all. In the South, with no prospect of freedom under patriot rule, invading British armies offered a means for personal liberation. One way or another, the American Revolution resulted in the first great emancipation of enslaved Blacks in the New World, with some finding freedom under the British banner and others gaining it from a liberty-inspired retrenchment of slavery in the North. The outcome was far from uniform as northern states moved fitfully toward abolition and southern states doubled down on slavery. Daniel Payne witnessed the contradiction firsthand. Having fled George Washington's plantation when British troops invaded Virginia in 1780, Payne found freedom in British-occupied New York. He then watched from one of the last ships evacuating freed Blacks from the city as his former enslaver entered it as a liberator in 1783.

The tensions caused by differing conceptions of liberty and slavery in northern and southern states erupted at the Constitutional Convention, fractured state ratifying debates, and threatened to disrupt the first federal Congress. Southern leaders like South Carolina's C. C. Pinckney, a former Revolutionary War general and future two-time Federalist Party nominee for president, believed that these episodes left state-sanctioned slavery on a secure footing and primed for expansion westward. Others, like Virginia's Patrick Henry, feared for the future of slavery in a federal union dominated by antislavery northerners.

Building on what came before, these episodes left an enduring legacy: a distinctively American heritage of liberty and slavery—two intertwining strands of the national DNA. For all Americans living through those three decades, particularly for enslaved and free Americans of color, it became a time of promises kept and promises broken; hopes fulfilled and hopes dashed. Congress spoke to those promises in 1792, when the first law authorizing American coins decreed that each bear the singular motto "Liberty," an aspirational affirmation that survives to this day. Along with the long shadow of slavery, the promises and hopes for liberty endure, firing the struggle for an enhanced American inheritance going forward.

EJL

New Haven, Connecticut

March 14, 2022

Crèvecoeur's Question

"What Is an American?"

"In the beginning all the world was America." So wrote the gaunt, sharp-nosed English philosopher John Locke in his 1689 *Second Treatise of Government* about a place he never saw but played a major role in shaping.[1] This sentence encapsulated Locke's theory that people originally found nature vacant and uncultivated, and made it their property by occupying and improving it. Created free and equal, as Locke theorized, people later exchanged some of their natural liberty to form governments for the protection of their civil liberty and private property, which in turn upended social equality. "The natural liberty of man is to be free from any superior power on earth," he maintained. "The liberty of man, in society, is to be under no other legislative power, but that established, by consent, in the commonwealth."[2]

Locke's allusion to America drew on the view, ascendant in Britain at the time, that because Native Americans held land in common and did not improve it, Britons could make America their own through occupation and cultivation.[3] Locke knew that, because native peoples lived in America, occupying cultivators could not take it as readily as they presumably once took the original vacant earth, but the allusion worked well enough to convey meaning to Britons who saw a rare opportunity in their occupation of New World colonies. The Spanish, Portuguese, and French held similarly self-serving views about European claims to New World lands but, by giving more weight to initial "discovery" by the agent of a Christian monarch rather than occupation, and to papal sanction, they produced somewhat more multiracial societies in their colonies. Whether by "discovery" or occupation, Europeans transformed America into their property and, more controversially, by capturing Native Americans, they made them their property too. Christopher Columbus said as much about the land and its people in the diary of his first voyage to the New World, and successive generations of Europeans in America put his words into practice.[4] Doing so gave a sense of liberty (or at least empowerment) to European Americans but meant slavery for Native Americans.

An influential English Whig theorist, who like other Whigs of his era championed parliamentary supremacy over royal rule, Locke wrote his *Treatise* in opposition to the claim that God gave absolute authority to monarchs. Under his theory, at some point in the past, people voluntarily formed governments to protect life, liberty, and property. Laws "ought to be designed for no other end ultimately, but the good of the people," he declared, and governments "must not raise taxes on the property of the people, without the consent of the people, given by themselves, or their deputies."[5] Individuals cannot choose to become enslaved because it violates the natural law of liberty, Locke reasoned, and in a like manner, they have a duty to revolt against governments enslaving them by taking their property or civil liberties without consent. "The reason why men enter into society, is the preservation of their property," he wrote, and "whenever the legislators endeavour to take away, and destroy the property of the people, or to reduce them to slavery under arbitrary power, they put themselves into a state of war with the people, who are thereupon absolved from any further obedience."[6] For Locke, the term "legislators" surely included monarchs, with the absolutist, seventeenth-century British Stuart kings foremost in his mind.

From the English Civil War, which ended the life of one Stuart king, through the Glorious Revolution, which ended the reign of another, English revolutionaries and Whigs freely used "slavery" as a metaphor for a lack of political liberty or agency. Drawing on classical writings glorifying the civic virtues of late republican Rome but (unlike the Romans) usually divorced from personal experience with chattel slavery, the English portrayed it as the predictable consequence of unchecked power in the hands of state or church officials. For people genuinely held in perpetual bondage, the metaphor might seem outrageous when applied to less onerous impositions like taxation without representation. Still, it had the rhetorical force to engage listeners and potentially change the way they viewed burdens placed on them by the king or Parliament. Metaphors matter because they both convey meaning and shape understanding.

Actual slavery existed—in fact, over two million enslaved Africans had been shipped to the Americas for sale by 1700 (an estimated one-sixth of these in British ships)—and as an investor in the slave-trading Royal African Company, Locke profited from it. In his *Treatise*, Locke noted that lawful conquerors could enslave captives. He termed this "the perfect condition of slavery."[7] Further, as personal secretary to one of the founding proprietors of the Carolinas, Locke helped to draft the colony's initial 1669 constitution, which established Black slavery there by positive law. "Every freeman of Carolina," it stated, "shall have absolute power and authority over his Negro slaves."[8] Both in theory and in practice, liberty and slavery stood as polar opposites in Whig political philosophy, with the one giving meaning to the other by way of contrast. In Locke's wake, they took similar form in Revolutionary American thought with liberty as the dream and slavery the nightmare.

For Locke in the late 1600s, America offered an example of embryotic processes of political formation happening in real time. By the mid-1700s, Americans saw in his *Treatise* the sanction to take those processes to their logical ends in revolution and independence. Locke's teachings seemed clear on civil liberty, taxation without representation, and the right to revolt and form new governments. On chattel slavery, however, colonists could take what they wanted from his mixed messaging about an institution that violated natural law but could exist by statute. "Britons will never be slaves," citizens of the United Kingdom sang in the refrain of "Rule, Britannia!," a popular anthem from 1740, but those same British citizens (at least in the colonies) might enslave others.[9] Race offered a way for them to enslave others without the fear of becoming enslaved themselves.

If Britons could not become slaves, then who could? Long before Europeans reached America and for over three centuries thereafter, slavery persisted in the Western Mediterranean, which divided Christian Europe from Islamic North Africa. In that region, Christians captured and enslaved Muslims; Muslims captured and enslaved Christians; and both trafficked in Black Africans. During the late 1450s, traders from the two principal Catholic nations engaged in this process, Portugal and Spain, started shipping enslaved Blacks directly from Africa to their New World colonies. By the 1500s and operating within some religious restraints, both nations adapted this practice to their new American domains by enslaving native people. In his 1493 letter of discovery to his Spanish monarchs, Columbus offered to ship "slaves, as many as they order to be shipped and who will be from the idolaters."[10] Most of these enslaved indigenous peoples remained in America to work on colonial plantations. As they died from overwork and Old World diseases or escaped into lands still held by their people, Africans replaced them as enslaved labor. This occurred first in the Portuguese and Spanish areas of South America, then on the British, Dutch, and French islands of the Caribbean beginning in the early 1600s, and finally in British and Dutch North America by the late 1600s. Unrestrained by religion, local custom, or natural law, these European Americans created a form of chattel slavery for Blacks harsher than any known precedent.

The sheer numbers stagger the imagination. For the New World as a whole from 1500 to 1800, an estimated 2.5 million Europeans moved there by choice and 12 million Africans by force. For mainland British

North America, those numbers stood at about one-half and one-third of a million, respectively. Many in both groups died young from disease, especially early in the settlement process, but on the mainland and much more so in the Caribbean, Blacks had higher mortality rates than whites. As a result, every mainland British colony in North America except South Carolina had more free whites than enslaved Blacks—in most cases considerably more.

Black slavery in British North America began at Jamestown, Virginia, the first permanent English settlement in the New World. In 1619, as this story goes, twelve years after the founding of Virginia, privateers anchoring at a nearby port took twenty enslaved Blacks seized from a Portuguese slave ship to Jamestown for sale. Unlike the colony's first white settlers, who famously included John Smith, no one now knows the names of the first Black Virginians and none of their descendants joined the First Families of Virginia.

Slavery had died out in England by then, and at first, no laws defined the status of those enslaved in British North America. Their masters might treat them akin to indentured servants (but with fewer rights and held for life) or subject them to a perpetual bondage that carried on to descendants. That same year, 1619, Virginia received permission to form its House of Burgesses, the first self-governing legislature in the colonies. Through this body, Virginia could enact its own laws covering slavery, culminating with its comprehensive slave code of 1705. Until that occurred, those enslaved in the Virginia colony lived in a netherworld where some remained in hereditary servitude and others gained freedom for themselves or their descendants over time, through work, or with payment. A small free Black community emerged on the fringes of society. In time, similar processes took place elsewhere in British North America, resulting in a mix of enslaved and free Blacks in every colony.

The gradual nature of this process, particularly as it unfolded along the Chesapeake's Eastern Shore, where at least some free Blacks secured a measure of social status, prompted some historians to posit that chattel slavery fueled anti-Black racism rather than the reverse—that slavery was born of racism. Poor whites worked alongside enslaved Blacks in early Virginia and "there are hints that the two despised groups initially saw each other as sharing the same predicament," the eminent historian Edmund Morgan wrote in his 1975 book, *American Slavery American Freedom*. "If freemen with disappointed hopes should make common cause with slaves of desperate hopes," he noted, colonial elites had reason to fear for their property, power, and position. "The answer to the problem," Morgan asserted, "was racism, to separate dangerous free whites from dangerous slave blacks by a screen of racial contempt." Enactment of racist slave codes and legal limits on all Blacks "successfully dissociated them from whites," he argued, and consolidated Blacks "in a single pariah group." In short, Morgan wrote, the Virginia "assembly deliberately did what it could to foster the contempt of whites for blacks."[11]

A different origins story for American slavery emerged in South Carolina, where Locke's constitution anticipated African slavery. By the time of that colony's founding in 1670, Barbados had emerged as the richest and most populated British colony in the New World. Sugar and slavery were the bases of its prosperity. During the 1500s, the center of sugar production for the European market had migrated from Spanish and Portuguese islands off the African coast to Portuguese Brazil, taking Black slavery with it. Again carrying Black workers along, it expanded in the 1600s to include the West Indies, starting with British Barbados. Established in 1627 on a fertile island with few native inhabitants at the extreme southeastern end of the West Indies, the colony struggled until the introduction of sugar cane, sugar-processing technology, and enslaved Blacks from Brazil in 1640. A capital-and-labor-intensive industry with brutal work in harsh conditions, sugar production flourished on large plantations using slave labor.

During the 1660s, Barbados dealt with its influx of Black labor by adopting a series of statutes making it the first British domain anywhere to authorize chattel slavery. Enslaved Blacks and their descendants (through the mother) became the absolute and perpetual property of their masters. For Britons (who "will never be slaves") to accept these laws, they must have viewed Blacks differently from whites because no such British statutes ever applied to whites, even the much-maligned Irish, and in Barbados such laws (targeted and applied only to Blacks) appeared almost spontaneously upon the arrival of the first Black workers. In short, to paraphrase Morgan, Black Africans came to America as a pariah group: slavery did not make them one. The Irish and other Europeans might become indentured servants but never enslaved; Africans typically became enslaved rather than indentured.

All this mattered for South Carolina because, casting about for settlers to populate their new colony and hoping to create a lucrative plantation economy, its proprietors recruited British Barbadian smallholders pushed off their land by the expansion of large sugar plantations. Enticed by Locke's constitution, which assured each of them "absolute power and authority over his Negro slaves," and promises of extra land for everyone they brought, these white Barbadians began arriving in South Carolina with their enslaved Blacks and slave-code experience as early as 1680.[12] At the time, no one even knew what plantation crop could thrive in the marshy low country around Charleston. By 1690, they found it in rice, which proved as brutalizing to produce as sugar and similarly dependent on slave labor. That year, Carolina enacted a slave code modeled on Barbadian law. From South Carolina, those laws spread to other mainland colonies in the American South, including Virginia.[13]

By the Revolutionary era in America, it little mattered which came first, racism or slavery. The two existed side by side and reinforced each other. British Americans, like Britons everywhere, proclaimed that they "will never be slaves." By direct experience, they knew better than did Britons in the United Kingdom precisely what slavery meant. Yet they generally accepted it for Blacks. Indeed, returning to London from a missionary trip to Virginia and Barbados around 1670, an English minister noted that the "two words, *Negro* and *Slave*" had "by Custom grown Homogenous and Convertible" there.[14] By the start of the American Revolution, enslaved Blacks made up over one-fifth of the population in the thirteen rebel colonies. South Carolina counted three enslaved Blacks for every two free whites. In Virginia, the ratio stood at two to three. Enslaved Blacks constituted a third or more of the non–Native American population in Georgia, North Carolina, and Maryland as well. The ratio stood at over one in ten in New York, where the original patroons, drawing on the Dutch colonial experience in the Caribbean, emphasized plantation agriculture. New York had more Black residents than any other northern colony. Each colony had its own local laws authorizing and governing slavery, with those in the American South most closely following Caribbean models. From its informal beginnings at Jamestown in 1619 through its development as a fundamental component of the plantation economy in the southern colonies, African slavery had become a distinctive feature of law and society throughout British North America by the mid-1700s.

Beginning in the 1760s during the run-up to the American Revolution, in speeches, essays, promulgations, and private letters, patriot leaders demanded their liberty as British subjects while denouncing their alleged enslavement by Parliament. Although they meant these cries for white audiences, enslaved Blacks heard them too. Joined by free Blacks, they turned the rhetoric of liberty against their masters. In 1765, for example, as white colonists paraded through Charleston, South Carolina, protesting British stamp taxes with chants of "*liberty liberty*," the future Revolutionary leader Henry Laurens wrote, some enslaved Blacks turned out and "mimick'd their betters in crying out '*Liberty*'"—causing anxious civic officials to put the city under guard for a week.[15]

Many white Americans saw little connection between freedom for themselves and slavery for Blacks. "It has been, of late, a very general practice to talk of slavery among those who are setting at defiance every power that keeps the world in order," English lexicographer Samuel Johnson sneered about American patriots in 1775. "It would be vain to prohibit the use of the word *slavery*; but I wish it more discretely uttered" by those who actually practiced it.[16] Some Americans agreed. "Where is the difference between the British Senator who attempts to enslave his fellow subjects in America, by imposing Taxes upon them contrary to Law and Justice; and the American Patriot who reduces his African Brethren to Slavery, contrary to Justice and Humanity?" Philadelphia patriot Benjamin Rush asked in 1773.[17] Can we "reconcile the *exercise of* SLAVERY with *our professions of freedom?*" Quaker loyalist Richard Wells added a year later. "Can we suppose that the people of England will grant the force of our reasoning, when they are told, that *every colony* on the continent is deeply involved with the inconstant practice of *keeping their own fellow creatures* in *perpetual bondage?*"[18]

Even as the number of enslaved Africans reaching British North America surged during the three decades leading up to the American Revolution, immigrants poured into the colonies from Germany, Ireland, Scotland, and Wales. Prior to 1700, except for pockets of Dutch, French, and Swedish settlers, virtually all white colonists came from England; thereafter, especially with the 1707 Acts of Union between England and Scotland, immigration to the thirteen mainland colonies became more ethnically diverse, at least with respect to peoples of white, western European ancestry. Early in the 1770s, the French American writer J. Hector St. John de Crèvecoeur took up the new white ethnic diversity of America by posing the question, "What is an American?" His answer helps to explain the widespread disregard for the rights of Africans and African Americans, as well as Native Americans.

"He is *either* an European, or the descendant of an European; hence that strange mixture of blood, which you will find in no other country," Crèvecoeur wrote. "I could point out to you a family whose grandfather was an Englishman, whose wife was Dutch, whose son married a French woman, and whose present four sons have now four wives of different nations. He is an American, who, leaving behind him all his ancient prejudices and manners, receives new ones from the new mode of life he has embraced, the new government he obeys, and the new rank he holds."[19]

Crèvecoeur published these words in a book of letters from a fictional

Pennsylvania farmer named James to an English correspondent. Capturing the simple pleasures of life in a new land, the book became a literary classic, with these sentences as its best-known passage. Even though one letter depicted Native Americans (their numbers reduced by Old World diseases and their lives degraded by alcohol abuse) living alongside white colonists, and another letter mentioned James's own well-cared-for "negroes," Crèvecœur identified *only* Europeans and their descendants residing in the colonies as "Americans"—members of an all-white melting pot.[20] Under his definition, patriot appeals for "American" liberty and denunciations of enslaving Americans applied only to European Americans.

The affable scion of Norman nobility, Crèvecœur went to Canada as a French mapmaker and officer during the Seven Years' War (known locally as the French and Indian War) and stayed on as a farmer, writer, and surveyor in New York's Hudson River valley after France lost. With the Revolution he married into a loyalist family and had three children before returning to Europe with one son after the warfare made the borderlands between British-occupied New York City and the rebel-held upstate unsafe. Stopping in London, Crèvecœur arranged for publication of his *Letters from an American Farmer*, which made his name as a writer and led to his return to New York in 1784 as the French consul, a post he held until the revolution in France.

Reflecting a viewpoint widely shared by Enlightenment-era Europeans and Americans alike, Crèvecœur's *Letters* contrasted the liberty of ordinary Americans with the quasi-slavery of European peasants, serfs, and land-bound workers. "Here man is free as he ought to be," Crèvecœur wrote of whites in America. "We are strangers to those feudal institutions which have enslaved so many." The change came from moving to America, he exclaimed, where cheap farmland abounded. "From being the slave of some despotic prince, to become a free man, invested with lands to which every municipal blessing is annexed! What a change indeed! It is in consequence of that change that he becomes an American."[21]

Despite never having visited the American South, Crèvecœur slipped a sensational first-person account of chattel slavery in South Carolina into his *Letters*. "While all is joy, festivity and happiness in Charles-Town, would you imagine that scenes of misery overspread in the country?" he wrote in one letter about whites living in the capital of what he depicted as the richest province in North America. "Their ears by habit are become deaf, their hearts are hardened; they neither see, hear nor feel for the woes of their poor slaves, from whose painful labours all their wealth proceeds."[22]

In this and other letters, Crèvecœur contrasted the brutish life of plantation slavery in the American South with the idyllic (but also fictional) lot of enslaved Blacks in northern colonies. About his own enslaved Blacks and others like them in the North, he wrote in one letter, "In health and sickness, they are tenderly taken care of" by their masters "and are, truly speaking, a part of our families."[23] In another letter, he quotes James's wife boasting about households like hers, "Look how fat and well clad their negroes are."[24] Still, Crèvecœur did not count even these northern Blacks—whether enslaved or free—among the people that he called Americans. Indeed, as much as he might bemoan their inhumane treatment under chattel slavery in the South, he accepted the enslavement of Blacks at least in the North where, as he put it, "They participate in many of the benefits of our society without being obliged to bear *any* of its burdens," whether of citizenship or simply of being an American.[25] In short, he might extend some measure of human dignity to Blacks but not true English liberty. To Crèvecœur, they were not Americans.

In some sense, Blacks remained children in Crèvecœur's mind, happier as well-cared-for enslaved workers than if they bore the burdens of liberty. Like many white Americans of his day, Crèvecœur used the words "slave," "Black," and "Negro" interchangeably. Despite the presence of some free Blacks in their midst, they equated Blacks with slavery and slavery with Blacks. White colonists never saw themselves as enslaved, or at least not until the British government tried to tax them directly. To the contrary, their liberty made them Americans.

Something similar appears in the writings of three key Revolutionary era leaders: Benjamin Franklin, James Otis Jr., and Thomas Jefferson. Representing different backgrounds and places, all agreed in the whiteness of the American experiment in liberty. Their mention here should not single them out for censure but instead suggest the pervasiveness of their views.

Whereas his thoughts on race evolved so much that he came to favor the abolition of slavery, Franklin initially espoused an even whiter vision of Americans than Crèvecœur. "There are suppos'd to be now upwards of One Million English Souls in North-America," Franklin wrote in a widely reprinted essay first published in 1755. "Why should the Palatine [German] Boors be suffered to swarm into our Settlements, and by herding together establish their Language and Manners to the Exclusion of ours? Why should Pennsylvania, founded by the English, become a Colony of *Aliens*, who will shortly be so numerous as to Germanize us instead of our Anglifying them?" Turning from culture to race, he added, "All Africa is black or tawny. Asia chiefly tawny. [Native] America (exclusive of the new Comers) wholly so. And in Europe, the Spaniards, Italians, French, Russians and Swedes, are generally of what we call a swarthy Complexion; as are [most] Germans." Positing that only the British and the Saxon were truly white, Franklin asked, "Why increase the Sons of Africa, by Planting them in America, where we have so fair an Opportunity, by excluding all Blacks and [non-native] Tawneys, of increasing the lovely White and Red?"[26] By Red, he meant the native peoples.

During the run-up to the American Revolution, in one of the most influential and often republished patriot pamphlets of the era, Boston lawyer and politician James Otis Jr. followed Franklin in equating Americans with white colonists of British stock. Britain's North American colonies, he stressed, "are well settled, not as the common people of *England* foolishly imagine, with a compound mongrel mixture of *English*, *Indian*, and *Negro*, but with freeborn *British white* subjects."[27] Otis's comment was truer of late-eighteenth-century Massachusetts, which had the lowest percentage on non-English residents of any large colony, than elsewhere in British America, but even Massachusetts had over four thousand Blacks and a residual population of Native Americans. Other colonies had considerably more of both groups, and Otis knew it. Indeed, in the same pamphlet, the liberty-loving Otis declared that enslaved Blacks have "the same right to freedom and the sweet enjoyment of liberty and life as their unrelenting taskmasters," but that did not make them Americans.[28]

In his 1785 book, *Notes on the State of Virginia*, Jefferson expressed similar sentiments about the race and ethnicity of the American people as Franklin and Otis. Widely quoted, this book presented the new republic as rooted in the concept of liberty and its creed as "a composition of the freest principles of the English constitution, with others derived from natural right and natural reason." Much as Franklin had expressed alarm about non-English immigrants disrupting the American experiment in liberty, so Jefferson worried about the impact of "foreigners" generally— by which he meant those not raised within the Anglo-American tradition. "Suppose 20 millions of republican Americans thrown all of a sudden into [absolutist] France, what would be the condition of that kingdom?" he asked. "If it would be more turbulent, less happy, less strong, we may believe that the addition of half a million of foreigners to our present numbers would produce a similar effect here."[29]

If Jefferson saw British Americans as a people of liberty, then what about the half million enslaved Africans living among them? "Many of their advocates, while they wish to vindicate the liberty of human nature, are anxious also to preserve its dignity and beauty," he wrote. This left those advocates with two logical choices according to Jefferson: *either* countenance the continuance of slavery and invite the "wrath" of a just God *or* "emancipate all slaves" and colonize them "beyond the reach of mixture" with whites.[30] Jefferson rested this conclusion on the premise, which he in turn based on supposedly objective observations, "that the blacks . . . are inferior to the whites in the endowments both of body and mind."[31] As such, he found them incapable of liberty on a par with whites.

Without accepting the inferiority of their race, given their treatment some Blacks did feel like aliens in America. "We have . . . No Country!" a Black petitioner named Felix exclaimed on behalf of "many Slaves" to the Massachusetts legislature in 1773.[32] In her Revolutionary era writing, enslaved Boston poet Phillis Wheatley regularly referred to herself as an African or Ethiopian rather than as an American. In one poem, for example, she wrote of the British evangelist George Whitefield preaching in America to "Americans" and "Africans."[33] In another poem, she wrote of "English blood" flowing in American veins.[34] "'Twas mercy brought me from my *Pagan* land," Wheatley wrote of her passage to America that led to her Christian conversion, yet here and elsewhere, she referred to Africa, not America, as "my" land or country.[35] Even when embracing American ways, Wheatley recognized her outcast status. In a similar manner, in their narratives as Blacks once enslaved in America and living as free persons in Britain by the 1770s, James Albert Ukawsaw Gronniosaw and Olaudah Equiano referred to Africans in Africa, not the white people of America or Britain, as their "countrymen."[36]

At once the culmination of colonial times and a beginning for antebellum America, the Revolutionary era built on old ways of thinking even as it forged new ones. Like many people of that era, Crèvecœur, Franklin, Otis, and Jefferson struggled to reconcile the promise of liberty for Americans with the reality of slavery for Blacks. One resolution lay in limiting the definition of Americans along racial lines to include only those of English, British, or European ancestry (or at least to exclude Blacks). Thus Crèvecœur could say of Americans, "They are a mixture of English, Scotch, Irish, French, Dutch, Germans, and Swedes. From this promiscuous breed, that race now called Americans have arisen."[37] A French immigrant living in a formerly Dutch county of a British colony, he saw people much like himself as true Americans and projected their image on the face of liberty. Africans were enslaved.

Another resolution lay in extending the principle of liberty to include Blacks in America, which gained impetus during the Revolutionary era mainly in the North, where it drew in the likes of Franklin and Otis, and gained under a program of gradual emancipation in most northern states. As principles or practices deeply rooted in every British American colony, however, liberty and slavery were conjoined at the nation's birth and remained so through the Civil War era, particularly in the southern states. As such, they continued as critical and often divisive components of American politics, culture, and society well into the nineteenth century. The shadow of slavery has hung over the United States ever since. Despite the opposing meanings of those words, the American Revolution and the new American nation became less about liberty or slavery than about liberty and slavery.

CHAPTER ONE

"A Rabble of Negros &c."

The First Shots for Liberty, 1770

"I heard a Bell ring, upon which I ran toward the Town house," Bostonian Robert Goddard testified following the massacre on March 5, 1770. "I went & stood near the Centry Box by the Custom house; I saw an Officer come toward the Box, with a party of Men, having a drawn Sword in his hand heard him frequently repeat 'Clear the way.'"[1] The officer was Captain Thomas Preston, then serving with one of two regular British army regiments stationed in Boston. His party consisted of some seven armed British soldiers dispatched to protect a lone British sentry, Private Hugh White, besieged by rowdy boys and men outside the Custom House on Boston's King Street.

"The Party then drew up near where the Centinel stood, and [Preston] order'd his men to stand with their Bayonets charg'd," Goddard noted. After quoting Preston as ordering the taunting crowd to "stand off," this witness added, "A sailor then struck the Officer, upon which he said 'damn you I will not be us'd in such a manner' immediately he said Fire, upon which the Soldiers stood for a short space. The officer then said 'Damn your Blood Fire.'" At first one, and then more soldiers discharged their muskets, Goddard testified, after which he "saw four men laying on the ground one of which was the deceas'd Crispus Attucks."[2] Several witnesses depicted Attucks as the first to fall, and two portrayed him as leading a party of sailors near the scene. One witness, but not Goddard, had Attucks striking at Preston.[3] In all, three civilians died on the spot and two later of their wounds. Musket balls struck six more. No soldier suffered grave injury.

In a page-long article denouncing the episode as a "horrid Massacre," the partisan, pro-patriot *Boston-Gazette* identified Attucks as a "mulatto" sailor "who was born in Framingham, [Massachusetts,] but lately belonged to New-Providence [Bahamas] and was here in order to go to North Carolina." Calling him a "stranger" to Boston, the newspaper reported that Attucks died instantly with "two balls entering his breast, one of them in special goring the right lobe of the lungs, and a great part of the liver most horribly."[4] An earlier article in the *Boston Chronicle* had misidentified him as Michael Johnson, apparently because, as a fugitive from slavery serving as a free sailor, Attucks sometimes used that alias.[5] Later accounts described him as part African and part Native American, roughly forty-six years old with a stout or imposing build, and over six feet tall.[6]

The *Gazette* depicted the massacre as the climax of several days of rising tensions between off-duty soldiers and young local workers.[7] A foot of snow blanketed Boston that evening and a waxing quarter-moon illuminated the surface with a silvery sheen. Following various skirmishes, the errant ringing of a fire bell drew a mixed-race crowd to the Custom House around nine o'clock. Some in the throng began hurling insults and snowballs at the lone sentry.[8] More snowballs and ice chucks greeted Preston and his men when they arrived, and perhaps sticks and stones as well. Depending on which eyewitness one believed, Attucks either charged the soldiers or stood to one side leaning on a stick.

No one ever ascertained why Attucks joined those at the Custom House that evening. Witnesses reported seeing him leave dinner as the commotion outside grew, brandish a club-like stick of cordwood, and lead a menacing party of sailors. Over a century later at the dedication of a monument to those killed in the massacre, historian John Fiske simply said of Attucks and his part in the events of March 5, 1770, "From this time until independence was won, there was hardly a struggle in which brave men of his race and color did not nobly acquit themselves."[9] This much was true, and Fiske stated it well without committing to Attucks's role in the massacre. Attucks could have been a Revolutionary leader who died in the defense of liberty; he could have been a large and looming participant targeted for his race; or he simply could have been in the wrong place at the wrong time when the shooting started.

Attucks left no written record. One African sailor working on American merchant ships plying the same waters at the same time as Attucks, Olaudah Equiano, wrote a memoir that showed how zealously an enslaved Black could embrace the cause of liberty. Claiming to have been born free, as Attucks may have been, Equiano became the enslaved servant of a Philadelphia ship owner. After seeing and suffering the immense cruelties of slavery in the British Caribbean and American South, through remarkable personal effort Equiano purchased his own freedom from his Quaker owner in the late 1760s, shortly before Attucks died. "I, who had been a slave in the morning, trembling at the will of another, was become my own master, and completely free," he wrote of his manumission. "I thought this was the happiest day I had ever experienced." While questions surround some aspects of his memoir, none relate to the author's desire for liberty. In his account, Equiano used the word over twenty times, including declaring his "love of liberty" and that to him, "life had lost its relish when liberty was gone."[10] Perhaps Attucks had a similar love of liberty—many Revolutionary era African Americans did.

Even though the violence outside the Custom House quickly subsided after the soldiers returned to their barracks and acting Massachusetts governor Thomas Hutchinson used promises of prosecutions to induce townspeople to disperse, the Boston Massacre later gained significance as a pivotal event in the run-up to the American Revolution. The British troops triggering the massacre had arrived in Boston eighteen months earlier to enforce the Townshend Act, which the British Parliament enacted in 1767 to raise revenue through tariffs on imports into the American colonies. Although these tariffs fell solely on colonists and thereby triggered their objections to taxation without representation, Chancellor of the Exchequer Charles Townshend had proposed them as external taxes paid upon the arrival of goods into the colonies rather than internal taxes on goods produced there.

The Townshend Duties replaced internal stamp taxes levied by Parliament in 1765 on printed, legal, and business documents produced only in the colonies. These caused so much unified and at times violent opposition that Parliament quickly repealed them. Resistance focused on taxes imposed without the direct or indirect consent of anyone paying them. Even though colonists lacked representation in the House of Commons, a general tax levied by Parliament on all British subjects at least carried the assent of representatives for some people paying it, whose interests stood in for others. Absent even this form of indirect representation, colonists feared that Parliament could freely take any of their property and thereby effectively enslave them. These fears spawned a militant reaction in Boston, leading to the forming of the Sons of Liberty resistance group there, and spread through Committees of Correspondence to other colonies. Non-importation agreements served as the opposition's main tool. Dwarfing any revenue raised by taxing colonists, the money flowing to Britain through trade with the colonies served as the foundation and justification for empire. By hobbling trade, colonial boycotts of British imports could affect policy.

No taxation without representation had been the cry against the Stamp Act, and it became so again against the Townshend Act, with Boston the seat of greatest resistance on both occasions. Indeed, mobs attacked the homes of Hutchinson and his brother-in-law, the colony's stamp agent, during Stamp Act riots in 1765. After those riots, when members of Parliament asked Benjamin Franklin, the agent for Massachusetts and several other colonies in London, about sending troops to enforce the Stamp Act, he replied, "They will not find a rebellion; they may indeed make one."[11] In 1770, having sent troops two years earlier to enforce the Townshend Act—four regiments at first, reduced to two in 1769—Parliament learned the wisdom of Franklin's comment.

The rebellion did not begin immediately, of course, but the presence of British troops contributed to a rebellious ill will between Bostonians and imperial officials. A standing army of twelve hundred in a city of sixteen thousand could do little to collect taxes and much to alienate citizens, especially because soldiers from both regiments, some with families in tow, lived in tents, rented houses, and temporary barracks scattered throughout the tightly packed urban area. "Soldiers quartered in a populous town, will always occasion two mobs, where they prevent one," John Adams said of the face-off. "They are wretched conservators of the peace!"[12] Even General Thomas Gage, the commander in chief of British forces in North America and an early advocate of using soldiers to enforce the law, came to realize the futility of that effort. "The People were as Lawless and Licentious after the Troops arrived, as they were before," he reported to his superiors in London. "The Soldiers were either to suffer ill usage and even assaults upon their Persons till their Lives were in Danger, or by resisting and defending themselves, to run almost a Certainty of suffering by the Law."[13] Taxes were bad enough. Using troops as tax collectors made matters worse.

In response first to the Stamp Act and then to the Townshend Act, Bostonians proclaimed their "liberty" at risk and warned of becoming "slaves" to Britain. "Our fore fathers came over here for liberty," John Adams railed against the Stamp Act in a 1765 newspaper essay that used common racist perceptions of Africans as enslaved to rally the opposition. "Providence never designed us for negroes, I know, for if it had it wou'd have given us black hides, and thick lips, and flat noses, and short woolly hair, which it han't done, and therefore never intended us for slaves."[14] Upon passage of the Townshend Act, his cousin Samuel Adams (who then served as the de facto leader of the Sons of Liberty) added in a 1767 open letter to Britain, "Slavery, my dear mother, we cannot think of: we detest it. If this be a crime, remember we suck'd it with your milk.

We boast of our freedom, and we have your example for it."[15] Having an enslaved person (even a fugitive one) die among the first martyrs to the cause could underscore the trope or, as the property of a colonist, undermine it. This tension soon became clear.

Boston had not even buried its dead before each side raced to put its own spin on the story. Already organized to resist the Stamp and Townshend Acts and firmly in control of the town government, local opponents of British imperial policy seized the initiative by gathering, publishing, and distributing a damning collection of ninety-six depositions from witnesses depicting a planned assault on townspeople, with only public restraint averting greater bloodshed. Defiantly titled *A Short Narrative of The horrid Massacre*, the pamphlet featured a blistering introduction placing full blame on the troops. Boston sent copies to nearby towns, other colonies, and London, where it fed into English Whig conspiracy theories of royalist plots to gain absolute power. Two Boston newspapers printed similar accounts. All three portrayed the "mulatto" Crispus Attucks as an innocent victim.[16] In a like manner, the report issued by the county coroner's jury on March 6 found that Attucks "was willfully and feloniously murdered . . . by a party of Soldiers to us unknown then and there headed by Captain Thomas Preston."[17] The resulting grand jury indictment charged that Preston and eight soldiers identified as with him, "being moved and seduced by the Instigation of the devil and their own wicked hearts, did . . . wilfully and of their malice aforethought assault one Crispus Attucks, then and there being in the peace of God."[18] The town took all nine into custody for trial by a local jury.

While these initial reports name all the victims, they only provide details about the deaths of two, Attucks and Samuel Gray. Those shootings stood out to witnesses, with some suggesting that the two men died first, and perhaps in targeted killings. "*The Captain then spoke distinctly, Fire, Fire!*" one witness testified. "I saw the Mulatto fall, and [as] Mr. Samuel Gray went back to look at him, one of the soldiers, at the distance of about four or five yards, *pointed his piece directly for the said Gray's head and fired*. Mr. Gray, after struggling, turned himself right round upon his heel and fell dead."[19] None of these depositions gave a reason for targeting Attucks, leaving readers free to speculate about a racist motive. In contrast, some of them had Gray among a group of young workers taunting off-duty soldiers during the days leading up to the massacre.

Led by Hutchinson, loyalists countered with a pamphlet of their own, *A Fair Account of the Late Unhappy Disturbance*. The title reflected the text: "fair" coverage, the authors opined, of an "unfortunate transaction." The pamphlet contained twenty-five depositions, all but five from British soldiers, and a cocksure introduction portraying townspeople as intentionally inciting a violent response from "ill-treated" troops, who acted strictly in "self-defense." In this loyalist account, the cry "Fire, and be damned," came from the crowd rather than Preston, who did all he could to restrain his men, and the first shot came from a soldier violently struck and made to stagger by a stick or chuck of hurled ice. The crowd became a "mob" and the victims nameless. Instead of appearing as a mixed-race person targeted for violence, Crispus Attucks vanished from the story.[20]

Without downplaying the violence, patriots also began altering the role ascribed to Attucks in the massacre. Within weeks of the event, the *Gazette*'s partisan account resurfaced in a broadside illustrated with an engraving by patriot silversmith Paul Revere that soon became the definitive visual depiction of the massacre. It shows soldiers with raised muskets purposely firing on unarmed citizens at close range upon an officer's command. All those pictured as dead or dying, which according to the article included Attucks, were white. No dark-skinned civilians appeared in this historically significant rendering of the event. Because the article plainly stated Attucks's race, Revere clearly chose to change it. Indeed, the dead appeared as random white victims of British violence.[21] In an elaborate public ceremony, Boston buried them as such in a common vault and, until the United States gained independence in 1783, commemorated the massacre with annual orations, only one of which named Attucks, and even this one, delivered by John Hancock in 1774, did not state his race. Like Samuel Adams, Revere and all of the early Boston Massacre orators including Hancock were prominent members of the Sons of Liberty.[22]

Thereafter, Attucks largely disappeared from published accounts of the massacre until around 1850, when the African American abolitionist William Cooper Nell rescued him from obscurity in service of pre–Civil War pleas for Black rights. "Colored Americans have ever been ready to worship at Freedom's shrine," Nell wrote in a typical passage. "The first martyr in the American Revolution was a colored man by the name of Attacks, who fell in King street, Boston."[23] Following Nell's lead, other abolitionists and some mainstream historians began citing Attucks to such an extent that he became a fixture in accounts of the Boston Massacre and the American Revolution. These new histories typically presented Attucks as Black rather than mixed-race and said little about his actual part in the episode other than his death by British musket fire.[24] Yet his prior treatment showed how Americans could airbrush race from the struggle for liberty.

Between his death as the mixed-race victim of British oppression and his resurrection as an African American hero, Attucks briefly played a racially defined role in the run-up to revolution before virtually disappearing from history for seven decades. By establishing the narrative that a horrid massacre had occurred in Boston, town leaders won the battle for public opinion locally, in the colonies, and to an extent in Britain. In a July 1770 letter to Franklin, eight of them, including Hancock and Samuel Adams, boasted of Boston's success in "preventing the Odium being cast on the Inhabitants, as the aggressors."[25] Most critical to this success, all the dead were townspeople and their bodies all but proved the crime. Revere's print added graphic detail. With Massachusetts aroused to a fever pitch and enmity rising elsewhere, Britain could either double down or retreat. "Measures more forceful must be taken," General Gage advised, or a total withdrawal effected.[26] British officials opted to move the troops from Boston to an offshore fort within days of the massacre and dispatched one regiment to New Jersey two months later. Further, news soon reached the colonies that Parliament had repealed most of the Townshend Duties in April 1770. As tensions cooled, the question arose about what Boston should do with the jailed officer and soldiers awaiting trial for the killings. The answer converted Attucks from victim to villain.

The trials began in October, long after both regiments had left Boston and most of the Townshend Duties had ended. Captain Preston was tried first and singly, with a joint trial of the eight soldiers to follow. By this time, town leaders had received letters from supporters in London urging them that, having won the battle for public opinion and secured their objective regarding troops and tariffs, they should not provoke Parliament by treating the accused harshly or conducting unfair trials.[27] John Adams and Josiah Quincy II, two of Boston's ablest young lawyers and patriot leaders, agreed to take the other side by defending Preston and the soldiers. "Above all," historian Serena Zabin notes, "Bostonians wanted to look moderate, fair, and high-minded."[28] Adams and Quincy would play their part.[29]

Preston's six-day trial turned on whether he had ordered his men to fire. Each side called twenty-three witnesses. Four declared that Preston definitely gave the order to fire, more testified that he definitely did not, and most said they did not know. No one in the courtroom or ever after could know for sure, and so Preston walked.[30]

Following Preston's acquittal, the soldiers could not effectively plead that they were simply following orders. Clearly some of them fired into the crowd—with the testimony suggesting that all but one of the eight had done so, but none more than once. Yet, somehow, musket balls hit eleven different people, two of them twice, and several shots missed. If the assailants acted as a group, then British law held them all liable regardless of who actually fired the fatal shots. The judges, however, all but instructed jurors to convict only those soldiers proven to have killed someone, and even then only if they had not acted in self-defense. Because everyone knew that the crowd assaulted the soldiers, the questions became, did the evidence tie any distinct death to any specific soldier and, if so, had that soldier reasonably acted "for the preservation of his own life."[31] These instructions advantaged the defense.

Between them, during the course of the soldiers' eight-day trial, the prosecution and defense called eighty-five witnesses. Most offered new testimony about what had happened. Taken together, that evidence credibly linked specific defendants to only the initial two deaths: Hugh Montgomery shot Attucks first; then Matthew Kilroy killed Gray. After those seemingly deliberate shootings, chaos descended on the scene, with random individuals felled by a brief flurry of shots—some possibly coming from unknown shooters within the Custom House. This testimony left the other soldiers relatively safe from a risk of conviction for specific deaths. Adams focused his courtroom arguments on defending Montgomery by maligning Attucks. In doing so, he manipulated the evidence in racist ways.

Attucks served Adams's purposes. At the time, white people in colonial Massachusetts still enslaved Blacks and, although Attucks had escaped bondage years earlier, at law he likely remained enslaved. Further, even free Blacks in the colony lacked basic rights held by whites, such as the rights to vote, hold public office, or serve in the militia. Finally, nonresident sailors (or "Jack Tars") aroused suspicion as untrustworthy transients, and Attucks was one. In all prior testimony and depositions, including those published in the initial pamphlet wars, no witness had placed Attucks in a threatening or hostile position at the massacre site. A few, however, recalled seeing him in the crowd at the Custom House, and two had him leading a group of sailors up nearby Cornhill Road from Dock Square shortly before the shootings.

At both trials, however, an enslaved Black man named Andrew gave vivid testimony about Attucks rushing forward "with a long cord wood stick" to strike at Preston and Montgomery, grabbing Montgomery's bayonet, and crying out, "Kill the dogs, knock them over." Then came the fatal shot.[32] Adams chose to rely heavily on this account even though no other evidence supported it and no one, not even Andrew, spoke of

Attucks leading sailors in a physical assault of anyone. "Unless all the other Witnesses were Stone-blind, or deprived of their Senses," the town counsel countered, Andrew's account "never had existence but in his own brain."[33] Called before the court to vouch for Andrew's credibility, his owner described him as "a fellow of a lively imagination."[34]

Adams built his defense by merging Andrew's testimony of what happened at the Custom House into a single story with that of two witnesses who saw Attucks leading sailors up Cornhill. Knowing that published reports of his arguments would reach far beyond the jury box, Adams wanted to defend his clients from murder charges in the court of law, and Boston in the court of public opinion from accusations that it had come under mob rule.[35] To his end, Adams needed enough mob action to justify the soldiers' responses but not so much as to discredit Boston.

"'Saw the Molatto seven or eight minutes before the firing, at the head of twenty or thirty sailors in *Corn-hill*, and he had a large cordwood stick,'" Adams quoted witness James Bailey as saying. "So that this *Attucks*, by this testimony of *Bailey* compared with that of *Andrew*, and some others, appears to have undertaken to be the hero of the night; and to lead this army with banners, to form them in the first place in *Dock square*, and march them up to *King-street*, with their clubs." Bailey had said nothing about banners, however, or that the group reached King Street. Further, Adams's own notes of Bailey's testimony confirmed, "It was not the Mollato that struck Montgomery." Yet Adams proceeded to say, "*Attucks* with his myrmidons comes round *Jockson's* corner, and down to the party by the Sentry-box." To this point, Adams depicted the troops as restrained. "Now to have this reinforcement coming down under the command of a stout Molatto fellow, whose very looks, was enough to terrify any person, what had not the soldiers then to fear?" Adams asked in reference to Attucks. "He had the hardiness enough to fall in upon them, and with one hand took hold of a bayonet." Here Adams reached his crescendo, "This was the behaviour of *Attucks*;—to whose mad behaviour, in all probability, the dreadful carnage of that night, is chiefly to be ascribed."[36]

Adams did not blame Attucks alone, but also the sailors he led and the mixed crowd he joined. Those club-wielding sailors could have killed all the soldiers, Adams declared. "Would it have been a prudent resolution in them, or in any body in their situation, to have stood still, to see if the sailors would knock their brains out, or not?" Without any testimony about their race, Adams depicted the sailors led by Attucks as "a rabble of Negros, &c." As for the crowd they joined, Adams dismissed it as "a motley rabble of saucy boys, negroes and molattoes, Irish teagues and out landish jack tarrs.—And why we should scruple to call such a set of a people a mob, I can't conceive, unless the name is too respectable for them."[37] None of the 222 different witnesses testifying about the massacre characterized the racial composition of participants in this way. Quite to the contrary, Attucks seemed to stand out in the crowd because of his dark skin.

But the *people* of Boston were not a mob, nor was the city under mob rule, Adams stressed. "The sun is not about to stand still or go out, nor the rivers to dry up because there was a mob in *Boston* on the 5th of *March* that attached a party of soldiers," he said. "Such things are not new in the world, nor in the British dominions, though they are comparatively, rareties and novelties in this town." Some black, brown, and Irish residents and sailors had rioted on March 5, Adams conceded, but no one should "ascribe all their doings to the good people of the town."[38] With these words, Adams did not simply remove people of color from the parade of American liberty; he portrayed them as impeding it.

As presented by the two defense attorneys, both prominent members of the Sons of Liberty, just and merciful jury verdicts should happily resolve the case.[39] In accord with instructions from the court, the jurors acquitted six of the soldiers and convicted Montgomery and Kilroy on the lesser charge of manslaughter.[40] The court then granted clemency to the two convicts as first-time offenders, and all eight soldiers left Boston to join their long-departed regiment.

A political crime with a political resolution, the Boston Massacre continued to play an outsized part in Revolutionary era politics. Although Bostonians acquiesced in the verdicts with little complaint, only months after the trials ended they began marking anniversaries of the massacre with popular public orations highlighting the price of liberty and the peril of slavery. Calling himself "an *American* Son of Liberty of true charter-principles," for example, the principal speaker at the first annual oration, Boston educator James Lovell, warned, "We are SLAVES 'till we obtain such *redress* thro' the justice of our KING as our happy *constitution leads us to expect*."[41] Another orator, physician Joseph Warren, later killed at the Battle of Bunker Hill, likewise exhorted Bostonians, "SCORN TO BE SLAVES" for your forebears "crossed the boisterous ocean, found a new world, and prepared it for the happy residence of LIBERTY."[42] Using the death of martyrs as text and drawing on Christian and classical themes, until the series of remembrances ceased following the end of the Revolutionary War in 1783, each subsequent oration hailed liberty as an absolute good, the quest for which gives purpose to life, and slavery as an ultimate evil that deprives life of all meaning.

These annual orations and the ongoing repressive British policies they highlighted kept the memory of Boston's massacre alive in the minds of Revolutionary era Americans. In 1773, after Parliament's Tea Act revived colonial opposition to the remaining tariff on tea, leading to the Boston Tea Party, the town's history of mob action gained new meaning—this time with prominent citizens leading the riot. Parliament responded in 1774 by sending troops back to Boston and imposing marshal law. The colonies countered by calling the First Continental Congress and reimposing non-importation agreements. Warren delivered the 1775 massacre oration before a crowd of 5,000 Bostonians and a watchful British officer fingering musket balls. "Standing armies always endanger the liberties of subjects," Warren declared, invoking the past massacre to speak to the present military occupation. "When the people on the one part, consider the army as sent to enslave them, and the army on the other, were taught to look on the people as in a state of rebellion, it was but just to fear the most disagreeable consequences."[43]

The predicted consequences came a month later when British troops fired on local militia defending Lexington and Concord, before enduring a blood-soaked march back to Boston, with some 350 casualties on the two sides. The siege of Boston ensued, with patriot leaders fleeing the city or (like James Lovell) suffering summary arrest while a large force made up mostly of New England volunteers bottled up the British army there. As the Second Continental Congress met in Philadelphia, and after the Battle of Bunker Hill all but dashed hopes for a peaceful settlement, patriot preacher Peter Thatcher gave the 1776 massacre oration in Watertown, beyond the reach of British troops. Speaking as much to the moment as to the massacre, Thatcher denounced the ambitious lord who would use force "to subvert every principle of liberty in the constitution of his government, and to render his people the most abject of slaves."[44] With Boston's John and Samuel Adams leading the charge, Congress declared independence four months later.

Looking back from a Bostonian's perspective, their massacre led in a series of steps through their tea party and their city's occupation to revolution and independence. "The 5th of March 1770 ought to be an eternal Warning to this Nation," John Adams observed in 1786, for "on that Night the foundation of American Independance was laid."[45] He had played his part in that episode by steering the defense of those charged away from an indictment of liberty-loving Boston.[46] Merged into one long war for American independence, the Boston Massacre served for some as an initial explosion rather than an isolated event. If so, a mixed-race fugitive from slavery named Crispus Attucks became the first martyr of that war and, with apologies to Ralph Waldo Emerson's "Concord Hymn," Hugh Montgomery fired the shot heard round the world.

While in the Revolution's aftermath Adams and some other New Englanders saw the Boston Massacre as a critical opening act or "foundation" for the independence movement, Adams in his diary for the period identified the Stamp Act crisis as beginning the break with Britain. "The

Year 1765 has been the most remarkable Year of my Life," he reflected at year's end. "That enormous Engine, fabricated by the british Parliament, for battering down all the rights and Liberties of America, I mean the Stamp Act, has raised and spread, thro the whole Continent, a Spirit that will be recorded to our Honour, with all future Generations."[47] With *liberty* as its objective, *slavery* became the activating metaphor invoked to inspire a revolution that carried mixed meaning for chattel slavery. Adams's "motley rabble of saucy boys, negroes and molattos" and Equiano's professed "love of liberty" formed the crosscutting subtexts shared by many in this formative era.

CHAPTER TWO

Imperial Protests and the Metaphor of Slavery

1765–1769

The spreading elm at the corner of Essex and Orange Streets in Boston's old South End had served as a local landmark for decades. At dawn on August 14, 1765, the patriot leader of the South End gang, shoemaker Ebenezer Mackintosh, signaled the start of organized violent resistance to the Stamp Act by hanging an effigy and a jackboot with a green sole from the tree. The effigy denoted the designated stamp agent for Massachusetts, Andrew Oliver, and bore the labels "A.O." and "in Praise of Liberty."[1] The boot symbolized the hated former British prime minister John Stewart, the Third Earl of Bute, who initiated the colonial tax policies carried on by his similarly reviled protégé and successor, George Grenville—hence the green sole. Known thereafter as the Liberty Tree, the great elm served as a rallying point for patriots until loyalists chopped it down in 1775 during the British military occupation of Boston following the Battles of Lexington and Concord.

Although the stamped paper had not yet arrived from London, nor Oliver's commission, and the Stamp Act would not take effect until November, a riotous crowd composed mostly of workers, at least some of whom came armed with clubs and staves, surrounded the tree that

August morning. Acting at the behest of the Loyal Nine—a clandestine committee of patriot artisans and merchants that soon expanded under the leadership of James Otis Jr. and Samuel Adams to become the Sons of Liberty—Mackintosh had united the rival North and South End gangs to make common cause against the Stamp Act.[2] Oliver's brother-in-law and fellow merchant, Lieutenant Governor Thomas Hutchinson—one of the most perceptive and powerful American-born British colonial officers in the colonies—immediately sensed trouble and directed the sheriff to remove the effigy. Objecting that his officers "could not do it without imminent danger of their Lives," the sheriff demurred.[3] Tensions rose as the day wore on without decisive action.

At dusk, leaders of the swelling crowd—which one local newspaper numbered at "some Thousands" in a town with under 16,000 people—took down the effigy and with mob in tow paraded it roughly a mile to Oliver's wharf.[4] There, rioters demolished a new brick building rumored to be the future office for distributing stamped paper. With the effigy and kindling from the demolished building, the crowd then passed by Oliver's stately home, which stood one block away at the base of Fort Hill. After beheading the effigy in plain sight of the house's occupants, protesters set it ablaze in a hilltop bonfire visible across town before storming the house, which Oliver and his family had just vacated. Helping themselves to Oliver's liquor, the rioters broke windows and mirrors, smashed furniture, tore down the fence, and made a mess of the place. Appearing in person to defuse the situation, Hutchinson and the sheriff tried to disperse the mob around eleven o'clock but were driven off in a shower of stones. The next day, to save himself from further injury, Oliver agreed to decline his commission as stamp agent and do nothing to execute the Act.

Word spread that Hutchinson and agents of the local customs office and admiralty court remained committed to enforcing the Stamp Act. The mob turned against them on the night of August 26, invading and trashing the homes of the comptroller of customs, the court's deputy register, and the lieutenant governor. At each stop, protesters pillaged papers, shattered windows and furniture, and took whatever money and silver plate they found. Noting that they worked three hours to rip the cupola off Hutchinson's roof, Francis Bernard, the colony's English-born royally appointed governor, wrote that the rioters left "the House a mere Shell from Top to Bottom."[5]

The militia finally turned out to keep the peace after the second night of rioting, but patriot leaders warned against jailing anyone for the attacks or more riots would follow.[6] No prosecutions ensued and Bernard, holed up offshore at the fort on Castle Island, let everyone know that he would not press the issue of stamps. "The Common talk is that the Stamp Act shall never be executed here; the person that Offers to sell a Stamp will be immediately killed; and if any troops shall be sent hither they will be effectually Opposed," Bernard reported to London. "These & other Things of the same kind I continually hear, not as coming from a Mob, but from Sober discreet People."[7] The Sons of Liberty ruled Boston.[8]

As news of these actions spread from Massachusetts, other British mainland colonies erupted. Stirred by fears of imperial plans to enslave them, colonial protesters fought stamp taxes as if their liberty as English people turned on this test.[9] Oliver's loyalist brother Peter later wrote of the Liberty Tree on Essex Street, "This Tree stood in the Town, & was consecrated for an Idol for the Mob to Worship."[10] Similar so-called liberty trees emerged across the colonies—a stately oak in New Jersey, for example, and a towering tulip poplar in Maryland—all rallying points for liberty.

As events in Boston suggested, the Stamp Act crisis seeded a spirit of liberty in the colonies that, as John Adams predicted, lived on in honor with future generations. Occurring in 1765, shortly after the tumultuous and disorientating Seven Years' War ended, it prompted mainland American colonists to fear for their liberty and property under British rule. It gave substance to widely circulating conspiracy theories, spun by opposition Whigs in England and spread by protesting colonists to implicate Parliament, about the supposed absolutist designs of Britain's Hanoverian monarchy to enslave its subjects. It led prosperous colonial lawyers, planters, and merchants from New England to the Carolinas, many of whom owned enslaved Blacks, to express apprehensions that they (to use their own racist formulation) would become Parliament's "Negroes."[11] As a result, the Stamp Act crisis of 1765 became a critical step in the march from colonialism to revolution and independence.

The crisis rested on a subtle difference repeatedly raised in pamphlets and essays. Colonists viewed themselves as subjects of the king with, as one Boston essayist wrote at the time, "the same essential privileges as they that live in Britain." Parliament, in contrast, viewed them as its subjects or, as that same essayist emphasized, "*subjects of the subjects*" of the king.[12] This difference might have remained academic had a new government in London not sought to balance the postwar budget on the backs of colonists by taxing them directly, with the proceeds used to fund its costs of administrating and defending the colonies.

"It is the inherent Birth-right, and indubitable Privilege, of every *British* Subject, to be taxed only by his own Consent, or that of his legal Representatives," the Pennsylvania Assembly resolved in defiance of the Stamp Act.[13] By imposing stamp taxes on them without their consent, however, Parliament treated colonists as its subjects. "You have been told by great authority, that *a respectful submission is your interest as well as your duty*," the Boston essayist counseled colonists in a deeply ironic tone. "And so it is with your brother Americans, the black inhabitants of the West India Islands. Their DUTY is certainly *to submit* to all the impositions of their masters; for we know they were created for no other end but, with the sweat of their brow, to support them in luxury and grandeur, and it is plainly their INTEREST, to bear fifty lashes without muttering, for fear of having a hundred."[14] For American readers familiar with race-based bondage, these words gave emotional force to the slavery metaphor.

A further difference in perspective compounded the problem. Britons knew that the Seven Years' War had cost them dearly in blood and treasure, but colonists felt the same way about their own wartime sacrifices. Britons knew their armies had fought in America to conquer Canada, but colonists remembered their militias doing so as well. British politicians emphasized that that conquest had removed the French threat from the colonies' frontier, but colonists saw themselves as partners in that victory. They also contended that Britain had gained the most, particularly after the Proclamation of 1763 barred colonial settlement west of the Appalachian Mountains, and the 1764 Quebec Act appended the Ohio Country to Canada. Colonists might not pay taxes directly to London other than the regulatory import tariffs that fell on Britons everywhere, but they paid taxes to their colonial governments, which in turn contributed to imperial coffers. Further, for general regulatory tariffs such as those imposed on imported woolen cloth and various agricultural products, the colonists had virtual representation in Parliament because all Britons paid them—but not for tariffs imposed only on them, for which Parliament could rely solely on its claim of sovereign authority over the colonies.

For each side, the stamp tax was a special case. Colonists saw it as an unprecedented internal tax imposed solely on them without their consent; Parliament as a modest contribution by colonists toward the cost of their internal security and governance. With the rise of first Lord Bute and then Grenville to the premiership following the ascension of George III to the throne in 1760, those in favor of imposing it gained the upper hand in Parliament.

Where earlier prime ministers adopted a sort of benign neglect toward the colonies by valuing them mainly as captive markets for trade, Grenville regarded them as subservient parts of an empire in need of revenue. The Seven Years' War, fought globally between the British and French empires but mainly over their New World colonies, left Britain deep in debt. The peace saddled it with the expense of militarily occupying such restive new domains as French Canada, Spanish Florida, and a Great Lakes region that erupted in a widespread uprising of native peoples initiated by the Ottawa leader Pontiac in 1763. Adding

to these costs, Grenville sought to ensure submissive colonial governors and officers by having London pay their salaries rather than leaving it to their colonial assemblies. Under his scheme, colonists would
pay for their own administration and defense through new import tariffs on goods entering the colonies and stamp taxes on paper used in the
colonies for legal documents, commercial transactions, and all manner
of printed items from newspapers to playing cards. Britain already had
domestic stamp taxes and other internal levies, but had not imposed
them on colonists.

Although he unveiled his full plan in 1764, Grenville, fearing opposition, delayed a parliamentary vote on the stamp tax until 1765. As he
hoped, presumably because they seemed like the standard regulatory tariffs, the new revenue measures spawned little initial opposition. Known
as the Sugar Act because of its tax on imported, non-British sugar, the
American Duties Act of 1764 generated protests from various colonial
assemblies, but only New York squarely raised the issue of taxation without representation with respect to it. Britain's Caribbean sugar colonies
did not object at all, because they benefited from a tax on sugar imported
to the mainland colonies from outside the empire.

Under Hutchinson's hand, Massachusetts, like most mainland colonies, focused its protest on the Act's impact on trade—particularly on
trade in Caribbean sugar, which served as an essential ingredient in the
production of rum by New England distilleries. Rum also lubricated the
transatlantic trade in enslaved Africans, with much of the liquid and
human cargo carried in New England ships. British taxation of trade
became an issue more generally because the 1763 peace with France had
not brought the colonies prosperity. Instead, the end of wartime spending
coupled with a bank panic produced an economic slump across America.
Britain's decision with the Currency Act of 1764 to protect its merchants
by barring colonies from issuing paper money made matters worse by
restricting the money supply that fueled the local economy. These acts
came on top of the Proclamation of 1763 restricting western settlement
in lands claimed by the colonies.

The development of opposition toward British measures that began with the Sugar Act, Currency Act, and Quebec Act in 1764 turned toward active resistance with passage of the Stamp Act in 1765. No one could disguise it as anything but a direct, internal tax on American colonists, which raised the legal issue of taxation without representation. Grenville did not seek cover. He wanted to establish the principle of parliamentary sovereignty over the colonies even in matters of taxes. The weak economy, high unemployment, and fall in farm prices made the situation more combustible. All this played into the hands of James Otis Jr., who had long spoiled for such a fight.[15]

A lawyer with a brilliant but unstable mind, Otis followed his father, James Otis Sr., up the ladder of Massachusetts politics as far as a leader of the so-called popular faction (dedicated to resisting encroachment on colonial rights) could rise in an elitist age. The rise made them ambitious; the ceiling made them rebellious; and the combination make them volatile. From a farming family in rural Barnstable, the senior Otis began as a worker and taught himself law, leading the proud Peter Oliver to depict him as a cordwainer who "work'd himself into a Pettifogger" with "a certain Adroitness to captivate the Ear of Country Jurors."[16] Elected to the colonial Assembly, he became its Speaker in 1760 and secured a promise from Governor Thomas Pownall of appointment to the next open seat on the colony's highest court. By then the junior Otis had joined his father as a rising politician and lawyer, with Pownall making him advocate general for the admiralty court. By the time that the next high court seat came open later in 1760, however, Bernard had replaced Pownall as governor and the judgeship went to Oliver in-law and sitting lieutenant governor Thomas Hutchinson. The Otises never forgave Hutchinson or Bernard, with the ensuing rivalries having a redounding effect on Massachusetts politics in the run-up to the Revolution.

In 1761, the first major case to reach the high bench after Hutchinson's appointment involved the issuance of general writs of assistance authorizing customs officers to search homes, shops, warehouses, and other private premises for contraband. Because such blanket writs carried royal authority, the death of George II in 1760 and ascension of George III required their reissuance—a seeming formality. As chief solicitor for the admiralty court, young Otis would submit the request, which the loyal Hutchinson would then grant. But smuggling had become a way of life in New England after the enactment of high regulatory tariffs on cheap sugar from the French West Indies under the 1733 Molasses Act, and colonists feared strict enforcement of those hated taxes under the new writs. Seeing a chance to stake out a popular position and put Hutchinson in an awkward one, Otis abruptly resigned as advocate general and offered, "whether under a fee or not, (for in such a cause as this I despise a fee)," to argue the case against the writs.[17] His brain ever oscillating between spells of mental acumen and illness, Otis often acted irrationally—a mental condition made worse after a violent blow to the head by a tax collector's cudgel in 1769 effectively incapacitated him. Carried off "raving Mad," as John Adams put it, Otis died by a bolt of lightning in 1783.[18]

"Otis was a flame of fire!" Adams wrote much later of the 1761 courtroom argument that he witnessed against reissuing the writs. "With a promptitude of Classical Allusions, a depth of research, a rapid summary of historical events & dates, a profusion of Legal Authorities, a prophetic glance of his eyes into futurity, and a rapid torrent of impetuous Eloquence he hurried away all before him. American Independence was then & there born."[19] In reality, Otis had a weak case at law even if a popular one with colonists. As a young lawyer freshly admitted to the bar, Adams attended the hearing and prepared an "Abstract" of the arguments—the principal contemporary record of an event that went unreported in newspapers.

According to Adams's abstract, Otis turned the rhetorical contrast between liberty and slavery long used by English Whigs to defend the "rights of Englishmen" generally to a defense of the rights of colonists in particular. "I will to my dying day oppose, with all the powers and faculties God has given me, all such instruments of slavery on the one hand,

and villainy on the other, as this writ of assistance is," Otis declared near the outset. "It appears to me the worst instrument of arbitrary power, the most destructive of English liberty, and the fundamental principles of the constitution, that ever was found in an English law-book." Distinguishing special writs issued for cause from general ones issued without cause, he warned, "Every one with this writ may be a tyrant: If this commission be legal, a tyrant may, in a legal manner also, control, imprison or murder any one within the realm." Claiming that no precedent existed in Britain for general writs, and that basic principles of English law weighed against them, Otis concluded, "No Acts of Parliament can establish such a writ; Though it should be made in the very words of the petition, it would be void. An act against the constitution is void."[20]

Strong words passionately delivered, Otis's assertion that courts in England did not grant general writs gave Hutchinson grounds to postpone a ruling until emotions cooled and he could inquire of London if English courts issued such writs. Four months later, when news came back that they did, Hutchinson issued them over scant protest.[21] Ignoring this outcome, Adams always portrayed the episode in triumphant terms.[22] "Mr. Otis's popularity was without bounds. In May 1761, he was elected into the House of Representatives, by an almost Unanimous vote," Adams wrote in 1817. "For ten years afterwards Mr. Otis at the head of his Countrys cause, conducted the Town of Boston & the people of the Province with a prudence & fortitude, at every sacrifice of personal interest."[23] Echoing a century of English Whig assaults against tyrannical Stuart and Hanoverian monarchs, Otis had turned the rhetorical device of liberty versus slavery against Parliament—the first American leader to do so.[24] This became his hallmark message and a feature of patriot oratory.

As time blurred his memory, Adams embellished the argument that Otis made in the writs case. "He asserted that every man, merely natural, was an independent sovereign," Adams wrote in 1818. "Nor were the poor Negroes forgotten. Not a Quaker in Philadelphia . . . ever asserted the Rights of Negroes in Stronger Terms. Young as I was and ignorant as I was, I shuddered at the doctrine he taught."[25] Otis later linked the slavery imposed by Britain on white colonists with that imposed by white colonists on Black ones, but not in 1761. It had little to do with the narrow case against the writs but much to do with a broad defense of liberty. As more colonists applied the metaphor of slavery to the Stamp Act and British tyranny, splits emerged about what that analogy meant for the actual institution of slavery. For American patriots, would liberty and slavery represent opposing points in a single continuum reserved for whites or, by including the third point of Black slavery in the Revolutionary discourse, would a doctrine emerge that might make even an elderly Adams shudder?

Following the writs case, Otis had the public standing and ready arguments to pounce once Parliament passed the Sugar Act in April 1764 along with a resolution declaring that, to defray the expenses of administrating the American colonies, "it may be proper to charge certain Stamp Duties in the said Colonies."[26] One of the first pamphlets published in response, and by far the best-known and most-often reprinted one, Otis's 1764 *The Rights of the British Colonies Asserted and Proved* denied the right of Parliament to impose either external revenue tariffs or internal stamp taxes on unrepresented colonists. "Every British subject born on the continent of America or in any other of the British dominions is . . . entitled to all the natural, essential, inherent, and inseparable rights of our fellow subjects in Great Britain," Otis declared. "No act of Parliament can deprive them of the *liberties* of such, unless any will contend that an act of Parliament can make *slaves* not only of one but of two millions of the commonwealth," the estimated colonial population. "The very act of taxing exercised over those who are not represented appears to me to be depriving them of one of their most essential rights as freemen," he wrote. "No man can take my property from me without my consent: if he does, he deprives me of my *liberty* and makes me a *slave*."[27]

In an introductory section on "natural rights," Otis now acknowledged the relevance of his argument to the institution of slavery, which still flourished in Massachusetts. "The colonists are by the law of nature freeborn, as indeed all men are, white or black," he wrote. "Will short curled hair like wool instead of Christian hair" prove otherwise, Otis asked in a series of queries pointing past superficial racial differences. "Can any logical inferences in favor of slavery be drawn from a flat nose?" Turning on the Caribbean "sugar islanders" who accepted the Sugar Act because it raised the price in America of sugar from other sources, he added, "It is a clear truth that those who every day barter away other men's liberty will soon care little for their own." Indeed, Otis warned, "for a little present gain" these "Creole" planters (as he called them) would make "white as well as black, worse slaves if possible."[28]

Following Otis's lead, in 1765, two other pamphleteers depicted the Stamp Act as a form of enslavement but, perhaps because (unlike Otis) both enslaved Blacks, without express reference to chattel slavery. This usage did not mean that these two prominent colonists—Rhode Island governor, merchant, and slave-ship owner Stephen Hopkins; and Secretary of Maryland, London-trained barrister, and slave-plantation owner Daniel Dulany—employed "slavery" merely as a trope to assail taxation without representation. While modern readers cannot read the word without thinking of Africans in chains, Hopkins, Dulany, and others like them ostensibly had something else in mind.

Hopkins opened his pamphlet by declaring, "Liberty is the greatest blessing that men enjoy, and slavery the heaviest curse that human nature is capable of." Without mentioning physical bondage, he then explained, "Those who are governed at the will of another, or of others, and whose property may be taken from them by taxes or otherwise without their own consent and against their will, are in the miserable condition of slaves."[29] In a similar manner four years later, South Carolina patriot leader Christopher Gadsden wrote in response to the Townshend tariffs, "We are as real Slaves as those we are permitted to command, and differ only in degree, for what is a slave, but one that is at the will of his master."[30] While these definitions of liberty and slavery echoed established English Whig usage, Hopkins and Gadsden relied on the prevalence of

Black slavery giving them added force in America.[31] At the time, South Carolina had more enslaved Blacks per capita than any other mainland American colony, and Rhode Island served as a center for the Atlantic slave trade. Over half of all Africans arriving in English North America during this period came on vessels operated by Rhode Island merchants, including sixteen ships owned by Hopkins and his brothers.[32]

Two of these brothers, Esek and either Stephen or William, appeared in the painting *Sea Captains Carousing in Surinam*, which captured the essential debauchery of the slave trade. The satirical canvas by Boston artist John Greenwood, then living in the Dutch Caribbean colony of Surinam, showed some twenty Rhode Island sea captains in bacchanalian excess far from home during the late 1750s, when legal restrictions on commerce with French colonies during the Seven Years' War led Americans to pass that trade through neutral Dutch ports. The indoor party featured drunken revelers, cheating gamblers, males dancing with males, passed-out drunks, retching men, and nude or seminude Black servers of both sexes (the only females shown). More than any other single product, Rhode Island rum bought the Africans resold in America. It flowed freely in this scene, with enslaved Blacks dispensing it, one captain pouring it over another, and others drinking it directly from serving bowls.[33]

More conservative than Hopkins and not a firebrand like Otis, the Cambridge-educated Dulany also gave a proper English meaning to "slavery." Perhaps for that reason, his pamphlet carried more weight in London than other colonial tracts and, along with the widespread protests and boycotts that ground tax collections to a halt, led Parliament to repeal the Stamp Act in 1766, less than a year after enacting it. "There may very well exist a *dependence* and *inferiority* without absolute *vassalage* and *slavery*," Dulany wrote with pinpoint emphasis. "In what the superior may *rightfully* control or compel, and in what the inferior ought to be at liberty to act without control or compulsion, depends upon the nature of the dependency and degree of the subordination."[34] Regarding the degree of subordination colonies owed Parliament, he argued, external regulatory tariffs did not cross the line but internal revenue taxes did.[35]

Dulany's conservative case against stamp taxes accepted subordination based on race and status. As if to make this clear, Dulany explained to "English readers" some facts he said they might not know about an English American colonist: "He may be neither black nor tawny, may speak the English language, and in other respects seem, for all the world, like one of them!"[36] Far from Otis's radical plea for universal natural rights or Hopkins's frank invocation of slavery, Dulany championed English rights for Englishmen like himself—a second-generation American of English stock. Thus constrained, the slavery metaphor carried the day. What eighteenth-century member of Parliament would enslave a white, English-speaking, Cambridge-educated barrister, he all but asked. Perhaps Dulany's approach helped—his pamphlet gained an audience in London, with some members of Parliament citing it in support of repealing the Stamp Act.

In accord with Dulany's view of the dependency of colonies on the mother country, however, Parliament paired its repeal of the Stamp Act with passage of the American Colonies Act of 1766. This so-called Declaratory Act avowed that Parliament had "full power and authority to make laws and statutes of sufficient force and validity to bind the colonies and people of America, subjects of the crown of Great Britain, in all cases whatsoever."[37] As face-saving words, these might not have mattered, but after Parliament proceeded under them to impose new revenue tariffs in 1767 and 1768, the slavery trope reappeared with a vengeance. While Dulany remained quiet and Otis struggled for sanity, Hopkins and others jumped into the fray.

Even during the Stamp Act crisis, and more so thereafter, the pamphlets by Otis, Hopkins, and Dulany did not stand out because they used the metaphor of slavery to assail British imperial policies. That usage was already common, if not ubiquitous. They stood out for their impact, which resulted from their effective use of revolutionary rhetoric, particularly the slavery metaphor. As these three pamphlets show, that metaphor did not always carry the same meaning or implications. For writers like Otis, it included chattel slavery as well as political enslavement and made them as one. For those like Dulany, who invoked the English Whig meaning, it spoke mainly of liberty for colonial elites. In Hopkins's usage, it carried mixed messages for readers and perhaps even for himself as he struggled with freeing his own enslaved workers at the urging of his Quaker wife and congregation.

Yet neither John Adams, who never owned a Black person, nor any other white American colonist at the time could use the metaphor without thinking in racial terms. A striking yet representative example appeared when, at the height of the Stamp Act crisis in 1765, Adams inveighed against British "enslavement" of white colonists: "We won't be their negroes."[38] Whatever meaning it carried in particular cases, the metaphor worked with white Americans *because* they did not want to be enslaved like "their negroes." Based on his reading of these and other patriot texts, historian Bernard Bailyn found that its meaning came from English Whig usage, where slavery denoted "loss of freedom."[39] Its unique power for colonists, however, came from the nightmare of Black slavery in their midst.[40]

The fury of the colonial response led so quickly to the repeal of the Stamp Act that, only a year after the publication of Hopkins's and Dulany's powerful pamphlets, the influential pastor of Boston's old West Church, Jonathan Mayhew, could hail its revocation in a 1766 sermon, which became a popular pamphlet, *The Snare Broken: A Thanksgiving Discourse*. For Mayhew, the Stamp Act represented the "snare" and "escaping" it cause for thanksgiving. A pioneer of the providential theism that inspired American Revolutionary leaders like Washington, Hancock, and Franklin, Mayhew attracted a wealthy, educated flock. He preached a rationalist, almost Lockean gospel of a creator God still active in creation, and personal salvation achieved through virtuous behavior, which included standing up for personal liberty and social betterment.

Allusions to slavery ran through Mayhew's thanksgiving closing sermon. News of the repeal of "the ugly Hag *Slavery*, the deformed child of Satan," and the return of the "celestial Maid, the daughter of God" Liberty, brought joy to all colonists, Mayhew proclaimed. Their "*emancipation*" resulted from their unified resistance in which "even," as he put it in a gendered aside, "devout women not a few" joined through participation in boycotts, protests, and other "kind of manly exertions, rather than live to propagate a race of slaves." More striking still, Mayhew added in a further aside, "Even our bought *Negro slaves* apparently shared in the common distress: for which one cannot easily account, except by supposing that even some of them . . . thought it would be more ignominious and wretched to be the *servants of servants*, than of free-men." Unlike Otis, whose plea for liberty included women and Blacks, Mayhew—a Lockean rationalist with slave-owning parishioners—acknowledged chattel slavery without renouncing it. Preserving liberty required vigilance, he drew on a gospel verse to warn, for "while men *sleep, then the enemy cometh*."[41]

Colonists could not rest long. With the Declaratory Act in hand and a mistaken sense that colonists accepted external taxes if not internal ones, the enemy sprang quickly. The turnover in British government offices under George III and heightened watchfulness in the colonies provided ready context for the next upheaval.

Repeal of the Stamp Act followed Grenville's fall in July 1765 and his replacement as prime minister by Lord Rockingham, an aristocratic Whig who supported constitutional rights for colonists and opposed the reassertion of royal power by George III. Rockingham lasted only one year in the post, however. With the Grenville-like Charles Townshend put in charge of tax matters as chancellor of the exchequer, Parliament in 1767 passed the so-called Townshend Act imposing revenue duties on tea, paper, glass, lead, and paint entering the colonies. Associated legislation created a Customs Board and Vice-Admiralty Court in Boston to enforce the new tariffs.

Once again declaring that taxation without representation violated their rights as British subjects, the colonists erupted anew. Repudiating now any distinction between internal and external taxes, patriot propagandists charged that all revenue measures imposed without consent constituted slavery. Effective in challenging stamp taxes, use of the metaphor exploded against the Townshend Duties.

With Otis by then increasingly sidelined by mental illness—John Adams would soon depict him as rambling and wandering "like a ship without a helm"[42]—John's cousin Samuel assumed the leading role within Boston's chapter of the Sons of Liberty and the far-reaching Committees of Correspondence. A gifted polemicist, his became the main voice of colonial resistance to the Townshend Act.[43] He used the slavery metaphor as sharply as Otis did against the British but without turning it against chattel slavery.

Having previously denounced the Stamp Act as reducing colonists "from the Character of free Subjects to the miserable State of tributary Slaves," Samuel Adams turned on the Townshend Duties with vengeance in 1767.[44] "Slavery, my dear mother, we cannot think of: we detest it," Adams wrote in a published letter to Britain, the mother country. "If this be a crime, remember we suck'd it at your milk. . . . Britons will never be slaves."[45] Adams carried on in this way into the 1770s, admonishing colonists in his trademark fashion, "Is it not High Time for the People of this Country explicitly to declare, whether they will be Freemen or Slaves?"[46]

Whether because he believed it or because he viewed it as an effective rhetorical tool, in an era when many Europeans lived in servitude or serfdom, Adams depicted the refusal to submit to slavery as a republican virtue largely reserved for the English. "No people ever groan'd under the heavy yoke of slavery, but when they deserv'd it," he wrote in 1771. "This may be called a severe censure upon by far the greatest part of the nations of the world who are involv'd in the misery of servitude: But however they may be thought by some to deserve commiseration, the censure is just."[47] This view gave grounds for English colonists fighting British bondage to accept slavery for those who did not fight hard enough for their freedom. For African Americans, Adams's words cut deep: The enslaved deserv'd their bondage. Although a lifelong opponent of chattel slavery, Adams broke with his Boston mentor James Otis by not presenting its abolition as part of the Revolutionary cause. Adams's approach spoke to white colonists appalled by the thought of their own enslavement without driving off those who enslaved Blacks or feared equality for people of all races.

Notwithstanding the overall influence of Adams's words and deeds, by many accounts the anonymously issued *Letters from a Farmer in Pennsylvania* had the greatest impact of any single publication or series of publications in steeling Americans against the Townshend Act. Ostensibly written by a simple farmer, the twelve letters, which appeared first serially in nineteen colonial newspapers beginning in 1767 and then together in pamphlets published in seven cities from Philadelphia to Paris in 1768, displayed legal acumen and a style that engaged readers of all stripes. Serving as a colonial agent in London, Benjamin Franklin reprinted them there—leading some to suppose that he wrote them. Only later did people learn that the author was Franklin's longtime Philadelphia political rival John Dickinson, a lawyer with landed wealth.

Born at Croisadore, his father's tobacco plantation in Maryland, and raised at Poplar Hall, the family plantation in Delaware that he inherited, Dickinson also held the Fair Hill estate in Pennsylvania through marriage to the wealthy Mary Norris. He worked his land with enslaved Blacks, owning more of them than anyone else did in the region. To the delight of patriots and the fury of loyalists, Dickinson turned the slavery metaphor against the Townshend Duties in his *Letters*, portraying himself and his ilk as the bondservants of Britain.[48]

Dickinson had used the metaphor earlier to assail the Stamp Act. Writing in 1765 as "a Gentleman in Philadelphia," he depicted stamp taxes (much like a master's lash) "drawing off, as it were, the last drops of their [prey's] blood." Noting that "Every drop of my blood is British," he later railed against the Act, the British nation should "be better pleased having their children speaking the language of freemen, than muttering the timid murmurs of slaves."[49] The metaphor worked better when attributed to a humbler hand in *Letters from a Pennsylvania Farmer*. "My farm is small, my servants few, and good," the first letter began. "I have a little money at interest; I wish for no more."[50] This opening hardly pointed toward the cool, conservative Dickinson, who had many enslaved servants and much cash, but his fictional farmer could make the metaphor sing for moderate Whigs and white artisans, shopkeepers, and small-farm owners.

"The parliament unquestionably possesses a legal authority to *regulate* the trade of *Great-Britain*, and all her colonies," Dickinson wrote in his second letter. "The single question is," he asserted, "whether the parliament can legally take money out of our pockets, without our consent? If they can, all our boasted liberty is but 'Vox et praetera nihil': A sound, and nothing else."[51] In letter seven, he declared, "Those who are taxed without their own consent expressed by themselves or their representatives, are slaves. *We* are taxed without our own consent given by ourselves, or our representatives. *We* are therefore—I speak it with grief—I speak it with indignation—we are slaves."[52]

The Townshend Act and related measures reduced colonists to a state of "abject slavery," Dickinson twice asserted. "Is it possible to form an idea of a slavery more complete, more miserable, more disgraceful, than that of a people, where justice is administered, government exercised, and a standing army maintained, at the expense of the people, and yet without the least dependance on them?" he asked readers in letter nine.[53] The loyalist writer J. Hector St. John de Crèvecœur would take Dickinson to task for this by depicting the literal horror of plantation slavery in his answering essays, *Letters from an American Farmer*.[54] Drawing on the same Bible passage as Mayhew, Dickinson closed his last letter by urging colonists: "Let us take care of our rights, and we therein take care of our prosperity. 'Slavery is ever proceeded by sleep.'"[55]

As knowledge of who wrote the wildly popular *Letters from a Pennsylvania Farmer* leaked, in June 1768 Dickinson contributed a song to two Philadelphia newspapers. He took the tune from the British navy anthem "Heart of Oak" that addressed sailors, "To honour we call you, as freemen not slaves." Dickinson repurposed the tune against the British with a rousing chorus that followed all eight verses:

> In FREEDOM we're BORN, and in FREEDOM we'll LIVE.
> Our Purses are ready,
> Steady, Friends, steady,
> Not as SLAVES, but as FREEMEN our Money we give.

The verses admonished "AMERICANS all" that "By *uniting* we stand, by *dividing* we fall" and "To DIE we can *bear*—but to SERVE we *distain*—For SHAME is to *Freemen* more dreadful than PAIN."[56]

Read by southern planters and northern farmers, in New York pubs and London clubs, by the colonial elite and the working poor, Dickinson's *Letters* had much the same impact on public debate over the Townshend Duties as Dulany's pamphlet had regarding stamp taxes. Written from a conservative perspective, both crystallized the issues at stake in terms of English liberty versus abject slavery, and awakened colonists to the patriot cause. From his vast Virginia plantation, George Washington wrote to George Mason early in 1769, "At a time when our lordly Masters in Great Britain will be satisfied with nothing less than the deprivation of American freedom, it seems highly necessary that something shou'd be done to avert the stroke and maintain the liberty which we have derived from our Ancestors."[57] Each one the owner of over one hundred enslaved Blacks, and both having read Dickinson's *Letters*, by mid-1769 they had organized in a boycott of British goods by Virginia planters and merchants with the goal, in Washington's words, of drawing Parliament's "attention to our rights & priviledges . . . by starving their Trade & manufactures."[58] Patriot leaders in other colonies did likewise around the same time, with remarkable effect. Trade in taxed goods plummeted and smuggling soared.

Matters only became worse after resistance to the Townshend Act in Boston led the British to dispatch warships and troops to enforce compliance there. The result was the bloodshed of March 5, 1770, described in Chapter One. Although the news had not reached America by the time of the Boston Massacre, in response to the ongoing boycotts, Townshend's successor as chancellor of the exchequer and by 1770 also prime minister, Lord North, had already engineered partial repeal of the Townshend Duties. To maintain the principle of its sovereignty, however, Parliament retained the tariff on tea. That, coupled with outrage over the Boston Massacre, kept the situation in the colonies fluid, with the Committees of Correspondence urging a sustained boycott everywhere. Crispus Attucks and four others had died, but Samuel Adams, Paul Revere, and the Sons of Liberty had whitewashed the episode. They were not staging a revolt of enslaved Blacks but rather, in their rhetoric, of enslaved colonists.

Into the 1770s, however, prominent patriots persisted in protesting their enslavement by Britain in passages explicitly laced with the imagery of Black slavery. "Those from whom we have a right to Seek protection are endeavouring by every piece of Art & despotism to fix the Shackles of Slavry upon us," Washington complained about the British in June 1774.[59] Parliament, he added two months later, sought to make colonists "as tame, & abject Slaves, as the Blacks we Rule over with such arbitrary Sway."[60] In his influential *Letters from a Freeman*, South Carolina planter William Henry Drayton exclaimed that same year, "It is as clear as the Sun at Noon, that the taxation of America" by Parliament serves "to compel America to bow the neck to Slavery!"[61] By accepting taxation by Parliament, John Adams chided Bostonians a year later, "You would not only be slaves—But the most abject sort of slaves to the worst sort of masters!"[62] With British troops occupying Boston in 1775, Harvard president Samuel Langdon depicted colonists' plight as "the vilest slavery, and worse than death."[63]

Following Dickinson, a wide array of patriot essayists employed the slavery metaphor: Virginia planter Thomas Jefferson, New York lawyer Alexander Hamilton, Philadelphia writer Thomas Paine, South Carolina merchant Christopher Gadsden, and more. No longer merely common, its use became ubiquitous. That this sampling includes two persons with and two without enslaved Blacks of their own underscores that ubiquity. To use the metaphor, it scarcely mattered whether one accepted or rejected chattel slavery.

Words drove the opening phase of the American Revolution, most historians agree, until the violence of it, especially on the western frontier and in the southern colonies, became its own driver. "The Revolution was in the Minds of the People, and this was effected, from 1760 to 1775," John Adams later wrote to Jefferson. "The Pamphlets [and] Newspapers in all the Colonies ought be consulted, during that Period, to ascertain the Steps by which the public opinion was enlightened and informed concerning the Authority of Parliament over the Colonies."[64] At least for white colonists, whether slaveholders or not, those revolution-inspiring words featured slavery as an absolute evil without necessarily condemning its continuance for Blacks.

As the quoted passages also suggest, patriot invocations of slavery were often not philosophical arguments based on abstract notions of freemen in a state of nature. They were intensely emotional appeals that relied for their force on a familiarity with chattel slavery and an equation of Blacks with such bondage.[65] "There are but two sorts of men in the world," John Adams declared, "freemen and slaves."[66] In their mind's eye, Americans were *either* Dickinson's white yeoman farmers living securely on a bit of investment income, *or* in a state of abject chattel slavery living like Blacks without recourse or property rights. If we accept taxation without representation, Joseph Warren warned in his 1772 Boston Massacre oration, we "must admit at once that we are absolute SLAVES, and have no property of our own."[67] One act of Parliament (backed by a few British troops) could change everything. The metaphor of slavery drove the call to arms.

That metaphor never worked better for this purpose than on March 23, 1775, when the spellbinding Virginia orator, country lawyer, and rising plantation slaveholder Patrick Henry stood at an unsanctioned meeting of his colony's Assembly to demand armed resistance to ongoing acts of British tyranny. "The question before the House was one of awful moment to this country. For his own part, he considered it as nothing less than a question of freedom or slavery," Henry reportedly began, speaking in the third person before shifting to the first. "Shall we acquire the means of effectual resistance, by lying supinely on our backs, and hugging the delusive phantom of hope, until our enemies shall have bound us hand and foot?" he asked in a clear allusion to chattel slavery. "No," he exclaimed. "There is no retreat, but in submission and slavery! Our chains are forged. Their clanking may be heard on the plains of Boston!" Then came the haunting close: "Is life so dear, or peace so sweet, as to be purchased at the price of chains, and slavery? Forbid it, Almighty God!—I know not what course others may take; but as for me, give me liberty or give me death!"[68] For Henry and many others caught up in the rush toward revolution, slavery was not an option. Some of their enslaved Blacks agreed, including ones owned by Washington, Jefferson, and Henry. They used the revolutionary tumult to make their break for liberty.

CHAPTER THREE

A Practice "So Odious"

The Legality of Slavery, 1770–1774

James Somerset heard the patriot cries for liberty and against slavery because the patriots of Virginia and Massachusetts directed them against his master, Charles Steuart, more than any other single colonist. Somerset, Steuart's human property under Virginia law, had duties that included traveling with Steuart from their homes in Norfolk and Boston and, independently of him, delivering messages and running errands. Steuart trusted Somerset with money and finding his way in cities and to distant places and back. Although Somerset left no written record and may not have been able to write, Steuart left one that frequently mentions Somerset in familial terms. In this record, Somerset appears intelligent, resourceful, and self-reliant. Steuart certainly did not want to lose him.

Steuart's white colleagues and business partners also knew Somerset, perhaps as a messenger bearing letters to and from Steuart. In their letters, they sometimes asked Steuart to pass along their warm regards, and those of their enslaved persons, to "our friend Somersett," as one of Steuart's white associates once put it.[1] Somerset made acquaintances easily and won the esteem of others. Steuart's financial records suggested that Somerset dressed smartly for his role—with silk clothes, fine stockings, and ribbons—and nothing in Steuart's papers hints at any particularly cruel treatment other than, of course, the ultimate cruelty of enslavement. Indeed, Steuart never gave an inch on slavery, doggedly pursued his enslaved persons who escaped, and threatened severe punishment for any who betrayed him. These traits made Steuart an ideal tax collector and imperial agent at a time of colonial upheaval. Even when encased in a soft fur glove, his hand had an iron grip that would not let go easily.

By his own lights, Steuart came upon Somerset honorably, although Somerset would have thought the transaction as dishonorable as possible. Steuart bought Somerset as his human property on August 1, 1749, in Norfolk, Virginia. The prior year British slave traders on the West African coast had kidnapped or otherwise secured Somerset, then a boy aged about eight with a name that no one thought to record, and placed him on a slave ship bound for Jamaica. No reports survive of that voyage, but it was likely similar to the one endured a few years later by the kidnapped African youth Olaudah Equiano. "The closeness of the place, and the heat of climate, added to the number in the ship, which was so crowded that each had scarcely room to turn himself, almost suffocated us," Equiano wrote of time spent in the ship's hold. "The shrieks of the women, and the groans of the dying, rendered the whole a scene of horror almost inconceivable." Historians estimate that between 1500 and 1800 some ten million enslaved Africans embarked on this hellish "Middle Passage" to the New World, with up to ten percent dying en route. Equiano, who saw others throw themselves overboard, wished to die as well.[2]

Like Equiano, Somerset went first to the British Caribbean, where enslaved persons vastly outnumbered free ones even though up to a third of the Africans there died from disease within a few years of their arrival. He then went on to Virginia, which only a small fraction of transported Africans reached. There Steuart, a merchant who traded in large lots of enslaved persons, acquired the bright, young Somerset as a personal body servant. Born on Scotland's remote Orkney Islands, Steuart had moved to Virginia in 1741 at age sixteen to work for a Scottish tobacco trader. He then moved on to Boston for a better job with his uncle, and back to Virginia first under one merchant and then in partnership with others, before establishing himself in his own mercantile business during the 1750s. Buoyed by a rapidly expanding economy, Steuart lived the life of a rising white colonist in British America. He began acquiring human property for personal services and perhaps as investments once he resettled in Virginia, even though he never married or had a plantation. Steuart owned at least seven other enslaved servants but trusted Somerset most and relied on him during business trips.[3]

For Steuart, and ultimately for Somerset, the big break came in 1762, when a disabled ship bound from Cuba to Spain found safe harbor in Norfolk, Virginia. The ship carried high-ranking refugees from Havana, including senior naval officers and a titled lady, sailing under official protection after the fall of that city to the British during the Seven Years' War. As a Norfolk merchant with formal port duties, Steuart took charge of the ship and its passengers. He showed remarkable loyalty in the face of unruly colonists when, by some accounts aided by an armed Somerset at his side, he stood off a drunken mob stirred by wartime xenophobia to demand death for the Spaniards.[4] This represented precisely the sort of fidelity to the mother country that British officials valued at a time of colonial unrest.

Steuart's defense of the Spaniards won recognition in London, including an audience with the king and appointment by the much-hated (at least in America) prime minister George Grenville as receiver general of customs for the eastern central district of British North America and, in 1765, as paymaster general of the American Board of Customs. These posts put Steuart in charge of enforcing first the disliked Sugar Act duties and then the despised Townshend tariffs in the colonies, with the second post leading to his relocation to the center of patriot resistance, Boston, and to widespread travel. Somerset accompanied Steuart as a personal servant on each move and many trips. Amid growing protests and spreading boycotts, they heard the calls for liberty and against slavery everywhere—with Steuart a target of abuse. Perhaps those calls affected Steuart and Somerset differently—stiffening the former and inspiring the latter. If so, Steuart seemed neither to notice a change in Somerset nor to lose faith in his fidelity.

Steuart's loyalist sentiments animated his exchanges with other imperial officers. "I am sorry to find the Bulk of the People still disputing the Authority from home," the comptroller of the colonial post office reported to his superior in London after conferring with Steuart and his top aide in 1766. The Americans "begin to imagine both the Post-Office and Custom-House are like Grievances: With Respect to Custom-House Officers they were always look'd on as such, but never disputed, till now." Referring to Steuart and his aide, the comptroller added, "*They are*, I should have said, *we are* all afraid of the Populace—for the Tail is where the Head should be: The Spirit of Independance is too prevalent, it does not subside much, and but little real Gratitude appears yet."[5]

At the time of this meeting, Parliament had just repealed the Stamp Act and had not yet imposed the Townshend tariffs, but grievances still festered over the Sugar Act. Distrust grew on both sides. The Townshend Act would compound the problem. "I can Struggle thro' Misfortunes, and brave Adversity itself, but unkind Returns of Friends, or those I thought so, and have been friendly to, cuts me deep," the post office official lamented.[6] Steuart too lost many of his American friends.

With the Townshend tariffs in place by the summer of 1768, Steuart had enough of America and Americans. He requested leave to do his work from London while recuperating from exhaustion and taking charge of three nephews after their father's death. By this time, the Boston-based Customs Board had sought military assistance in enforcing the Townshend tariffs, with the fifty-gun warship HMS *Romney* arriving in May. Custom officers seized the sloop *Liberty* owned by John Hancock in June on charges of smuggling, leading to riots that forced British officials in Boston, presumably including Steuart along with Somerset, to seek refuge at the fort on Castle Island. The first regiment of British army soldiers arrived in Boston to enforce order on October 1, allowing those holed up at the fort to leave it. On that very day, Steuart and Somerset sailed for London, where they settled into a house at Baldwin's Gardens, Holborn, near the fashionable heart of the city. Although they never returned to America, their impact on it continued.

Given his Scottish upbringing and colonial administrative experience, Steuart surely knew that he ran a risk of losing Somerset by taking him to Britain. Slavery had died out in England following the Norman Conquest in 1066. A form of feudal serfdom called villeinage remained lawful, but it created bondservants with more rights than enslaved persons and had effectively ended as well. The last known case of English law involving villeinage dated from 1618, and it freed the villein.[7] Still, as if to emphasize the point, Lord Holt, the chief justice of the Court of King's Bench, wrote in a 1701 ruling, "One may be a villein in England, but not a slave."[8] Citing Holt, William Blackstone's 1765 *Commentaries on the Laws of England* declared that the "spirit of liberty is so deeply implanted in our constitution, and rooted even in our very soil, that a slave or a negro, the moment he lands in England . . . becomes *eo instanti* a freeman."[9]

Although English monarchs and Parliament had granted charters and passed laws facilitating slavery in the mainland American and Caribbean colonies and authorizing the African slave trade, these never applied to the British homeland. Britain's New World colonies filled in the gap by adopting local statutes (or "positive law") legalizing slavery within their borders, with the sugar-rich Caribbean colonies and mainland plantation colonies of the American South enacting full-fledged chattel slave codes. If for no other reason than fear of popular upheaval, Parliament left the judge-made common law (which did not recognize slavery) in place for Britain. Slavery thrived where law and conditions allowed, with southern and Caribbean colonies offering both. Britain offered neither. It had a large underemployed workforce and a people who identified with liberty. By 1770, the British had corrupted the refrain of their unofficial national anthem to declare, "Britons never, never shall be slaves." This, as they sang, "was the charter of their land," and they would not suffer returning colonists to undermine it by bringing in their human property to breed an alien institution.[10]

The establishment of slavery in British America and the rising wealth and power of colonial slaveholders raised vexing legal questions. Despite what Blackstone wrote, could those slaveholders visit or move to Britain with their enslaved servants even if they could not have initially enslaved them there? If so, could British residents visiting places with legalized slavery acquire and bring back human property? Partisans on either side raised various analogies. People legally married elsewhere remained so when visiting or moving to Britain, slavery proponents noted, and the same should apply to slavery. Not if (like slavery) the marriage was polygamous or otherwise contravened fundamental British principles, opponents countered.[11] Further, persons who legally owned domesticated animals still did so if they brought them to Britain, proponents added, and that should follow for human property. Under English law, opponents replied, the ownership of a captured wild animal ended if the animal escaped and enslaved persons were more like captured wild animals than domesticated ones because slavery violated natural law and owning pets and livestock did not.[12]

Without a statute resolving the matter, the few relevant common-law rulings only deepened the confusion regarding the status of enslaved Blacks brought into England by their owners. Between 1697 and 1706, three King's Bench opinions by Holt held against their continued enslavement: "The common law takes no notice of negroes being different from other men," he wrote in the final one.[13] A 1677 ruling by the same court but before Holt joined it held otherwise, as did a scattering of lower-court decisions involving unbaptized Blacks legally purchased in the colonies.[14] An earlier, 1569 case, often cited during the 1700s but not found in any original reports, involved an English court purportedly freeing someone purchased in Russia by a visiting Briton named Cartwright. "England was too pure an Air for Slaves to breathe in," the judge supposedly said.[15] Running through these cases but never cited as dispositive in any, a sense persisted that no one could enslave a Christian in Britain, which led enslaved Blacks seeking freedom to obtain baptism.[16]

Faced with these conflicting rulings, colonial slaveholders secured an advisory opinion in 1729 from two British officials, Attorney General Philip Yorke and Solicitor General Charles Talbot. It stated that an enslaved person brought to Britain "doth not become free" by baptism and, while perhaps not allowed to remain enslaved in Britain, "the master may legally compel him to return to the plantations."[17] Only friendly lawyers working with confused precedent could reach such a twisted conclusion, but it was not patently wrong. Somerset and Steuart walked into this legal morass when they disembarked in 1769 and, by the fortitude of the former and the intransigence of the latter, resolved the status of slavery in England but complicated it for America.

Some enslaved persons in England and America understood the confused state of British slavery law. Somerset learned about it after his arrival if he did not know about it before. He did not bolt immediately, however, but continued to serve Steuart for nearly two years as a personal messenger and body servant traveling widely within London and throughout Britain, going on his own as far afield as Bristol and Edinburgh.[18]

At the time, an estimated 15,000 enslaved Blacks lived in Britain. Most resided in London, which then had about three-quarters of a million people (many of them poor) crowded into seven square miles, making it the largest city in Europe. Like Somerset, most of these Blacks came to England with their colonial masters and, if they tried to escape, ran the risk of their masters sending them back to the colonies. A small community of escaped and free Blacks lived on the fringes of London society at places like Black Boy Court and Blackmoor's Alley. A nascent network of white British abolitionists, most of them Quakers or radical Anglicans, helped these Blacks secure or maintain their freedom, and worked to end the slave trade. In London, a devoutly religious moral crusader named Granville Sharp pushed the legal fight against slavery in England while Philadelphia Quaker Anthony Benezet propelled it in America.

The freedom to travel on his own likely allowed the amiable Somerset to establish friends within London's Black community and among its abolitionist supporters. Three of those white abolitionists signed as his godparents when Somerset obtained baptism at an Anglican parish church in Holborn, a rite possibly performed to assist his escape and surely done without Steuart's knowledge or consent. Then, on or around October 1, 1771, James Somerset—described in his baptismal record as "an adult black male about thirty years old"[19]—left Steuart's house, perhaps on an assigned errand, and never returned.

Steuart quickly set out an alarm by engaging slave chasers, posting a reward, or both. Jealous of his reputation, Steuart (according to a popular magazine of the day) viewed Somerset's escape as "insulting his person."[20] He wanted that insult punished and Somerset pursued, much as he had pursued those who fled his bondage in Virginia.[21] Unlike many enslaved persons in London, Somerset did not wear a metal collar or bear a distinct brand on his flesh, but his taller than average height probably made him stand out in the city's Black community. Bounty hunters found him within two months. Steuart did not want him back, however. He no longer trusted him. Further, the uncertainties of slave law in Britain meant that keeping an unwilling person in bondage raised an ongoing risk of flight. In line with the Yorke-Talbot legal opinion, Steuart ordered those who caught Somerset to take him to a ship, the *Ann and Mary*, preparing to depart for Jamaica. There its captain, John Knowles, would resell him. For a middle-aged person used to household duties like Somerset, work in the Caribbean sugar fields likely meant a quick death.

Speed now became critical. Once the ship left Britain for the colonies, slavery effectively reattached. Somerset's only hope lay in a rescue by the abolitionist network before the ship sailed. His three godparents promptly petitioned the chief justice of the King's Bench, Lord Mansfield, for a common-law writ of habeas corpus requiring Knowles to produce Somerset and show cause for his detention, which Mansfield granted on the spot.[22] When Knowles complied, Mansfield released Somerset subject to the promise of sureties, presumably his godparents, to pay if Somerset failed to appear in court on the question of whether Steuart rightfully detained him.[23] Mansfield set the hearing for the next judicial term in January 1772. Somerset then turned for help to Granville Sharp, who secured a team of able young barristers to argue the case pro bono.[24] With wealthy Caribbean planters paying his costs, Steuart hired the best lawyers money could buy, including one who earlier had worked with Sharp.[25] Both sides recognized the potential significance of the case. The press followed it closely.

Mansfield, already the most respected common-law judge of his day and destined to become one of the most esteemed ever, had played the judge's role in this deadly serious game of cat and mouse before. Indeed, he had just concluded a similar case over a captured Black named Thomas Lewis, whom Sharp had rescued by a habeas corpus action from a ship bound for Jamaica. After Lewis's purported owner did not press the legality of slavery in Britain by contesting the writ, Lewis and Sharp tried to force the matter by charging him with false imprisonment. Mansfield dodged that overarching issue by having the jury find that the defendant never owned Lewis, which mooted the question of whether anyone could own a Black in Britain. "I hope it never will be finally decided," Mansfield commented in a cynically pragmatic aside, "for I would have all masters think [their Blacks] were free and all negroes think they were not because then they would both behave better."[26]

This comment spoke volumes about both Mansfield and British policy toward slavery. The son of a Scottish lord, Mansfield married the daughter of an English earl and served in Parliament and as attorney general before becoming lord chief justice of the King's Bench in 1756. A reform-minded royalist, Mansfield sought to yank the English common law from its feudal, agrarian roots and replant it in the soil of a modern commercial empire by making it more attuned to current business practices than medieval agricultural customs. Legal precedent should bend to national policy and moral principle, he believed, and property rights mattered more than anyone's status. This made Mansfield a wild card on the issue of slavery. On the one hand, he loathed destroying the property rights of colonial slaveholders living in Britain, especially when the custom of merchants recognized slavery.[27] On the other hand, he did not want to normalize such a status-based institution as slavery in the industrializing homeland.[28] The absence of common-law precedents and the presence of policies on both sides left Mansfield free to factor in such fundamental legal principles as liberty, property rights, free trade, individual justice, and natural rights.

These principles cut both ways too but, despite Mansfield's conservative leanings, Sharp placed enough hope in the jurist's sense of justice to push for a decision rather than accept a settlement that freed Somerset without resolving the issue of slavery in Britain.[29] Relying on Mansfield's reverence for property rights, Steuart and the colonial slaveholders backing him also refused to settle despite the jurist twice urging them in open court to do so.[30] At least one Caribbean planter feared a loss, however. Asked to predict the fate of Somerset, the planter reportedly replied, "He will be set free, for Lord Mansfield keeps a Black in his house which governs him and the whole family."[31]

The planter referred to a child named Dido Elizabeth, the out-of-wedlock daughter of Mansfield's nephew, Royal Navy Captain (later admiral) Sir John Lindsay, and an enslaved African whom Lindsay took from a captured Spanish ship in 1760. Lindsay then sent the pregnant woman to England, where Mansfield and his wife raised the child almost as part of their family. "He knows he has been reproached for shewing a fondness for her," former Massachusetts governor Thomas Hutchinson said of Mansfield when Hutchinson met Dido at the jurist's estate in 1779.[32] Aged ten at the time of the *Somerset* case and later freed by Mansfield with an annual allowance and inheritance, the girl may have weighed on the jurist's mind. Would he want someone to own her? The planter thought not, and that this personal interest would influence Mansfield's ruling.

At the time, the King's Bench typically disposed of cases quickly—a dozen or more a day during four fixed annual terms of roughly three weeks each. Juries deliberated on the spot; judges rattled off oral rulings. Without official transcripts or written opinions, lawyers and journalists struggled to write down what the barristers and judges said, leading to differing versions of what actually happened.

Habeas corpus actions usually went especially fast because the petitioner could not dispute the cause given for detention. If the respondent gave a plausibly valid reason for holding the petitioner, the court reinstated detention. Somerset's case was different because the agreed cause for his detention—slavery in Britain—stood at issue, and only the court (acting without a jury) could decide its legality. Presumably either side could have raised relevant factual issues, such as whether Steuart and Somerset had moved from Virginia to Massachusetts and then to England, so that Virginia's slave code no longer applied to them.[33] This could have freed Somerset without resolving the issue of whether anyone could bring an enslaved person into Britain even on a visit. Neither side chose to. "By the laws of Virginia this man is a slave; but I submit that the laws of Virginia extend to Virginia alone," Somerset's counsel declared in court. English "air is too pure for him to breathe in."[34]

Far from passing quickly, Somerset's case played out over five hearings stretched over three judicial terms running from January to June 1772. Seven barristers argued the cause for or against slavery in England, the audience growing as London's newspapers trumpeted the case. Five lawyers supporting Somerset pulled forward for liberty while two hired by Steuart pushed back for property—the common law's twin pillars set at odds. England's pure air met calls for colonial comity. Rights versus reality. "Neither the air of England is too pure for a slave to breathe in, nor have the laws of England rejected servitude," Steuart's lawyer declared. He mocked the servants who would defy their masters by saying, "The first step on this happy land sets all men on a perfect level."[35] Somerset's counsel warned that if Steuart prevailed, "Domestic slavery, with its horrid train of evils, may be lawfully imported into this country, at the discretion of every individual foreign and native. It will come not only from our own colonies . . . but from Poland, Russia, Spain, and Turkey."[36] Steuart's team countered with the specter of freedom-seeking slaves from the colonies overrunning Britain: "The means of conveyance, I am told, are manifold."[37]

Somerset's lawyers pressed to prolong the case, perhaps to build public support and steel the judge. Mansfield complied in an apparent hope for a settlement that would free Somerset without setting a precedent for others. He worried aloud in court about the effect of freeing 15,000 enslaved Blacks in Britain, and alternately suggested that Somerset's sponsors buy and free him or that Steuart drop the case.[38] At the hearing in May, Mansfield pointedly warned in legal Latin, "If the parties will have judgement, 'fiat justitia, ruat caelum'; let justice be done whatever be the consequence."[39] Steuart foresaw the result but let it happen. Near the end, he commented about the tone of public opinion. "The papers," he wrote to a friend, "have been tolerably decent with respect to me; but I am sorry for the load of abuse thrown on L[or]d M[ansfield] for hesitating to pronounce judgement in favor of freedom."[40]

Mansfield announced his ruling on June 22, 1772. "The state of slavery is of such a nature, that it is incapable of being introduced on any reasons, moral or political, but only by positive law" or statute, he declared. "It is so odious, that nothing can be suffered to support it, but positive law. Whatever the inconveniences, therefore, may follow from the decision, I cannot say this case is allowed or approved by the law of England; and therefore the black must be discharged."[41] Mansfield did not rest his judgment on immutable constitutional principles, however, but solely on the mutable common law. If they wanted to keep their human property in Britain, he advised colonial slaveholders to seek relief from Parliament.[42]

On balance, Britons welcomed the ruling in Somerset. "As soon as Lord Mansfield had delivered the opinion of the court," one observer noted, Somerset ("who was present at the court"), and "a great many other blacks" there with him, "came forward, and bowed first to the judges, and then to the bar with symptoms of the most extravagant joy."[43] The following Monday, hundreds of Blacks celebrated the ruling at a local tavern.[44] London newspapers generally hailed the result and interpreted it as ending slavery in Britain. According to one disgruntled master, Somerset himself spread that news to enslaved persons whom he knew, leading some to escape.[45] After making the ruling, Mansfield tried to walk it back by claiming it "went no further than to determine the Master had no right to compel the slave to go to a foreign country."[46] In court, however, he and counsel on both sides said that a ruling for Somerset would end slavery in Britain and, despite efforts by colonial slaveholders to evade that result, commentators and the public mostly saw it that way.[47] Proposals in Parliament to allow colonists to keep their enslaved servants in Britain failed.[48]

In England, the *Somerset* case fit into a popular narrative of expanding liberty. By the 1770s in America, however, that narrative clashed with the overriding one of British oppression. With many colonists already in arms about the British Parliament's taking their financial property through taxation, some now worried that the British courts would take their human property by decree. The animus toward American slavery expressed during *Somerset* deepened colonial concerns. "The horrid cruelties, scarcely credible in recital, perpetuated in America, might, by the allowance of slaves amongst us, be introduced here," one of Somerset's lawyers warned in court. "Could your lordship, could any liberal and ingenuous temper, endure, in the fields bordering on this city, to see a wretch bound for some trivial offense to a tree, torn and agonizing beneath the scourge?"[49] Was this how Britons viewed American slavery, colonists asked in reply, and if so, how long would they suffer it to continue? "Have the laws of Virginia any more influence, power, or authority in this country, than the laws of Japan?" another of Somerset's lawyers asked, making the American colonies seem as foreign from Britain as the heathen fiefdom of a god-emperor.

The public debate in Britain over American slavery spawned by *Somerset* mirrored what went on in the courtroom. Even some favoring the institution criticized American excesses while critics of it doubled down against colonial norms. Within weeks of Mansfield's ruling, when an Anglican leader issued a pamphlet defending slavery in the colonies, Sharp shot back with a tract of his own. "We must not, for . . . the supposed advantage or imaginary necessities of our American colonies, lay aside our *Christian charity*," he wrote, "because, whenever we do so, we certainly deserve to be considered in no better light than as an overgrown society of robbers, a mere banditti."[50] Two years later, royalist writer Samuel Johnson complained about the Americans, "How is it that we hear the loudest yelps for liberty among the drivers of negroes?"[51]

No one quite knew what *Somerset* meant for America. On its face, the ruling did not free anyone where local statutes allowed slavery, which included every American colony, but it raised that risk. If slavery "was repugnant to the law in England," one colonial slaveholder living in Britain asked, how could slavery "be the law of America" since an English statute provided that colonial laws could not be "repugnant to the laws of England?"[52] American critics of slavery would press the point. In 1774, for example, Philadelphia Quaker merchant Richard Wells stated in a long, published essay, "We declare with a joint voice, that ALL *the inhabitants of America* are entitled to the privileges of the inhabitants of Great-Britain; if so, by what right do we support slavery?" Then, paraphrasing the widely reported arguments from *Somerset*, he declared, "The instant a slave sets his foot in England he claims the protection of the laws, and puts his master at defiance; if British rights extend to America, *who* shall detain him in bondage?"[53] Further, even if the common law of England did not overcome colonial slavery statutes, under the Declaratory Act, if Parliament could impose taxes in the colonies, it could also end slavery there as well.

At the very least, *Somerset* outraged colonial slaveholders who felt that they had a right to take their property with them to England.[54] By his holding, Chief Justice Mansfield answered a resounding no to his rhetorical question, "Whether any dominion, authority or coercion can be exercised in this country, on a slave according to the American law?"[55] As such, he upheld Blackstone's view of the colonies as dependent domains.[56] Regardless of the views of Americans on slavery, this played into their fears of British tyranny.

Colonial newspapers closely covered the proceedings in *Somerset* and exploded with a flurry of articles when Mansfield issued his ruling. "The late decision with regard to Somerset the Negro," the *Boston News-Letter* predicted, "will occasion a greater ferment in America ... than the Stamp Act itself."[57] An essay in another Boston newspaper warned about the ruling, "A fermentation must be dreaded from so great an alternation of the conditions of men as will ensue from robbing a master" in two ways: "First of his money given for the slave ... and then ... the moneys" taken by taxes.[58] Favorable reports on *Somerset* appeared mainly in loyalist newspapers that defended all things British.[59]

Having turned against Britain by this time, as sharp a critic of slavery as Benjamin Franklin could see little good in *Somerset*. "Pharisaical Britain," he wrote in a published editorial, "to pride thyself in setting free *a single Slave* that happens to land on thy coasts, while thy Merchants in all thy ports are encouraged by thy laws to continue a commerce whereby so many *hundreds of thousands* are dragged into slavery."[60] In a letter to Philadelphia abolitionist Anthony Benezet, Franklin fumed against the hypocrisy of Britain "for promoting the Guinea Trade, while it piqu'd itself on its Virtue Love of Liberty, and the Equity of its Courts in setting free a single Negro."[61]

Reinforcing American perceptions of British hypocrisy over slavery, the *Somerset* case coincided with a royal veto of a widely publicized colonial effort to rein in the transatlantic slave trade. In March 1772, Virginia's House of Burgesses had passed a bill designed to restrain the importation of enslaved persons into the colony by a prohibitive tariff.[62] It did not limit slavery within Virginia, of course, nor the export of enslaved people from the colony. At the time, Virginia held more people in bondage than any other mainland colony, with their owners profiting from breeding and selling them. Indeed, nearly half of all Blacks in British North America lived there, most them enslaved, while slave-holding white planters controlled the legislature. The burgesses had long wanted to bar the entry or import of more Africans to boost the value of those already there. But to maintain the lucrative slavery trade, the king had vetoed such bans. Now, with its 1772 law, the burgesses sought to use their tax powers to obtain that result through prohibitive tariffs on the unwanted trade.

The burgesses had tried this once before, in 1769, only to have a coalition of English merchants, who would lose business under the restrictive tariff, secure a royal veto. They argued that Virginia lawmakers simply wanted to raise the value of their own human property by limiting imports.[63] Taking advantage of the growing popular sentiment against the transatlantic slave trade, the House of Burgesses submitted its 1772 bill along with a petition condemning the "great Inhumanity" of that trade and suggesting that they passed this bill to curtail it.[64] To no avail. The king's veto came even as the King's Bench decreed slavery too odious for England's pristine air.

Already aggrieved by British taxes and troops, colonists could not help but feel a slap. Slavery, too odious for the English, appeared fine for colonists so long as it served imperial interests. Certainly, in their petition, the burgesses whitewashed their motives, but some powerful white Virginians did oppose the Atlantic slave trade and a few (including physician Arthur Lee, planter George Mason, and Quaker activist Robert Pleasants) opposed slavery. In a 1764 essay disparaging the "cruelty, cunning, perfidy, and cowardice" of Africans that "fitted" them for slavery, for example, Lee condemned the institution itself as a violation "of justice and humanity" and "always an enemy to virtue and science."[65] Two years after George III vetoed the Virginia tariff, in a pamphlet that burnished his credentials as a patriot, Thomas Jefferson listed "his majesty's negative" as a key grievance against the king. By depicting the tax, which he claimed would "exclude all further importations from Africa," as a calculated step toward "the abolition of domestic slavery," Jefferson all but blamed American slavery on Britain.[66]

One group of Americans did embrace *Somerset*, however: free and enslaved Blacks. Some bolted for England, or at least tried to, though no one will ever know how many succeeded. Escaping slavery in America was hard enough—passage from America to England even harder for Blacks not taken there as servants. In one of the most outlandish arguments by either side in *Somerset*, Steuart's chief counsel warned that Blacks would flood into Britain from the colonies should the court free Somerset. "Most negroes who have money (and I think that description will include nearly all)," the lawyer asserted about American Blacks, will "make interest with the common sailor to be carried hither."[67] Evidence exists that the "notion," as one Virginia planter then put it, of escaping to England became "prevalent" within the enslaved population and that at least some Blacks attempted it—but that route to freedom never became common.[68]

A Somerset-like story of escape appeared in a June 30, 1774, notice placed in the *Virginia Gazette* by Gabriel Jones, a rich frontier lawyer then serving in the House of Burgesses. Bacchus, whom the notice described as Jones's thirty-year-old "Negro Manservant," had run away on June 16 wearing dress clothes, "neat Shoes [with] Silver Buckles," and "a fine hat cut and cocked." Jones depicted Bacchus as a cunning fellow, "very capable of living alone," and familiar with the region, "having constantly rode with me for some years past." He had trusted Bacchus with money, Jones noted, and "thought [Bacchus] had proved his Fidelity." He "will probably endeavour to pass as a Freeman under the Name of *John Chapman*," Jones wrote, "and get on Board some Vessel bound for Great Britain, from the Knowledge he has of the late Determination of *Somerset's* Case."[69] The same notice ran in later issues of the newspaper, suggesting that Bacchus remained free for some time, if not indefinitely.[70]

Rather than seeing escape to England as a viable option, however, some American Blacks sought to extend *Somerset*'s reach to the colonies even though, by its terms, it did not apply there. Massachusetts offered the most hope because, while its laws allowed hereditary slavery for Blacks and Native Americans captured in war or sold into bondage, those enslaved people retained standing to sue in court and petition the government for redress—two basic English rights not usually held by the enslaved in America. Individuals in the colony regularly filed freedom suits challenging the basis of their enslavement or seeking to enforce manumission contracts, and often succeeded if they could prove their claims. John Adams witnessed such a trial in 1767—his first—and commented on it with wonder. "This is call'd suing for Liberty," Adams wrote in his diary, "the first Action that ever I knew, of the Sort."[71]

Freedom suits multiplied in Massachusetts after *Somerset* but differed from that landmark case because *Somerset* asserted that slavery violated English common law while plaintiffs in freedom suits argued that their particular enslavement did not comply with their colony's slavery statutes. They might claim to have a free mother, for example, or to have fulfilled agreed terms for their manumission. Accordingly, these lawsuits turned on the facts of each case, which jurors (rather than judges) decided. At least after *Somerset*, Massachusetts jurors tended to favor the enslaved.[72] "I never knew a Jury by a Verdict to determine a Negro to be a Slave," Adams later said of this revolutionary era in colonial law. "They always found them free."[73] Still, the process only freed one person at a time, and their outcome need not have reflected a popular repudiation of slavery. At the time, Massachusetts required slaveholders to post a £50 surety bond for each individual that they manumitted. Estates needed to post this bond for anyone freed in a will. If not posted, the slaveholders or their heirs might later try to renege on the manumission—leading to a freedom suit. The process of informal manumissions also made it difficult to determine when individuals like John Hancock or Samuel Adams, who consistently opposed slavery, actually freed the enslaved household workers that they inherited or acquired by marriage and kept on as paid, free employees.

Because *Somerset* upheld slavery where statutes authorized it, enslaved Blacks in Massachusetts increasingly looked toward their colonial legislature or "General Court" for relief. The Assembly had tried to halt the importation of enslaved persons into the colony by legislation in 1771, but in line with British policy, the loyalist royal governor, Thomas Hutchinson, vetoed it.[74] Then, following *Somerset*, an enslaved Bostonian named Felix, on behalf "of many slaves" in and around Boston, filed a freedom petition with the General Court on January 6, 1773. "We have no Property! We have no Wives! No Children! We have no City! No Country!" the petition exclaimed. "We pray for such Relief only, which ... to us will be as Life from the dead."[75] Freedom.

Though the Assembly took no action on it, Felix's petition generated at least some public comment. "For this People to be *talking* of *Liberty*," the preface to a printed edition of the petition noted about the people of Massachusetts, "and, at the same Time to be importing and making *Slaves* of whole Cargoes of their Fellow Creatures [is] ... a Solecism of Language."[76] Linking the petition to *Somerset*, a newspaper essayist added, "All People who should *ever* inhabit within the Province, should enjoy the same *Liberties* and *Privileges* as if in *England*."[77]

Encouraged by the response to his first petition, Felix (now identified as Felix Holbrook), along with three other named Black petitioners, submitted a second, bolder, appeal to the General Court on April 20, 1773. "The divine spirit of *freedom*, seems to fire every humane breast on this continent, except" those lawmakers who resisted extending it to those actually enslaved. The plan proposed in this second petition included not only freedom for enslaved Blacks but also their transport "to some part of the Coast of *Africa*."[78] After several towns in Massachusetts instructed their representatives to support the petition with a program of gradual emancipation, Holbrook and other unnamed Blacks, "on behalf of all those who ... are held in a state of SLAVERY within the bowels of a FREE country," sent a third petition in June 1773.[79] Declaring that slavery deprived them "of every thing that has a tendency to make life even tolerable," in addition to restating their prior requests for freedom and transport to Africa, the petitioners asked in the alternative for "some part of the unimproved land, belonging to the province, for a settlement."[80]

The freedom petitions posed problems for patriot lawmakers in Massachusetts. By then in control of the General Court and at loggerheads with the royal governor, they sought to unite white colonists against enslavement by Britain, not divide them over the enslavement of Africans. The British were already scoffing at Americans for demanding their liberty while enslaving Blacks, and beginning to use *Somerset* to seek support among Black Americans. Further, like the Quakers of Pennsylvania and perhaps inspired by the Revolutionary rhetoric of liberty, a growing number of New England Congregationalists were turning against slavery. Their voice came through in some of the towns instructing their legislators to support the freedom petitions. Most white colonists probably still supported slavery, however, or at least opposed freeing Blacks to live in their midst. This may account for the proposal to transport freed Blacks to Africa or an unsettled part of the colony. "This scheme," the June petition noted, "will remove all rational objections to our freedom."[81]

Equivocating, the General Court referred the June petition to a committee that included such prominent patriots as John Hancock and Samuel Adams who, while opposed to slavery, cared more about closing ranks against the British.[82] "I will not be a slave," Hancock had declared at the height of the Stamp Act crisis in 1765—a time when he likely still owned three Blacks inherited in 1764 from his uncle.[83] Adams spoke in similar terms while holding one Black given as a marriage present to his wife in 1764. By 1773, both men had freed those servants but still dodged the issue of abolishing slavery for fear of alienating whites from the patriot cause. Seeking time to weigh its response, the committee deferred debate on the petition until the next legislative session in January 1774.[84] By then, the Boston Tea Party had scrambled patriot politics and upended the colony's government.

The Tea Party resulted from the ill-advised passage by Parliament of the Tea Act in May 1773. In the face of colonial boycotts of taxed British goods, Parliament had repealed the hated Townshend tariffs three years before, but preserved, on principle, the one on tea. With colonial boycotts of British tea continuing even as other factors crippled the East India Company, Parliament, under the leadership of Lord North, passed the Tea Act to lower the price of the company's tea in America below that of smuggled tea without repealing the Townshend tariff. The Sons of Liberty saw the Act as a scheme to gain American acceptance of the tax, which in part it was, and organized to stop the tea from reaching American consumers. Having prevented the company from offloading its tea from ships in Boston Harbor, on December 16, 1773, patriots lightly disguised as Native Americans and led by Hancock and Adams boarded the ships and dumped 46 tons of loose tea into the harbor—reportedly enough to taint the water brown.

"There is a Dignity, a Majesty, a Sublimity, in this last Effort of the Patriots, that I greatly admire. The People should never rise, without doing something to be remembered—something notable And striking," John Adams wrote in his diary on the day following the tea's destruction. "What Measures will the Ministry take, in Consequences of this?—Will they resent it? will they dare to resent it? will they punish Us? How? By quartering Troops upon Us?—by annulling our Charter?—by laying on more duties? By restraining our Trade? By Sacrifice of Individuals, or how."[85] The British did them all, and more.

Under North, Parliament responded forcefully to the Boston Tea Party with the so-called Intolerable Acts. These new statutes closed the port of Boston until colonists paid for the tea, revoked the colony's charter, made the General Court's upper house appointed by the crown rather than elected by colonists, and authorized the transfer of criminal trials for royal officers to London. Reaching beyond Massachusetts to all the American colonies, the Acts empowered royal governors to quarter troops in privately owned buildings, and transferred the Ohio Country from the jurisdiction of the older, more rebellious colonies extending from Virginia to Massachusetts to the newly acquired, more docile colony of Quebec. Finally, Britain replaced Hutchinson as the governor of Massachusetts with General Thomas Gage, who concentrated over 3,000 British troops and a large naval presence in Boston.

With these matters unfolding, the General Court took up the freedom petition in January 1774. The petitioners added a memorial addressing the changed conditions. "The many steadfast resolutions made by this large province to maintain their liberties and privileges," the memorial began, "gives us . . . great expectations of your taking up our last petition . . . and give us the thousands of poor unhappy Africans their freedom, which we as men, and by nature have a right to demand." It closed with a plea "that his Majesty would hear your prayers, and that you would hear ours."[86] Instead, turning the slavery issue against the British without splitting patriot ranks, on the committee's recommendation, the General Court responded to the petition by passing another bill barring the importation of enslaved persons into the colony.[87] To avoid the *Somerset* issue, the restriction would not apply to visitors or short-term residents who brought along a "Negro or other such Person or Persons as necessary servants."[88] As patriot lawmakers surely foresaw, in line with imperial policy, Gage rejected the measure and thereby appeared to put Britain on the side of slavery.[89] Check and checkmate in the game of patriot politics without a single Black going free.

The petitioners then focused their attention on Gage with a petition to him in May 1774, followed by a similar one to the General Court in June. "Your Petitioners apprehind we have in common with all other men a naturel right to our freedoms," the May petition began. "But we were unjustly dragged by the cruel hand of power . . . and Brought hither to be made slaves for Life in a Christian land." The May petition asked Gage to "cause an act of the legislative to be pessed that we may obtain our Natural right [to] our freedoms and our children be set at lebety."[90] The June petition renewed the plea for a remote tract of land where "each of us may quietly sit down under his own fig tree."[91]

The June petition had barely arrived when Gage dissolved the Assembly for appointing delegates to attend an intercolonial convention called to coordinate American resistance to the Intolerable Acts. Meeting from September 4 to October 26, 1774, in Philadelphia, this First Continental Congress brought together representatives from twelve colonies, including Samuel and John Adams of Massachusetts, Rhode Island's Stephen Hopkins, John Dickinson of Pennsylvania, and Virginia's George Washington and Patrick Henry.

With normal political processes disrupted, nothing more came of the effort by the enslaved people of Massachusetts to obtain their freedom until after the American Revolution. Gage authorized the election of a new assembly in 1774, but its members refused to meet with an appointed upper house and instead convened an extralegal provincial congress outside Boston under the protection of the colonial militia. Soon, British officials in Massachusetts could not venture beyond the range of Royal Navy guns without the protection of armed British troops.[92] The shooting war would begin the following spring, when Gage sent troops to capture the colonial armory at Concord.

In the meantime, Cæsar Sarter, a free Black living north of Boston, drew on the freedom petitions to publish an address in the August 17, 1774, issue of his local newspaper, the *Essex Journal*, uniting the causes of American and African liberty. Born free in Africa, transported as a youth to America, and enslaved for two decades before regaining his freedom, Sarter addressed his appeal to slaveholders in Massachusetts. "At this time of great anxiety and distress among you, on account of the infringement not only of your Charter rights; but of the natural rights and privileges of freeborn men," he began, "permit [me] . . . to tell you" about slavery and liberty.

"As Slavery is the greatest, and consequently most to be dreaded, of all temporal calamities: So its opposite, Liberty, is the greatest temporal good," Sarter declared. Turning their own rhetoric against them, he asked white patriots, "Now, if you are sensible, that slavery is in itself, and in its consequences, a great evil; why will you not pity and relieve the poor, distressed, enslaved Africans?" With twelve relatives still in bondage, Sarter linked the cause of white colonists to that of their enslaved servants. "Would you desire the preservation of your own liberty?" he asked. "As the first step let the oppressed Africans be liberated; then, and not till then, may you with confidence and consistency of conduct, look to Heaven for a blessing on your endeavours to knock the shackles with which your task masters are hampering you, from your own feet."

Sarter posed the question for a revolutionary age: Would white Americans embrace liberty for some and slavery for others, or liberty for all? "If in this attempt to serve my countrymen, I have advanced any thing to the purpose," he closed his appeal without differentiating whether by "my countrymen" he meant Africans or Americans, "I pray it may not be the less noticed for coming from an African."[93]

CHAPTER FOUR

The Declaration of Liberty

1774–1776

The day after Cæsar Sarter published his address in the *Essex Journal*, the *New-York Journal*, New York's leading patriot newspaper, featured a "new song" titled "The Glorious SEVENTY FOUR" to the old tune of a popular Royal Navy anthem. Appearing as they did in late August 1774, after most colonists had come to reject the Intolerable Acts as incompatible with their rights as British subjects, these two pieces reflected the new landscape of American politics as seen through the eyes of Blacks and whites.

Read with hindsight, Sarter's essay all but recognized the futility of reconciling with Britain and linked liberty for all with American independence. Massachusetts legislators, "to their immortal honor," had voted to end the slave trade, Sarter noted. "That they have not succeeded in their laudable endeavours was not their fault," he wrote, but that of the royal governor, who vetoed the measure. Free from British rule, liberty for all could follow, Sarter suggested: "I need not point out the absurdity of your exertions for liberty, while you have slaves in your houses." He never questioned that the British had enslaved Americans;

he only asked that Americans learn from their "present calamities" not to enslave Africans.[1]

Written with foresight, the *New-York Journal*'s new song also seemingly acknowledged the futility of such a reconciliation and welcomed a new era of American liberty. The first verse railed against slavery in a distinctly British American fashion:

> COME, *come, my brave boys, from my song you shall hear,*
> *That we'll crown Seventy-four, a most glorious year;*
> *We'll convince* Bute *and* Mansfield *and* North *tho' they rave,*
> *Britons still like themselves spurn the chains of a slave.*[2]

This version of the song included a reworked first verse that called out Bute for initiating taxation without representation and North for championing the Intolerable Acts. Known in America for the *Somerset* case, Mansfield perhaps bore censure for infringing on the liberty of colonists to own slaves. At the time, the *New-York Journal* regularly ran advertisements offering rewards for the return of escaped enslaved and indentured servants. One such notice appeared across the page from its new song spurning slavery's chains.[3]

Along with Sarter's address and the *Journal*'s new song, the late August issues of these papers included articles originating from New England to the Carolinas of colonists meeting to choose or dispatch delegates for the intercolonial congress called for September in Philadelphia.[4] Such reports, echoed in hundreds of articles in dozens of newspapers from New Hampshire to South Carolina, displayed the anticipation and enthusiasm generated by the First Continental Congress. The American colonies had met in congress twice before—once in Albany during the French and Indian War and once in New York to protest the Stamp Act—but nothing like this had ever happened.[5] Aside from those two congresses, both brief and having little impact, and a few ongoing ties among neighboring colonies in New England, astride the Delaware River, or around the Chesapeake Bay, British colonies in North America radiated like spokes of a wheel outward from London. Britain favored this arrangement because it fostered dependency and discouraged independency. Now, in the shadow cast by ten years of taxation without representation and darkness resulting from the Intolerable Acts, the colonies were assembling with broad popular support and in defiance of their royal governors.

Staging the new Congress raised constitutional questions that touched on matters of liberty and slavery. On whose authority did the Congress assemble and act, for example, and if on the peoples' authority, which people? The English Board of Trade had called the Albany Congress in 1754, with the acting royal governor of New York presiding. Seven colonies attended. In 1765, without seeking approval from British officials, the patriot-led Massachusetts Assembly had initiated the Stamp Act Congress by inviting other colonial assemblies to send delegates to a joint meeting. Representatives from nine colonies showed up, with many of them chosen over the objection of their royal governors at ad hoc or extralegal meetings of assembly members. Unable to prevent it from meeting, the host state's acting royal governor denounced the Congress as illegal.

As news of the Intolerable Acts reverberated through the colonies during the spring and summer of 1774, calls for another intercolonial congress arose from many quarters. The Massachusetts Assembly managed to elect delegates before Governor Gage disbanded it for doing so. The two colonies with elected governors and charters that did not rely on British authority, Connecticut and Rhode Island, also chose delegates through normal processes. Elsewhere, extralegal conventions, committees, or meetings—some elected for the purpose as in New Jersey, some composed of assembly members as in Virginia, and some simply gatherings of citizens as in South Carolina—named delegates. Only the royal governor of far-off Georgia successfully kept his colony's patriot faction from sending delegates to the Congress.[6]

Tying sovereignty to the crown, loyalists denounced the entire process of calling and staging the Continental Congress as unconstitutional. Inclined to lodge sovereignty in the people, however, patriots increasingly saw their actions as fundamentally constitutional and the Intolerable Acts, particularly the ones revising the Massachusetts charter and closing Boston Harbor, as gross violations of law and liberty. Yet, if sovereignty lay in the people, no evidence shows that anyone other than property-owning white males participated in the mechanisms leading to the selection of delegates. For patriot purposes, free white men represented the people.[7]

Despite its limitations, the First Continental Congress set the stage for how the various colonies (or later, states) would work together during the Revolution. From the start, the restrictions on Massachusetts imposed by the Intolerable Acts stood as the rallying point for delegates and the people from all the colonies. "Be comforted ye oppressed Bostonians!" came news from the public meeting held in Charleston, South Carolina, to elect delegates. "And tremble ye minions of slavery!—a blow will soon be struck, if you urge us to that extremity, which will convince you, that one soul animates three millions of brave Americans." Described in this account as "the largest body of the most respectable inhabitants that had ever been seen together upon any public occasion here," the South Carolina assemblage (acting by ballot open to "every free white person residing in the province") chose three delegates—all slaveholders—and approved aid for Boston, which suffered privation with its port closed. The crisis brought on by the Intolerable Acts united every "free born American, and overlooked all distinctions" of personage, the report stated, except apparently those of race and slavery.[8]

Such distinctions persisted in Massachusetts too. Only one of the Bay Colony's delegates to the Congress, Thomas Cushing, came from a slaveholding family; but none of the others—Samuel Adams, John Adams, and Robert Treat Paine—had taken a public stand against slavery, even though the freedom petitions of Black residents had helped to make abolition a public issue in Massachusetts. Making "a splendid show," as one observer wryly commented, the Massachusetts delegates rode to Philadelphia in Cushing's carriage drawn by four horses. Trailing them in servant's livery, two Black attendants rode on horseback and two walked.[9] Throngs cheered the party along its way, with the accompanying Black attendants adding to the show. "No Governor of a Province, nor General of an Army was ever treated with so much Ceremony," John Adams wrote at the time with obvious delight.[10] "We are universally acknowledged the Saviors and Defenders of American Liberty."[11]

Massachusetts remained at center stage when Congress convened in September, particularly after Paul Revere arrived on horseback with a series of resolutions from Boston's home county of Suffolk. Repeatedly invoking the slavery metaphor to assail Britain, the Suffolk Resolves stopped short of calling for war. Instead, after denouncing the Intolerable Acts "as the attempts of a wicked administration to enslave America," and placing them in the context of an extended parliamentary plot to impose the "curses of slavery upon us, our heirs and their heirs forever," they urged a purely economic response. "The fate of this new world, and of unborn millions," depends on standing for liberty and not to "yield to voluntary slavery," the Resolves roared. "Until our rights are fully restored to us," they then purred, "we will, to the utmost of our power, and we recommend the same to the other counties [in Massachusetts], to withhold all commercial intercourse with Great-Britain."[12] Congress approved the Suffolk Resolves on September 18 and, after a further month of fitful debate, adopted a similar approach for the colonies as a whole. Then it abruptly adjourned. If Bostonians were not ready for war, the Congress would not start one.

By this point, trade boycotts had become the standard American response to imperial infractions of colonial rights. Even the largely ineffectual Stamp Act Congress proposed one. When dispatching delegates to the new Congress, virtually every colony directed them to orchestrate an effective economic response to the Intolerable Acts, and did so in more specific terms than the Suffolk Resolves. "The colony was ready to go into resolutions of non-importation and non-exportation" if decreed by the Congress, the meeting naming South Carolina's delegates declared, and every merchant present pledged not to import "British or East India goods, wines and slaves" in the meantime.[13] The convention of deputies choosing North Carolina's delegates adopted similar resolutions, with imports to end in January and exports to follow in October.[14] A meeting of Fairfax County, Virginia, freeholders chaired by George Washington added a pledge against the sale or consumption of British goods "until American grievances be redressed."[15]

Despite the growing abolition movement centered in Boston and the censure of colonial enslavement expressed by the Suffolk Resolves, those resolutions never raised the issue of chattel slavery—not even to criticize Gage for vetoing legislation to end the slave trade. In this respect, the southern colonies went further than Massachusetts. "We will neither import any slave or slaves, nor purchase any slave or slaves, imported or brought into this province by others, from any part of the world" so long as the grievances lasted, North Carolina's convention resolved.[16] Making a similar pledge, the Fairfax County freeholders added, "We take this opportunity of declaring our most earnest wishes, to see an entire stop forever put to such a wicked, cruel, and unnatural trade."[17] These and other instructions to the assembling delegates made the Atlantic slave trade a necessary agenda item for the Congress. Ending it would not only put America on the side of liberty but would also hurt British and British West Indian interests without freeing any enslaved Americans. Indeed, it could raise their value to their owners, which could account for the readiness of southerners to embrace limits on the widely vilified Atlantic slave trade.

Always impatient, John Adams went from euphoria at the outset when Congress confirmed its support for Massachusetts by approving the Suffolk Resolves—"one of the happiest Days of my Life," he noted in his diary for September 17—to frustration by the end when the delegates did little more for liberty.[18] "In Congress, nibbling and quibbling—as usual," Adams wrote about his fellow delegates on October 24. "These great

Witts, these subtle Cricticks, these refined Genius's, these learned Law-yers, these wise Statemen, are so fond of shewing their Parts and Powers, as to make their Consultations very tedius."[19] Expressly attributing their grievances to "a ruinous system of colonial administration, adopted by the British ministry about the year 1763, calculated for inslaving these colonies," the delegates concluded their work by creating a "Continen-tal Association." By its terms, the Association would enforce a boycott of British imports beginning December 1774; restrictions on the con-sumption of British goods after March 1775, and a suspension of exports in September 1775. "We will neither import nor purchase, any slave imported after the first day of December next," it stated, "after which time, we will wholly discontinue the slave trade."[20] Adams wanted a mil-itary response as well but concluded regarding other delegates, as he put it in a private letter, "They will not at this Session vote to raise Men or Money, or Arms or Ammunition. Their opinions are fixed against Hos-tilities and Ruptures."[21]

Beyond approving the Suffolk Resolves and adopting the Associa-tion—its principal acts of immediate significance—the First Continen-tal Congress debated and ruled on two matters that affected the cause of liberty and the case of slavery going forward. It began by debating whether each colony would have equal or proportionate weight in voting and, if the latter, how to factor in enslaved persons. "Will not People com-plain," Patrick Henry asked, "10,000 Virginians have not outweighed 1000 others?"[22] In the end, Congress resolved to give one vote to each colony because it lacked "proper materials for ascertaining" their rela-tive weight.[23] The uneven distribution of disenfranchised Blacks would complicate the issue of representation throughout the Revolutionary era.

The delegates also struggled to identify the sources of their rights as British colonists before ultimately naming three: "the laws of Nature, the principles of the English Constitution, and [colonial] charters and compacts."[24] As even a casual reader of Locke's *Second Treatise of Gov-ernment* and Mansfield's *Somerset* decision knew—and many of these delegates studied such authorities closely—slavery fared differently depending on which of these sources controlled. What Nature might abhor, an unwritten constitution could ignore, and local charters and statutes allow. Invoking all three sources for American liberty left the legitimacy of slavery uncertain. With Virginia planter Peyton Randolph serving as its president and most of its other members also slaveholders, the First Continental Congress never debated abolition or manumission.

One final matter the Congress did address became its most significant action. On October 22, four days before voting to adjourn, it called for a Second Continental Congress to convene in Philadelphia beginning the following May.[25] This became the fateful one, but even John Adams did not see that coming. "Took our Departure in a very great Rain, from . . . Phyladelphia," he noted in his diary for October 28. "It is not very likely that I shall ever see this Part of the World again."[26] Riding snugly in a closed carriage, he never mentioned the liveried Blacks trailing behind in the pouring rain. By this point, the non-slaveholding delegates from Massachusetts had forged alliances with slaveholding ones from Virginia—particularly the Adamses and the Lees—with liberty for the colonies taking precedence over all else.[27]

Perhaps blinded by hope, many Americans thought that, faced with stiff resolve and a punishing boycott, Parliament would repeal its imperial edicts, or at least relax them. Leading patriots let on that Americans might pay for the tea if the British would thereafter treat them like subjects of the crown rather than slaves of the Ministry then in control of Parliament. "Admit that the Ministry . . . should be able to carry the point of taxation, and reduce us to a state of perfect humiliation and slavery," Congress asked in a letter to the British people. "May not a Ministry with the same armies inslave you?" Liberty should prevail, it reasoned, not power. "The cause of America is now the object of universal attention," the letter concluded with patriotic bravado.[28]

Congress had drawn a line in the sand and left it for Britain to respond. "The Colonists have now taken such grounds that Great Britain must relax, or inevitably involve herself in a civil war," Pennsylvania delegate John Dickinson wrote during Congress's final week. "I wish for peace ardently, but . . . the first act of violence on the part of Administration in America, or the attempt to reinforce General Gage this winter or next, will put the whole Continent in arms."[29]

When the British government showed no signs of relenting by year's end, hopes for peace began to fade in beleaguered Boston. Depicting Gage's occupying army as the "Nursery of Slavery," James Otis's wise and witty sister, Mercy Otis Warren, warned in December 1774, "I behold the civil sword Brandish'd over our Heads & an innocent Land Drenched in Blood."[30] About that same time, her friend Abigail Adams wrote about the impasse, "We consider it as a struggle from which we shall obtain a release from our present bondage by an ample redress of our Grieveances—or a redress by the Sword. The only alternative which every American thinks is of Liberty or Death." Repeating the slavery metaphor, she declared that Americans had "all the Horrours of a civil war threatning us on one hand, and the chains of Slavery forged for us on the other."[31]

Writing to her husband John at the Congress during September 1774, Abigail Adams had equated the cause of liberty from political enslavement for Americans with that of liberty for those physically enslaved by Americans. "I wish more sincerely there was not a Slave in the province," she observed. "It allways appeared a most iniquitious Scheme to me— fight ourselfs for what we are daily robbing and plundering from those who have as good a right to freedom as we have." John had remained silent on the issue and Abigail here suggested that she had pressed him on it before by adding, "You know my mind on this Subject."[32] Like her brother James and her friend Abigail, Mercy Otis Warren also linked the two causes of liberty by speaking out against the enslavement of colonists by Britain and of Blacks by colonists. "I am more and more convinced, of the propensity in human nature to tyranize over their fellow man," she wrote in 1775, and thus to banish "the ideas of native freedom, and the equal liberty of man" from America.[33] Defending equal liberty became her lifelong goal.

Liberty seemed even more in peril after the January 1775 publication in America of the king's speech opening a new session of Parliament. Denouncing the "most daring spirit of resistance" prevailing in Massachusetts and the encouragement given to it by other colonies, George III assured Parliament of his "firm and steadfast resolution to withstand every attempt to weaken or impair the supreme authority of this Legislature over all the dominions of My Crown."[34] Suddenly, in patriot eyes, the king became as much an enemy to liberty as Parliament. "The die is cast," Abigail Adams wrote to Mercy Otis Warren upon reading the king's speech. "Yesterday brought us such a Speech from the Throne as will stain with everlasting infamy the reign of George the 3. . . . It seems to me the Sword is now our only, yet dreadful alternative." The published replies from the Houses of Commons and Lords praising the speech made matters worse, she added. "The Friends of Liberty" in America, she wrote, "will rather chuse no doubt to die the last British freemen, than bear to live the first of British Slaves."[35]

The beginning of April brought the further news that, in a February address to the king, the two houses of Parliament had declared Massachusetts in open rebellion to British authority. Further, the prime minister had proposed dispatching 10,000 troops and 14 frigates with 2,000 sailors to Boston.[36] "All things wear a warlike appearance here," James Warren wrote to his wife Mercy Otis Warren from the patriot command center at Concord. "This Town is full of Cannon, stores, ammunition, etc., and the [British] Army long for them and they want nothing but strength to Induce an attempt on them. The people are ready and determined to defend this Country Inch by Inch."[37] By this time, patriot congresses or conventions had assumed effective control of governance in most colonies and chosen delegates to a second Continental Congress scheduled to begin in May 1775.

"The last Address of the Two Houses has extinguished every spark of hope," the renowned and revered Harvard professor John Winthrop wrote on April 10 to British Enlightenment philosopher and abolitionist Richard Price. "They say, the Americans will never have the courage to fight, but . . . when they see themselves treated like a parcel of slaves on a plantation, who are to work just as they are ordered by their masters, . . . and then judge whether it be likely that such men will give up every thing dear and valuable to them without a struggle."[38]

By this point, rumors had enslaved Blacks taking different sides in the looming battle. Abigail Adams, for example, warned her husband of a supposed "conspiracy of the Negros" to tell Gage that "they would fight for him provided he would arm them and engage to liberate them if he conquerd."[39] Other reports had Blacks joining patriots resisting the British occupation of Boston.[40] In the coming war for freedom, enslaved Americans had to choose which side best served their interest in liberty.[41]

The widespread practice of chattel slavery in British America shaped the war in other ways as well. From the outset, for example, mainland patriots sought to recruit British Caribbean colonists in Jamaica, Barbados, and elsewhere to their cause. In theory at least, the Stamp Act and the Declaratory Act "enslaved" white colonists there as much as those on the mainland, but the former never joined the latter in active resistance. With the Intolerable Acts bringing matters to a head in Massachusetts by early 1776, however, the Jamaican colonial assembly weighed in with a petition to the king that laid bare the constraints imposed by slavery on the so-called sugar colonies.

Jamaica (as much as Massachusetts) wanted "to avert that last greatest of Calamities, that of being reduced to an abject State of Slavery" by acts of Parliament, the petition stated. "Its very small number of white inhabitants, and its peculiar situation from the incumbrance of more than Two Hundred Thousand Slaves" ruled out "resistance," however. Twelve thousand whites in Jamaica could not keep twenty times that number of Blacks in bondage and, at the same time, fight for their own freedom, the petitioners all but stated. Jamaica could only "humbly approach the Throne" and "beseech" the king "to become a Mediator" between his "American Subjects" and Parliament.[42]

The petitioners penned their plea without a hint of irony because they felt none. Their rights were due them under the "English Constitution" as "a part of the English people," the petition explained, and so presumably did not extend to their enslaved Blacks. And their rights mattered, the petitioners added in an unwittingly revealing appendix, because of the economic "importance of the Island of Jamaica, to the Kingdom of Great Britain"—an importance they explicitly tied to the products of enslaved labor.[43] Slaveholding, the petitioners as much as admitted, constrained their actions and, in this way, restricted the Revolutionary movement to the mainland colonies. Further, as events played out, the relative "importance" of all of its so-called sugar colonies would lead Britain to prioritize their defense over the reconquest of its mainland colonies in the ensuing war for American independence.

Slavery also affected how some colonists viewed the patriot cause, particularly in Massachusetts. Presenting as dark a picture of imperial oppression as any patriot pamphleteer, for example, a sermon by Baptist minister John Allan, then serving a church in Boston, blamed slavery for America's enslavement. "With what face can you look up to the ALMIGHTY," Allan asked in a published sermon from 1774, "and beg of him his aid and assistance in our political affairs, while we are oppressing our *African* brethren ten thousand times as much by keeping them in slavery for life?" He called on the people of Massachusetts to abolish "this vile custom of slave-making, either by a law of the province, common law, (which I am told has happily succeeded in many instances of late) or by a voluntary releasement."[44] Similar pleas came from Quaker abolitionists in Pennsylvania and a community of Scottish Calvinists in Georgia. "We hereby declare our disapprobation and abhorrence of the unnatural practice of Slavery in America," the Georgia resolution declared, "a practice founded in cruelty and injustice, and . . . laying the basis for that liberty we contend for upon a very wrong foundation."[45]

No published argument of this sort carried more weight in America than *A Dialogue Concerning the Slavery of the Africans* by New England theologian Samuel Hopkins, the most influential Congregationalist minister of the era and a disciple of the early eighteenth-century neo-Puritan or "New Light" theologian Jonathan Edwards. With Edwards, Hopkins had developed the distinctly American theology of "disinterested benevolence," which held that acting out of Christ-like, selfless love for others represented the only certain evidence of salvation. Moving beyond Edwards, who died in 1758 still owning slaves but opposing the Atlantic slave trade, Hopkins embraced abolitionism as a practical and pressing form of practicing disinterested benevolence toward enslaved Blacks. The impact of his arguments appeared in the rising opposition to slavery among members of the established Congregationalist churches of Massachusetts and Connecticut.

"If the slavery in which we hold the blacks, is wrong; it is a very great and public sin; and therefore a sin which God is now testifying against in the calamities he has brought upon us," Hopkins wrote in his *Dialogue*. Drawing on the jeremiads of his Puritan predecessors, Hopkins in his 1775 *Dialogue* used scripture to suggest that "this woe [of revolutionary warfare] has fallen heavily upon us" as divine punishment for enslaving Africans. "Woe to that man by whom the offense cometh," Lincoln would say about slavery; and what hope for relief but by ending slavery, Hopkins declared. Patriot use of the metaphor of slavery accentuated the sin, Hopkins added. "While the poor negroes look on and hear, what an aversion we have to slavery, and how much liberty is prized," he wrote, "and behold the *Sons of Liberty*, oppressing and tyrannizing over many thousands of poor blacks, who have as good a claim to liberty as themselves, they are shocked with the glaring inconsistence."[46] Printed in time for the Second Continental Congress, Hopkins had copies of his *Dialogue* distributed to its members in Philadelphia.[47]

On April 19, 1775, as delegates from twelve mainland colonies began traveling toward Philadelphia for the new Congress, the standoff in Boston between local patriots and occupying forces exploded into open warfare. Acting under orders from London authorizing military action, General Gage dispatched seven hundred troops on a seventeen-mile march from Boston to destroy the patriot arsenal in Concord. Forewarned by express riders from Boston, first minutemen soldiers and then whole militia companies gathered (much as Warren had predicted) to defend the countryside inch by inch. Alarmed residents, seeing the soldiers pass, radiated outward, summoning the militia of nearby towns. Some sent their enslaved workers to spread the news. In Needham, a Black man named Abel Benson awakened the town to danger with a trumpet blast.

The first skirmish occurred at the ten-mile mark on the commons in Lexington, where eight militia soldiers died and dozens more incurred injuries in a hail of British musket fire. One of the injured, Prince Estabrook, was an enslaved Black minuteman. A larger battle occurred at a bridge outside Concord where, according to American lore, the embattled farmer militia "fired the shot heard round the world."[48] Several members of that militia were Black.[49] By then, scarcely any arms or ammunition remained for the British to destroy, and a long line of red-coated soldiers began marching back to Boston on a winding road bordered by hedges, walls, and buildings.

Augmented by militia companies from the surrounding region, the minutemen took their revenge on the road back to Boston. Firing from protected positions along the route, they pelted the withdrawing British with musket fire. By nightfall, the British had suffered 250 casualties compared with under 100 for the colonists. Within days, a 15,000-soldier-strong patchwork militia army drawn from every New England colony bottled up Gage's much smaller force in Boston. Only Royal Navy ships in the harbor kept the patriots at bay. The resulting standoff lasted for nearly a year.

"Unhappy it is though to reflect," Virginia delegate George Washington wrote from the Congress after hearing details of the engagement, "the once happy and peaceful plains of America are either to be drenched with Blood, or Inhabited by Slaves. Sad alternative! But can a virtuous Man hesitate in his choice?"[50] John Adams provided those details to Congress after inspecting the battlefield before departing for Philadelphia. "The Die was cast, the Rubicon crossed," he wrote of his feelings at the time, "if We did not defend ourselves they would kill Us."[51] A new urgency confronted the assembling delegates. A war for liberty (if not yet for independence) had begun with slavery perceived by many to hang in the balance.

The Second Continental Congress convened in Philadelphia on May 10, 1775, with fifty-eight delegates from twelve colonies. Virtually all of them had attended the First Continental Congress as well, though Pennsylvania added to its delegation the illustrious Benjamin Franklin, freshly returned from serving for ten years as a colonial agent in London. Massachusetts included John Hancock, who became the Congress's president ten days later when Peyton Randolph left to serve as Speaker of the Virginia Assembly. These changes put a non-slaveholder in the chair and added an opponent of slavery from Pennsylvania, but both Hancock and Franklin were successful entrepreneurs turned pragmatic politicians who had owned a few enslaved house servants earlier in their careers. Most other delegates still owned some. Twelve or more delegates, mainly from the South, built their wealth on plantation agriculture using enslaved labor. This became the Congress that proclaimed America's liberty from Britain. The addition of representatives later in 1775 from the thirteenth colony, Georgia, further increased the number of slaveholders present.

Although it met continually for six years and served as a de facto central government until 1781, with a war to fight against Britain, the Second Continental Congress never took a stand on domestic slavery. Unlike many later political revolts, the American Revolution did not involve an uprising rooted in the lower classes to gain liberty, but instead was led by local elites (mainly lawyers, planters, and merchants) to retain liberty. One of these, a wealthy young lawyer and slaveholding planter sent by Virginia to replace Peyton Randolph, ultimately engaged more openly with the issues of liberty and slavery than any other member: Thomas Jefferson.

Trained as a lawyer, Jefferson inherited 5,000 acres of land with over 50 enslaved workers from his father and, through his wife Martha, two more plantations with another 135 enslaved persons from his father-in-law, John Wayles. Among the enslaved coming with the Wayles estate in 1773 was a mixed-race infant called Sally fathered by Wayles with his longtime, mixed-race, enslaved mistress Elizabeth Hemings. A half-sister of Martha, Sally Hemings became Jefferson's mistress at some point after his wife died in 1782. Prior to acquiring the Wayles's estate and giving up his law practice in 1774, Jefferson brought a number of so-called freedom suits to secure liberty for mixed-race children born of a free mother—slavery in Virginia passed through the mother—and championed legislation allowing owners to emancipate those they held in bondage without government consent. Much later, Jefferson used the law to free two of his children by Hemings. He informally freed Hemings and her other children.[52] Given their parentage, these children would have been seven-eighths white by blood but fully enslaved by law.

Scholarly by nature and well versed in legal theory, Jefferson leaped to the fore of patriot propagandists with his 1774 pamphlet, *A Summary View of the Rights of British America*. This masterly tract mixed soaring claims of rights with lurid charges of their violation. "Single acts of tyranny may be ascribed to the accidental opinion of the day," he wrote, "but a series of oppressions, begun at a distinguished period, and pursued unalterably through every change of ministers, too plainly prove a deliberate and systematical plan of reducing us to slavery." Among these oppressions, Jefferson stressed the veto of colonial legislation to bar or tax the importation of enslaved Africans—a bill he cast as a first step toward ending slavery. "The abolition of domestic slavery is the great object of desire in those colonies," Jefferson claimed without basis. "But previous to the enfranchisement of the slaves we have, it is necessary to exclude all further importations from Africa; yet our repeated attempts to effect this by prohibitions, and by imposing duties which might amount to a prohibition, have been hitherto defeated by his majesty's negative."[53]

To the end of his life in 1826, Jefferson maintained (as he declared in this 1774 pamphlet) that slavery violated natural law.[54] Much like many other white patriots, however, he never budged beyond a wholly unrealistic plan of gradual emancipation. First, as stated in the pamphlet, stop the importation of enslaved Africans.[55] Then improve the lives of those already in America.[56] Once sufficiently prepared to care for themselves, free those born into bondage thereafter and transport them to Africa or the Caribbean.[57] His 1774 pamphlet (which incorporated this plan) helped Jefferson to gain an appointment to Congress in June 1775 and, one year later, a seat on the committee drafting the Declaration of Independence.

Despite his objections to slavery, Jefferson never believed in racial equality. Quite to the contrary, he saw whites and Blacks as distinct races that could not freely coexist.[58] This view did not dominate in Congress, however. Many members either never betrayed such fixed views on the matter or actively disagreed with Jefferson. New York delegate John Jay, for example, later founded the New York Manumission Society and, as governor, signed legislation for the gradual abolition of slavery in his state. Based on his experience with the education of Black children, Franklin had long held that Blacks and whites had equal mental capability.[59] In a 1773 pamphlet, Pennsylvania delegate Benjamin Rush, a well-known physician, dismissed as unfounded any claim that Blacks and whites differed in intellect, "their capacity for virtue and happiness," or beauty.[60] "Ye ADVOCATES for American Liberty," he pleaded, "rouse up and espouse the cause of Humanity and general Liberty" by ending slavery. "The plant of liberty is of so tender a Nature, that it cannot thrive long in the neighbourhood of slavery," Rush warned.[61] After arousing resistance only among a few religious sects in colonial America, chattel slavery began to encounter rising opposition on many fronts during the Revolutionary era.

After the Battles of Lexington and Concord, as Britain slowly but steadily prepared an empire for war against its rebellious provinces, local patriots rose up across America, drove off royal officers, and effectively took control from New Hampshire to Georgia. Even highly fortified places fell. In May 1775, for example, militia forces from New England seized the British forts at Ticonderoga and Crown Point in northern New York, leading to an invasion of Lower Canada six months later.

Using cannons from those forts, patriot forces composed mostly of New Englanders but placed by Congress under the command of the experienced Virginia regimental officer, George Washington, drove the British from Boston in March 1776.

Done to unify the war effort and make it more fully continental, Washington's appointment as commander in chief also highlighted regional differences, particularly regarding race and slavery. Well known for his military exploits during the French and Indian War, Washington inherited Mount Vernon, his father's tidewater plantation, and its enslaved Blacks after the death of his older half-brother Lawrence. He gained control of more lands and enslaved Blacks through marriage to the wealthy widow Martha Dandridge Custis. By way of these acquisitions and aggressive purchases, Washington became one of the leading landowners and largest slaveholders in Virginia by the early 1770s. Fiercely opposed to the Townshend tariffs, he freely used the slavery metaphor during this period to condemn British imperial policies without ever questioning his own use of enslaved workers. This alone put him in an incongruous position when he arrived with liveried enslaved attendants outside Boston, where slaveholding had become a divisive issue in local revolutionary politics.

Regional difference over race played out in military affairs. Although Virginia military officers (including Washington) often took their own enslaved servants along during their tours of duty, and Blacks sometimes served the colony's troops in menial capacities, those Blacks virtually never bore arms. Not so in New England. Upon taking command during the siege of Boston in July 1775 following the Battle of Bunker Hill, Washington found free and enslaved Blacks serving alongside whites in the lower ranks of the New England militia. One Black soldier, Salem Poor, had received a citation for bravery at Bunker Hill, and others served there with notable distinction.[62] John Trumbull's iconic painting, *The Death of General Warren at the Battle of Bunker's Hill*, depicts an enslaved Black, later identified as Asaba, holding a musket alongside his wounded master, Lieutenant Thomas Grosvenor. Despite the success of patriot forces in containing the British army in Boston and their dogged defense of Bunker Hill, Washington, in reports back to Congress, criticized the lack of discipline in the patchwork army he inherited and complained about the "Number of Boys, Deserters, & Negroes" in the Massachusetts militia.[63] He set about addressing both issues with training, recommendations, and new orders.

Although in overall command, Washington faced the daunting task of leading divided forces. Congress authorized forming a Continental Army, which Washington organized and led, but colonies also fielded their own provincial regiments and local militias. Together, these independent bodies composed the domestic land forces defending America. Battles required their coordinated action. Working with governors and legislators, Washington became as much a political general as a military one.

From the outset, Washington did not want to include Blacks in the Continental Army. He discussed the matter with his general staff on October 8, 1775. Minutes of that meeting state, "Agreed unanimously to reject all Slaves, & by a great Majority to reject Negroes altogether."[64] A visiting delegation from Congress endorsed the policy two weeks later.[65] Free Blacks already in the army objected to their exclusion from continued service, however, and Washington relented. "It has been represented to me that the free negroes who have Served in this Army, are very much disatisfied at being discarded," Washington wrote to Congress President John Hancock in December. "I have presumed to depart from the Resolution respecting them, & have given Licence for their being enlisted."[66] Congress approved the revised policy in January 1776 while reaffirming the ban on new free Black recruits and the service of any enslaved Black soldiers.[67]

John Adams and other New England delegates faced hostile comments from their colleagues in Congress about Blacks serving in the regimental and militia forces raised to liberate Boston. "It is represented in this City by Some Persons, and it makes an unfriendly Impression upon Some Minds, that in the Massachusetts Regiments, there are great Numbers of Boys, Old Men, and Negroes," John Adams wrote from Philadelphia to Massachusetts major general William Heath on October 5, 1775. "It is natural to suppose there are some young Men and some old ones and some Negroes in the service, but I should be glad to know if there are more of these in Proportion in the Massachusetts Regiments, than in those of Connecticutt, Rhode Island and New Hampshire."[68]

Heath's reply gave a picture of the racial makeup of New England provincial forces. "There are in the Massachusetts Regiments Some few Lads and Old men, and in Several Regiments, Some Negroes. Such is also the Case with the Regiments from the Other Colonies, Rhode Island has a Number of Negroes and Indians, Connecticut has fewer Negroes but a number of Indians. The New Hampshire Regiments have less of Both," he wrote. "But the Troops of our Colony are Robust, Agile, and as fine Fellows in General as I ever would wish to see in the Field."[69] In line with congressional policy, however, beginning with Massachusetts in January 1776, the New England colonies began restricting the recruitment and retention of Blacks in their regiments and militia—though these policies did not always apply in practice.[70] The middle colonies followed suit, with Pennsylvania exempting non-whites from a general requirement for able-bodied males to receive military training, and New Jersey ordering Black soldiers to turn in their weapons.[71]

In the southern colonies, where enslaved Blacks made up a third or more of the population, whites rarely trusted Blacks with arms and generally barred them from service in colonial or state forces. In the coming war, southern Blacks had to look elsewhere for their freedom and, as historian Benjamin Quarles wrote, "Whoever invoked the image of liberty, be he American or British, could count on a ready response from the blacks."[72]

Following *Somerset*, the winds of war carried persistent rumors of enslaved Blacks offering their services to the British in return for their emancipation, or simply fleeing toward the British lines in the hope they would find freedom there. Some of these stories had a basis in fact but many did not.[73] To win over wavering whites, southern patriots augmented these rumors with stories of their own about British officials urging the enslaved to turn on their patriot masters, but virtually all of these lacked any basis in fact.[74] The British could hardly hope to keep their Caribbean colonies in tow and, at the same time, foment racial warfare within the empire. Debating the king's October 1775 speech to Parliament outlining the deployment of troops to put down the rebellion in America, William Lyttelton, a former royal governor of South Carolina then serving in the House of Commons, suggested using Blacks to suppress rebels in the southern colonies. "If a few regiments were sent there, the negroes would rise, and embrue their hands in the blood of their masters," he declared.[75] No members of Parliament endorsed Lyttelton's proposal, and another former southern governor serving in the Commons, George Johnstone, damned it as "too black and horrid to be adopted."[76] The sitting governor of Virginia, however, put such a scheme into practice.

Having previously rejected offers of support from enslaved Virginians, after fleeing the colonial capital of Williamsburg in June 1775 for the safety of navy ships in Chesapeake Bay, the embattled royal governor of Virginia, Lord Dunmore, turned to them with a remarkable offer. "I do require every person capable of bearing arms to resort to his Majesty's STANDARD," he wrote in a November 7, 1775, proclamation declaring martial law in Virginia. "And I do hereby further declare all *indented servants, Negroes,* or others (appertaining to rebels) *free*, that are able and willing to bear arms, they *joining his Majesty's troops.*"[77] Within two months, roughly 800 enslaved men, some with women and children, flocked to the royal standard at Dunmore's redoubt in Norfolk, with more trickling in thereafter. The governor formed some 300 of them into a unit commanded by white officers called the Ethiopian Regiment. Ill trained, poorly armed, and prematurely sent into battle, these hastily assembled troops proved no match for the patriot militia and a smallpox epidemic that killed hundreds of uninoculated Blacks in Dunmore's camp.[78] Retreating eventually to Gwyenn Island on the advice of army physicians, a remnant held on in Virginia with Dunmore until after Congress declared independence in July 1776.

By that time, Dunmore's proclamation probably had done more to boost the patriot cause than the loyalist one. "If [the British] Administration had searched thro the world for a person the best fitted to ruin their cause, and procure union and success for these Colonies," Virginia delegate to Congress Richard Henry Lee observed following the proclamation's issuance, "they could not have found a more complete Agent than Lord Dunmore."[79] In a similar vein, South Carolina delegate Edward Rutledge wrote about the proclamation "tending in my judgment, more effectively to work an eternal separation between Great Britain and the Colonies,—than any other expedient, which could possibly be thought of."[80] Anticipating a similar move by their embattled royal governor, in 1775 South Carolina patriots cleared free and escaped Blacks from Sullivan's Island, where they reportedly had gone in search of British protection.

Rutledge's comment hit on the critical issue. Dunmore's proclamation not only drove some previously neutral and loyalist-leaning white colonists, particularly in South Carolina and Georgia, into the patriot camp, it also pushed more patriots everywhere toward backing independence.[81] These patriots did not necessarily view themselves as fighting a war to preserve slavery—likely few if any of them did—but recruiting enslaved Blacks to subdue their white masters struck many as an unconscionable example of imperial effrontery.[82] This alone made Dunmore's proclamation significant and telling: significant in how it affected the war for independence and telling for what it said about Black slavery in America as a means for white empowerment. The British in turn fostered or repudiated slavery as best served their imperial purposes.

By the fall of 1775, Lee, the Adamses, Franklin, and some other delegates favored independence, but they could not get a majority in Congress to that point. Even as Congress voted to support armed resistance to Britain in July 1775, it sent the Olive Branch Petition to the king inviting reconciliation on pre-1763 terms. In August, the king proclaimed the colonies in "an open and avowed Rebellion," yet Congress still held back.[83] Dunmore's proclamation helped to turn the tide.

Patriot propagandist Thomas Paine quickly incorporated it into his hugely influential pamphlet *Common Sense*. First published two months after Dunmore's proclamation and selling some 150,000 copies by July 1776, *Common Sense* replaced the lawyerly arguments for English rights that marked earlier patriot pamphlets with passionate appeals for independence. It also assailed the king rather than Parliament. "A government of our own is our natural right," Paine wrote, and soon most Americans seemed to agree.[84] "My Countrymen," Washington wrote in April, "will come reluctantly into the Idea of Independancy; but time, & persecution, brings many wonderful things to pass; & by private Letters which I have lately received from Virginia, I find *Common Sense* is working a powerful change there in the Minds of many Men."[85]

"Ye that oppose independance now, ye know not what ye do," Paine wrote in his passage from *Common Sense* invoking Dunmore's proclamation. "There are thousands, and tens of thousands, who would think it glorious to expel from the Continent, that barbarous and hellish power, which hath stirred up the Indians and Negroes to destroy us."[86] Raised in a Quaker family and instinctively opposed to slavery, Paine, in his plea for American independence, could not resist denouncing England for offering freedom to the enslaved in exchange for their service suppressing the Revolution. A master polemicist, he knew the charge would inflame his readers. Paine also turned sentiment against Britain by his use of the slavery metaphor, at one point warning, "When republican virtue fails, slavery ensues." Unlike such patriot pamphleteers as James Otis, however, in *Common Sense* Paine never risked alienating white readers by condemning slavery or challenging the republican credentials of patriot slaveholders.[87] Paine may have hated American slavery, but he hated the British monarchy more.

Dunmore's proclamation and Paine's pamphlet having set the stage for separation, a coordinated, three-prong reinvasion by British forces finally turned a colonial revolution for rights into the war of American independence. Beginning in May 1776, one British army reclaimed Lower Canada. In June, patriot troops repulsed a second, smaller British force sent to subdue the Carolinas, leaving Dunmore's dwindling mixed-race units isolated in the South. Then, on July 2, some 32,000 troops drawn from across the British empire and hired from Germany began coming ashore on Staten Island with the aim of seizing New York and splitting the colonies. Supported by half of the ships in the Royal Navy, this massive force had nearly twice as many soldiers as the entire American army. On the day of that first landing—July 2, 1776—Congress voted for independence and opened three days of debate on a declaration drafted by Jefferson to explain and justify that radical move.

A gifted wordsmith, Jefferson drew on his 1774 pamphlet, *A Summary View of the Rights of British America*, in composing his draft Declaration of Independence. As such, it asserted rights and leveled charges. Like his earlier tract, the draft blamed American slavery on British policy and denounced the king for vetoing colonial efforts to curtail the Atlantic slave trade. Then, attributing Dunmore's proclamation to royal policy and using convoluted logic, the draft leveled one of Jefferson's harshest charges against the king. "He is now exciting those very people to rise in arms among us, and to purchase that liberty of which *he* has deprived them, by murdering the people upon whom *he* also obtruded them," the draft asserted, with "them" and "those people" referring to enslaved Blacks and "us" to free white Americans. Adding emphasis, the passage went on to depict the king as "thus paying off former crimes committed against the *liberties* of one people, with crimes which he urges them to commit against the *lives* of another."[88]

Too much for the delegates from South Carolina and Georgia to accept, Congress deleted the draft's entire paragraph on slavery. "Our northern brethren also I believe felt a little tender under these censures," Jefferson later noted, "for tho' their people had very few slaves themselves yet they had been pretty considerable carriers of them to others."[89] Congress would fight for liberty without opposing slavery.

Despite the omission of the tortured paragraph on slavery, the lyrical heart of Jefferson's draft remained. "We hold these truths to be self-evident," proclaimed the key sentence of the approved 1,320-word-long text, "that all men are created equal, that they are endowed by their Creator with certain inalienable Rights, that among these, are Life, Liberty, and the pursuit of Happiness."[90] Only time would tell if "all men" included Blacks, Native Americans, and women, or if being "created equal" precluded human slavery.

CHAPTER FIVE

"Liberty Is Sweet"

An Illusive Promise, 1776–1778

During the winter of 1775–76, George Washington, the slaveholding commander of American forces in a war for liberty, confronted something new for him: Blacks demanding the same sorts of rights he demanded for himself and other white colonists. It should not have been new for him. Washington had dealt with many enslaved and some free Blacks in Virginia, and they surely desired their liberty as much as other Americans did. Some white Virginians had sensed this about Blacks by then, but no evidence exists that Washington had.

A year in New England forced Washington to see at least some Blacks differently. The region was home to fewer Blacks than the South, but more of them could read and write, attend church, and enjoy some basic rights even if enslaved—and relatively more were free. Having initially barred all Blacks from serving in the army, Washington relented in December, at least with respect to those already in arms, in response to their pleas and petitions and, presumably, reports of their notable service at the Battles of Concord and Bunker Hill. Then, early in 1776, Washington received a letter and poem from a recently freed Black woman, with the poem featuring the sorts of classical allusions and heroic tone that delighted and impressed him.

The only Black American of her day with an international reputation, Phillis Wheatley showed the possibilities and limits of living enslaved in northern colonies during the Revolutionary era.[1] Born in West Africa, perhaps near the island of Gorée, and enslaved as a child, Wheatley arrived in Boston on the slave ship *Phillis* in 1761 as a seven-year-old. John Wheatley, already the owner of other enslaved household servants and a wealthy merchant with patriot leanings, bought the girl at the docks as an attendant for his wife Susanna, who named her after the ship that carried her to America. Later, Phillis took the surname of her owners.

According to Wheatley family lore recorded sixty years later by Susanna's great-grandniece, Susanna quickly recognized Phillis's "uncommon intelligence." The Wheatleys' daughter Mary taught Phillis to read and write.[2] Phillis especially liked poetry and began writing her own in the neoclassical style of Alexander Pope by 1765. Two years later, her writing first appeared in print when a Rhode Island newspaper published her poem about the harrowing escape of a ship from a storm at sea.[3] The same issue that printed those verses "by a Negro Girl" ran ads for the sale of an enslaved "Negro Girl" about Phillis's age, and for the return of an escaped "Negro Man named *James*."[4]

That year, 1767, Wheatley wrote a poem about Harvard College that reflected her rejection of African animism for the Christian faith of her owners. It began,

> *'Twas not long since I left my native shore*
> *The land of errors, and* Egyptian *gloom:*
> *Father of mercy, 'twas thy gracious hand*
> *Brought me in safety from those dark abodes.*

The poem admonished Harvard students to shun sinful revelry ("An *Ethiop* tells you 'tis your greatest foe") and embrace learning.[5] Tutored at home by her owner's daughter, Wheatley studied Latin and read Roman poets in their original tongue. Soon her poetry began expressing an American patriot's view of liberty—"Why weeps americus why weeps my Child," she penned in 1768 about the hated Townshend Act. She invoked a sense of Black dignity in another poem that year: "Remember, *Christians*, *Negros*, black as *Cain*, / may be refin'd, and join th' angelic train."[6] In the former poem, Wheatley included herself, an African, within the lineage of English liberty by asking about Britain's withholding rights from its American colonists, "What no more English blood? / Has length of time drove from *our* English veins."[7]

Wheatley's fame reached Britain in 1771 when her poetic eulogy on the death of English evangelist George Whitefield (who had carried the Great Awakening to America by preaching to vast audiences of whites and Blacks in the colonies) appeared as a broadside on both sides of the Atlantic. "Take HIM, 'my dear AMERICANS,' he said," Wheatley wrote of Jesus's appeal in the mouth of Whitefield, "Take HIM ye *Africans*, he longs for you; / Impartial SAVIOUR, is his title due."[8]

This poem brought her to the attention of Whitefield's evangelical benefactor, the Countess of Huntington, who had long supported missionary work among Native and African Americans. In 1772, the countess agreed to sponsor publication of a volume of Wheatley's poems by an abolitionist-minded religious printer in London, making Wheatley the first African American woman and the third female American to publish a book. The Countess wanted the poet's image displayed on the frontispiece, leading to a painting of Wheatley generally attributed to the enslaved Black artist Scipio Moorhead—the first known portrait of a named African American.[9] Only prints made from an engraving of the work exist, with these showing a pensive woman with quill in hand posed in a manner suggestive of paintings by the then-popular Boston portraitist John Singleton Copley.

To oversee publication of her book, Wheatley sailed on one of her owner's merchant ships to England in May 1773. There she met with the secretary of state for the colonies Lord Dartmouth, Massachusetts colonial agent Benjamin Franklin, Granville Sharp, and other prominent abolitionists then living in London. "Should you, my lord, while you peruse my song, / Wonder from whence my love of *Freedom* sprung," Wheatley wrote at this time in a poem dedicated to Dartmouth. Linking the cause of American liberty with a cry for her own freedom, she added:

> *I, young in my life, by seeming cruel fate*
> *Was snatch'd from Afric's fancy'd happy seat:*
> *What pangs excruciating must molest,*
> *What sorrows labour in my parent's breast? . . .*
> *Such, such my case. And can I then but pray*
> *Others may never feel tyrannic sway?*[10]

News of her mistress's mortal illness caused Wheatley to return to Boston in July, before a planned audience with the king. Publication of her book that year led a London literary journal to scoff, "We are much concerned to find that this ingenious young woman is yet a slave. The people of Boston boast themselves chiefly on their principles of liberty. One such act as the purchase of her freedom, would, in our opinion, have done more honor than hanging a thousand trees with ribbons."[11]

Appeals from those Wheatley now called "my friends in England" prompted her master to free her after her return to America in September 1773, but the Boston Tea Party later that year and the ensuing British occupation of Boston disrupted her life and enjoyment of liberty.[12] After Susanna Wheatley died the following March, the remaining Wheatleys, like many patriots, fled Boston, with Phillis accompanying the Wheatleys' then-married daughter Mary to Rhode Island. Despite remaining in the Wheatley household, letters from Phillis to the abolitionist minister Samson Occom after her manumission testify to her commitment to liberty for enslaved Blacks and censure of white slaveholders. "In every human Brest," she wrote to the Native American Occom, "God has implanted a Principle, which we call Love of Freedom; it is impatient of Oppression, and pants for Deliverance; and by the Leave of our modern Egyptians I will assert, that the same Principle lives in us."[13]

Phillis Wheatley surely knew that Washington remained one of those slaveholding modern Egyptians. Yet, when he arrived in 1775 to lead the patriot siege to recapture Boston, Wheatley sent him a poem—a refugee's plea really—for deliverance. "Your being appointed by the Grand Continental Congress to be Generalissimo of the armies of North America, together with the fame of your virtues, excite sensations not easy to suppress," Wheatley's cover letter to Washington stated. "Wishing your Excellency all possible success in the great cause you are so generously engaged in."[14] The letter and poem did not reach the general until early in 1776.

Depicting the American colonies as "the land of freedom's heaven-defended race" and never mentioning Washington's ownership of some three hundred enslaved Blacks, Wheatley's poem hailed the general as "Fam'd for thy valour, for thy virtue more." It concluded with the prayer,

> *Proceed, great chief, with virtue on thy side,*
> *Thy ev'ry action let the goddess guide.*
> *A crown, and mansion, and a throne that shine,*
> *With gold unfading, WASHINGTON! be thine.*[15]

The first tribute expressing such unqualified veneration for the newly commissioned general, the poem, published in 1776, renewed Wheatley's fame in America. Washington replied with a polite letter thanking "Mrs Phillis," as he called her, for her "elegant Lines" that "exhibit a striking proof of your great poetical Talents."[16] Washington invited Wheatley to visit him at his headquarters in Cambridge, but no contemporary evidence points to such a meeting. He would have left by the time she returned to Boston. No other letter exists from Washington to a Black person, and none by Washington addressing any women other than his relatives by their first names. She had signed her letter to him, Phillis Wheatley, and so Washington surely would have addressed her as Miss Wheatley if she were white. Still, Wheatley's poem, like the pleas to remain in the Continental Army by free Black soldiers, caused Washington to see at least some Black Americans as something other than enslaved servants. They remained the exceptions for Washington, however, not the rule.

In having her portrait painted, Phillis Wheatley also stands out as an exception to the rule of African anonymity in colonial America. Before the advent of photography and the mass media during the 1800s, etching and printing, painting or drawing, and sculpture served as the principle means to record and preserve someone's likeness. Only very rich, powerful, or famous people left multiple images in various media. Qualifying on all three counts, Washington became the subject of countless printed images, some three dozen portraits, and numerous marble, metal, or plaster sculptures during his lifetime.[17] By the time of his death in 1799, most Americans and many Europeans could have recognized him by sight. Through his portraits, people all over the world still know his face. Among Revolutionary era Americans, only Franklin, Jefferson, and perhaps John Adams were similarly recognizable then and now.

The vast majority of white Americans of the period never had their portraits painted. Their faceless names endure, if at all, in a handful of written documents. Free Blacks typically left an even thinner written record than whites did. Phillis Wheatley not only survives in multiple poems and letters, but modern Americans know her face through her portrait. No other named Black American of her day survives in this way.

Enslaved Americans generally did not even leave a written record, much less identifiable portraits. Most of them could neither write nor participate in the sorts of activities that left a paper trail, like church baptisms and burials, voting and government service, or land ownership. Blacks sometimes populate landscape paintings of colonial plantations but never with their names recorded. Those names never mattered to the artist. A few individual enslaved Blacks might appear in paintings of their owners, such as two portraits of Washington with a servant once thought to be his valet, Billy Lee, but now known to be anonymous black models.[18] Historians once believed that an individual portrait existed for the general's enslaved chef, Hercules Posey. Later research disproved the attribution, leaving no pictorial record for Posey. When Martha Washington's enslaved attendant Ona Judge ran away in 1796, her owners could only describe her in the notice offering $10 for her recapture. "A light mulatto girl, much freckled, with very black eyes and bushy black hair," the ad read.[19] No known picture of Judge ever existed.

Like Judge in 1796 and Posey a year later, an enslaved stable hand called Harry escaped from the Washington family in a successful bid for liberty. Born in the Gambia River region of West Africa around 1740 and transported to America as a boy, Harry first worked for George Washington in 1764 on land being drained to cultivate rice in Virginia's Great Dismal Swamp. From there, Harry moved on to jobs at Mount Vernon. Never reconciled to slavery, Harry first ran away in 1771, but Washington recaptured him after offering a reward for his return.[20] With Washington away for nine years serving as the American commander in chief during the American Revolution, the war offered Harry another chance for liberty. He took it, leading to an eventful second half of his life. Like Judge, Posey, and virtually every other enslaved American, however, no image of Harry exists and only a scanty written record.

According to his own account, recorded when the British evacuated him from New York in 1783, Harry fled Mount Vernon in the months following the November 1775 offer by Virginia royal governor Dunmore of liberty for any able-bodied enslaved or indentured servants of rebel masters willing to fight for Britain. "There is not a man of them, but woud leave us, if they believe'd they coud make there Escape," Mount Vernon's plantation manager wrote to Washington about the response of those on the estate to Dunmore's proclamation. "Liberty is sweet."[21] Harry took the surname of his former owner in the "Book of Negroes" compiled by the British in 1783. "Harry Washington, 43, Stout fellow," this record noted, "Formerly the Property of General Washington, left him Seven years ago."[22] Plantation records have Harry escaping in 1781, along with sixteen other enslaved persons, when a British warship anchored at the estate, but another record has "three of George Washington's servants" taken aboard a British navy vessel in July 1776, which likely included Harry.[23] The discrepancy in the timing of Harry's departure from Mount Vernon underscores the anonymity of plantation slavery in the American South and the disruption caused by war.

Based on his own account, Harry initially would have served in Virginia as part of Dunmore's Ethiopian Regiment. Rejecting warnings by patriot slaveholders that Dunmore would never free them, and evading patriot patrols sent to stop them, about 300 enslaved Blacks reached Dunmore's base at Norfolk or ships in the Chesapeake by early December 1775. Among them was a "run away" from New Jersey named Titus who would later become Dunmore's most famous recruit.[24] Dunmore armed incoming Blacks capable of military service but never had time to train them. Some accounts had them outfitted in uniforms inscribed with the motto "Liberty to Slaves."[25] Their only formal military engagement occurred on December 9 at Great Bridge, where the patriot militia had assembled in preparation for an attack on Norfolk.

Dunmore's battle plan called for using the raw Ethiopia Regiment as a diversion while white troops launched a preemptive frontal assault on the patriot position. The Black soldiers received conflicting orders, however, and the frontal assault collapsed before the entrenched patriots. The Ethiopian Regiment survived intact but Dunmore abandoned Norfolk and operated thereafter from ships in the Chesapeake or island camps. Enslaved Blacks continued to arrive, perhaps another 500 (including Harry Washington) by the middle of 1776, but Dunmore mainly used them to forage for food and supplies in raids targeting the plantations of patriots.[26]

Dunmore had originally hoped that 2,000 Blacks would join his 300 white soldiers, and predicted great success with that force. With reduced numbers, he could do little more than sail up and down coastal waterways harassing patriots. "I have been endeavouring to raise two regiments here—one of white people, the other of black," Dunmore wrote in a March 1776 report to London. "The former goes on very slowly, but the latter very well, and would have been in great forwardness had not a fever crept in amongst them, which carried off a great many very fine fellows."[27] That fever, smallpox, "carried off an incredible number of our people, especially blacks," he reported in June.[28] By then, he had only 150 Blacks left in service, with a continuing trickle of new arrivals maintaining the force.

In August 1776, Dunmore gave up his efforts in Virginia after his last island base fell to the patriots, and a lackluster British effort to open a second front in the South failed at the Battle of Sullivan's Island, near Charleston. Dunmore scuttled half his fleet of some one hundred ships and boats, and sent his white loyalist followers with their still-enslaved servants south to the British Caribbean. He took his remaining soldiers (including about 150 Blacks) north to join the massive British army forming in Nova Scotia during the spring of 1776 under General William Howe to invade New York beginning in July. Harry Washington went with this small, largely Black force to join Howe's large, overwhelmingly white one.

First under Howe and later under General Henry Clinton, members of the Ethiopian Regiment joined other British army units in noncombat roles. Many became part of a newly formed company of Black Guides and Pioneers (or service workers), the only predominately Black unit in Britain's North American army, charged with such duties as moving supplies, chopping firewood, digging trenches, and erecting, maintaining, and striking camp.[29] Some, like Harry Washington, found positions as unarmed laborers in British or Hessian units. Washington served in the Royal Artillery Department; many more were teamsters or stable hands in the Wagon Master General's Department. As members of regular army units, these and other Blacks formerly enslaved by patriots received housing, clothing, rations, and pay roughly on par with enlisted white soldiers.[30] Other escaped Blacks became the free servants of British officers or found civilian jobs.[31] Clinton never allowed Blacks and whites to serve together in integrated combat units but did promise to free enslaved Blacks (or at least those with rebel owners) in return for their service.

If joining the British offered better prospects for freedom to enslaved southern Blacks than remaining with their patriot masters, the opposite seemed true in New England, where a nascent abolitionist movement had taken root among both Blacks and some whites before the war and gained momentum from patriot cries for liberty. This sentiment appeared most clearly among Blacks in the freedom petitions of Felix Holbrook and other Massachusetts Blacks, Cæsar Sarter's 1774 essay, and the willing service of free and enslaved Blacks in the New England militia forces fighting the British. Among whites, it came through in the letters of Abigail Adams and Mercy Otis Warren, James Otis's 1764 pamphlet, and perhaps most clearly in the sermons of John Allan and Samuel Hopkins. All suggested that, at least in the North, the revolutionary spirit demanding freedom from British tyranny could ask the same or something similar for enslaved Blacks. This stark contrast between the spirit of liberty in the North and in the South surfaced too in that, at about the same time as Harry Washington fled Mount Vernon for his liberty, Phillis Wheatley welcomed its owner, George Washington, to lead the fight for liberty outside British-occupied Boston.

By then free, Wheatley continued to embrace the patriot cause as a fight for liberty. Her solemn odes lamenting the British capture of American general Charles Lee during the retreat from New York in December 1776, and the death of American general David Wooster a year later during a small battle in Connecticut, added to her renown as a patriot poet. She returned to Boston with John Wheatley following the British surrender of the city in 1776, married a local free Black grocer named John Peters, and began a new life as a free Black wife and mother in white-dominated New England. Meanwhile, the war moved on to other fronts.

By mid-1776, with the Wheatleys back in Boston, Harry Washington and Dunmore's Ethiopian Regiment transferred to New York, and George Washington with his entire army entrenched in New York and New Jersey, the American Revolution entered a distinct second phase that would last until mid-1778. No more major battles occurred in Massachusetts. The patriots abandoned Canada to the British. With 19,000 troops, the American army focused on defending New York from a massed force of about 24,000 British soldiers, 8,000 Hessian mercenaries, and a Royal Navy armada determined to divide the states and subdue the revolt. A regional conflict had become a continental war for independence. For two years, liberty hung in the balance. Phillis Wheatley captured the scene in her poem to Washington. "Fix'd are the eyes of the nations on the scales," she wrote, "For in their hopes Columbia's arm prevails."[32]

On July 2, 1776, General Howe began landing British troops on undefended Staten Island, across the harbor from Manhattan. "We expect a very bloody Summer of it at New York," Washington had predicted a month earlier, "as it is there I expect the grand efforts of the Enemy will be aim'd."[33] Despite an order from Congress directing Washington to defend the city, its extended coastline and open terrain made it indefensible against a seaborne invasion. Howe had amassed over 20,000 soldiers by late August, included Dunmore's small mixed-race unit from Virginia. For the Americans, disaster followed disaster beginning with the August 27 Battle of Long Island in which Washington's outmaneuvered army suffered over 2,000 casualties to under 400 by the attacking British.[34]

Fearing such an outcome, New Jersey patriot leader Jonathan Dickinson Sergeant, who had recently left Congress to help draft a new constitution for his state, wrote to Congress's Board of War member John Adams in mid-August about forming "a Negroe Battalion" for the defense of his state. At the time, New Jersey and New York had more Black residents than other northern states, with only a tiny fraction of them in uniform. Admitting that the plan might "be heretical," Sergeant proposed it as a desperate measure.[35] Adams worried more about the internal divisions it would cause. "Your Negro Battallion will never do," he wrote back to Sergeant only days before New York fell to the British. "S. Carolina would run out of their Wits at the least Hint of such a Measure."[36] With insufficient troops to defend the region, the Battle of Long Island proved only the first of many setbacks.

A rapid succession of defeats drove Washington's army from its initial defensive lines in Brooklyn Heights, out of Manhattan and the lower Hudson Valley, across New Jersey, and into eastern Pennsylvania by December 1776. With units of Howe's army having reached the Delaware River by then, Washington warned Congress on the 9th about Philadelphia, "The Enemy might . . . march directly in and take Possession."[37] Congress moved to Baltimore. Meanwhile, a British force under Henry Clinton took and held the strategic harbor at Newport, Rhode Island. Between captures, casualties, disease, and desertion, Washington's army had dwindled to roughly 3,000 men fit for duty, with the terms of enlistment for most of these remaining soldiers due to expire on December 31. "In a word," Washington declared, "if every nerve is not straind to recruit the New Army with all possible Expedition I think the game is pretty near up."[38] Increasingly, Black soldiers would play a role in that new army.

The enlistment deadline forced Washington to improvise. On Christmas night, 1776, he took this army back across the ice-chocked Delaware River to New Jersey. Washington captured the Hessian garrison at Trenton, held off a British counterattack at Assunpink Creek, and routed a British force in Princeton before retiring with his remaining troops to Morristown for the winter. There, he began accepting more Blacks into his ranks. Howe, for his part, settled his army into winter quarters in New York as Black recruits from across the region flocked to his standard in the hope of liberty.

While the victories at Trenton and Princeton boosted American spirits, they could not dissipate the gathering gloom as white soldiers left the Continental Army in droves once their commissions expired. All told, after pulling in men from other units, Washington encamped in Morristown with about 3,000 soldiers, while Howe had ten times that number in New York.[39]

Washington used the bleak winter at Morristown to reassess and revise his army's structure and strategy. Both were faulty. "The misfortune of short Inlistments, and an unhappy dependance upon Militia, have shewn their baneful Influence at every period," he wrote in January 1777, but "at no time, nor upon no occasion were they ever more exemplified than since Christmas."[40] Washington wanted what amounted to a standing army with more soldiers, multiyear terms of enlistment, and severe penalties for disobedience and desertion. For the Continental Army, those extended terms typically became three years or the duration of the war. To fill its ranks on those terms recruiters increasingly turned to Blacks.

With short terms and service close to home offered by state militias and regiments, many free whites willing to serve the patriot cause chose those options instead of long commitments with the Continental Army. To boost enlistment, Congress acted in 1777 to impose a troop quota on each state—essentially shifting the burden to the states for supplying added troops to the Continental Army. The northern states responded in part by sending free Blacks when enough whites did not sign up for service. Many states used conscription to meet their quotas, with most allowing conscripts to send substitutes in their place— further boosting the numbers of free Blacks in the Continental Army. In 1777, for example, Connecticut passed laws exempting draftees who supplied substitutes and relieving slaveholders from legal liability for persons they freed. Taken together, these laws encouraged Connecticut conscripts to free enslaved Blacks and send them to war as their substitutes. Massachusetts reached a similar result when it authorized the enlistment of freed Blacks in 1778. Desperate to fill its regiments, New Hampshire paid bonuses to slaveholders who freed Black recruits.

The fall of Newport to the British in December 1776 made it exceptionally difficult for Rhode Island to meet its troop quotas. After a year of struggling to recruit and retain white soldiers, the commander of Rhode Island forces, James Mitchell Varnum, proposed combining the state's two depleted battalions in the Continental Army into a single full-sized one and then recruiting a new battalion composed largely of Blacks led by white officers from the old units. Although Rhode Island's Black population was relatively small and mostly enslaved, Varnum, knowing the appeal of freedom in exchange for service, wrote to Washington about the proposal in January 1778, "It is imagined that a Battalion of Negroes can be easily raised."[41] Washington forwarded the proposal to Rhode Island governor Nicholas Cooke, who submitted it to the state legislature.[42] It quickly passed a month later.

"History affords us frequent precedents of the wisest, the freest, and bravest nations having liberated their slaves, and enlisting them in the defense of their country," the Rhode Island Slave Enlistment Act stated. It added that the British capture of a large part of the state "rendered [it] impossible for this State to furnish recruits for [its] two battalions" any other way.[43] Explaining how the measure would work, Cooke wrote to Washington in February, "Liberty is given to every effective Slave to enter the Service during the War, and upon his passing Muster he is absolutely made free, and entitled to all the Wages, Bounties and Encouragements given by Congress to any Soldier inlisting into their Service. The Masters are allowed [compensation] at the Rate of £120 for the most valuable Slave, and in Proportion for those of less Value." Cooke estimated that up to 300 Blacks would enlist under these terms.[44] Under the act, any "able-bodied negro, mulatto, or Indian man slave in the State" could volunteer, but each would have to pass muster under the white colonel in charge of the battalion. Enlistment did not require a master's consent.[45]

Eighty-eight enslaved Rhode Islanders actually joined the mixed-race regiment by June 1778, when the state stopped the program in part due to its cost and refocused on recruiting whites. Forty or so free Blacks may have joined the regiment as well, making it half or more Black in August 1778, when it joined the failed American and French effort to drive the British out of Newport in the Battle of Rhode Island.[46] The American commander, John Sullivan, later praised the regiment for its role during the battle. Its soldiers checked the British counterattack that

threatened to destroy the American forces left exposed by the departure
of the French fleet after a severe storm at sea.

By this time, free Black soldiers composed up to one-tenth of the Continental Army, with most of them restricted to menial tasks and few
rising above the rank of private. Their presence, however, freed white
soldiers to fight. Enslaved Blacks, in contrast to free Blacks, never served
as armed members of the Continental Army, though some conscripted
whites freed Blacks specifically to take their place in the army. Having
typically signed on for the war's duration, Black soldiers continued to
serve in significant numbers in the Rhode Island regiment and the overall Continental Army until the end of active combat in 1783, by which
time an estimated 5,000 had served in the army. As the war wore on,
some militia units from states as far south as Maryland resumed or began
enlisting free (and sometimes enslaved) Blacks as well. As it turned out,
Blacks and whites would not again serve together in integrated units of
the United States Army until 1948.

At the start of its 1777 summer offensive, Britain had a large army in
Canada and a larger one in New York. The United States countered with
the remnant of the force that once invaded Canada holed up in upstate
New York and Washington's main (but much reduced) army at Morristown. Fully expecting to suppress the rebels by fall, the British began
their offensive in June with John Burgoyne's northern army moving
south from Montreal through the Lake Champlain Valley. With the veteran general Horatio Gates assuming command of patriot forces there
and militia troops streaming in from New England, the Americans in
upstate New York regrouped in the forested regions around Saratoga.
They hoped to stop the British advance before it reached the lower Hudson Valley and split the states in two from Montreal to Manhattan.

Political and military uncertainty in the region had permitted the
New England settlers of the New Hampshire Grants in what became
Vermont to declare their independence from New York earlier in 1777.
This issue dated from 1749, when the colonial governor of New Hamp-

shire began surveying towns and issuing grants for land north of Massachusetts and west of the Connecticut River in a region claimed by New
York. Up to 10,000 white colonists lived in the disputed region by 1770,
most of them under land grants issued by New Hampshire even though,
in 1764, the crown had ruled in favor of New York's claim to the area and
New York refused to recognize the New Hampshire Grants.

In 1770, the New England settlers of the New Hampshire Grants
organized their own militia, the Green Mountain Boys, to defend their
claims against New York. Elements of this force joined the patriot side
in some early Revolutionary activity, including the capture of the British
fort at Ticonderoga in May 1775. A year later, representatives of the New
Hampshire Grants petitioned the Continental Congress for recognition,
but New York blocked the request, leading to the declaration of Vermont's independence in January 1777. Six months later, with Burgoyne's
army bearing down on the region, delegates from the various grants hur-
riedly assembled to draft a state constitution in the hopes that this step
might lead to the admission of Vermont to the union.[47] Although largely
copied from Pennsylvania's new constitution of 1776 and never debated
at length or subject to a public ratification process, the Vermont constitution added a revolutionary provision abolishing slavery—the first written constitution in the world to include such a proviso.

"All men are born equally free and independent, and have certain natural, inherent and unalienable rights, amongst which are the enjoying
and defending life and liberty," the first article of the Vermont constitution's Declaration of Rights stated. "Therefore, no male person, born
in this country, or brought from over sea, ought to be holden by law, to
serve any person, as a servant, slave or apprentice, after he arrives to the
age of twenty-one Years, nor female, in like manner, after she arrives to
the age of eighteen years."[48] Urged by Congress to establish new governments based on popular rather than royal authority, ten states had
adopted new constitutions by this point, but none of them barred slavery.[49] The Pennsylvania constitution had identical language regarding
people being "born equally free" with "unalienable rights" to liberty, but

even that state's otherwise radically democratic charter did not specify the implications of those rights for chattel slavery.[50]

No record survives explaining why the Vermont delegates took that added step. Many of the state's founders, including Governor Thomas Chittendon and the brothers Ethan and Ira Allen, used the metaphor of slavery to rail against the oppressive policies of New York and Britain, and, as we have seen, at least some patriot leaders had recognized a link between that metaphor and the actual practice of slavery by this time. Vermont's founders may have as well. At least one of them, Ebenezer Allen, freed his two enslaved workers shortly after the constitution's adoption. Evidence suggests that others did not, including perhaps Ethan Allen, whose household continued to count Black "servants" among its members.[51] The constitutional provision did not include an enforcement mechanism and its wording did not cover enslaved minors. Further, census records suggest that fewer than fifty Blacks (and still fewer enslaved ones) lived in Vermont at the time, so ending slavery would not affect many Vermonters. Whatever the actual impact on individuals, the Vermont constitution of 1777 sent a message that resounded throughout New England, even though its adoption did not deter New York from continuing to block Vermont's admission to the union.[52]

Massachusetts felt the shock waves first. Having deferred the task of drafting a state constitution for two years due to the British occupation of Boston, shortly after Vermont adopted its charter in 1777, Massachusetts launched the process by convening its legislators as a convention to frame one. They failed miserably.

Completed early in 1778 and sent to town meetings across the state for ratification, the draft constitution did not include a bill of rights, even though in 1641 Massachusetts was the first colony to enact one. Further, despite rising popular opposition to slavery in the state, the draft constitution not only failed to restrict the practice but limited voting to free, white, tax-paying, adult males "worth sixty pounds," and expressly disenfranchised "negroes, Indians and mulattoes."[53] In doing so, legislators followed the counsel of John Adams. "Do you intend to make every Man of 21 a Voter?" he asked in a letter from his perch in Congress to the state legislature's presiding officer. "I fear you will find a Fountain of Corruption, in making So many Voters." He favored property requirements for voting—at the time, ten states imposed such limits and the others required tax payments—but presumably not the racial restriction incorporated into the draft—only three states (Virginia, South Carolina, and Georgia) then barred free Blacks from voting. Turning to a proposal to end slavery in Massachusetts, however, Adams noted in his letter, "The Bill for freeing the Negroes, I hope will sleep for a Time. We have Causes enough of Jealousy Discord and Division [among the states], and this Bill will certainly add to the Number."[54] Whatever his own views on slavery, Adams did not want to disrupt the concord between New England and the southern states during the Revolutionary crisis.

Adams made his comment on abolition in response to a petition submitted to the legislature early in 1777 from a self-described "Great Number of Blackes detained in a State of slavery in the Bowels of a free & Christian Country." In reality, not all of the petition's eight signers were enslaved—some had received their freedom—but they consciously signed on behalf of the state's enslaved population. These eight included Peter Bestes, who had signed the April 1773 freedom petition and, two years later, joined fourteen other free Blacks in forming the first African American Masonic lodge. By this time, the all-male Masonic movement (or freemasonry) had spread throughout western Europe and British North America as a secretive, loosely networked, fraternal organization that tended to attract civic-minded merchants, artisans, large landowners, and aristocrats. George Washington, Benjamin Franklin, and John Hancock were active Masons, as were many British military officers. Indeed, after Boston's all-white Masonic lodge refused to admit Bestes and the other Black applicants in 1775, they formed their own all-Black lodge under the auspices of one attached to a British infantry unit then occupying Boston. Four of the eight signers of the 1777 petition were members of this Black lodge, including Prince Hall, a free Black tanner who supported the patriot cause and likely drafted the petition. With the legislature then composing a new state constitution, the petitioners implored lawmakers to address the rights of enslaved Blacks.

"To Be sold Like Beast of Burthen & Like them Condemnd to Slavery for Life," the petitioners declared, "is far worse than Nonexistence." Reflecting on the Revolutionary struggle for liberty and urging legislators to end "the inconsistancey of acting themselves the part which they condem and oppose in others," they added, "Every Principle from which America has Acted in the Cours of their unhappy Dificultes with Great Briton Pleads Stronger than A thousand arguments in favours of your petioners." Freedom, the petition declared, "is the Naturel Right of all men." While asking for an immediate end to slavery, the petitioners pleaded that at least "their Children who wher Born in this Land of Liberty may not be heald as Slaves after they arive at the age of twenty one years."[55] Even though this petition failed to persuade legislators to follow Vermont's lead on the matter, it influenced the ratification process.

At roughly the same time and also in Massachusetts, Lemuel Haynes—the freeborn, mixed-race disciple of New England theologian Samuel Hopkins and future pastor to white churches—wrote a fiery address denouncing slaveholding as incompatible with both the American ideology of liberty and the disinterested benevolence that stood at the heart of Hopkins's neo-Puritan theology. Born of a white mother—possibly a servant or the servant's mistress—Haynes was raised as the indentured servant of a devout Massachusetts farmer who educated the boy and exposed him to revivalist preaching of New Light Calvinists. When his indenture ended in 1774, Haynes joined a local patriot militia that saw some limited service in the siege of Boston and the occupation of Fort Ticonderoga, where he contracted the typhus that ended his military service. Returning home, he studied for the ministry, and received a license to preach in the state-established Congregational Church in 1780. Five years later he became the first ordained Black minister in America.

Slavery had its origins in hell, Haynes declared in his address, but liberty in heaven. Vividly describing this "hell upon Earth," he pleaded,

"Even an affrican, has Equally as good a right to his Liberty in common with Englishmen." Paraphrasing the biblical golden rule, Haynes declared, "We should not impose anything upon Others, But what we should Be willing should Be imposed upon us." Although born of a Black father and never a slave owner, Haynes depicted the enslaved as "others" and slaveholders as "us" in his address. While hailing Americans for fighting for freedom from British oppression, he condemned them for condoning the "much greater opession" of slavery. "Liberty is Equally as precious to a *Black Man*, as it is to a *white one*," Haynes wrote before reaching his core religious message. "Let that pity, and compassion, which is peculiar to mankind," he exclaimed, "no Longer Lie Dormant to your Breast: Let it run free thro' *Disinterested Benevolence*. then how would these iron yoaks Spontaneously fall from the gauled Necks of the Opress'd!"[56] Although his only known address devoted wholly to the topic of abolition, Haynes continued to champion racial harmony as a minister in western New England and upstate New York.

Faced with a draft state constitution that did not include a bill of rights and heaped further restrictions on free Blacks without liberating enslaved ones, Massachusetts voters gathered in town meetings across the state and rejected the document by large margins. In their official returns of vote totals to the state, most towns did not explain why their voters opposed the constitution but virtually all that did cited the lack of a bill of rights. Seventeen of these twenty-three towns also condemned the article imposing high property qualifications and racial restrictions on voting. A few cited the draft for failing to abolish slavery. Referencing the 1777 petition from Bestes, Hall, and other Black advocates of freedom, for example, the return from Hardwick decried slavery as "very Contrary to the Law of god and Liberty that we Profess" and "a Crying Sin which has Brought Gods Judgments upon the Land."[57] Appealing to natural and biblical law, the return from Boothbay declared, "We know of no reason in nature, or in revelation, to justify our depriving the Africans and their descendants (whose long continued Shameful and unchristian Slavery reflects dishonor and Endangers the curse of heaven on our public Struggles for our own rights) of a natural privilege of all men."[58]

Several Massachusetts towns denounced the constitution for tying voting rights to skin color.[59] "We are contending for our freedom—Let us all be equally free," the return from Essex pleaded.[60] Barring even free, property-owning Blacks from voting "appears to us to wear a very gross complextion of slavery," the town of Sutton declared. "This is manifestly ading to the already acumulated Load of guilt lying upon the Land in supporting the slave trade."[61] Black slavery had joined white liberty as voting issues in Massachusetts, with the ongoing war for independence shaping the debate. When John Adams returned to Boston in 1779, state leaders would try again to make a constitution. Like Adams, many of those leaders were trimmers seeking to balance their liberty against Black slavery in an unbalanced time. Not everything was possible in Revolutionary America, but the response of Massachusetts voters to the draft constitution of 1778 reflected a significant new popular perspective on slavery and race at least in some northern states.

In the meantime, as Burgoyne's army marched south into Vermont and upstate New York in June 1777, Washington and other patriot leaders fully expected Howe to send forces north from New York City to relieve Burgoyne's overextended forces. Burgoyne thought so too and did not keep his supply lines open to Canada—hence his need to forage supplies in and around Bennington by August. Instead, Howe dithered until mid-July trying to lure Washington into an open fight and, when this failed, he loaded two-thirds of his soldiers onto ships to invest Philadelphia from the south. As Congress fled, the British occupied the city in September. A company of 172 Black Pioneers accompanied this invasion force.

Taking Philadelphia without capturing Congress or crushing Washington's army represented a hollow victory for General Howe. The city had little strategic value, no established defensive perimeter, and many indifferent Quaker residents. Once the operation ended without Howe decisively defeating the Continental Army, London recognized his blunder and replaced him with Henry Clinton, who withdrew the British army to New York in the summer of 1778. He later dispatched much of it to retake the southern colonies and defend the British Caribbean.

Worse still for Britain, without relief from Howe, the position of Burgoyne's army in upstate New York became untenable. With winter setting in and no help in sight, it surrendered to Gates at Saratoga in October 1777. After word of this American victory reached Paris, representatives of France and the United States signed treaties in February 1778 recognizing American independence, opening formal trade between the two countries, and establishing terms for their military cooperation. These treaties did not win the war—that process would take five more years—but they made victory possible. The prospect of American independence offered hope to Blacks like Phillis Wheatley who embraced the patriot cause, but complicated the situation for those like Harry Washington who had sided with the British in their quest for freedom. The case of Titus, or "Colonel Tye" as he became known, exemplified their dilemma, as we shall see.

CHAPTER SIX

"Contending for the Sweets of Freedom"

1778–1781

The American Revolution entered a distinct third phase in June 1778 when General Clinton began moving the sole remaining British army in the rebelling states from Quaker Philadelphia to loyalist-leaning New York City. If the contrasting actions of Harry Washington and Phillis Wheatley exemplified differing approaches of Black Americans to the Revolution during its prior phase, then those of Colonel Tye and William Lee illustrated those options for its decisive third phase. Both saw action, or at least saw the action, at the inconclusive Battle of Monmouth in New Jersey on June 18, 1778.

"THREE POUNDS Reward," the 1775 newspaper advertisement had read. "RUN away from the subscriber, living in Shrewsbury, in the county of Monmouth, New-Jersey, a NEOGRE man, named Titus, but may probably change his name." The ad described Titus as "about 21 years of age, not very black, near 6 feet high," and wearing a homespun coat.[1] His owner, a Quaker farmer named John Corlies who spurned church teachings against slavery, dated his notice November 8, 1775— one day after Dunmore's proclamation offered freedom for the enslaved who left their patriot owners to fight for the crown. Titus apparently escaped to Virginia, became part of Dunmore's Ethiopian Regiment, and in August 1776 went with Dunmore to join the British army occupying New York. There, Titus—perhaps by then called Tye—would have worked as a "Pioneer," or service worker. A company of about 200 Black Pioneers followed the British army under the command of General William Howe from New York to Philadelphia in 1777, and (its numbers expanded by Pennsylvania Blacks seeking freedom) then back to New York in June 1778 after Henry Clinton replaced Howe as the commander in chief of British forces in North America.[2] By one name or another, Titus or Tye likely served in this unit.

The return march (or retreat, as patriot propagandists called it) took Titus through his home county of Monmouth, New Jersey, where a vanguard of the pursuing American army caught up with the rear guard of the New York–bound British force on the 28th. In overall command for his first battle since the failed defense of Philadelphia the prior autumn, George Washington had sent some 4,500 soldiers ahead to harass the British rear guard as he followed with his remaining troops. Washington found the vanguard falling back before a superior British force by the time he reached it. He rallied units of the vanguard just long enough for his main force to form a solid line on rising ground behind the retreating troops, who then fell back to join it. This hastily formed line stopped the British advance. The two armies then pushed back and forth across the battlefield until nightfall, when the British resumed their march to New York.

At the time, Washington traveled with his enslaved, mixed-race valet William Lee, whom Washington bought in 1767 from the estate of John Lee, the then-young manservant's likely father. Washington favored light-skinned servants for household duties and paid a premium for "Mulatto Will," as Washington called him in his accounts ledger.[3] As a noncombatant, Lee accompanied Washington throughout the war. He appeared in Moorish servant's garb alongside the uniformed general in a full-length portrait showing a scene from the New York campaign. Painted from memory in London five years later by Washington's former aide-de-camp John Trumbull in the European "orientalist" style then popular for depicting Black subjects, the picture may not accurately depict Lee.

According to the published recollections of George Washington Parke Custis, Martha Washington's grandson by a son from her first marriage, Lee led a "corps of [officer's] valets" to a hilltop viewpoint to watch the Battle of Monmouth. "See those fellows collecting on yonder height," Washington supposedly said of the group, "the enemy will fire on them to a certainty." When British cannon fire scattered the valets, Custis later reported in what had become Washington family lore, it "caused even the grave countenance of the General-in-Chief to relax into a smile." In his telling of it, Custis branded the episode as "ludicrous" and mocked Lee as "a square muscular figure . . . riding pompously" at the head of the parade of valets.[4]

By the time Custis related this account in a Washington, DC, newspaper during the mid-1800s, he had become the self-appointed keeper of George Washington's legacy. He had joined the Washington household as an infant when his father died in 1781, and later billed himself as Washington's "adopted son" even though never formally adopted.[5] Washington often expressed frustration with Custis and, after the boy dropped out of school for a third time at age seventeen in 1798, sent him back to his mother. "He appears to me to be moped & Stupid," Washington wrote to her about Custis, "says nothing—and is always in some hole or corner excluded from Company."[6] Inheriting several plantations from his father's estate at age twenty-one, Custis followed his father (Martha's son), grandfather (Martha's first husband), and great-grandfather (Martha's father) in raping enslaved Black women and siring children by them. Although part of this world, the best evidence suggests Washington never engaged in such practices.[7]

Along with a dark-skinned attendant in a red servant's vest long thought to represent Lee (at right), Custis as a boy in a red suit (at left) frames Edward Savage's celebrated group portrait of the First Family circa 1790. That Lee appeared (or supposedly appeared) in two major paintings of Washington suggests the ties linking the general and his valet. Custis's account of the episode at Monmouth may have captured Washington's attitude toward Lee—laughing at his pratfalls—or Custis's view of Lee (or Blacks in general) as childlike. Either way, it offers a window on slavery in the American South during the Revolutionary era. For Washington's part, the general seemed to think more highly of Lee than of Custis.

Titus's experience at the Battle of Monmouth differed markedly from Lee's. Also there as a noncombatant in a servile capacity—but with the British rather than the American army—Titus took advantage of his familiarity with the area to capture an officer of the patriot militia and take him prisoner to New York. With a sizable local population of both patriots and loyalists, by this time northern New Jersey had become a contested borderland in a civil war dividing neighbors and splitting families. Loyalists held the upper hand until January 1776, when patriots ousted Royal Governor William Franklin (Benjamin Franklin's loyalist son) and took control of New Jersey, only to lose its northern part to British troops by year's end. Washington contested this advance but fell back to Pennsylvania in 1777. Clinton's decision to concentrate British forces in New York City after 1778 left New Jersey to the patriots. With each shift in fortune, local patriots or loyalists (whichever held power) exacted revenge on the other, while those out of power engaged in fifth-column guerrilla-style resistance. By capturing a patriot officer without any account of how he did it, Titus became something of a hero to loyalist New Jersey refugees in British-occupied New York.

Then in his mid-twenties, Titus half-emerged at this point from the obscurity of American slavery to assume a shadowy role as Colonel Tye, a freelance loyalist raider with an assumed title and adopted name. For two years, Tye joined or led raids in and around Monmouth County, foraging food and terrorizing patriots from a base on New Jersey's British-controlled Sandy Hook peninsula. His raiding parties included dozens of Blacks and at least some whites.[8] Other loyalist paramilitary units operating in the region, such as Thomas Ward's 400-member force, had Black combatants as well.[9] These raids often targeted patriot militia leaders and slaveholders, with some executed on the spot and others turned over to the British for bounties. Rustled cattle and horses also netted rewards from the British.

A rich agricultural region dotted with small farms (many with a few enslaved field hands) and wedged between opposing armies in chronic need of supplies, northern New Jersey proved a breeding ground for bitter reprisals. Resident Blacks sometimes aided the raiders and occasionally escaped with them to New York. Injured in a raid on the home of a New Jersey patriot known for his brutal treatment of loyalists, Tye died from his wounds in September 1780, having won his freedom through combat for a brief but bloody period.[10] "The famous negro *Tye*," the patriot *New Jersey Gazette* reported after his death, was "justly much more to be feared and respected, as an enemy, that any of his brethren of the fairer complexion."[11]

No portrait exists of Tye. No one ever made one. The only surviving description of his appearance appeared in the 1775 ad offering a reward for his recapture. For years, historians believed that Lee, for his loyalty to his owner, enjoyed the favored fate of having his image preserved in two celebrated portraits of Washington. The obscurity of slavery cloaks even this most famous of enslaved Americans, however. While a Black man in servant's livery hovers deferentially behind Washington in these portraits, the artist did not identify the servant as Lee, and recent research suggests that neither image could be his.[12] If any dark-skinned model could stand in for the role, it was an illustration of an enslaved Black's marginal status in Revolutionary America as much as no image at all.

Following the Battle of Monmouth in 1778, Washington spread his troops in a wide arc around the city from northern New Jersey to western Connecticut, successfully enveloping but never dislodging the British from New York City. From 1778 to 1781, northeastern New Jersey and the lower Hudson River valley became a no-man's-land between entrenched armies—a scene of bloody borderland skirmishes and nighttime raids (like those led by Tye) initiated by both sides. Washington anchored his southern flank in Morristown, New Jersey, with sizable portions of his army enduring two hard winters there in 1778–79 and 1780–81. Adding to the suffering caused by a lack of food, shelter, and clothing, the collapsing value of continental paper money and the inability of Congress to pay the troops made matters worse than before. The ongoing stalemate, coupled with disputes over the length of service for members of the Pennsylvania and New Jersey regiments, led to near mutinies at Morristown during the winter of 1780–81, ending in the summary execution of some ringleaders. Liberty had its costs, and limits.

The disputes over the length of military service turned on whether signing up for "three years or during the war" meant a fixed term or for the war's duration. Enlistment contracts for the Continental Army began using that phrase in 1777, so its meaning gained urgency when the war extended beyond 1780. Some enlisted soldiers wanted out or bonuses to remain after three years; their officers demanded they stay. Black recruits, in contrast to white soldiers, generally enlisted for the duration of the war, often had fewer alternatives, and sometimes needed to stay in to secure their emancipation.[13] Although complete figures for the number of free and enslaved Blacks serving in the Continental Army do not exist, in his study of the topic, historian Benjamin Quarles estimated the total at around 5,000, with increasing numbers over time.[14] By 1781, the final year of active warfare, a visiting French officer observed that Blacks made up about a quarter of the soldiers in the army assembled in and around Washington's headquarters in the lower Hudson River valley.[15] In 1778, the only year for which such rolls survive, the percentage of armed and unarmed Blacks serving with individual regiments of the Continental Army ranged from a low of 6 to a high of 13 percent.[16]

Throughout the war, Black soldiers in the Continental Army and state regiments typically served as privates in the infantry with non-arms-bearing duties. They generally supported combat operations without participating in them except as drummers. "Other than orderly duties" for officers, Quarles noted, "Negro soldiers were often assigned to such semi-domestic occupations as those of waiter and cook."[17] Many served as wagoners, foragers, or manual laborers. In regimental rolls listing soldiers by name, Blacks sometimes appeared anonymously as "A Negro name not known" or "Negro name unknown."[18] A published directory of Revolutionary War soldiers and sailors from Connecticut compiled from muster rolls lists hundreds of Blacks by only their first names, and seven solely by their race.[19] It identifies the complexion of over a third of the sailors on the Connecticut-based Continental Navy frigate *Trumbull* as "Dark," "Negro," or "Brown."[20]

Throughout the 1700s, both free and enslaved Blacks (like Crispus Attucks and Olaudah Equiano) found jobs as sailors on merchant and military ships, usually in the lowest ranks and occupations. Led by Stephen Hopkins's brother Esek, the Continental Navy eventually had some fifty warships. Several states formed their own navies. Congress flooded the sea with authorized privateers. All these ships needed crews, and many Blacks had the requisite experience.[21] At the time, some critics depicted the life at sea of an ordinary sailor as a form of bondage, but at least the local laws and conventions of formal enslavement did not apply. With the launching of American navies and a surge in privateering, this sort of employment on ships exploded during the war, with up to an estimated 1,000 Africans and African Americans serving in the fleets assembled by Congress and the states, or on privateers operating under letters of marque from Congress.[22]

By all accounts, more Blacks served on the British side than with the Continental Army during the American Revolution—as much as three times as many.[23] Dunmore's Ethiopian Regiment and extralegal loyalist raiding parties aside, Black members of formal British and official loyalist military units were even less likely to bear arms than those in patriot forces. Clinton never allowed it in his ranks—yet he never lacked for Blacks serving in noncombat roles. They undergirded his army.

Perhaps hearing about the 1775 proclamation issued by Dunmore in

Virginia or the earlier *Somerset* case from England, or possibly simply drawn to any place beyond the reach of their patriot masters, enslaved Blacks seeking liberty flocked behind British lines. New York became a magnet for enslaved and free Blacks alike because of its occupation from 1776 to 1783 by the main British army in North America and its large size and many jobs. Manhattan Island already had a significant number of Black residents—a 1771 census put the number at over 3,000, or about 14 percent of the population—and the reported influx of Black people during the British occupation raised the total.[24] At the time, one local loyalist judge estimated that influx as "at least 2,000 men, women, and children."[25] Some of them found work doing menial tasks for the British army or as personal attendants to British officers; others in civilian occupations open to Blacks, such as household servants, day laborers, sailors, and teamsters. Those with construction skills could find jobs rebuilding portions of the lower west side destroyed in a fire that began shortly after patriots evacuated the city.[26]

The British never issued a general decree freeing enslaved Blacks in New York or other occupied areas. Those enslaved by loyalists remained enslaved, which included many who stayed in New York with their owners after the British occupied the city in September 1776. Loyalist slaveholders could also enter the city to recover their runaways. The British refused to return enslaved Blacks who had escaped patriot owners, however, and treated them as free Blacks.[27] On June 30, 1779, Clinton formalized this policy by issuing the so-called Philipsburg Proclamation from his headquarters in Westchester County. "I do most strictly forbid any Person to sell or claim Right over any NEGROE, the Property of a Rebel, who may take Refuge with any Part of this Army," Clinton decreed, "and I do promise to every NEGROE Who shall desert the Rebel Standard, full security to follow within these Lines, any Occupation which he shall think proper."[28] Clinton's proclamation went beyond Dunmore's decree by covering all runaway enslaved Blacks behind British lines rather than only able-bodied ones joining the British army, but it still applied only to those enslaved by patriots, not loyalists. Nevertheless, the proclamation resulted in the most widespread emancipation of Blacks in America to that time—at least 3,000 from occupied New York City alone.

The Philipsburg Proclamation, which applied throughout the thirteen rebellious states, gained added meaning because of Clinton's so-called Southern Strategy. After establishing his headquarters in easily defended New York, Clinton sent over half of his troops south, by ship, to defend Britain's sugar-rich Caribbean colonies from the French, tie down the French in the defense of their own Caribbean colonies, and try to subdue the American South. The decree did not apply in the British Caribbean, which never rebelled, but it did in Georgia, the Carolinas, and Virginia, where enslaved Blacks made up nearly half of the non–Native American population.

After British troops, aided by a local Black guide, captured Savannah without much effort in December 1778, Clinton arrived with more soldiers to lead the assault on Charleston beginning in February 1780. Harry Washington went along as a corporal in a corps of some sixty Blacks in the royal artillery. Clinton counted on local white and Black loyalists to rally behind the royal banner and supply intelligence about patriot operations. Many did, with able-bodied white males organized into loyalist military units and five hundred Black men put to work building earthworks to besiege Charleston. During the six-week-long siege of the city, formerly enslaved Blacks also did the backbreaking work of portaging boats, draining marshes, and maintaining camp for 13,500 British and Hessian soldiers. Harry Washington presumably helped transport and emplace the cannons that forced the Americans to surrender the city on May 12. Some Blacks served as spies or informal informants, passing in and out of the besieged city collecting and conveying information.[29]

Within days after Charleston fell, so many enslaved Blacks had responded to Clinton's proclamation that he advised his chief field officer, Lord Cornwallis, to discourage any more from attaching themselves to the British army.[30] Nevertheless, before turning over leadership of ongoing operations in the South to Cornwallis in June and returning to his headquarters in New York, Clinton reiterated his policy in a memorandum to Cornwallis and the British commandant at Charleston. In occupied Charleston and the American South generally, the British would return the enslaved Blacks of loyalists to their owners on the condition that they would not suffer for having left. Enslaved Blacks escaped, captured, or confiscated from "rebel" owners would become "public" property subject to work for the British army in menial, noncombat roles so long as the war lasted. If they faithfully served until the war's end, the British would free them.[31]

Under these terms of engagement, leaving a detachment that included Harry Washington's artillery unit to defend Charleston, Cornwallis led the main British army west to subdue the interior of South Carolina before turning north to retake North Carolina and Virginia. Everywhere it went, enslaved Blacks flocked to Cornwallis's army by the hundreds, with some supplying useful intelligence, serving as guides, or put to work, but most simply following the army from place to place. "Their property we need not seek," one British officer reported at the time about patriot slaveholders and their human property, "it flies to us."[32] One account put the number of Blacks taken by the British from South Carolina patriots at over 5,000, some received as individuals, some in families, and some as communities.[33]

During the Revolutionary War, Americans never responded in kind to the British offer of freedom for enslaved Blacks who ran away from owners on the opposing side. Of course, like the British, if Americans recaptured runaways claimed by someone on their side, they returned them.[34] Unlike Clinton, Washington did not use his powers as commander in chief to free those owned by the enemy or enemy supporters even if they reached his lines or offered to serve in his army. He left the matter largely to the states, which typically treated the captured or confiscated human property of loyalists as the spoils of war.

Virginia, for example, put Blacks captured or confiscated from loyalists to work at its state-owned lead mines producing the musket balls needed for the war effort. South Carolina gave them to white soldiers as enlistment bounties or rewards for service. Maryland auctioned them off and kept the proceeds. At various times, Georgia traded enslaved Blacks confiscated from loyalists for war supplies, put them to work as laborers, and used them to pay the governor and other white officials. Often, southern state militia officers and soldiers simply kept enslaved Blacks that they captured from loyalists as private booty—the plunder of war.[35] Rather than obtaining liberty, for most southern Blacks, escaping the bond of loyalist owners simply led to the whips of new patriot ones.

After resisting suggestions to arm enslaved Blacks for the first five years of the war, Congress responded to Clinton's Southern Strategy in 1779 by adopting a resolution recommending that Georgia and South Carolina raise several battalions of Black troops. Savannah had fallen to the British by this time and Charleston appeared in jeopardy. The initiative began a year earlier with John Laurens, the European-educated son of South Carolina merchant-planter and Continental Congress delegate Henry Laurens. Only twenty-four years old at the time, the younger Laurens served as an aide-de-camp to George Washington. Laurens took his idea to his father, however, rather than to Washington. Enlisting enslaved Blacks "would advance those who are unjustly deprived of the Rights of Mankind to a State which would be a proper Gradation between abject Slavery and perfect Liberty," Laurens wrote to his father early in 1778. "Men who have the habit of Subordination almost indelibly impress'd on them, would have one very essential qualification of Soldiers."[36] In line with the practices of ancient Rome, which would free the enslaved to join its legions in desperate times, Laurens viewed military service by enslaved Blacks as a stepping-stone to emancipation as well as a means to defend South Carolina.

Henry Laurens initially dismissed the scheme as a "Quixotism," as he put it, of his high-minded son, but promised to consider it. "I have been cautious of speaking openly of the project," he wrote from Congress, "but hitherto I have not heard one person approbate the Idea from the

The Bloody Massacre perpetrated in King Street Boston on March 5th, 1770, engraving by Paul Revere, 1770, showing all victims as white. *Courtesy of Princeton University Library, WHS 115.5*

Abigail Adams, print after portrait by Gilbert Stuart, c. 1830–60. *Courtesy of Library of Congress*

The Political Cartoon for the Year 1775, political cartoon from *Westminster Magazine*, May 1, 1775, showing George III and Lord Mansfield leading Britain into war with America. *Courtesy of Library of Congress, PC 1-5288A*

Olaudah Equiano, frontispiece engraving from Olaudah Equiano, *The Interesting Narrative of the Life of Olaudah Equiano, or Gustavus Vassa, the African, Written by Himself*, 1794. RB 426765, The Huntington Library, San Marino, California

Sea Captains Carousing in Surinam, including the Hopkins brothers of Rhode Island and enslaved Black servants, oil on bed ticking by John Greenwood, c. 1752–58. *Saint Louis Art Museum, Museum Purchase 256: 1948*

Left: *Benjamin Franklin*, engraving by Charles Willson Peale made during the Constitutional Convention, 1787.   *Courtesy of Mount Vernon Ladies' Association*

Right: Benjamin Lay, early Quaker abolitionist, print after portrait by William Williams, c. 1750.   *Courtesy of Library of Congress*

Lemuel Haynes, frontispiece from Timothy Mather Cooley, *Sketches of the life and character of Rev. Lemuel Haynes, A.M.* (New York: Harper & Brothers, 1837).   *Courtesy of Sterling Memorial Library, Yale University*

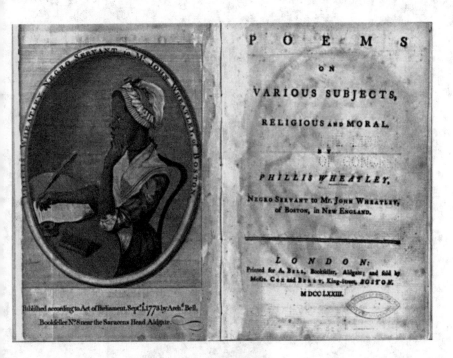

Above: Phillis Wheatley, frontispiece engraving and title page after portrait by Scipio Moorhead, 1773. *Courtesy of Library of Congress*

Left: *George Washington and William Lee*, oil on canvas by John Trumbull, 1780. *Bequest of Charles Allen Munn, 1924 (24.109.88), Metropolitan Museum of Art*

Charles Cotesworth Pinckney, proslavery federalist, engraving,
c. 1862.   *Courtesy of Library of Congress*

Patrick Henry, proslavery antifederalist,
print after painting by George Bagby
Matthews, c. 1904.   *Courtesy of Library of
Congress, D416-9855*

Gouverneur Morris, antislavery
federalist, engraving, 1783.
Courtesy of Library of Congress

George Bryan, antislavery antifederalist and author of Pennsylvania's
gradual abolition statute, print after
portrait, c. 1770.   *Courtesy of University Archives and Records Center, University
of Pennsylvania, UARC20040326003*

Left: James Madison, from *Pendleton's Lithography* after portrait by Gilbert Stewart, c. 1828. *Courtesy of Library of Congress*

Below: *The Washington Family*, engraving by Edward Savage, 1797, showing unidentified enslaved Black servant. *Courtesy of Mount Vernon Ladies' Association*

Thomas Jefferson, print by Cornelius Tiabout after painting by Rembrandt Peale, c. 1801, holding a copy of the Declaration of Independence next to a bust of Benjamin Franklin. *Courtesy of Library of Congress*

Banneker's Almanack for 1795, front cover with portrait of Benjamin Banneker, 1794. *Courtesy of Maryland Center for History and Culture, RN 2241*

hints which I dropped in order to gain opinions." Most enslaved Blacks would not choose to serve as soldiers in exchange for the promise of liberty, he opined, and "if you have any dependence upon free Negroes *depend* upon it you will be deceived."[37] They would not serve, he felt.

Laurens persisted in badgering his father about the idea and, as the military situation in South Carolina worsened by early 1779, the senior Laurens threw his qualified support behind it—qualified in that he left the final decision to his home state's legislature. By this point, the younger Laurens had secured a leave of absence from Washington to go south and join in the defense of South Carolina, with the dashing junior officer hoping to raise a regiment of Black soldiers under his personal command.[38] "For my part," he wrote to his father, "it will be my duty and my pride, to transform the timid Slave into a firm defender of Liberty and render him worthy to enjoy it himself."[39] Although seemingly quixotic, a father's love embraced it.

Passing through Philadelphia on his way south, John Laurens delivered a letter endorsing his project from his close friend and comrade-in-arms Alexander Hamilton to the new president of Congress, John Jay. "The contempt we have been taught to entertain for the blacks, makes us fancy many things that are founded neither in reason nor experience," Hamilton wrote in support of enlisting the enslaved to defend America. "An essential part of the plan is to give them their freedom with their muskets. This will secure their fidelity, animate their courage, and I believe will have a good influence upon those who remain, by opening a door to their emancipation." The prospect of widespread manumission of enslaved Blacks, Hamilton confided to the abolitionist-minded Jay, "has no small weight in inducing me to wish the success of the project; for the dictates of humanity and true policy equally interest me in favour of this unfortunate class of men."[40]

In March 1779, with his son's proposal presumably forefront in his mind, Henry Laurens asked Congress to appoint a committee on ways and means to defend the southern states and secured his own appointment to it.[41] By then, South Carolina governor John Rutledge had sent his state's commander in chief, Isaac Huger, to implore Congress for added Continental troops. "Continuing the Militia or Yeomanry of So Carolina in the field for any considerable time will be attended with fatal consequences," Huger reportedly advised the committee, "by affording temptation to negro Slaves to rise in Rebellion or at least to desert to & strengthen the hands of the Enemy."[42] Most of South Carolina's militia members must "remain at home," the committee reported to Congress, "to prevent insurrections among the negroes."[43] By this convoluted reasoning, the committee proposed that South Carolina and Georgia, "if they shall think the same expedient," recruit 3,000 able-bodied Blacks and form them into battalions "to be commanded by white commissioned and non commissioned officers." Congress would pay $1,000 to the owner of each recruit, but "no pay or bounty be allowed to the said negroes." Every Black who served until the war's end "shall then return his arms, be emancipated and receive the sum of fifty dollars." In a final bit of Revolutionary nepotism, the committee recommended that John Laurens receive a commission of lieutenant colonel and lead the Black battalions.[44]

In response to an inquiry from Henry Laurens, Washington expressed grave doubts about the scheme. Freeing some enslaved Blacks would "render Slavery more irksome to those who remain in it," he observed, and he never envisioned freeing all of the enslaved. Arming some of them would lead the British to arm others, he added, "the upshot then must be who can Arm fastest—and where are our Arms?"[45] Nevertheless, with the key caveat that the proposal only represented a recommendation that John Laurens would carry to South Carolina and Georgia, Congress approved it.[46] New Hampshire delegate William Whipple, who had freed his enslaved household servant Prince to serve as a soldier, hailed its passage. "This will," he wrote in an overly rosy assessment, "lay a foundation for the emancipation of those poor wreches in that Country & I hope be the means of dispensing the Blessings of freedom to all the Human Race in America."[47] By then, his own former enslaved servant Prince had served at the Battles of Saratoga and Rhode Island.

Seven decades later, in a historical sleight of hand designed to suggest a diversity of people supporting American liberty, the republican-minded German artist Emanuel Leutze put Prince Whipple (as he called himself after his emancipation) near the front and a Native American at the rear of the boat in the iconic painting *Washington Crossing the Delaware.* There is no evidence of either person having been there.[48]

Never venturing as far as Georgia, John Laurens repeatedly pressed the recommendation for arming enslaved Blacks on the South Carolina governor and legislature in 1779 and 1780.[49] "If implicit obedience to the commands of Superiors, if bodily strength and activity—if constitutions proof against fatigue, watchings, fastings and the intemperatures of seasons are essential qualifications in soldiers these men are superiorly qualified for that station," he explained in a 1779 letter to the governor's Privy Council.[50] State officials dismissed the proposal out of hand.[51] "We are much disgusted here at Congress recommending us to arm our Slaves," Lieutenant Governor Christopher Gadsden wrote to Samuel Adams, his friend from the First Continental Congress and Committees on Correspondence. "It was received with great resentment, as a very dangerous and impolitic Step."[52] Among the rights that many white South Carolinians fought for in the American Revolution, few ranked higher than their established legal property rights in enslaved Africans.

With the British still entrenched in Charleston, John Laurens tried again in 1782 with the added support of Nathanial Greene, the Yankee Continental Army general sent by Washington to help the South break free of British occupation. Rather than ask for enslaved Blacks from local patriots, this time Laurens proposed raising the units from enslaved Blacks confiscated from loyalist estates. Whites would still lead the units.

Again, both the Privy Council and the state legislature rejected the proposal. "The single voice of reason," Laurens reported to Washington on his own efforts, "was drowned by the howlings of a triple-headed monster in which Prejudice, Avarice & Pusillanimity were united."[53] Instead, the legislature voted to send those confiscated Blacks to serve as laborers for

Greene's existing white units.[54] The legislators defeated the proposal "not because they objected to the expence (for they give a most enormous bounty for white men, and pay in Slaves)," Greene noted, "but from an apprehension of the consequences"—presumably their fear that confiscated Blacks would bear arms and receive their freedom.[55] Laurens died in battle three months after his letter to Washington. His proposal died with him.

Prince Whipple, the enslaved Black man freed to fight for New Hampshire, and many others like him, would not let the idea of emancipation die, however, and it endured in the North. In 1779, Whipple (by then a veteran of the Continental Army's stunning victory at Saratoga) joined nineteen other enslaved or formerly enslaved New Hampshire Blacks in petitioning the state legislature to abolish slavery.

"Here we know that we ought to be free agents!" the petitioners exclaimed. "Here we feel the dignity of human nature. Here we feel the passions and desires of men, though checked by the rod of slavery. Here we feel a just equality. Here, we know that the God of Nature made us free!" For the sake "of injured liberty" in the midst of a war for liberty, they asked legislators to "enact such laws . . . whereby we may regain our liberty and be ranked in the class of free agents and that the name of slave may no more be heard in a land gloriously contending for the sweets of freedom."[56] The legislature read the petition during its next session but ruled it "not ripe for determination" and postponed the matter indefinitely.[57]

Despite years of agitation by abolitionists in New England, New Hampshire had nearly as many enslaved Blacks in 1780 as before the Revolution; Massachusetts and Connecticut likely had more. Of all the New England states, only Rhode Island with its large Quaker population and Black military regiment had fewer. Still, the New Hampshire legislature ignored the petition. The state's post-independence constitution, adopted in 1776, said nothing about the rights of anyone—free, enslaved, male, or female—and would not do so until redrafted in 1784.[58]

The same year, 1779, the legislature of nearby Connecticut received two quite different freedom petitions. The first, in May, came from two

Blacks, Prime and Prince, enslaved by patriot owners, petitioning on behalf of themselves and other Blacks in Fairfield County. The second came from Pomp, whose loyalist master and family fled the state with British troops in July.

"Altho our Skins are different in Colour, from those who we serve, yet Reason & Revelation join to declare, that we are the Creatures of that God who made of one Blood, and Kindred, all the Nations of the Earth," Prime and Prince declared in their petition. Seeking their liberty in the context of a war for liberty, they asked legislators to consider "whether it is Consistent with the Present Claims, of the united States to hold so many Thousands, of the Race of Adam, our Common Father, in perpetual Slavery. Can human Nature endure the Shocking Idea?"[59]

Pomp took a different tack, but one still situated in the context of the American Revolution. "Being unwilling to go with [his] master over to the Enemy," Pomp wrote, he "made his Escape" and now sought his freedom, which only the legislature could grant. Describing himself as "Thirty Years of Age and of a firm and healthy Constitution," Pomp assured lawmakers that he could "well-provide for himself and a Wife and Child," who were already free.[60] Legislators ignored the petition of Prime and Prince, but granted the one from Pomp.[61] Otherwise, as the confiscated property of an absconded loyalist, the state would have sold Pomp and pocketed the proceeds. By freeing him, Pomp could take care of his free wife and children.

Regardless of outcome, such petitions illustrated the continued revolutionary agitation for liberty among Blacks in the northern states, especially New England. Many whites in the North, particularly Quakers in Pennsylvania and Congregationalists in Massachusetts, joined them in depicting abolition as an integral part of the patriot cause. Those two states, then the second and third most populous in America, took initial steps toward ending slavery in 1779.

In Massachusetts, the process began in September 1779 when the General Court (or legislature) convened a formal constitutional convention after voters rejected the draft constitution crafted by legislators. Voting by towns in meetings where they voiced their objections, the lack of a bill of rights, high property qualifications for voting, and (for some) no limits on slavery coupled with a bar on voting by Blacks stood out as the main reasons for disapproving the prior draft. Composed chiefly by John Adams, the new constitution addressed those concerns in measured terms. Property qualifications on voting dropped from a net worth of sixty pounds to either that net worth or an annual income of three pounds, and racial restrictions on voting disappeared.[62]

Without expressly barring slavery, the new constitution opened with a thirty-article Declaration of Rights that began with the ringing affirmation in Article I, "All men are born free and equal."[63] The returns of the various towns submitted over the spring of 1780 indicated that nearly every voter approved of this first article, with many of them believing that, if properly construed, it would abolish slavery in the state.[64] That, of course, would await judicial interpretation of the article. The constitution took effect in June 1780; the first freedom suits under it followed a year later.

Of all the initial state constitutions of the Revolutionary era, only the Pennsylvania constitution of 1776 (and the one based on it adopted in 1777 by the purported fourteenth state of Vermont) contained similarly expansive language about "all men" being born free.[65] Most of the other state constitutions did not include a bill of rights, and those that did generally guaranteed those rights only to "freemen."[66] The bill of rights adopted with the Virginia constitution, as drafted by the iconoclastic critic of slavery George Mason (who nevertheless owned at least three hundred enslaved Blacks), began with expansive language. Before approving that draft, as Virginia governor Edmund Randolph later explained, a "certain set of aristocrats" led by Robert Carter Nicholas inserted a phrase guaranteeing those rights only to those who "enter into a state of society."[67] Under the social-contract political theories of the day, Nicholas (a slaveholding lawyer whose mother came from the state's wealthiest family) understood this amended wording to exclude Africans and Native Americans, who supposedly lived outside society and thus did not possess civil rights. For generations, Virginians applied their bill of rights in this manner. In contrast, Pennsylvanians, like the Vermonters who abolished slavery in their constitution, took their expansive declaration of rights seriously and did not wait long to begin applying it to "all men."[68]

In August 1778, two months after the British had evacuated Philadelphia along with much of the city's Black population and many white loyalists, the State Assembly received a bill freeing all future children born of enslaved parents, "by which a gradual abolition of Servitude for life would be obtained."[69] Assembly members tabled that bill, but the state's Executive Council soon endorsed the concept of gradually ending slavery. "No period seems more happy for the attempt than at present, as the number of such unhappy characters, ever few in Pennsylvania, has been much reduced by the practices & plunder of our late invaders." This act, the council added, would impress all in Europe "who are astonished to see a people eager for Liberty holding Negros in Bondage."[70]

George Bryan, an architect of the 1776 Pennsylvania constitution and leader of the radical Constitutionalist faction in state politics—named for its support of the hyper-democratic state constitution—led this crusade. Serving on the council as the acting governor (or "president") in 1778, he likely authored its plea for gradual abolition. Remaining on the council in 1779 as vice president, he secured a renewed call for action in a February 1779 message to the Assembly. Denouncing the practice of slavery as a disgrace "to those who have been contending in the great cause of liberty," the council asserted, "honored will be that state in the annals of history, which shall be the first to abolish this violation of the rights of mankind." Recognizing the opposition that had stalled the prior bill, the message suggested that any new plan incorporate "such restrictions and regulations as to not injure the community," which included minimizing its economic impact on slaveholders.[71]

The Assembly promptly appointed an ad hoc committee of legislators representing both urban abolitionist and rural slaveholding interests to draft the measure.[72] Bryan worked with this group to prepare legislation for the next Assembly session. The initial draft, released for comment in March 1779, called for freeing future children born into slavery upon reaching age eighteen if female or age twenty-one if male, thus breaking the cycle of hereditary slavery without liberating anyone already enslaved. To prevent the introduction of more enslaved persons into the state, owners would have to register those currently there. Anyone not registered within seven months of the act's passage would become free. Further, the bill ended colonial-era restrictions on free and enslaved Blacks by granting them equal rights with whites to assemble and access the courts. Placing its scheme for gradual abolition within a Revolutionary context, the bill stated, "It becomes those who contend for their own freedom, to promote the liberty of others."[73]

A successful merchant and politician, Bryan recognized the complexity of Pennsylvania's becoming the first free state in a union of slaveholding states. His bill granted exceptions for enslaved servants transported into Pennsylvania by members of Congress sitting in Philadelphia or foreign diplomats, and, for up to six months, by nonresidents passing through or visiting the state. It offered no protection for runaways or fugitives legally enslaved in other states. It retained the state's colonial-era ban on interracial marriage and cohabitation.[74] Given the deep hostility to slavery by the state's Quaker community and growing opposition to it among urban workers, the measure or something like it would likely pass despite the objections of some farmers and mine owners who still held enslaved workers. An active and devout Presbyterian lay leader, Bryan worked with mixed success to rally rural members of his denomination behind the measure.

The draft legislation featured an expansive preamble placing the measure squarely in the context of the American struggle for liberty. "WHEN we contemplate our abhorrence of that state, to which the arms and tyranny of Great-Britain were exerted to reduce us," the preamble began, "we conceive it to be our duty, and rejoice that it is in our power to extend a portion of that freedom to others." Addressing the contentious issue of racial equality in a religious context, it noted, "It is not for us to enquire into the reasons why, in the creation of mankind, the inhabitants of the several parts of the earth, were distinguished by a difference of feature or complexion. It is sufficient to know that all are the work of one Almighty hand."[75]

When its 1779–80 session opened in the fall with the Constitutionalist faction holding a commanding majority, the Assembly voted overwhelmingly to print the bill for public discussion.[76] Based on comment already received, this printed draft raised to twenty-eight the age for freeing all future children born to enslaved mothers, purportedly to allow owners to recoup the cost of rearing those children, but also serving to keep them enslaved during their prime working and childbearing years. On the other hand, it now repealed the colonial-era ban on interracial marriage. The measure still did not liberate anyone already enslaved, but by cutting off the flow of further enslaved persons into the state through birth or importation, it sought to end slavery gradually. That result, however, would take a lifetime. Because it did not deprive slaveholders of their existing enslaved property, and allowed them to retain children born of their enslaved females for twenty-eight years, the bill did not compensate them.

Petitions for and against the bill flooded the legislature, with a heated one from Lancaster County assailing it in terms that the lawmakers rejected as indecent.[77] After several delays, the Assembly gave its initial assent to the bill in February 1780 and, by a margin of 34 to 21, its final approval in March. All of the representatives from the city of Philadelphia supported the measure, even though they came mainly from the minority Republican, or anti-Constitutionalist, faction. Legislators from rural counties cast virtually all of the votes against it, but even members from these regions did not uniformly oppose the bill. Indeed, a significant majority of the representatives from only two counties—Westmoreland in the state's iron-making region and Lancaster in the rural, largely German southeast—voted no.[78] Both of these counties had a higher ratio of enslaved workers than most in Pennsylvania, and tended to stand apart culturally and politically.[79]

Riddled with loopholes and glacial in process, the 1780 Pennsylvania act served as the model for how most northern states ended slavery. Illustrating its limits, the same local newspapers that reported on its progress simultaneously ran paid notices advertising the sale of Blacks and offering rewards for returning runaways. For example, directly below a February 17 article reporting on the initial passage of the bill—an "act of humanity, wisdom, and justice," the article commented—the *Pennsylvania Packet* ran a notice declaring, "TO BE SOLD, A NEGRO LAD, about eighteen years of age, who is very handy at waiting on table and doing house-work."[80] The next page offered for sale, "A LIKELY, healthy NEGRO WENCH, eighteen years of age, has had the small pox and measles."[81] Under the new law, neither of these eighteen-year-old youths would ever gain their freedom. Several similar ads appeared in local newspapers immediately after the bill's final passage. "To be sold a hearty NEGRO MAN," one of them read, "between twenty and thirty years of age, who understands farming."[82] The new law offered this man nothing except the prospect that any of his later-born children would be free.

In a public statement, dissenting, mostly rural, lawmakers objected to the act for disrupting harmony among the states and legalizing interracial marriage. Whatever "the humanity and justice of manumitting slaves in time of peace," the dissenters contended, "we cannot think this the proper time, since the seat of war is likely to be transferred to the Southward."[83] In politics as in war, delay often becomes the last defense for the defeated. Although Bryan's Constitutionalist faction lost control of the Assembly in the next election—a response to the radical measures they adopted—an effort made in the next session to extend the date for registering enslaved persons and thereby reenslave some already freed failed by vote of 27 to 21.[84] Urban Republicans remained supportive. Bryan had made the necessary compromises to help the bill survive and become a model for ending slavery in other northern states.

If right about nothing else, the dissenters did predict the war's southward course. After securing Savannah and Charleston and despite defeat in a skirmish at Cowpens and stalemate in a battle at Guilford Courthouse early in 1781, the British army pushed relentlessly north into Virginia. There, Cornwallis hoped to join with other British army and navy units and carry the battle to the heartland of patriot resistance, home to some 220,000 Blacks, most of them enslaved and many living on the plantations of prominent patriots. Washington, Jefferson, Henry, Mason, and the Lees all resided there and derived their wealth from enslaved labor. Deprive Virginia patriots of their enslaved workers, one British officer commented, "and famine follows."[85] Responding to the threat, in February 1781 the Virginia legislature authorized bonuses for new recruits and existing soldiers serving until the war's end: either one healthy Black between the ages of ten and thirty, or 60 pounds in specie.[86] Unwilling to free Blacks to fight in its defense, Virginia used enslaved people as bounties to entice and retain its white defenders. As governor, Jefferson signed the bill into law.

Cornwallis's strategy worked to a point. Until American and French troops arrived from the north, the British army moved virtually at will though Virginia, burning the capital of Richmond, raiding Charlottesville, and destroying up to ten million pounds of cured tobacco, the lifeblood of the state economy. Everywhere the British army went, enslaved Blacks fled to their lines—often individually but sometimes as large groups from plantations. Washington lost sixteen in one day from Mount Vernon and another twenty-two from his plantation in Virginia's Great Dismal Swamp.[87] James Madison heard from his cousin about the impact on plantations around Richmond: "Some have lost 40, others 30, every one a considerable Part of their Slaves."[88] According to a lawmaker in Richmond, State Assembly Speaker Benjamin Harrison, a former member of Congress and signer of the Declaration of Independence, lost "all his valuable Negroes."[89] Jefferson, the sitting governor, later reported his personal losses for 1781 as "about 30 slaves." Overall, he wrote, "From an estimate I made at that time on the best information I could collect, I supposed the state of Virginia lost under Ld. Cornwallis's hands that year about 30,000 slaves." Other estimates placed the total lower, but always in the thousands.[90]

Whatever the exact number, with some 8,000 troops, the British, Hessian, and loyalist forces in Virginia could not put so many Blacks to use in noncombat roles and refused to use them in combat. "Every soldier had his Negro, who carried his provisions and bundles," the Hessian officer Johann Ewald noted in his diary. "Every officer had four to six horses and three or four Negroes, as well as one or two Negresses for cook and maid." Over 4,000 more Blacks trailed behind the troops, he wrote. "Any place this horde approached was eaten clean, like an acre invaded by a swarm of locusts."[91] In July, when Cornwallis moved his army to Yorktown, at the Chesapeake Bay mouth of the York River, under orders to settle in and await resupply from the British navy, he put thousands of Blacks to work building embankments and redoubts to fortify the village and nearby Gloucester as a secure base for ongoing British operations in Virginia.

Continually on the move until entrenched at Yorktown and often traveling in family groups with insufficient food and clothing, the Blacks accompanying Cornwallis, like those who remained on pillaged patriot plantations, suffered enormously. Making everything much worse, the smallpox endemic within the British army became epidemic among the Blacks accompanying it. Most British and Hessian soldiers had received inoculations against the deadly airborne virus that spreads easily from person to person. Most Black Virginians had not. The result was catastrophic. Jefferson later recalled that virtually all of his escaped Blacks died from the disease, though actually only about half of them did.[92] Still, the death rate was enormous.

A concurrent outbreak of typhoid fever among Blacks and whites and countless cases of malaria added to the horror. Hunger stalked the base at Yorktown as well. Black foraging parties scoured the area for food but not enough remained to feed Cornwallis's large army, much less accompanying civilians. One party found only burned corn unfit for human consumption. Cornwallis never incorporated runaway Blacks into his fighting forces and forbade any Blacks from carrying firearms, even when foraging. Perhaps 4,000 settled in with his army at Yorktown.

Near the end of a narrow peninsula surrounded on three sides by navigable water, Yorktown offered a safe refuge for Cornwallis's army so long as the Royal Navy controlled access by sea. There, British ships could resupply and (if necessary) evacuate the troops. On September 5, however, a French fleet from the Caribbean defeated the British one sent to defend Cornwallis and closed off resupply and escape by sea. In the bold stroke that decided the war, a combined Franco-American army nearly twice the size of Cornwallis's force and composed largely of troops shifted south by Washington from the encirclement of New York soon blocked land access to Yorktown. These troops included the mixed-race regiment from Rhode Island, which had been serving in the bloody borderland between American and British forces in the lower Hudson River valley, where it lost eight Black soldiers and its commanding officer in a surprise attack by loyalist militia in May 1781. Working together, the French and Americans entrapped Cornwallis's army in Yorktown much as Washington once hoped to capture Clinton's army in New York. Then Washington tightened the noose through classic siege operations that put his troops and artillery ever closer to the British.

On October 9, the French siege cannons let loose a fearsome barrage that continued until the British capitulated. The situation in Yorktown became horrific, with cannonballs raining down, buildings exploding into fire, and stench rising up from the diseased, dead, and wounded. Unable to feed the horses, on October 14 Cornwallis ordered them slaughtered, with their bodies cast into the river. The tide brought back their carcasses, adding to the nauseating smell. In desperation, he expelled first those infected with smallpox and then Black camp followers, many of whom hid in the woods to escape capture by the patriots, or sought out French units for protection. By October 17, the British had exhausted their supplies of ammunition.

If war is hell, then Yorktown became the ninth circle of that inferno for the Blacks trapped there. Half or more died from disease, malnutrition, or wounds—with smallpox taking the most. When the British finally laid down their arms on October 19, the articles of capitulation stipulated that Americans could recover all their lost property from the British at Yorktown and the nearby fort at Portsmouth, including any runaway, captured, or confiscated enslaved Blacks who still survived. No rules governed the process other than the order supplied by Virginia law governing the recapture of runaways, which addressed conflicting claims among white owners more than the rights of captured Blacks. Slaveholders and their agents descended on Yorktown to make their claims, with some hiring American soldiers to hunt down Blacks hiding in nearby woods. Washington recovered two of his; Jefferson five.[93] Cornwallis spirited away some of those who had helped him the most on the one Royal Navy ship allowed to sail to New York without examination.

Although the British held on in New York City, Charleston, and Savannah, with Black loyalists in all three cities, the combat phases of the Revolution concluded with the surrender at Yorktown in 1781. A new British government soon opened the negotiations that led to its acceptance of American independence, and the states began working out their postwar social and political norms. Northern and southern states moved in divergent directions on the future of Black slavery in a free, predominately white republic. The choices made then profoundly affected Americans ever after.

CHAPTER SEVEN

A House Dividing

Liberty and Slavery under the Confederation, 1781–1787

"Oh God! It is all over!" British prime minister Lord North reportedly exclaimed upon hearing the news from Yorktown.[1] He was right. Following the patriot victory there in October 1781, the British military footprint in the United States, already reduced to Savannah, Charleston, and New York, shrank in stages over the next two years before vanishing altogether in November 1783. The British simply lacked the will to fight on in America with so little to show for their effort and pressing concerns elsewhere in the empire. As their losses mounted in the Caribbean and the Mediterranean, with the French taking St. Kitts, Montserrat, Nevis, and Minorca, they focused on holding the colonies that mattered most to them: Jamaica and Barbados.

Defections from his Tory Party cost North his majority in Parliament and, in February 1782, opposition Whigs led by longtime supporter of American rights Lord Rockingham passed a motion to end offensive operations in North America. Having first served as prime minister in 1765, when his repeal of the Stamp Act quieted the colonies, Rockingham replaced North in March 1782 and sued for peace. Rockingham's death in July did not derail the process, as his successor, Lord Shelburne, assigned peace negotiations to the elderly Scottish merchant and slave trader Richard Oswald, who hoped to buy a plantation in South Carolina after the war.

British forces left Savannah first, completing their evacuation on July 11, 1782, when the final British warships sailed from port. Some five thousand Blacks went with them or on other British or Tory transports leaving the city over the previous weeks.[2] Most of these Blacks departed with their white loyalist owners bound for resettlement on vacant land in British East Florida or the Bahamas. Some went with army units to New York or Jamaica, but because of limited space on the warships, the general in charge of the evacuation, Alexander Leslie, ordered civil government departments not to take away local Blacks who had worked with them. Although Leslie refused requests from patriot slaveholders to enter the city to reclaim their runaways before his troops departed, an unknown number of Blacks remained behind for white Georgians to reenslave.[3] As soon as the British left, the Georgia legislature voted to authorize "every Citizen, having property with the British to go down [to Savannah] and make claim thereof."[4] All told, roughly two-thirds of the estimated 15,000 enslaved Blacks living in Georgia before the Revolution either died or departed during it, leaving the white residents eager to acquire more after the war.[5] The transatlantic trade in enslaved Africans soon resumed.

Next came Charleston, a much larger city than Savannah with many more British and Hessian troops, local loyalists, and free and enslaved Blacks. Begun in August 1782, the evacuation did not conclude until December 14, 1782, when the last of several hundred British ships left the wharves in Charleston. Among the ships departing on the final hectic days, fifty sailed with Hessian and loyalist troops for New York, fifty with British regiments for Jamaica, and twenty with wounded and demobilized soldiers for London. All of these fleets plus smaller ones heading for East Florida, Nova Scotia, and St. Lucia carried loyalists and Blacks fleeing the city.[6] The officers in charge on the American and British sides carefully choreographed a peaceful transfer of control, with the British threatening to destroy the city if not allowed to depart safely.[7] That did not prevent some loyalists remaining behind by choice or accident from suffering reprisals.[8] For their part, South Carolina officials vowed to confiscate loyalist property and repudiate debts owed to London bankers if the British carried away enslaved Blacks claimed by patriots.[9] Nevertheless, over 10,000 Blacks left with the British, though most of them traveled as the enslaved property of loyalists headed for East Florida and the British Caribbean.

"The struggle and conflict has been long and severe," the Continental Army's southern commander Nathanial Greene reported to Congress about retaking Charleston in December 1782. "But when it is considered that the enemy had upwards of 18,000 regular troops, besides several thousand militia and negroes, employed for the reduction of the southern states, I hope it will be found that the progress of the southern army has been no less honorable than important."[10] Beyond the thousands of Blacks taken away from South Carolina with their white loyalist owners, Alexander Leslie insisted on evacuating all runaway Blacks who had joined the British in response to an offer of liberty or, by their service to the British, would suffer reprisals from their former owners.[11] Due to his long service to the royal artillery, George Washington's former enslaved worker Harry qualified for evacuation as a free man and left Charleston with the final transport to New York.

In an effort to keep disputes over the evacuation of Blacks from reigniting armed combat as the British drew down their forces, the two sides agreed to form a joint commission to review the applications of Blacks seeking to leave Charleston as free people. It quickly collapsed as hundreds sought interviews and distrust mounted on all sides. The British wanted to clear "almost every Negro, man, woman and child, that was worth carrying away," the American commissioners complained.[12] For their part, local British officers refused to deliver nearly half of those marked by the commission for return to their American owners. It became a four-way tug of war with few good options for the thousands seeking liberty. Patriot slaveholders demanded "their" Blacks back. White loyalists sought those Blacks as compensation for property taken from them by patriots. Some British officers, soldiers, and privateers wanted to retain those same Blacks either as their servants or as booty of war destined for sale in the Caribbean slave markets. Under orders from Guy Carleton, the new British commander in chief for North America in New York, Leslie struggled to honor prior promises to free the Blacks who had sought refuge behind British lines or aided the British war effort. In the end, only about 15 percent of the some 10,000 Blacks evacuated from Charleston went as free people, with most of those going to New York or London.[13]

The obstacles impeding the departure of Blacks during the evacuation of Charleston paled in comparison to those arising in 1783 as the British prepared to leave New York, their final and largest base in the United States. Compounding the problem, this final British evacuation of an American city took place after word reached New York of the preliminary peace treaty signed by British and American negotiators in Paris on November 29, 1782. Joining the American delegates in Paris on the final day of negotiations for this preliminary deal, Henry Laurens insisted on adding a clause to the completed but unsigned treaty to bar the British from "carrying away any Negroes, or other Property of the American Inhabitants."[14] The other American negotiators, Benjamin Franklin, John Adams, and John Jay, came from northern states and opposed slavery. They had not asked for such a provision, yet Oswald, the chief British negotiator, readily agreed to Lauren's demand without offsetting concessions. For a quarter century, Oswald had served as a named partner in the firm operating the Bunce Island slave station in West Africa that shipped enslaved Blacks to Charleston, where Laurens served as the firm's agent. Laurens and Oswald had grown rich in this joint enterprise, and Laurens later presented the clause as a similar joint effort.[15]

News of the peace treaty "diffused universal joy among all parties, except us, who had escaped from slavery, and taken refuge in the English army," wrote Boston King, who then lived behind British lines in New

York after fleeing enslavement in South Carolina. "A report prevailed at New-York, that all the slaves, in the number 2000, were to be delivered up to their masters," he recalled. "This dreadful rumour filled us all with inexpressible anguish and terror."[16]

New York then harbored a remnant of the most loyal and useful Black soldiers to join the British side during the Revolution, numbering perhaps 3,000 persons. Carleton refused to renege on the vows made to them by his predecessors. He unilaterally interpreted the clause in the treaty about not carrying away enslaved Blacks as to exclude those freed by serving or seeking refuge with the British prior to the treaty's execution. "It could not have been the Intention of the British Government by the Treaty of Peace to reduce themselves to the Necessity of violating their Faith to the Negroes who came into the British Lines under the Proclamation of his Predecessors in Command," Carleton explained to a fuming George Washington at a conference on May 6, 1783. Anything else, Carleton added, would constitute "a dishonorable Violation of the public Faith pledged to the Negroes."[17] They stood by us in war, he effectively said, and we stand by them in peace by issuing each a certificate of freedom. Indeed, he informed Washington, some Blacks had already departed New York as free people, with most bound for settlement in the sparsely populated British colony of Nova Scotia.

Washington vigorously contested Carleton's interpretation of the treaty both at the conference and in an ensuing letter. Any embarkation of Blacks from New York, he wrote to Carleton, "is totally different from the Letter & Spirit of the Treaty." In line with it, Washington urged Carleton "to prevent the future carrying away of any Negroes or other Property of the American Inhabitants."[18] To this end, Washington had already asked an American agent in New York to look for his own runaways among the departing Blacks. "I will be much obliged by your securing them, so that I may obtain them again," he wrote.[19]

On this point of principle, Carleton would not budge. "The negroes in question, I have already said, I found free when I arrived at New York," Carleton replied to Washington. "I must confess that the mere supposition, that the King's Minister could deliberately stipulate in a treaty, an engagement to be guilty of a notorious breach of the public faith towards people of any complection seems to denote a less friendly disposition than I could wish."[20] Conceding defeat, Washington wrote to Virginia governor Benjamin Harrison, who had asked Washington to track down his own runaways among the Blacks in New York, "The Slaves which have absented from their masters will never be restored to them. Vast numbers of them are already gone to Nova Scotia."[21]

"Vast numbers" reflected Washington's fears rather than reality, but thousands of Blacks and tens of thousands of loyalists did leave New York over the seven months leading up to the final British evacuation of the city on November 25, 1783. The first fleet left New York with loyalist refugees bound for Nova Scotia in April. By September, a report came back from Nova Scotia, "There is now about 1500 refugees there, one half of which are Negroes."[22] In October, a patriot essayist from New York writing under the name Brutus complained of the British and their "Tory" followers, "How many thousand negroes, the property of citizens of these States, have already been carried off in your fleets?"[23]

The British kept meticulous records of the Blacks that they evacuated from New York. The total came to 2,990 free Blacks and a lesser number of enslaved ones traveling with their white owners—not as many as from Charleston, but a higher proportion of them free.[24] Boston King and Harry Washington left on July 31 aboard *L'Abondance* bound for Birchtown, a new settlement for freed Blacks in Nova Scotia. "Every family had a lot of land," King wrote, "and we exerted all our strength in order to build comfortable huts before the cold weather set in."[25]

As Brutus's essay suggested, patriots had difficulty believing (or at least admitting) that these newly freed Blacks left of their own accord—yet they did.[26] After the peace became official and before the British departed, southern slaveholders and their agents swarmed into New York trying to persuade their former enslaved workers to return south, but most who obtained certificates of freedom from the British opted to evacuate. King wrote of their "joy and gratitude" in leaving.[27] Countless others slipped through the porous boundaries of occupied New York to melt into the countryside or towns of northeastern states where slavery was in retreat. A committee composed of British and American representatives charged with overseeing the evacuation of Blacks from New York collapsed as quickly as the one had in Charleston, again because the American members felt powerless in the process. "Finding that merely the superintendance of Embarkations, (and that only when called upon by the British) without the power of restraining the Property of the Inhabitants of the United States from being carried away, could be of little utility—having been also informed that the *departure* of all Negroes (who choose to go away) indiscriminately and without examination, in private Vessels, is, if not publickly allowed, at least connived at," Washington complained to Congress, "I cannot think there will be much advantage in continuing our Commissioners any longer at New York."[28] In a later letter, he called the entire committee process "little more than a farce."[29]

Rushed at the end, the British evacuation of New York concluded in late November when the last Royal Navy ships cast off, awaiting fair winds to set sail. While embarking all of the British and Hessian troops wishing to go, the arbitrary deadline set by the British for their departure left behind some loyalists and divided families. Judith Jackson, for example, who had defected to the British in response to Dunmore's proclamation and worked with the Royal Artillery Department, waited for the last transport to Birchtown in hopes of recovering her daughter from their former owner. Carleton ruled in Jackson's favor but time ran out for her daughter.[30] Also on one of the last ships to leave New York, Daniel Payne, who fled Mount Vernon when the British invaded Virginia in 1780, could watch from the *Concord* in New York Harbor as fireworks lit up the night's sky welcoming George Washington, his former owner, back to New York following seven years of British occupation. Payne was one of three Blacks listed on the evacuation records as formerly owned by Washington.[31] For all of its limitations, one historian has called the

British evacuation of the United States culminating in their departure from New York "the most significant act of emancipation in early American history."[32]

While the British departure from New York may have seemed too rapid for Jackson and some loyalists, it felt too slow to Washington and his troops. Following the peace agreement with Britain, they waited for months north of New York for the British to leave the city before entering it. During that period, strapped for funds, Congress sent most of the soldiers home so that only a skeleton force remained by November. Still, when Washington finally entered the war-ravaged city leading a parade of officers and officials down Broadway to the Battery on November 25, it was all about the dawn of liberty and the demise of political slavery. A formal address to Washington from patriots returned to the city from voluntary exile declared, "In this place, and at this moment of exultation and triumph, while the engines of slavery still linger in our sight, we look to you, our deliverer, with unusual transports of gratitude and joy."[33] By "engines of slavery," these returning patriots meant the British warships remaining in the harbor, not the shackles of actual slavery present in the city.

To Payne and other Blacks watching the liberation of New York from ships in the harbor, it may not have seemed like the beginning of liberty for either themselves or America. Most of the more than 15,000 Blacks leaving the United States after the American Revolution went as the property of white loyalists to Florida or the British Caribbean, where they typically faced a slavery even harsher than before. When Britain turned over Florida to Spain in 1783, loyalists resettled there faced a second remove to the Bahamas or the Caribbean. Meanwhile, most of those like Payne and Harry Washington, who departed as freed Blacks under the proclamations of Dunmore or Clinton, went first to the wastelands of Nova Scotia, where harsh weather, poor soil, and hostile treatment all but broke them. Rather than small farmers, many became the servants of local whites.

Moved by reports of appalling conditions for freed Blacks in Nova Scotia and familiar with the grinding poverty of many who made it to

London, British abolitionists led by Granville Sharp, the acknowledged
mastermind of the *Somerset* lawsuit, began a well-meaning but ill-planned
effort to resettle freed Blacks from Canada and Britain in Africa. In
1786, they chose a spot on the Sierra Leone River near Oswald's Bunce
Island slave station, which ultimately made the settlement a target for
slave traders. Looking for any chance to improve their lot, thousands of
Blacks signed up for resettlement, beginning with 377 on the first transports from London in 1787. Harry Washington and Boston King joined
their number from Nova Scotia five years later. Until pushed out in a dispute over white oversight of the new settlement, the noted Black writer
and former enslaved sailor Olaudah Equiano served as the public face
for the movement in London. Sharp lost control of the enterprise in 1791,
after Parliament issued a new charter empowering an all-white board in
London to run the colony.[34]

In 1796, when the British directors imposed an annual tax on what
settlers viewed as their land, Harry Washington joined hundreds of the
settlers in attempting to set up their own Black colonial government in
Sierra Leone. "Who could say that now they were not slaves?" the colony's embattled white governor reported one Black settler as asking about
the tax in a rhetorical question reminiscent of patriot protests against
taxation without representation in America.[35]

With military reinforcements and a new colonial charter from London, Sierra Leone's white governor suppressed the Black revolt in 1800,
concluding with the execution of two settlers and banishment of thirty
more, including Washington. Having embraced the back-to-Africa movement as a partial solution to their own race issues, white Virginians at
the College of William and Mary (where faculty members and students
alike held enslaved servants) duly awarded Sharp an honorary degree in
1791, before learning of his removal as the effort's leader.[36] Meanwhile,
with his banishment into the African interior, all record of Harry Washington (then sixty) ended, though some sources have him becoming a
leader of the exiled group even as it too faded from the historical record.[37]
Sierra Leone endured as a white-ruled British colony.

After a week celebrating the departure of British troops from New York in November 1783, George Washington began a circuitous two-week journey through New Jersey, Pennsylvania, Delaware, and Maryland to appear before Congress, then meeting in Annapolis, and resign his commission as commander in chief before returning to his slave plantation. Celebrating his triumphs and hailing his retirement, tributes awaited Washington at every stop on his way. Liberty became the common thread. "When we Consider that leaving us in the full possession of liberty and Independence, Your Excellency is returning to your Native State," the citizens of one New Jersey town addressed the general, "We congratulate you."[38] By your example, the Pennsylvania Assembly added when he reached its state, "You have shown us how to preserve, by wisdom and justice, that liberty and honour, which, as our natural inheritance, we maintained by arms."[39] When its turn came, the Wilmington, Delaware, town council hailed Washington's "glorious Endeavours" as "crowned with the noble award of Liberty."[40] At the retiring general's final stop, the slave state of Maryland formally proclaimed that Washington had "saved a dear country and millions of fellow citizens, and millions yet unborn, from slavery."[41] One of Virginia's largest slaveholders had become the face of liberty for America.[42]

"Having defended the standard of liberty in this new world," the president of Congress declared upon receiving Washington's resignation at a packed ceremony on December 23, 1783, "you *retire from the great theatre of action* with the blessings of your fellow citizens."[43] The formalities over, Washington rode away on a fast-riding horse to reach Mount Vernon in time for Christmas.

Although he faced the daunting task of restoring his plantation to profitability after eight years away, Washington was then only fifty-one years old and did not view American liberty as secure. Shortly before his retirement, in his last official communication to the states as commander in chief, he sent a "circular letter" to all the governors in June 1783 and asked them to distribute it widely. It urged the states to reform the central government into "an indissoluble Union of the States under one federal head." Under the Articles of Confederation, Washington wrote, that government tended toward "Anarchy and confusion"—"Liberty abused to Licentiousness," he termed it—due to a lack of central authority. Withholding from Congress any power to act directly on states or individuals, the Articles had created little more than a league of friendship among thirteen sovereign states. "There should be lodged somewhere, a supreme power to regulate and govern the general concerns of the confederated Republic, without which the Union cannot be of long duration," he declared.[44] For Washington, these core matters of general concern included regulating international and interstate commerce, taxing and spending for the common defense, repaying the nation's war debts, and opening the western frontier for settlement. Just as certainly, they would not include internal domestic matters such as slavery.

This letter thrust Washington into the forefront of the budding movement to forge a new government for the United States by replacing the Articles of Confederation with a national constitution. Newspapers throughout the states published his letter; people discussed it; speakers read it aloud at public events. More than his wartime leadership, Washington wrote, this call for constitutional reform "may be considered as [my] Legacy" to the American people. Once again, as in his support for armed revolution, now in his call for constitutional reform, Washington stressed, "Liberty is the basis." Measures that "have a tendency to dissolve the Union, or contribute to violate or lessen [central] Sovereign Authority, ought to be considered as hostile [to] the Liberty and Independancy of America," he wrote, "and the Authors of them treated accordingly."[45]

The rhetoric of liberty served many purposes during the Revolutionary era, with patriots and loyalists, nationalists and partisans of state sovereignty using it to advance their ends. At various stops on his journey from New York to Annapolis, Washington employed it in reiterating his call for preserving liberty through a national government.[46] From then until the nation adopted a new constitution a half-decade later, Washington maintained a steady drumbeat in his private letters to state leaders and members of Congress. Liberty required a new charter, he argued; lax national sovereignty would lead back to political slavery.

With no effective general government, the various states separately addressed the issues of liberty and slavery inside their borders as independent republics within a confederation of sovereign states. This encouraged the state experimentation and regional differentiation that began tearing at the fabric of the unity that Washington desired, with nothing separating northern and southern states more than their respective stances on slavery. "The States were divided into different interests not by their difference of size," James Madison would declare at the Constitutional Convention in 1787, "but principally from the effects of their having or not having slaves."[47] This was not true prior to the Revolution, when every state allowed slavery, or even during the Revolution, when only Pennsylvania and the putative state of Vermont moved toward abolishing it. With peace, other northern states—little dependent on slavery economically—proceeded in that direction even as southern states steadily expanded their reliance on enslaved labor, creating the fundamental divide that Madison detected by 1787.

In the post-Revolutionary North, Massachusetts began the process of abolition through a popular consensus that scarcely required legal action and never involved legislation. During the Revolution, John Adams and other patriot leaders had resisted the tide toward abolition in Massachusetts for fear of disrupting the wartime union with slaveholding states.[48] Peace broke that dam.

Going back at least as far as James Otis's powerful 1764 pamphlet, *The Rights of the British Colonies Asserted and Proved*, the Revolutionary movement in Massachusetts had linked the rights of whites and Blacks. "Colonists are by the law of nature freeborn, as indeed all men are, white or black," Otis wrote and others believed.[49] Whether free or enslaved, Massachusetts Blacks embraced this creed. Unlike in most other colonies, they had always had the right in Massachusetts to petition the government and use the same courts as whites.

During the 1770s, Blacks in the state increasingly used their rights to petition the legislature to abolish slavery and to seek their own emancipation through freedom suits in court. While these suits typically employed some pretext for liberty, such as the plaintiff claiming to have had a free mother or been promised his liberty by a prior owner, during the Revolutionary era courts virtually always granted the request. Indeed, John Adams later observed, "I never knew a Jury by a Verdict to determine a Negro to be a Slave."[50] That would never have happened in Virginia, but in Massachusetts, it became the norm—and slaveholders knew it. Whether because of religious beliefs or revolutionary principles, slavery had lost its purchase in Massachusetts. Of course, even at its height during colonial times, slavery contributed little to the Massachusetts economy, whereas it supplied the engine of production in Virginia.

While long practiced there, slavery always had a slippery legal footing in Massachusetts. Under English law, which controlled the colonies prior to 1776, and confirmed in the *Somerset* decision, it took a local enabling statute to maintain slavery. Whereas elaborate codes established the institution in most colonies, in Massachusetts it rested on the slender reed of the 1641 Body of Liberties. It provided that "There shall never be any bond slaverie, villinage or Captivitie amongst us unless it be lawfull Captives taken in just warres, and such strangers as willingly selle themselves or are sold to us. . . . And these shall have all the liberties and Christian usages which the law of God established in Israell concerning such persons doeth morally require."[51] Captives taken in just wars, the legalistic leaders of Massachusetts reasoned, covered Native Americans captured in combat. Enslaving Africans relied on an expansive reading of the "sold to us" language, those leaders knew, because Blacks surely had neither sold themselves nor been taken in a just war.

The opening phrase of the 1780 state constitution, "All men are born free," undermined whatever legal authority the Body of Liberties (which itself was meant to extend rather than limit rights) gave for slavery in Massachusetts.[52] Lawyers, judges, lawmakers, and citizens seemed to assume this at the time, and this meaning of the constitution became settled law by 1783.[53] Only in retrospect did a few then-obscure legal cases appear important to the process of abolishing slavery in America's second most-populous state.

The case of an enslaved Black woman known as Mum Bett offers a prime example. By 1781, the wife of John Ashley, Bett's owner, had hit Bett one too many times—the last time leaving a lasting scar from a scalding-hot fire shovel. Bett vowed to win her freedom and sought help from Theodore Sedgwick, a young lawyer in her western Massachusetts town of Sheffield. "I heard that paper read yesterday, that says, 'all men are born equal,'" she reportedly told Sedgwick, "won't the law give me my freedom?"[54] A conservative patriot then serving in the state legislature, Sedgwick agreed to take her case. Failing to find any of the standard grounds for a successful freedom suit, such as a purported promise of manumission, Sedgwick argued Bett's case for freedom solely based on the state constitutional guarantee of individual rights. It worked. A local trial-court jury (whose members likely knew all the parties involved) found for Bett. Recognizing the futility of fighting to overturn the jury verdict, Ashley dropped his appeal and accepted the court's judgment. Bett changed her name to Elizabeth Freeman and took a job working as a paid household servant for Sedgwick.

The 1781 ruling in *Bett v. Ashley* attracted little notice at the time. It might have been groundbreaking elsewhere, but it was unremarkable in Massachusetts, where public opinion ratified by the constitution of 1780 had effectively ended slavery even if no law formally declared it. People remember the case today because Sedgwick later became Speaker of the U.S. House of Representatives and a national Federalist leader. Long after his death, during the run-up to the Civil War, his daughter resurrected this early case to burnish his memory as an abolitionist, even though in reality he was just a lawyer who on various occasions represented different sides in freedom suits.[55]

Another series of cases from 1783, nearly as obscure as *Bett v. Ashley* at the time, was even more lionized later for having ended slavery in Massachusetts. Unlike in the *Bett* case, a former owner had promised to free an enslaved man, Quock Walker, when he reached age twenty-five. That owner died, however, and Walker passed to the owner's son-in-law, Nathaniel Jennison, who refused to honor the promise. Walker left anyway, and took a job with his former owner's son, John Caldwell. After Jennison pursued, beat, and kidnapped him, Walker sued Jennison for his injuries and capture; Jennison sued Caldwell for lost profit from Walker's services; and the state indicted Jennison for criminal assault. Everything turned on whether Walker remained enslaved to Jennison because, under Massachusetts law, a slaveholder cannot be liable for injuring his own property.

Unremarkably, the jury found for Walker based on his prior owner's promise. To this point, Walker's case represented a standard freedom suit, and Jennison did not press his appeal. The criminal case against Jennison proceeded to the Supreme Judicial Court of Massachusetts in 1783, however, where Chief Justice William Cushing, a former slaveholder, instructed the jury regarding Walker's status in Massachusetts, "The idea of slavery is inconsistent with our own conduct and Constitution." Under that state constitution, he observed, slavery is "as effectively abolished as it can be."[56]

As monumental as Cushing's words sound, he said them in court to a jury. No one reported them at the time, and even Cushing's brother, the clerk of courts, later commented that the slavery question had never come before the state's supreme court. Perhaps some judges and lawyers heard of the ruling and relied on it, but no reported court decision cited it until after the Civil War. By then, a legal scholar had uncovered the Walker litigation and, in an 1866 book, selectively quoted a statement depicting it as "a mortal wound to slavery in Massachusetts." Previously, he noted, "the received wisdom in Massachusetts" held that the 1780 state constitution, "by its own force and efficacy," ended slavery.[57]

The constitution might not have achieved this end alone, but in conjunction with popular sentiment, it sufficed. Reflecting on this development near the time, Massachusetts abolitionist Jeremy Belknap concluded in 1795, "Slavery hath been abolished here by *publick opinion*." After then noting the role played by religion and revolution in turning the people against slavery, and by the constitution in confirming it, Belknap added a critical ingredient. "Many of the blacks, taking advantage of this *publick opinion* and of this general assertion in the bill of rights, asked their freedom, and obtained it. Others took it without leave."[58] *They* ended slavery in Massachusetts. In 1790, the first federal census found nearly 700,000 enslaved persons in the United States. It reported "none" in Massachusetts, the only fully free state.[59]

With domestic slavery abolished in Massachusetts, one further case from 1783 dealt with *Somerset*-like claims of nonresident slaveholders there. At the time, Massachusetts stood as one in a confederation of thirteen states, with each pledged by the Articles of Confederation to respect the rights of the "free citizens" of the other twelve. In particular, the Articles provided, no state may "prevent the removal of property imported into any State, to any other State, of which the owner is an inhabitant."[60] Four years earlier, thirty-five enslaved Blacks taken by British privateers from patriot-owned plantations in South Carolina had, through the vicissitudes of war, ended up in Boston. Their owners quickly retrieved all but about ten.

The remaining ten, from rich rice plantations on the marshy west side of South Carolina's coastal Waccamaw Neck, likely spoke Gullah, a creole tongue, and only had first names—or at least early reports listed only their first names: Quosh, Affa, Kate, George, and the like. Urban Boston would have been as foreign to them as the American South had been to their African ancestors. Perhaps because they viewed patriot-held Boston as more secure from raiders than coastal Carolina, the owners of these ten, brothers Anthony and Percival Pawley, waited until after the war's end in 1783 to try to recover them. By then, the ten had blended into Boston's free Black community and did not wish to return to slavery in Waccamaw Neck.[61]

After an agent sent by the Pawley brothers had the ten (or at least the nine he could find) detained in a local jail, someone—perhaps the individuals themselves or perhaps others in the community—filed the necessary habeas corpus actions for their release. The cases went directly to the Supreme Judicial Court, which promptly ordered their release without addressing the issue of their status as enslaved or free. Since they had committed no crime, the court ruled, the state could not hold them.

Incensed by this supposed breach of their property rights, the Pauley brothers complained to their governor, who dispatched an angry letter to Massachusetts governor John Hancock, who passed it on to Chief Justice Cushing for a reply. "If a Man has a right to the Service of another, who deserts his service, undoubtedly he has a right to take him up & carry him home to Service again," Cushing explained, but he has no right to the state's help.[62] Although far from a *Somerset*-like repudiation of nonresident slavery in Massachusetts, when agents of the Pauley brothers failed to capture any of the ten without local assistance, it sufficed to leave all of them living as free Blacks in or around Boston.

Massachusetts had satisfied the bare requirement of the Articles of Confederation by not *preventing* the Pauley brothers from removing their property from the state, but it outraged them by not helping effect that removal. A series of heated protests followed, including an idle threat by South Carolina to take the matter up with the Confederation Congress, but nothing happened. In official statements, South Carolina denounced the act as a religiously motivated violation of its state sovereignty—charges that Cushing dismissed as incomprehensible.[63] Congress lacked any enforcement mechanisms whatsoever and could not have done anything anyway. Southern slaveholders would need an effective federal fugitive-slave law to get runaways back from free states like Massachusetts, but that would require a stronger central government than provided by the Articles of Confederation. Whatever legal rights the Pawley brothers retained in their human property residing in Massachusetts meant little. The 1790 census found several of them living openly as free persons in Boston, with George having taken Pauley as his surname and Affa married to Prince Hall.[64]

The immediate abolition of slavery in Massachusetts and its gradual abolition by statute in Pennsylvania—the second and third most populous states in the United States—posed problems for slaveholders in other states. Before the Revolution, every British colony in America authorized slavery by local law. This left no safe place for fugitives or runaways from slavery. They might hide on the frontier or go to sea as sailors, but they could not live openly anywhere in America without fear of capture and reenslavement. By 1783, however, they could seek refuge in two large states with significant free Black populations, and live openly there like Boston's Affa Hall and George Pauley. In 1784, Connecticut and Rhode Island joined Pennsylvania in passing laws providing for the gradual abolition of slavery for future generations. Although never given teeth by court decisions, the broad language in the 1783 New Hampshire constitution declaring, "all men are born equal," suggested to many that the state had followed Massachusetts in ending slavery. The 1800 census reported only eight enslaved persons in New Hampshire, and the 1810 census listed none. While not a state until 1791, Vermont had banned slavery by its 1777 constitution.

Five states thus stood as free or on the way toward gradual freedom by 1784, with two more—New York and New Jersey—soon to follow, which would make a majority of the original thirteen. Immediately south of them, Virginia, Maryland, and Delaware continued their wartime limits on the Atlantic slave trade, and passed laws allowing owners to free persons from bondage without getting permission from the state legislature.[65] Only the lower South stood foursquare for maintaining and expanding slavery.

Drafted in 1777 when every state allowed slavery but not ratified until 1781, when some no longer did, the Articles of Confederation offered little guidance for resolving divisions created by a government half slave and half free. South Carolina officials naturally considered taking the interstate dispute over the Waccamaw Blacks to the Confederation Congress, but concluded not to bother.[66] Congress could not have resolved the matter over the objections of either South Carolina or Massachusetts, and likely would have declined to intervene.

Although slavery existed across the republic, the Articles of Confederation did not use that word or refer explicitly to the enslaved people living within the union it created. Expressly entered into by the states "for their common defense, the security of their liberties, and their mutual and general welfare," the Articles created "a firm league of friendship" among otherwise independent entities.[67] "Each state retains its sovereignty," the compact declared, "and every power, jurisdiction, and right, which is not by this Confederation expressly delegated to the United States."[68] Those express powers related mostly to military and foreign affairs and did not cover slavery. The Articles did not even give Congress the power to impose taxes; instead the Articles vaguely stated, "Expenses that shall be incurred for the common defense or general welfare . . . shall be defrayed out of a common treasury, which shall be supplied by the several States in proportion to the value of all land within each State."[69] Congress could ask the states for funds, which it regularly did, but had no power to force them to supply the requested amounts, which they often paid late and only in part.

As originally drafted by John Dickinson in 1776 at the request of the Second Continental Congress, the Articles would have given more authority to Congress by reserving to the states only those powers "that shall not interfere with the Articles of this Confederation."[70] Some delegates worried that such language gave Congress too much power over property rights. Expressing his fear of the "leveling Principles" of northerners in Congress and the "fluctuation of Property" that might result if they held the power to make laws "bend to what they call the good of the whole," South Carolina delegate Edward Rutledge "resolved to vest the Congress with no more Power than what is absolutely necessary."[71] After Rutledge left Congress in November 1776, North Carolina delegate Thomas Burke took credit for pushing through the amendment holding "that all sovereign Power was in the States separately." Under the prior draft, he wrote, a future Congress could "make their own power as unlimited as they please."[72] Protecting slavery in their states, these southern slaveholders suggested, served as one reason to limit the power of Congress. The South Carolina legislature did its part in 1783 by reenacting its harsh colonial slave code to ensure that independence had not somehow voided it by ending royal rule.[73]

Further, rather than using land value as the basis for allocating the funds due from each state, Dickinson's original draft Article XI would have used "the Number of Inhabitants of every Age, Sex and Quality, except Indians not paying Taxes," as a proxy for wealth in imposing requisitions.[74] In July 1776, however, when the belligerent Maryland slaveholder Samuel Chase instead proposed having the Articles use only the number of "white inhabitants" for fixing such payments rather than the whole number of people, enslaved or free, Congress erupted into its first-ever sectional dispute over slavery.[75]

"Negros are property," Chase said about enslaved Blacks. "There is no more reason therefore for taxing the Southern states on the farmer's head, and on his slave's head, than the Northern ones on their farmers' heads and the heads of their cattle."[76] Chase, never one to mince his words, here frankly equated enslaved Blacks with livestock.

"The numbers of people were taken by this article as an index of the wealth of the state and not as subjects of taxation," John Adams of Massachusetts shot back. "It was of no consequence by what name you called your people whether by that of freemen or of slaves. that in some countries the labouring poor were called freemen, in others they were called slaves: but that the difference as to the state was imaginary only."[77] Adams presented enslaved workers here as simply the laboring poor by another name—a form of serf, perhaps. Little wonder that he had so readily overlooked slavery in pursuit of wartime unity. New England had its laboring poor too, and since Adams never saw the American Revolution as overturning its economic hierarchy, he would leave the South's alone as well.

James Wilson of Pennsylvania, an opponent of slavery who never-theless owned an enslaved household worker, broadened the north-ern assault on Chase's motion and turned it squarely against slavery. Given the high cost of war, he declared, exempting enslaved workers in computing the requisitions exacted to pay for it "will be the great-est encouragement to continue slavekeeping, and to increase it, that can be." Wilson then leveled various arguments against slaveholding. As a practical matter, presumably by creating a source of internal resistance, he declared, enslaved workers "increase the burthen of defence, which [under Chase's amendment] would of course fall so much the heavier on the Northern [states]." As a moral issue, Wilson invoked the widely con-demned Atlantic slave trade to declare it "our duty to lay every discour-agement on the importation of slaves." America does not need enslaved workers, he told his southern colleagues. "Dismiss your slaves and free-men will take their place," he claimed. Holding them "is attended with many inconveniences."[78]

Wilson's claim brought an intemperate retort from South Carolina planter Thomas Lynch. "Freemen cannot be got to work in our Col-onies; it is not in the ability or inclination of freemen to do the work that the negroes do," he declared in making the affirmative economic case of slavery for southerners. "If it is debated, whether their slaves are their property, there is an end of the confederation." His state would not remain in a federal union that endangered slavery, Lynch warned his colleagues—the first of many such threats from southerners over the coming years. "Our slaves being our property, why should they be taxed more than . . . sheep?" he asked.[79]

"There . . . is some difference between them and sheep," Benjamin Franklin answered in support of Wilson's point. "Sheep will never make any insurrections."[80] If this insight did not defuse the tension in the room, then no compromise could bridge the sectional divide over slavery.

Cooler minds prevailed when two compromises surfaced on the issue of state requisitions, one prophetic but deeply problematic and one seem-ingly attractive but ultimately unworkable. "Slaves did not do so much work as freemen," Virginia delegate Benjamin Harrison, the owner of some one hundred enslaved Blacks, conceded. Perhaps "two effected more than one," but he "doubted" even that. As a "compromise" then, Harrison proposed, "two slaves should be counted as one freeman" for the purposes of taxing the states.[81] He never suggested that enslaved Blacks had half of the moral worth of free whites, or any moral worth at all. Harrison spoke only to their relative contribution to the wealth of a state and therefore its due share of war costs. With this remark, he opened the door to the future compromises over the fractional count- ing of the enslaved. In the meantime, New Jersey's John Witherspoon, the scholarly president of Princeton College, suggested that Congress use land value rather than population to allocate each state's payments. "This is the true barometer of wealth," he noted.[82]

Congress chose land values as the basis for allocating requisitions under the Articles of Confederation, with the states ratifying this approach in 1781. But assessing relative land values across the states proved unwork- able.[83] By 1783, Congress began fishing for a more readily ascertainable method of allocating requisitions based on wealth under the Articles. A committee composed of delegates from northern and southern states returned to Harrison's proposal of using population, with enslaved Blacks counting as one-half of "white Inhabitants." Southern delegates generally supported this approach. Northern delegates countered with a "two-thirds" ratio more favorable to their economic interest.[84]

In March 1783, Virginia delegate James Madison then offered the infamous three-fifths compromise as "a proof of the sincerity of his pro- fessions of liberality." South Carolina's Rutledge seconded Madison's motion. Pennsylvania's Wilson agreed to "sacrifice his opinion to this compromise."[85] With only Rhode Island dissenting, Congress accepted it as a proposed amendment to the Articles but, when sent to the states for ratification, the compromise failed to get sufficient support to become law.[86]

Although not implemented at this time, this so-called federal ratio remained in the minds of Madison and other members of Congress for future applications. They did not see it as a measure of the relative human worth of enslaved Blacks and free whites, only of their relative economic value to the state for purposes of payments due Congress.[87] Under the Articles, the ratio never came up as a means for allocating representation among the states because each had one vote regardless of population.[88] It would carry different meaning as a method of calculating representation under the Constitution.

On one issue of race in the Articles of Confederation, all the states agreed. No matter how much greater the military burden on northern states *versus* southern ones—and it was considerable—none of them voted to encourage arming Blacks for war. From Dickinson's first draft of the Articles penned at the Revolution's outset through the final text approved in the midst of battle, Congress set the quota of soldiers from each state "in proportion to the number of *white* inhabitants in such State."[89] This nearly doubled the quotas for northern over southern states. No state complained, not even Massachusetts, which in absolute terms under the Articles bore the brunt of battle more than other states. Race mattered in bearing arms.

Given the Confederation Congress's lack of jurisdiction over matters involving slavery, the issue rarely arose during the mid-1780s under the Articles. In one telling case from 1786, however, when Congress sought added authority over foreign commerce, Georgia insisted that this power "not extend to prohibit the importation of negroes."[90] In their wartime boycotts of trade with Britain, both the first and the second continental congresses urged the colonies or states to stop importing enslaved Africans. At least for a time, all did. With the war over, the Revolutionary consensus against the Atlantic slave trade collapsed. In its effort to recover from its wartime losses of enslaved workers and expand their numbers further, Georgia asserted its "liberty" to import more enslaved Blacks from Africa and the Caribbean. South Carolina followed suit and North Carolina eventually did as well. Slavery's hold on the lower South never wavered during the Revolutionary era. In the first two calendar years after the liberation of Savannah and Charleston in 1782, slave ships carried over 10,000 Africans into bondage in Georgia and South Carolina.[91] By 1790, the enslaved population in the American South had increased by nearly half from before the Revolution.

While the Articles of Confederation effectively precluded Congress from tampering with slavery in the states, it left open congressional jurisdiction over slavery in the western territories. The United States did not have any western territories when Congress drafted and twelve states ratified the Articles. Under their colonial charters, some of the seaboard states claimed vast swaths of the trans-Appalachian West, with Virginia claiming the most. Others, like Maryland, claimed none. With each state sovereign under the Articles, as the frontier opened for settlement the states with western lands would increasingly dwarf those without any. All thirteen states needed to ratify the Articles for them to take effect, and Maryland held out until other states ceded to Congress their claims to lands northwest of the Ohio River. Virginia did so preliminarily in 1781 and conclusively in 1784. Congress would not retain these lands indefinitely, however. Under the cession agreement, Congress would divide this vast territory into units roughly the size of other states and, as their population warranted, admit them as states on an equal footing with the original ones rather than as colonies of an imperial realm.[92]

When the 1783 peace treaty with Britain set the western boundary of the United States at the Mississippi River, vast frontier lands largely unsettled by whites came under the domain of Congress. Virginia delegate Thomas Jefferson, who owned hundreds of enslaved Blacks but believed slavery harmed both slaveholders and the enslaved, promptly proposed that Congress discourage the further expansion of slavery into western lands by banning it there after 1800.[93] He envisioned the West as a reserve for the sort of white yeoman farmers that he saw as essential to sustain a free republic.

Congress named Jefferson to chair the congressional committee charged with drafting legislation for the orderly admission of new, coequal states from western lands ceded to Congress. He inserted his proposal for barring slavery in that region after 1800 into what became the Ordinance of 1784.[94] Although this provision survived in committee, Congress struck it out on a strictly sectional vote, with every northern state present voting yes but not any southern ones.[95] At the time, passage of any provision required a majority of all thirteen states, not just a majority of those present, and each state cast its vote in accord with the majority will of its delegates. States could have between two and seven delegates, and for that vote, Virginia had three delegates present. Although voting yes, Jefferson could not even carry his home state because both of the other Virginia members voted no. Only one other southern delegate, Hugh Williamson of North Carolina, voted for the antislavery provision, but his lone vote could not carry his state. In the end, every northern delegate present voted yes and all but two southern delegates voted no, leaving the provision to fall one vote short of the seven needed for passage.[96] As amended, the measure then passed without it.[97]

As drafted and enacted, the Ordinance of 1784 applied to all territories "ceded or *to be ceded* by individual states to the United States."[98] At the time of its passage, this ceded region included only the trans-Appalachian West north of the Ohio River. Delegates expected future cessions of lands south of the Ohio River from Virginia, the Carolinas, and Georgia, and the measure would then apply to them as well. Although few white settlers lived in western lands north of the Ohio River in 1784, and most of those were holdovers from the era of French rule, many southern whites had moved into the Kentucky and Tennessee regions of Virginia and North Carolina, some taking enslaved Blacks with them. Jefferson's antislavery provision (which would have operated as a form of gradual abolition to take effect sixteen years later while discouraging the expansion of slavery in the meantime) could have applied to them.[99] The uniform votes of southern states to strip Jefferson's antislavery provision from the Ordinance of 1784 showed not only that their delegates did not view slavery as dying out in Revolutionary America but also that they wanted it to expand westward and take root in future states.

The issue arose again the following year, when Congress passed the Land Ordinance of 1785 to establish mechanisms for surveying and selling its ceded lands. Deeply in debt from wartime expenditures, Congress desperately needed revenue from these sales, and the most promising purchasers for land north of the Ohio River came from New England and the Northeast. The former quartermaster general of the Continental Army, Thomas Pickering of Massachusetts, represented many of these potential buyers and lobbied Congress to ban slavery there to facilitate its settlement by small farmers rather than large plantation owners. "It will be infinitely easier to prevent the evil [of slavery] at first than to eradicate it or check it at any future time," Pickering wrote to Massachusetts delegate Rufus King in March 1785. "For God's sake, then, let one more effort be made to prevent so terrible a calamity."[100] King tried but failed to add an antislavery provision to the Ordinance of 1785, which again would have applied to all states carved from territory "ceded or to be ceded" to Congress, even though this time the proposal added a clause allowing for the recapture of fugitives from slavery "in any one of the 13 origl states."[101] The states from Virginia southward uniformly opposed King's proposal.[102]

This issue reached the Confederation Congress again two years later in the Northwest Ordinance of 1787, which dealt solely with lands north of the Ohio River. This statute, widely considered one of the premier achievements of the Confederation Congress, formally created the Northwest Territory from the lands already ceded to Congress and provided for its subsequent division into states. As proposed by committee in September 1786 and later submitted to Congress in May 1787, the measure said nothing about slavery and thus left the matter to the new territory or, in keeping with the prevailing practice, later states for resolution.[103] During the bill's second reading on July 12, 1787, its lead author, Nathan Dane of Massachusetts, offered an added article six. "There shall be neither Slavery nor involuntary Servitude in the said territory otherwise than in the punishment of crime," the article stated, "provided always that any person escaping into the same, from whom labor or service is lawfully claimed in any one of the original States, such fugitive may be lawfully reclaimed."[104]

"When I drew the ordinance which passed (a few words excepted) as I originally formed it I had no idea the States would agree to the sixth Art. prohibiting slavery," an astonished Dane wrote to Rufus King on July 16. "But finding the House favourably disposed on this subject, after we had completed the other parts, I moved the art[icle]—which was agreed to without opposition."[105] All eight states present, five of them from the South, approved it.

After the failure of more modest antislavery articles for the ordinances of 1784 and 1785, no one has ever conclusively determined why southern delegates accepted this one without dissent. Of course, it only applied to lands north of the Ohio River, and some read it as tacitly authorizing slavery south of that divide.[106] Less than a month after the measure passed, Virginia delegate William Grayson wrote to his congressional colleague James Monroe, who missed the vote, "The clause respecting slavery was agreed to by the Southern members for the purpose of preventing [the plantation crops of] Tobacco & Indigo from being made on the N.W. side of the Ohio, and as well as for sevl. other political reasons."[107] He added that its passage promptly led to the sale of over five million acres of the land to the New England consortium then led by Manasseh Cutler.

Cutler, like Pickering before him, had lobbied to exclude slavery in the region. Congress certainly needed the money that Cutler brought to the table, and securing favorable terms for the sale could have spurred delegates to add the antislavery provision.[108] Still, it seems improbable that revenue alone would have won over every southern delegate when only some would have sufficed to carry the provision. Other commentators have suggested that the "other political purposes" referred to by Grayson included securing the complex compromises over slavery then under negotiation at the Constitutional Convention.[109] Assessing that factor involves unpacking those compromises, which the next chapter addresses.

Whatever the cause, enactment of the 1787 ordinance set the five states later carved from the Northwest Territory on a free-labor course that, over time, tipped the nation toward ending slavery. One of those states, Illinois, became the home of Abraham Lincoln; another, Ohio, produced the abolitionist senator and governor Salmon P. Chase. Chase, whom Lincoln made his secretary of the treasury, later called the ordinance's sixth article, "the last gift of the congress of the old confederation to the country."[110] In his classic 1911 history of American slavery, Ulrich Phillips depicted the article's enactment as "the first and last antislavery achievement by the central government" during the Revolutionary era.[111] It set a precedent for Congress, under the Constitution, to restrict slavery in the territories, which led to the Missouri Compromise of 1820, the "fire bell in the night" that put the states on a path toward disunion.[112] By the time the ordinance passed in July 1787, however, the focus of political attention had shifted from the Congress in New York to the Constitutional Convention in Philadelphia. There, with the sectional divide over slavery deepening and each side having a path to expand its social, political, and economic regime westward, the future of American liberty hung in the balance.

CHAPTER EIGHT

The Compromised Convention

1787

During the Revolutionary era, no one fought longer, harder, or with more foresight for an effective union of the American colonies or states than did Benjamin Franklin. His legacy on slavery, however, remained more equivocal. Intuitively seeing collective action as the way to solve political problems, Franklin first outlined his thoughts for unifying the colonies in a 1751 letter to a New York newspaper editor. As he then framed it, a congress with proportional representation from the various colonies should manage "every Thing relating to Indian Affairs and the Defence of the Colonies."[1] Three years later, the military threat to the colonies mounting with French incursions into the Ohio Country, Franklin published a plea for a defensive union in his newspaper, the *Pennsylvania Gazette*. He punctuated this appeal with the first editorial cartoon ever printed in an American newspaper. Of his own design, it showed a rattlesnake cut to pieces with the name of a colony on each severed part. "Join, or Die," the caption read.[2]

Chosen by Pennsylvania as one of its delegates to a congress of the colonies called in 1754 for Albany by the lieutenant governor of New York, Franklin used the occasion to turn his ideas on colonial cooperation into a formal plan for a united government. Under it, each colony would retain authority over its internal affairs. A "General Government," however, with a "President-General" appointed by the king and a Grand Council composed of representatives from the colonies, would assume control over defense of the coast and frontier, settlement of the West, and relations with Native Americans. For these purposes, that central government could raise an army, launch a navy, and levy taxes.[3]

Although this congress endorsed Franklin's Albany Plan of Union, the colonies were not yet willing to give up their sovereignty over military affairs and the frontier. Rejecting Franklin's plan, they struggled on separately until the crisis over British taxation without representation led to some coordination of resistance through joint boycotts of British goods proclaimed by the Stamp Act Congress in 1765 and the First Continental Congress in 1774. Then the Intolerable Acts and military suppression of colonial rights by Britain led the Second Continental Congress to form a unified Continental Army in June 1775 and, with support from Franklin, to appoint George Washington as its commander in chief.[4] The two had worked together during the French and Indian War as leaders of the militias of their respective colonies.[5] Although surprising choices for these roles in 1755, given Washington's youth at twenty-three and Franklin's age and lack of military experience at fifty, both proved quick learners and able commanders. Even though by 1775 Franklin personally opposed slavery, to liberate America with a united force he endorsed the choice of a slaveholder from Virginia to lead an army already composed of a significant number of New England Blacks. Indeed, later in 1775, Franklin served on the three-member congressional delegation that (as noted in Chapter Four) approved Washington's recommendation to purge that army of Black soldiers.[6]

Once Congress approved a joint army in June 1775, Franklin introduced a draft constitution for "*The United Colonies of North America.*" This draft contained concepts that he later supported at the Constitutional Convention, including proportional representation in Congress and centralized power over commerce, war and peace, foreign affairs, western lands, and such domestic matters as thought "necessary to the General Welfare."[7] In a concession to federalism, Franklin added a clause with no parallel in his earlier Albany Plan, "That each Colony shall enjoy and retain as much as it may think fit of its own present Laws, Customs, Rights, Privileges, and peculiar Jurisdictions within its own Limits," which clearly protected state-sanctioned slavery but left open the status of fugitives from slavery. Further, the draft stated that the colonies formed their union for "the Security of their Liberties *and Propertys*," which presumably included their properties in people, though only time would tell how this related to the liberties of Black people.[8] Finally, the draft allocated representation and financial contributions among the colonies based on the number of their male voters, which would not count any enslaved Blacks or many free ones because they could not vote.[9] Without using the word "slavery," the draft accommodated it in the states without rewarding it at the federal level.

Thinking the colonies not yet ready to formalize their union, Franklin did not immediately press Congress to take up his proposal, but he circulated it widely among the delegates. In June 1776, with Franklin serving on one congressional committee writing the Declaration of Independence, another led by John Dickinson took up Franklin's draft and transformed it into the Articles of Confederation that, after much debate and some amendment, passed Congress in November 1777.[10]

While Dickinson's version did not name the security of property as one of its goals, it retained Franklin's slavery-friendly assurance, "Each Colony shall retain and enjoy as much of its present Laws, Rights and Customs, as it may think fit."[11] At the time, Dickinson (unlike Franklin) still held people in bondage, owning about sixty enslaved Blacks at his Delaware plantation. Perhaps with this small state in mind, Dickinson's draft (and the final Articles) gave one vote to each state regardless of size.[12] Until leaving Congress in December 1776 to serve as its minister to France, Franklin took part in the debates over the Articles, arguing for proportional representation in Congress and, as a means to discourage slavery without banning it, counting the enslaved as people for purposes of fixing the per-capita contribution (but not representation) of each state.[13] These matters resurfaced at the Constitutional Convention, where the issue of slavery split the states.

In 1785, at age seventy-nine, Franklin returned in triumph to Philadelphia from Paris. There, virtually singlehandedly, he had secured the financial and military support from France needed to win the Revolutionary War. Working with John Adams, John Jay, and Henry Laurens, he negotiated the treaty with Britain that recognized American independence and, in principle at least, ceded to the new nation all of the territory south of the Great Lakes and north of Florida, west to the Mississippi River. With these monumental achievements, Franklin had become an American hero and a unifying figure in his home state. Once a leader of anti-proprietor, pro-tradesperson partisans in Pennsylvania politics, Franklin now united all sides in that highly factionalized state and was elected without opposition as governor (or "President") for three consecutive one-year terms from 1785 to 1788. This post made him the host governor for the Constitutional Convention when it convened in May 1788 at the State House in Philadelphia.

Like Washington, Franklin played a crucial behind-the-scenes role in staging the convention. Entrepreneurs with interstate business operations—Franklin as a printer and publisher, Washington as a planter and landowner—both men had long favored uniform commercial regulations for the states. In 1785, Washington hosted delegates from Maryland and Virginia at a conference at Mount Vernon called to coordinate commerce between the two states as a step toward opening a canal across them connecting the Potomac and Ohio Rivers. The success of that meeting led Virginia to call another one for Annapolis, Maryland, in October 1786, charged with reducing trade barriers among the states generally. Delegates from five states attended, including James Madison from Virginia and Washington's brilliant former aide, Alexander Hamilton of New York. From Pennsylvania, Franklin sent Tench Coxe, a well-bred merchant of high social standing with such facility for switching sides at opportune moments that critics dubbed him "Mr. Facing Both Ways."

Even before the delegates met, Madison and Hamilton thought that any meeting limited to matters of trade could not solve the complex problems of lax central authority plaguing America under the Articles of Confederation. They wanted the Annapolis convention to lead to another that would forge a truly national government rather than a feeble league of sovereign states.[14] When the Annapolis convention failed to attract delegates from enough states to deal effectively even with trade barriers, Hamilton suggested and the delegates agreed that those present should propose holding a second convention and go home. Their closing resolution urged their states to appoint delegates "to meet at Philadelphia on the second Monday in May next, to . . . devise such further provisions as shall appear to them necessary to render the constitution of the Federal Government adequate to the exigencies of the Union."[15]

In December 1786, Virginia became the first state to endorse this call and name delegates to the convention. By year's end, acting on the recommendation of Franklin as its governor, Pennsylvania became the second big state to appoint delegates. Both states chose committed nationalists who would dominate the proceedings. Indeed, as the only delegates to reach Philadelphia on time, while waiting for enough others to trickle in to make a quorum, they jointly devised the framework for a strong national union, the so-called Virginia Plan, which set the tone for the ensuing deliberations. But the delegates from these two states differed sharply over slavery, which Pennsylvania had voted to abolish and Virginia steadily expanded.[16] Dividing North and South as it had not prior to the Revolution, slavery would become a central point of contention and compromise at the convention.[17]

The slavery issue placed Franklin in a conflicted position. He urgently wanted the convention to succeed in unifying the states under an effective central government. Almost as dearly, he wanted to end slavery and the Atlantic slave trade.

Franklin had come to his views on slavery gradually. As early as 1729, he began publishing the writings of Quaker abolitionists in Pennsylvania—decades before those views became Quaker dogma.[18] Franklin not only published abolitionist views, he listened to them, particularly to those of Benjamin Lay, whose portrait hung in his house, and Anthony Benezet, who became a close friend.[19] "We fetch and steal them out of their own Country," Lay wrote about enslaved Africans in a book published by Franklin, "and in taking of them murther many, very many, and serve them that we take alive ten times worse; steal Husband from Wife, Wife from Husband; steal the Children from their Parents." Their new American masters "work 'em, whip and starve 'em almost to death," Lay added. "Be these Christians, and Ministers too, that encourage and plead for these Things? It must be all a Lie, and that is of the Devil."[20]

Religious pleas alone could not persuade a rationalist like Franklin. The manifold horrors of the Atlantic slave trade had turned him against that enterprise by 1770, when he called it a "Wickedness" in print.[21] Only during his time in France during the American Revolution, however, did the Enlightenment era arguments of such philosophes as Claude-Adrien Helvétius and Marquis de Condorcet fully persuade Franklin that slavery itself—not just the slave trade—should end. "A celebrated Philosophical Writer remarks," Franklin wrote with approval in 1773 about Helvétius, "that when he consider'd the Wars made in Africa for Prisoners to raise Sugar in America, the Numbers slain in those Wars, the Number that being crowded in Ships perish in the Transportation, & the Numbers that die under the Severities of Slavery, he could scarce look on a Morsel of Sugar without conceiving it spotted with Human Blood."[22] Two years after returning in 1785 to a Philadelphia almost cleansed of slavery, Franklin accepted the presidency of the Pennsylvania Abolition Society, the first American association dedicated to ending slavery. No one then could doubt his stance.[23]

After Pennsylvania chose Franklin as one of its delegates to the Constitutional Convention, members of the Abolition Society petitioned him to raise the issue of limiting slavery, or at least of ending American participation in the Atlantic slave trade, at the proceedings. They entrusted Coxe, then the Society's secretary, to deliver the petition to Franklin. A trimmer known for his expediency, Coxe, by his own account of the episode, delivered the paper along with his personal "opinion that it would be a very improper season & place to hazard the Application," apparently because it would disrupt the convention by driving off the southern states.[24] Bring those states under an effective national government first, Coxe may have reasoned, and then have that government work toward ending slavery. Regardless of whether this tactic originated with Coxe, Franklin appeared to follow it. While debates over slavery roiled the convention, Franklin neither initiated nor pressed them as he later would before Congress on the Society's behalf after the Constitution took effect.

On May 13, 1787, one day before the scheduled start of the convention but nearly two weeks before it actually began, Washington arrived in Philadelphia by carriage with three enslaved servants: his mixed-race valet William Lee and two liveried Black postilions, Giles and Paris. As his first formal act, Washington called on Franklin at his home two blocks from the convention site. By all accounts, they stood as the two indispensable authors of American independence and, with Thomas Jefferson and John Adams serving abroad as ambassadors, key partners in framing a new constitution. Although their views on governmental structure differed, with Franklin favoring a strong legislature and Washington a strong executive, both agreed that the United States needed a strong central government to defend liberty. Four weeks earlier, Franklin wrote about the convention to Jefferson, whose views on it were largely shaped by his friend and regular correspondent Madison, "If it does not do Good it must do Harm, as it will show that we have not Wisdom enough among us to govern ourselves."[25] Similarly, in the run-up to the convention, Washington frequently warned that without a new constitution, American liberty would be lost.[26]

For his part, Franklin threw himself into the work of the convention.[27] Despite his gout and gravel (as he termed his nearly incapacitating kidney stones), Franklin would miss only one session of the four-month-long marathon proceedings, sometimes being borne from his home to his place inside the assembly hall on a sedan chair. As word of the convention spread among republican-minded European intellectuals, English polymath Erasmus Darwin wrote to Franklin, "Whilst I am writing to a Philosopher and Friend, I can scarcely forget that I am also writing to the greatest Statesman of the present, or perhaps any century, [w]ho spread the happy contagion of Liberty among his countrymen."[28] In America and Europe, many friends of liberty (as they called themselves) looked on the convention as the next stage for establishing a working model for popular rule. Washington certainly thought so, as did Madison.[29]

The convention formally opened on Friday, May 25, when the necessary majority of delegates from the needed majority of states met to elect Washington as the convention's president. Commencing with just twenty-nine delegates from nine states, the gathering ultimately comprised fifty-five white, male members representing every state except Rhode Island. All men of substance and standing, most delegates came and went over the course of the convention and, by those movements, some states gained or lost representation over time.[30]

South Carolina planter Charles Pinckney, at twenty-nine the fourth-youngest member of the convention and one of its richest, with some two hundred enslaved Blacks at his plantations, then moved to create a committee to draw up rules for the convention. After naming Pinckney, Hamilton, and Virginia's George Wythe to that committee, the convention recessed until the next week.

Tuesday, May 29, proved crucial to all that followed at the convention. Having adopted the rules proposed by Pinckney's committee, including that each state would have one vote and that a majority of the states then represented could decide any question, the convention voted to proceed in secret, with nothing "printed, or otherwise published, or communicated" outside the hall.[31] Washington then called on Virginia governor Edmund Randolph to introduce the Virginia Plan for, as the convention's journal depicted it and the plan itself stated, "The establishment of a *national* government."[32] After Randolph finished his speech and delegates referred his Virginia Plan to a committee of the whole convention, Pinckney offered his own "draught of a federal government," which the delegates also referred to committee.[33] Similar in many respects, these two plans raised a key issue that would occupy the delegates for the next six weeks: both called for some form of proportional, rather than equal state, representation in both houses of Congress. Everything would turn on how the convention handled this issue.

In a letter to Washington one month earlier, Madison had explained the need to change from equal to proportional representation in Congress. Under the Articles of Confederation, he noted, "in which the intervention of the States is in all great cases necessary to effectuate the measures of Congress," equal voting did not matter because the acts of Congress served as little more than recommendations to the states, each of which controlled how those acts were implemented within its borders. Under a system where Congress acted directly on states and people, however, only proportional representation reflecting the "weight and influence" of each state could work. Expressing a rosy optimism that "such a change will not be attended with much difficulty," Madison wrote, "To the Northern States it will be recommended by their present populousness; to the Southern by their expected advantage in this respect" through rapid growth in Georgia, Tennessee, and Kentucky. With sectional interests overriding considerations of size, smaller states would yield to larger ones, he predicted, and proportional representation "will obviate the principal objections of the larger States to the necessary concessions of power."[34]

Madison's letter is telling in two respects. First, it suggested that the principal divide at the convention would pit not large versus small states but northern versus southern ones, with slavery as a pivotal issue.[35]

Second, while Madison wrote that representation should turn on each state's relative weight and influence, he equated these to population, with northern states then having more people than southern ones, but with faster growth on the frontier in the slaveholding Southwest than the still-closed Northwest. Madison failed to anticipate either the obstinacy of small states on the issue of representation or the disagreements of delegates from northern and southern states over how to count people. Taken together, on May 29, the Virginia Plan and Pinckney's draft laid the second matter bare by offering three different ways to represent population proportionally.

Breaking with the Articles, the plans presented by Randolph and Pinckney both provided for proportional representation in the lower branch of Congress. Befitting a proposal advanced by delegates from two different large states—Virginia with the most enslaved people of any state and Pennsylvania with the most free ones—the Virginia Plan straddled the fence on slavery. Using the neutral phrase "quotas of contribution," which those present understood to mean counting all people (enslaved and free) as a rough gauge of state contributions to the union, the proposal read, "Legislature ought to be proportioned to the Quotas of contribution, *or* to the number of free inhabitants, as the one or the other rule may seem best in different cases."[36] In short, the Virginia Plan left it to the convention to decide the key issue of counting all people or just free people for purposes of representation. Counting all people would favor southern states; counting only free people would favor northern states. Compounding the impact of any rule of representation for the lower branch of Congress, the Virginia and Pinckney plans had that chamber selecting the upper one (or Senate) and the entire Congress picking the president, so all power turned on how the lower branch was apportioned.[37]

Whip-smart and direct—a fellow delegate would say that he spoke with great "perspicuity . . . without running into prolixity"—Pinckney, representing only himself and his state, cut to the chase in his plan.[38]

Reaching back to a 1783 congressional compromise for allocating financial requisitions among the states, Pinckney proposed that the lower
branch of Congress *"consist of one Member for every ____ thousand
inhabitants 3/5 of Blacks included."*[39] Drawing on the 1783 compromise,
by "Blacks" he meant enslaved people (whether Black, Native American, or mixed-race) and not free Blacks. This ratio, Pinckney presumably
reasoned, would net southern whites as much added representation for
their enslaved people as they could expect in a convention dominated by
northern states. Of course, he did not envision enslaved Blacks casting
three-fifths of a vote. No Blacks, free or enslaved, could vote in Virginia,
Georgia, or (after 1790) South Carolina, and yet free Blacks there, like
women, children, and non-landowning whites—who could not vote in
most states—would count as a full person for purposes of representation.

Modern commentators generally agree that, while the three-fifths
compromise made some sense as a measure of a state's wealth for assign-
ing contributions, it was arbitrary as a rule of representation.[40] At the
time, even critics of slavery like Franklin conceded that enslaved workers generated less wealth than free ones.[41] While delegates might believe
that the enslaved generated about three-fifths as much wealth as free
people, all of them knew that no enslaved Black would receive any representation under the three-fifths compromise. It empowered slaveholders,
not the enslaved.

As arbitrary as it was, the three-fifths compromise acted like a riptide
sucking in delegates no matter how much they tried to swim against it.[42]
Setting aside Pinckney's proposal to work through the Virginia Plan resolution by resolution, the convention reached the rule on representation
on May 30, only to postpone its consideration after Hamilton moved to
base representation solely on the number of each state's "free inhabitants," which would favor the North.[43]

The issue resurfaced on June 11 when Connecticut's Roger Sherman
made the proposal for counting only "free inhabitants" for representation.[44] Prepared this time, John Rutledge of South Carolina immediately
countered with the alternative "quotas of contribution" method, which

would effectively count slaves along with others and thus benefit the South.[45] As if on cue, Charles Pinckney and Pennsylvania's James Wilson then chimed in with the three-fifths compromise.[46] At this point, the only stated objection to this compromise came from the irrepressible Elbridge Gerry of Massachusetts, a short, wiry, small-town merchant who never owned an enslaved person. After noting for dramatic effect, "Blacks are property, and are used to the southward as horses and cattle to the northward," Gerry sneered about southern states, "why should their representation be increased to the southward on account of the number of slaves, than horses or oxen to the north?"[47] For his part in this set piece, Franklin sought to bridge the divide by observing, "Representation ought to be in proportion to the importance of numbers or wealth," which left open fractionally counting the enslaved as a measure of wealth rather than population.[48] With little else said, the three-fifths compromise passed nine states to two, with only the small states of Delaware and New Jersey voting no to register their opposition to any form of proportional representation.[49]

With the sectional issue over representation in the lower branch seemingly settled, the convention turned its attention to the Senate, with Sherman declaring, "The smaller States would never agree to the [Virginia] plan on any other principle than an equality of suffrage in this branch."[50] Even though the large states united that day to defeat Sherman's motion for equal representation in the Senate by a slender five-to-six margin, delegates from small states persisted, including by offering the so-called New Jersey Plan, which would have kept the existing one-branch Congress where each state had one vote.

The ensuing back-and-forth over this divisive issue continued through June, with delegates on both sides threatening to walk away if they did not get their way.[51] At one point, the secular Dr. Franklin asked for prayer, and at another, the sharp-tongued Hamilton spoke of resorting to an "elective monarchy."[52] Ever the theorist, an exasperated Madison declared it all a distraction. "The States were divided into different interests not by their difference of size but . . . from the effects of having or not having slaves," he opined. Rather than have one branch of Congress with proportional representation and another equal, Madison now proposed (perhaps for effect) having the one apportioned based on free population only and the other on total population, free and enslaved.[53] This idea went nowhere but it did emphasize how deeply slavery divided the states.

A political nonissue before the Revolutionary era, slavery had become a defining moral one by the time of the Constitutional Convention. "The antislavery revolution of the Revolutionary era brought in a change in consciousness," historian Christopher Brown explained. "It inspired a shift in moral perception sufficient to unsettle the place of slavery in American life but insufficient to dislodge it from the social order."[54]

The matter of the Senate's composition came to a head on June 2 when, with a few strategic absences, the convention deadlocked, five-to-five with one state divided, on whether to use proportional or equal representation. "We are now at a full stop," Connecticut's Sherman declared with a bit of boast, "and nobody he supposed meant that we shd. break up without doing something."[55] The small states had held the line but had not yet won. Without better options, the convention then sent the matter to a committee composed of one member from each state and effectively led by the ever-resourceful Franklin. Two days before, he had admonished delegates, "When a broad table is to be made, and the edges of planks do not fit the artist takes a little from both ends, and makes a good fit. In like manner here both sides must part with some of their demands."[56] This spirit prevailed within the committee, which met at Franklin's home during the convention's July Fourth recess.

Following Franklin's lead, the committee returned on July 5 with the so-called Great Compromise of equal representation in the Senate, proportional representation using the three-fifths compromise in the lower branch, and money bills starting in the lower branch. This compromise met the minimum demands of the small states, but diluted the bargained-for gains of southern states from proportional representation under the three-fifths compromise, which no longer would apply to the Senate.

Solving one issue reopened others, which led Franklin to compare the moves at the convention to those of a chess game. "The players of our game are so many," he wrote, "their ideas so different, their prejudices so strong and so various, and their particular interests independent of the general seeming so opposite, that not a move can be made that is not contested."[57] Case in point, while still willing to accept the three-fifths compromise if applied to Congress as a whole, after small states won equal representation in the Senate, Pinckney now declared his preference that "blacks ought to stand on an equality with whites" in apportioning the lower branch.[58] The ensuing debate put the three-fifths compromise back in play when Pierce Butler and Pinckney's cousin, C. C. Pinckney, both from South Carolina, formally moved "that blacks be included in the rule of Representation, *equally* with the Whites."[59]

Slavery suddenly took center stage at the convention again, but the bitter battle over Senate representation gave a sharper edge to the discussion than before. Reviving the idea of tying representation to wealth, Butler said in defense of his motion for counting free and enslaved people equally in apportioning the lower branch, "The labour of a slave in S. Carola. was as productive & valuable as that of a freeman in Massts."[60] Northern delegates disagreed, of course, but now even senior Virginia delegate George Mason, the owner of more enslaved Blacks than either Pinckney (and they owned some two hundred each), spoke bluntly. "Slaves were valuable," Mason declared, but not "equal to freemen."[61] With this, the Pinckney-Butler motion failed, with Virginia, Maryland, and North Carolina joining the northern states in opposing it. Once resurrected, however, the issue of how to count enslaved people persisted.[62]

In the course of the two-week-long debate over the Great Compromise, William Paterson of New Jersey, who supported equal representation in the Senate, asked what many northern delegates must have wondered all along about the three-fifths compromise. "Has a man in Virga. a number of votes in proportion to the number of his slaves? and if Negroes are not represented in the States to which they belong, why should they be represented in the Genl. Govt."[63] Just as Charles Pinckney backed away from the compromise that he had offered, his original northern cosponsor now did so too. "Mr. Wilson did not well see on what principle the admission of blacks in the proportion of three fifth could be explained," Madison wrote in his notes for July 11. "Are they admitted as property? then why is not other property admitted into the computation?" he reported Wilson asking in a question that helped explain why southern delegates used the innocuous-sounding "quotas of contribution" language.[64] Ultimately, the Constitution would call them all "people," but for representation and direct taxes, count only three-fifths of those not free.[65]

At this point, Gouverneur Morris, Wilson's blunt-speaking and acutely perceptive colleague from Pennsylvania, declared "himself reduced to the dilemma of doing injustice to the Southern States or to human nature, and he must therefore do the former" because even fractionally counting enslaved Blacks would encourage the damnable Atlantic slave trade.[66] Others piled on and the three-fifths compromise crumbled on July 11, with a majority of the states (mostly from the North) voting against using it for the census needed to allocate representation.[67]

A night's reflection brought all sides back to the table. On July 12, one day after the delegates reneged on the three-fifths compromise and four days prior to their acceptance of equal representation in the Senate, the convention revisited the apportionment issue. "It was meant by some gentlemen to deprive the Southern States of any share of Representation for their blacks," North Carolina's mild-mannered William Davie said of the vote against the census counting enslaved Blacks as three-fifths of a person. "N. Carola. would never confederate on any terms that did not rate them at least as 3/5. If the [Northern] States meant therefore to exclude them altogether the business was at an end."[68]

If even Davie would walk, northern delegates reasoned, other southerners would as well. Randolph then moved to restore the three-fifths compromise, "urging strenuously," as Madison reported it, "that express security ought to be provided for including slaves in the ratio of Representation."[69] The motion passed with only Delaware and New Jersey voting no in accord with their ongoing opposition to any form of proportional representation. The three-fifths compromise remained untouched thereafter, and the delegates moved on to other matters. Two of these other matters produced concessions on slavery nearly as consequential as the three-fifths compromise: twenty-year protection for the Atlantic slave trade and a fugitive slave clause.

The three-fifths compromise alone might have supplied sufficient security for slavery to satisfy southern delegates, especially once the electoral-vote method of selecting the president incorporated it as well. Further, from the outset, delegates never seriously considered empowering Congress with authority to tamper with slavery in existing states—though the immediate precedent of the Northwest Ordinance arguably made territories a different matter. Still, two issues continued to concern southern delegates: the Atlantic slave trade and the return of fugitives from slavery. Some southern delegates feared that Congress might use its enhanced powers over international commerce to limit the importation of enslaved Africans, and hoped that a tighter union could help their citizens to retrieve fugitives who fled enslavement to other states. Southern delegates peppered the convention's remaining weeks with demands on both issues that suggested just how deeply slavery divided the country.

Importation came first. On July 26, after agreeing in detail on representation in Congress and in outline on the structure of the other branches and centralized powers, the convention sent the resolutions passed so far to a Committee of Detail to frame into a single document. When the committee submitted its draft constitution on August 6, one short section of it not in those prior resolutions reignited the slavery debate.

"No tax or duty shall be laid by the Legislature on articles exported from any State," that section stated, "nor on the migration or importation of such persons as the several States shall think proper to admit; *nor shall such migration or importation be prohibited.*"[70] A related section imposed a two-thirds majority requirement for enacting any limits on foreign trade.[71] Raising barriers to restricting trade while barring tariffs on exports favored states with a plantation economy using enslaved labor, which typically produced more products for export than one using free labor, but the main controversy centered on the further prohibition against taxing or limiting the Atlantic slave trade. The colonies had long used tariffs to curtail the importation of enslaved Africans and protested when the king vetoed them.[72] In 1774, the First Continental Congress called for a boycott of the Atlantic slave trade and, during the Revolution, eleven states banned it. Now a draft constitution purportedly designed to "secure the blessings of liberty" would protect that trade forever

"It was inconsistent with the principles of the revolution and dishonorable to the American character to have such a feature in the Constitution," the ebullient Luther Martin of Maryland declared as soon as the clause protecting the Atlantic slave trade reached the floor.[73] "Religion & humanity had nothing to do with this question—Interest alone is the governing principle with Nations," South Carolina's Rutledge shot back. "If the Northern States consult their interest, they will not oppose the increase of Slaves which will increase the commodities of which they will become the carriers."[74] The increased shipping for northern merchants that Rutledge hailed included not only transporting the products of enslaved workers but also the importation of those workers themselves. The share of the Atlantic slave trade carried on American ships to North America jumped from about one-sixth prior to the Revolution to nearly three-fourths after the war, with most of the share carried on vessels based in the North.[75]

Three South Carolina delegates and one each from Georgia and North Carolina then took the floor to declare that their states would never ratify any constitution that authorized Congress to limit slavery imports.[76] "In every proposed extension of the power of Congress," Charles Pinckney stated, South Carolina "has expressly & watchfully excepted that of meddling with the importation of negroes."[77] Georgia's Abraham Baldwin and Hugh Williamson of North Carolina made similar statements. Dickinson and Wilson doubted their resolve—"They would never refuse to Unite because the importation might be prohibited," Wilson said of the three lower South states—but most other delegates would not run that risk.[78]

George Mason and Gouverneur Morris joined Luther Martin in framing the issue in moral terms, and extended it beyond the Atlantic slave trade to domestic slavery as well. In arguing against importing any more enslaved Africans, for example, Mason spoke of the impact of Black slavery on free whites. "The poor despise labor when performed by slaves," he said. "They produce the most pernicious effects on manners. Every master of slaves is born a petty tyrant."[79] Mason had reason to know: upon reaching maturity at age twenty-one, he inherited some three hundred enslaved Blacks from the estate of his deceased father and never freed any of them. At least in Virginia, however, which already had an excess of enslaved Blacks and imposed its own ban on importing more, additional congressional limits would have little effect on domestic slavery other than the welcome one of reducing competition from foreign sources for the domestic market in enslaved Blacks.

For his part, Morris broadly assailed both the Atlantic slave trade and domestic slavery. Even before denouncing "the inhabitant of Georgia and S.C. who goes to the Coast of Africa, and in defiance of the most sacred laws of humanity tears away his fellow creatures from their dearest connections & damns them to the most cruel bondages," he disparaged the impact of slavery on those states. "The moment you leave ye NE. Sts, & enter N.York, the effects of the institution become visible," he declared. "Proceed Southwdly, & every step you take thro' ye great regions of slaves, presents a desert increasing with ye increasing proportion of those wretched beings."[80] Born into a wealthy New York slaveholding family, Morris refused to accept enslaved persons as his legacy and never owned any.

Even as Mason warned that slaveholding itself would "bring the Judgment of Heaven on a Country," several delegates from both northern and southern states protested that slavery was not at issue. "The morality or wisdom of slavery are considerations belonging to the States themselves," Connecticut's Oliver Ellsworth reminded his colleagues. "The old confederation had not meddled with this point, and he did not see any greater necessity for bringing it within the policy of the new one."[81] Of course, except for making recommendations, the old confederation had not meddled with the slave trade either, but that was because (under the Articles) it lacked power over trade. Other delegates supported Ellsworth's effort to keep the focus on the Atlantic slave trade by expressing the consensus view that, under any new constitution, slavery would remain a matter of state law. Nothing could deter Martin, Mason, and Morris from expressing their heartfelt hostility to slavery, however.

Speaking as a slaveholder who knew the institution's evils firsthand, Mason stressed the simple fact that enslaved Africans arriving "thro' S. Carolina & Georgia" would not remain in those states. They would overflow into the Southwest and "fill that Country with slaves." Further, all three delegates and some others warned that enslaved Blacks might support future foreign invaders and foment domestic insurrections, which would create costs for the general government. Rufus King of Massachusetts asked about the combined effect of not taxing exports or limiting the slave trade: "If slaves are to be imported shall not the exports produced by their labor [be taxed to] supply a revenue the better to enable the Genl. Govt. to defend their Masters?"[82] Others discounted this risk or suggested that the national economic benefits of slavery outweighed its economic costs. "What enriches a part enriches the whole," Ellsworth smugly said of these benefits.[83]

The structure of the debate over constitutional protections for the Atlantic slave trade differed from the one generated by the three-fifths compromise, but the basic dynamics did not change. The upper South, with its surplus of enslaved Blacks, now stood willing to side with most northern states—a point that C. C. Pinckney snidely made. "As to Virginia," he sneered, "her slaves will rise in value, & she has more than she wants."[84] The Connecticut delegates, however, seemed to have cut a deal with the South Carolinians to support the slave trade in return for requiring only a majority vote for limiting other imports, which could help promote manufacturing in the Northeast.[85] By stopping that trade, "we shall be unjust towards S. Carolina & Georgia," Connecticut's Ellsworth declared.[86] "It was better to let the S. States import slaves than to part with them," Sherman added.[87] Ultimately, that concern for unity—the same that carried the three-fifths compromise—prevailed, but this time with a twenty-year limit that the Carolinas and Georgia accepted. By 1808, as North Carolina delegate Richard Dobbs Spaight later explained to his state's ratifying convention, the states of the Deep South "would be fully supplied" with enslaved laborers.[88]

Most delegates cared more about drawing all the states into a fortified federal union than immediately stopping the Atlantic slave trade, which Georgia's Abraham Baldwin depicted as one of his state's "favorite prerogatives."[89] Slavery "is justified by the example of all the world," C. C. Pinckney added in an even broader defense of importing more enslaved Blacks. "In all the ages one half of mankind have been slaves."[90] Supported by this united minority front, the Atlantic slave trade endured for another generation.

"By agreeing to the clause, it would revolt the Quakers, the Methodists, and many others in States having no slaves," Virginia governor Edmund Randolph conceded. "On the other hand, two States might be lost to the Union," and he could not accept that loss.[91] The majority did secure both a limit of twenty years for the ban on ending the slave trade, by which time South Carolina and Georgia could catch up with Virginia in securing a surplus of enslaved labor for domestic export, and a nominal tariff "not exceeding ten dollars for each person" on imported Africans.[92] Indeed, after expressing his belief that his state would not stop "her importation of slaves *in any short time*," South Carolina's C. C. Pinckney personally offered the motion setting a twenty-year limit on constitutional protections for the slave trade.[93] During those two decades, over 200,000 enslaved Africans entered the United States through the Carolinas and Georgia—the only three states allowing such imports during the period—or nearly as many as imported into all thirteen colonies prior to the American Revolution.[94]

The final major concession won by the slaveholding states at the convention came in a flash, without dissent or discussion, on August 29 as the delegates raced to complete their work. It passed immediately after the southern states agreed to allow only a majority vote for enacting trade restrictions, a key concession to northern states also approved without dissent. "If any person bound to service or labor in any of the U— States shall escape into another State, he or she shall not be discharged from such service or labor," the motion offered by South Carolina slaveholder Pierce Butler read, "but shall be delivered up to the person justly claiming their service or labor."[95] Under this "Fugitive Slave Clause," the *Somerset* decision (or anything like it granting liberty to fugitives from slavery reaching a free state) would not apply within the United States. In particular, the Clause seemingly addressed concerns of this sort raised in 1779 by the rulings of the Massachusetts courts in the case of the Waccamaw Blacks and so vehemently but futilely protested under the Articles of Confederation by South Carolina. Presumably the clause in the Constitution protecting the "Privileges and Immunities" of each state's citizens should have addressed this concern, but that clause resembled one in the Articles that South Carolina found ineffective.[96]

After the strident debates over the three-fifths compromise and protection for the Atlantic slave trade, the delegates' silence on the Fugitive Slave Clause spoke loudly. In the shadow of *Somerset* and in light of the increasing number of free states in the North, many delegates must have known that the Clause could become crucial for maintaining slavery in the southern states. Some southern delegates claimed as much upon returning home. All should have known it even if they did not foresee that the enforcement of federal laws passed under the Clause would become flashpoints in the run-up to a civil war over slavery.

The fugitive-slave issue first arose late on the previous day, August 28, when Butler offered his motion as an amendment to an article requiring states to deliver up and return escaped felons from other states. Wilson complained at the time that extending the escaped-felon requirement to "fugitive slaves and servants," as Butler had asked, would impose expense on the states by creating an obligation for them to catch and return fugitives from slavery. Sherman added that, if they constituted property, then "he saw no more propriety in the public seizing and surrendering a slave or servant, than a [runaway] horse."[97] Delivering up such a fugitive might be appropriate, these comments suggested, but not an affirmative duty to capture them. Butler asked to withdraw and revise his motion. As offered the next day, it closely tracked the fugitive slave clause contained in the ordinance Congress had enacted six weeks earlier to create a slavery-free Northwest Territory.

Any sectional deal to incorporate a fugitive slave clause into the Northwest Ordinance of 1787 may have included adding it to the Constitution, as some historians suggest, or the prior clause may simply have served as a model for the convention delegates, as other historians surmise.[98] In either case, no evidence from the era shows that northern delegates accepted proslavery compromises in exchange for Congress's excluding slavery from the Ohio Country through the Northwest Ordinance. That deal, even though cut at the same time as the three-fifths compromise, arose from factors intrinsic to Congress, not the convention, such as securing land sales to New Englanders in the Ohio territory, and navigation rights for westerners on the Mississippi River.[99] Despite the precedent of the Confederation Congress's Northwest Ordinance, nothing in the Constitution expressly empowered the federal government to limit slavery in the territories.[100]

The Fugitive Slave Clause may have readily passed the convention because it exhibited a property (as opposed to a contract) view of slavery without explicitly defining enslaved people as property, which Madison had sought to avert by never using the words "slave" or "slavery" in the Constitution. Only express provisions in the property law of a slaveholding state, not its contract law, could account for the enforceable bondage of enslaved persons from birth or purchase without their prior consent. Having the Clause link fugitives from slavery with those from indentured servitude failed to defeat this presumption because no one asserted that an enslaved person (as opposed to an indentured one) had entered into a contract for their service. The property view of slavery generally held by Americans at the time may help explain the delegates' acceptance of the Fugitive Slave Clause. After all, aroused by the specter of taxation without representation, patriots had fought a revolution to defend their liberty *and* property.

By mandating the interstate repatriation of fugitives, the Clause came as close as anything else in the Constitution to sanctioning slavery at the federal level. Proslavery southerners would later claim that it recognized property rights in enslaved Blacks, which antislavery northerners had sought to avoid by having the Constitution consistently refer to such Blacks as persons.[101] With its inclusion, C. C. Pinckney returned to South Carolina boasting, "We have obtained a right to recover our slaves in whatever part of America they may take refuge, which is a right we had not before."[102] Perhaps he exaggerated in that, without further federal law, the Fugitive Slave Clause lacked an enforcement mechanism, but it did serve as authority for enacting such a statute in the coming years.

Along with these major compromises and concessions, other constitutional provisions indirectly bolstered state-sanctioned slavery. One clause entrenched the status quo on slavery by requiring three-fourths of the states to approve constitutional amendments. Another empowered states to call on the general government to suppress domestic violence and insurrections, including uprisings by the enslaved against their masters.

All this gave C. C. Pinckney reason to crow. Working with other delegates from Georgia and the Carolinas, he had won key concessions on slavery. He was able to do so because, on balance, southern delegates fought harder to defend and extend state-sanctioned slavery under the Constitution than northern delegates fought to contain and curtail it. In this respect, Pinckney and Franklin offered a telling contrast. Both able, practical politicians, the proslavery, pro-union Pinckney stood firmer for slavery than the pro-union, antislavery Franklin stood against it. Franklin cared most about establishing a strong general government, and southerners like Pinckney could force him to compromise on slavery to get it. In the end, Franklin got what he wanted most from the convention and so did Pinckney. The resulting Constitution embodied a pragmatic mix of lofty ideals and lowly compromises.

Years later, the leading abolitionist William Lloyd Garrison denounced the Constitution as "a covenant with death, and an agreement with hell."[103] Yet it passed the convention with all eleven states then represented voting for it, and only three individual members dissenting. At the time, no delegate—not even those like Gerry and Mason who voted no—viewed the Constitution in such stark terms. Gouverneur Morris at one point declared that, because of its concessions to slavery, he "would sooner submit himself to a tax for paying [to purchase and liberate] all the Negroes in the U. States than saddle posterity with such a Constitution," yet he still signed it.[104] Like Morris and Franklin, many other delegates opposed slavery. Some viewed it as an unavoidable evil, and perhaps a few as an avoidable one. Of the southern delegates, none portrayed slavery as waning in their region, and most of them fought to assure its expansion (at least into the Southwest) under an enhanced union.[105] Some considered slavery a positive good. At least twenty-five of the delegates, or about half, owned enslaved Blacks at the time of the convention, and some later bought more. There were shades of meaning even in the purpose of the union as stated in the Constitution's Preamble: it was in part to "secure the Blessings of Liberty to ourselves and our Posterity"—a phrase as indeterminate as "We the people of the United States."[106] Some opponents of slavery later maintained that this phrase supported abolition, but supporters of slavery never read it that way and wrote Blacks out of the Constitution.[107] During the Revolutionary era, "liberty" to some meant the freedom of all people; to others it meant the freedom to own Black people.

That it had come to this showed just how much America had changed since 1765. Prior to the Revolutionary era, only Quakers and a few other colonists had voiced moral objections to slavery. The institution existed in every colony; in many, it flourished. At the convention, however, Virginia's governor acknowledged that the delegates' compromises on slavery would alienate not only Quakers and Methodists but "many others in States having no slaves."[108] By this reference, he clearly meant states like Pennsylvania, Rhode Island, and Connecticut, then in the process of enacting a gradual abolition of slavery, as well as Massachusetts and New Hampshire, which had seemingly done so abruptly through their state constitutions. Revolutionary America had experienced a meaningful (if neither uniform nor conclusive) shift in white sentiment about slavery, with much more movement in the North than the South. Yet at the time, this shift did not bring Blacks into the conversation over constitutional reform. No state sent a delegate of color to Philadelphia, and with the doors to the convention closed to nondelegates, no people of color heard the debate or left written comments about it. As much as the Constitution would affect slavery in America, Black Americans did not join in framing it.

As a snapshot, the Constitutional Convention exposed the shift in sentiment about slavery by laying bare a stark sectional divide over the issue. That does not mean the Constitution itself advanced the process. Garrison certainly thought that it retarded the antislavery cause, and C. C. Pinckney suggested as much in his boasts about the Fugitive Slave Clause.[109] The majority of delegates showed their discomfort by refusing to use the words "slave," "slavery," or "enslaved" in the Constitution. New Jersey's Paterson pointed that way early in the debate when he noted that Congress in amending the Articles of Confederation "had been ashamed to use the term 'Slaves' & had substituted a description."[110] The delegates followed this approach at every turn, even when a mocking Morris tried to goad them into making the clause protecting the Atlantic slave trade bluntly authorize the "importation of *slaves* into N. Carolina, S— Carolina & Georgia" rather than discreetly allow in "such Persons as any of the States now existing shall think proper to admit." His text would "avoid the ambiguity" of using a euphemism, he declared.[111] Sherman replied that he liked using covert descriptions rather than terms "which had been declined by the old Congs & were not pleasing to some people."[112]

Rarely one to mince words, Luther Martin said of these euphemisms that the delegates "anxiously sought to avoid the admission of expressions which might be odious to the ears of Americans, although they were willing to admit into their system those *things* which the *expressions* signified."[113] Decorous words did not hide nefarious acts or prevent monstrous consequences. Seventy years later, debating Stephen Douglas as they confronted the expansion of slavery into the territories, Abraham Lincoln put the best spin possible on this use of euphemisms. The framers used "covert language," he said, so that "after the institution of slavery had passed from us—there should be nothing on the face of the great charter of liberty suggesting that such a thing as Negro slavery had ever existed among us."[114] If so, they failed. The use of euphemisms neither cleansed the charter's future face nor prevented the consequences of their compromises. The clauses remain in the text and their effects endure for the country and its people. Still, Lincoln had a point. The framers' refusal to use the word "slavery" made the Constitution less overtly supportive of the institution, and kept it from expressly declaring property rights in people.[115]

If, like Franklin, most delegates went to the convention with the principal goal of forming a more powerful federal union than existed under the Articles, then they succeeded. "I agree to this Constitution with all its faults," Franklin said in a closing speech that quieted the hall, "because I think a general Government necessary for us, and there is no form of Government but what may be a blessing to the people if administered well." With enhanced power, the resulting government could do more than the previous one to advance or to retard both liberty and slavery in post-Revolutionary America. Franklin knew this well because he went on to warn his fellow delegates that this new government "can only end in Despotism, as other forms have done before it, when the people shall become so corrupted as to need despotic Government, being incapable of any other."[116] Time would tell if those delegates had formed "a more perfect Union" as well as a more powerful one.[117] Under a republic, even a compromised one, the people would ultimately decide such matters and, with them, the future of liberty and slavery in the United States, even if that might require a civil war and fundamental changes to the Constitution.

CHAPTER NINE

"We, the States"

Ratifying Liberty and Slavery, 1787–1788

"We the People of the United States," the Constitution's Preamble begins, "in Order to . . . secure the Blessings of Liberty to ourselves and our Posterity, do ordain and establish this Constitution for the United States of America."[1] With some justification, Patrick Henry shot back at the Virginia ratifying convention in June 1788, "Who authorized them to speak the language of *We, the People*, instead of *We, the States*?"[2] Rarely one to miss the mark wholly and often able to hit a rhetorical bull's eye, Henry raised a perplexing question: Just what people ordained and established the Constitution?

The Constitution's lofty opening phrase clearly could not refer to the free, white, adult, male delegates who attended the convention that drafted the Constitution, because they did not represent "the people." State legislatures (not voters) chose them to represent their states, with these legislatures composed exclusively of free, white males. Further, only fifty-five of the seventy named delegates attended, with forty-one present for the final vote. Rhode Island sent no delegates to the convention, and a majority of those from New York left midway through it. With the delegates voting by state and each state having an equal vote no matter how small, the process represented Henry's "We, the States," more than the Preamble's "We the People."

The ratification process, which involved popularly elected delegates, came closer than the convention to validating the phrase, "We the People of the United States," but still fell short in several respects. The resolution transmitting the proposed Constitution from the convention to Congress urged that the document "be submitted to a Convention of Delegates, chosen in each State *by the People* thereof, under the Recommendation of its Legislature, for their Assent and Ratification."[3] Artfully written, the resolution did not require the approval of the Constitution by either Congress or state legislatures, though those legislatures could derail the process by not calling state conventions. In this respect, and by the provision in the Constitution requiring ratification by nine states (regardless of their population) rather than by a national process, it was the states rather than the people that ratified the Constitution.[4] Given the wide disparity in the number of people in each state—ranging from less than two percent of the American population in Delaware to over twenty percent of it in Virginia—nine states could ratify the Constitution without the ratifying states containing half of "We, the people of the United States."[5] None of these state conventions represented the American people as a whole; they represented states.

Further, delegates at these state conventions could only vote up or down on the document, which limited their role in the process. Amendments could come later, of course, but only after the Constitution took effect. This inability for a state to condition its ratification on amendments became a point of contention, with some delegates urging changes but federalists—the name taken by those supporting the new Constitution—insisting that no means existed for altering the document prior to its ratification. This view prevailed. "The Constitution requires an adoption *in toto*, and *for ever*," was how James Madison put it in a letter to fellow framer Alexander Hamilton.[6] In addition, each state set the procedures for electing delegates to its ratifying convention, with all of them limiting those voting to free, property-owning or tax-paying adults.

Some states added religious restrictions on suffrage, six states disenfranchised free Blacks, and only New Jersey permitted any women to vote.[7]
As a result, less than one in five Americans could vote for delegates to the
ratifying conventions, none of which had any Black or women members.
We, the people, were white, male landowners.

Although the resolution sending the Constitution to Congress proposed that the document "should afterward" go to the states, Pennsylvania's delegates could not wait that long.[8] As soon as the convention
ended on September 17, 1787, and before the proposed Constitution even
reached Congress, delegates from Pennsylvania raced upstairs in the
State House, where both the convention and the state Assembly met,
to notify state lawmakers that they "were ready to report" on the proposed new general government.[9] This put in motion the first state ratifying process, and one that set the tone for much that followed in other
states. Competing claims of liberty rang out on both sides—liberty won
or liberty lost—with George Bryan's populist Constitutionalist faction,
named for its support of Pennsylvania's radically democratic state constitution, leading an opposition that hardened into a nationwide antifederalist movement.

The debate over calling a state ratifying convention began the next
day. Caught off guard, Constitutionalists begged for time to review the
document. At least wait until Congress received the draft Constitution
and referred it to the states, they pleaded. Congress or other states might
offer amendments, the Constitutionalists argued, and hinted that those
amendments might restrict slavery.[10] Under George Bryan, Constitutionalists had secured the world's first gradual abolition law and still
prided themselves on that landmark achievement.

"Not so, sir, they must adopt *in toto* or refuse altogether for it must be
a plan that is formed by the United States," majority-party leader Daniel Clymer shot back against the claim that states could condition their
ratification on amendments. Alluding to amendments restricting slavery, Clymer noted, "Could it be expected that Virginia (the Dominion
of Virginia, as some people in derision call it, though I say it is the land

of liberty) . . . and the Southern States shall coincide with alterations made for the benefit of Pennsylvania?" No state could disrupt the compromises baked into the Constitution, he said, not even ones involving slavery. It was all or nothing, concessions for slavery and the Atlantic slave trade included.[11]

"As we have taken up this matter, let us go through," Clymer added, to garner for Pennsylvania "the honor of agreeing first to a measure, that must entitle to posterity security for their property . . . , security to their liberty, and security to their personal safety." He depicted these triple "blessings" of the new Constitution (with safeguarding property conspicuously listed before securing liberty) as ones that "will engage the gratitude of posterity to venerate your ashes."[12] Joining Clymer in the Assembly, his cousin George (who represented Pennsylvania at the Constitutional Convention) also called for a quick state convention and hailed the proposed Constitution as "a measure on which our future happiness, nay I may almost say, our future existence, as a nation, depends."[13]

Expressly objecting to the absence of a bill of rights protecting individual liberty in the proposed Constitution, which became a central issue at the Pennsylvania convention, minority-party members sought to delay the process of calling the convention by boycotting the Assembly and denying it a quorum.[14] After the Seargent at Arms forcibly corralled enough dissenting members for the Assembly to proceed, however, Clymer's partisans rammed through legislation calling the nation's first state ratifying convention for November 20, 1787. "It is," Daniel Clymer declared, "a subject which I almost adore."[15]

As elections for delegates proceeded and the date for the Pennsylvania state convention approached, a contest of words erupted with "liberty" on every tongue. Eighteen essays published under the pseudonym Centinel, widely thought to be by George Bryan but actually by his son Samuel, set the tone for the opposition. "All the blessings of liberty and the dearest privileges of freemen are now at stake," Centinel wrote in his first and most widely reprinted essay. A general government led by a Congress with "comprehensive" powers to tax and spend for the "general welfare" and unbounded by express guarantees for individual liberties would quickly overwhelm the "certain *liberties* and *privileges* secured to you by the constitution of this commonwealth," he warned. Adding, "A very extensive country cannot be governed on democratical principles," Centinel argued that the United States could not be "melted down into one empire" in a manner "consistent with freedom." Certainly, he contended, by creating an aristocratic Senate and a supreme, unelected judiciary, *this* Constitution failed to protect liberty and establish democracy.[16] Initially published in Philadelphia only days after the Constitutional Convention ended, Centinel's first essay ultimately appeared in nineteen newspapers from Massachusetts to Virginia.

Constitutional Convention delegate James Wilson, a Scottish-born and -bred lawyer with a philosophical bent and aristocratic bearing, answered Centinel and other critics. In a speech given outside the Pennsylvania State House on October 6 and reported in thirty-four newspapers across the country, he set out the arguments that would define the federalist case for ratification.[17]

A government with enumerated powers, as the Constitution would create, did not need a bill of rights, Wilson asserted, unless those named powers infringed on specific rights. "For instance, the liberty of press," he offered, would require express protection only if "a power similar to that which has been granted for the regulation of commerce, had been granted to regulate literary publications." In fact, Wilson added, an express declaration of rights could lessen liberties by implying that the Constitution took away those rights not listed. After replying to other criticisms with similarly lawyerly rejoinders that his opponents readily brushed aside, he turned on critics like George Bryan who held office or profited under the existing state-centered system. Without leveling any specific charges of corruption, Wilson declared that critics did not oppose the new Constitution "because it is injurious to the liberties of his country, but because it affects his schemes of wealth and consequence." "Regarding it then, in every point of view, with a candid and disinterested mind, I am bold to assert," he concluded, the Constitution "is the best form of government which has ever been offered to the world."

Although contesting claims of liberty featured foremost in Pennsylvania's public debates over ratification, arguments over slavery and the Atlantic slave trade appeared as well. The most vocal antifederalists at the state ratifying convention, John Smilie, William Findley, and Robert Whitehill, took turns bashing the new Constitution for extending protection of the slave trade until 1808.[18] Some opponents went so far as to claim that constitutional protection of the slave trade would lead to the reintroduction of slavery into Pennsylvania.[19] At the state ratifying convention, Wilson repeatedly responded with the equally preposterous claim that, by empowering Congress to end the slave trade in 1808, the new Constitution gave it the power to abolish slavery altogether. "If there was no other lovely feature in the Constitution, but this one, it would diffuse a beauty over its whole countenance," he declared. "Yet the lapse of a few years and Congress will have power to exterminate slavery from within our borders."[20]

Replying with similar excess, Pennsylvania antifederalists resorted to the standard Whig trope (familiar from the rhetoric used against the British during the American Revolution) of equating infringements on liberty with enslavement. Attacking the Constitution's broad delegation of authority to Congress without the guardrails of a bill of rights, for example, Whitehill warned, "We know that it is the nature of power to seek its own augmentation, and thus the loss of liberty is the necessary consequence of a loose or extravagant delegation of authority." Pleading to condition ratification on amendments designed to protect liberty, he declared, "It is our duty to employ the present opportunity in stipulating such restrictions as are best calculated to protect us from oppression and slavery."[21] Wilson countered by repeating the federalist credo, "We must take the system as a whole, and, as a result of the whole, ratify or not ratify."[22] With nearly twice as many federalists as antifederalists elected to the convention, delegates voted on November 26 to preclude amendments and on December 12 to ratify the Constitution, making Pennsylvania the first large state to do so. Only neighboring Delaware slipped ahead of it by virtue of a short convention that began after but ended before the one in Pennsylvania.

Two other small states, New Jersey and Georgia, joined Delaware in ratifying the Constitution by the end of 1787.[23] All three acted quickly, unanimously, and without leaving a formal record of their convention debates. With each of them allowing slavery at the time and Georgia still embracing the Atlantic slave trade, no surviving evidence suggests that constitutional provisions on those matters ever became an issue in these states, or deterred delegates at their state conventions from voting to ratify the Constitution. Indeed, in a letter to Georgia convention president John Wereat dated one week prior to his state's convention, Lachlam McIntosh, a Revolutionary War general from Georgia, suggested that the "20 years more" assured by the Constitution constituted "the proper time" for doing "what may be done" to resupply the state with enough enslaved workers to replace those lost during the Revolution.[24]

By this point, the leading public opponents of ratification had emerged as George Mason and Richard Henry Lee, both Virginia planters, and Elbridge Gerry, a merchant from Massachusetts. Mason and Gerry gained that status by refusing to sign the Constitution at Philadelphia and then broadcasting their objections. Lee joined them by his rearguard efforts to amend the Constitution in Congress. All three had stellar patriot credentials—Gerry and Lee as signers of the Declaration of Independence and Mason as an early critic of British tyranny. They all denounced the new Constitution for restricting the liberties that they had fought so long to secure, with the lack of a bill of rights and undue concentration of power in Congress chief among the objections. "Conceiving as I did, that the liberties of America were not secured by the system, it was my duty to oppose it," Gerry wrote in an open letter to his state's Assembly explaining his no vote at the Constitutional Convention.[25] Mason and Lee said much the same and joined in orchestrating the resistance to ratification in Massachusetts, Virginia, and New York—three big states essential for any viable federal union.[26]

In January 1788, attention shifted northward to Connecticut and Massachusetts as the first two New England states to hold ratifying conventions. Federalists viewed Connecticut as friendlier to their cause than Massachusetts, but both had strong antislavery sentiment that might prove problematic for passage. Anticipating this in Connecticut, which acted first, federalists sought to defang the liberty-based objections of Lee and Mason by branding them as slaveholders. In a letter ostensibly to Lee published in the *Connecticut Courant* two weeks prior to the state's convention, a federalist charged, "All your cant about liberty . . . is hypocritical" because never "have you been known as the guardian or protector of that depressed race of men whose toils have enabled you to live in affluence."[27] In a like manner and in the same newspaper, former delegate to the Constitutional Convention and future U.S. Supreme Court chief justice Oliver Ellsworth, writing under the pseudonym A Landholder, decried "the madness of Mason" who "vented his rage to his own Negroes and to the wind."[28]

These and other federalists argued that the Constitution did as much as possible to limit slavery. "All good men wish the entire abolition of slavery as soon as it can take place with safety to the public, and for the lasting good of the present wretched race of slaves," Ellsworth wrote in the *Courant*. "The only possible step that could be taken toward it by the Convention was to fix a period after which they should not be imported."[29]

In multiple essays published in Connecticut in advance of the state convention, federalists accused opponents of falsely appropriating the metaphor of slavery. "*If we reject the Constitution, we shall be free; if we adopt it, we shall be slaves,*" an essayist writing under the pseudonym A Freeman quoted an unnamed antifederalist as saying, and then proceeded to bludgeon this straw man. "Many have no other idea of liberty, but for everyone to do as he pleases—to be as honest as he pleases—to be as knavish as he pleases," A Freeman wrote. "Every government which is worth having and supporting must have a competent degree of power in it to answer the great ends of its creation—the happiness of the people, the protection of their persons, and the security of their property." By concentrating power, he argued, this Constitution "secures all our liberties that ought to be secured." "Liberty," he repeated, "is revered in the Constitution; and is totally different from licentiousness."[30] Echoing a view of civil liberty famously espoused 150 years earlier by John Winthrop, the founding governor of Puritan Massachusetts—"a liberty to that only which is good, just, and honest" he called it—this argument resonated in Connecticut, then widely considered the most religious of the states—a virtual Protestant theocracy.[31] Of course, Winthrop's Massachusetts deported and sometimes hanged religious dissenters, as did colonial Connecticut.

Making a similar argument at the state convention, Connecticut's devoutly religious governor Samuel Huntington stated, "The great secret of preserving liberty is to lodge the supreme power so as to be well supported and not abused." This, he said, the Constitution did.[32] Lieutenant Governor Oliver Wolcott agreed. The sole consideration in ratifying the Constitution is "whether it secures the liberties of the people," he noted. As "it is founded upon the election of the people," Wolcott noted, "this is all the security in favor of liberty which can be expected."[33] With little else said of substance, delegates to the Connecticut convention ratified the Constitution by a vote of 128 to 40 on January 9, 1788, after meeting for only five days.[34]

In stark contrast to the brief and noncontentious ratification in Connecticut, the massive, 364-member convention in Massachusetts lasted nearly a month, with its outcome in doubt until the end. Even federalists in the state worried that antifederalists might have the upper hand when the convention opened on January 9. "Many of those known to be elected, are in opposition," Boston federalist Christopher Gore commented about the town-by-town elections for delegates. "I really cannot yet form any judgment of the weight of members, or which side the pros or cons will preponderate."[35]

Resistance to ratification centered in the interior parts of Massachusetts and Maine, which remained part of the state until 1820, but reached the coast in some rural towns like Sandwich and Kittery. Antifederalists at the convention lacked organization, principal spokespersons, or an agreed agenda. They were largely leaderless when Elbridge Gerry lost his bid to serve as a delegate after having moved in 1787 from his hometown of Marblehead, which likely would have elected him, to federalist-friendly Cambridge. Most antifederalists rarely spoke at the convention, but those who did typically expressed a generalized concern that, by creating a powerful central government remote from their homes, the Constitution posed a grave threat to their personal liberty.[36]

The lack of a bill of rights, infrequent elections for members of Congress, and provision for a standing army stood out among the most-often expressed objections of antifederalists at the Massachusetts convention. Others, at least those who viewed God as the source of their liberty, objected to the absence of a Christian religious test for officeholders. "The power is unlimited in Congress . . . as much power as was ever given to a despotic prince," perhaps the most dogged of the opponents, Amos Singletary of Sutton, protested. "The only security is, we may have an honest man [in Congress], but we may not have—we may have an atheist, pagan, Mahommedan."[37] He did not actually fear that Massachusetts voters would elect a Muslim, however—he feared the Constitution. After apologizing for speaking again so soon, four days later Singletary exploded, "These lawyers, and men of learning, and monied men, that talk so finely and gloss over matters so smoothly, to make us poor illiterate people swallow down the pill, expect to get into Congress themselves . . . and then they will swallow up all us little folks."[38]

Singletary's outburst brought Jonathan Smith, a farmer from Lanesborough, to his feet. "I had been a member of the Convention to form our own state Constitution, and had learnt something of the checks and balances of power, and I found them all here," Smith said of the proposed Constitution. "I don't think the worst of the Constitution because lawyers, and men of learning and monied men, are fond of it. I don't suspect that they will want to get into Congress and abuse their power." Liberty was safer under this new Constitution than under the "anarchy" spawned by the existing confederation, Smith argued over the jeers of antifederalists in the hall. As an example he cited the recent violence of Shays' Rebellion—a debtors' revolt in central Massachusetts. "When I saw this Constitution, I found that it was a cure for these disorders."[39]

This became a standard federalist tactic at the convention. Whatever provisions in the Constitution antifederalists posed as a threat to liberty, federalists presented as a protection of it. "I readily grant all these reasons are not sufficient to surrender up the essential liberties of the people," Thomas Thatcher said about the value of an effective federal union and a common defense against foreign attack for example. "But do we really surrender them?" he asked regarding the broad delegation of federal power and the provision for a standing army. "The spirit of liberty [is] in the people," Thatcher assured the delegates, and "should any servants of the people, however eminent their stations, attempt to enslave them, from this spirit of liberty, such an opposition would arise, as would bring them to the scaffold."[40] Regarding a religious test for public office, Isaac Backus of Middleborough, a dissenting Baptist minister in a state dominated by Congregationalists, added, "Let the history of all nations be searched, from that day to this, and it will appear that the imposing of religious tests hath been the greatest engine for tyranny in the world."[41]

Massachusetts federalists could dance around other arguments, but the lack of a bill of rights stood as the one liberty-based objection to ratification that they could not shake, and their insistence on ratifying the Constitution as written posed a seemingly insurmountable problem until nearly the convention's end. Then they came up with a solution and placed it in the hands of the state's popular governor, John Hancock, who as the convention's presiding officer had stayed largely above the fray. Combining all the liberties that delegates seemed to demand into a draft bill of rights, this tactic proposed offering them as "*recommendatory* amendments" (as federalists dubbed them) for submission by the convention for Congress to consider after ratification.[42]

Agreeing to this tactic, Hancock settled on nine amendments calculated to address many of the rights-based objections raised by antifederalists without making the structural government changes they also wanted. Hancock offered them in convention on February 1, where they were seconded by Samuel Adams, another uncommitted delegate with impeccable patriot credentials. The convention sent Hancock's amendments to a committee composed of both federalists and antifederalists. After making minor revisions, that committee approved them with two antifederalists joining the federalists in voting yes.

Switching sides on ratification, Nathaniel Barrell, one of the antifederalists who supported the amendments in committee, assured the convention that the amendments, which became a basis for the later Bill of Rights, "will secure to us and ours that liberty, without which life is a burden."[43] The full convention approved the amendments on February 6 by vote of 187 to 168, and later that day ratified the Constitution by the same margin. "If amended (as I feel assured it will be) according to your proposals," Hancock told the delegates after the first vote and before the second, the Constitution "cannot fail to give the people of the United States, a greater degree of political freedom, and eventually as much national dignity, as falls to the lot of any nation on the earth."[44] Liberty, Hancock and Barrell agreed, had won the day.

While liberty lit up the Massachusetts ratifying convention and guided its outcome, slavery hid in the shadows. It went little mentioned at the convention, perhaps because Massachusetts had abolished slavery, and perhaps because there were no Black delegates and no contemporaneous comments on the ratification debates by Black observers. The state's proportion of enslaved Blacks—about two percent of its population and only one percent of those enslaved in all the states—had always been low. With even those people now free, delegates at the state convention focused on other matters. No delegate spoke up for slavery anywhere, and many openly deplored it everywhere, but few saw it in constitutional terms. "No gentleman within these walls detests every idea of slavery more than I do," a hero of the Revolution, General William Heath, declared at one point. "It is generally detested by the people of this Commonwealth,—and I ardently hope that the time will soon come, when our brethren in the southern States will view it as we do, and put a stop to it, but to this we have no right to compel them."[45] At another point, Samuel Thompson, a general in the Maine militia during the Revolution, snapped at a reference to the likely first president. "Oh! Washington, what a name has he had," Thompson lamented, "but he holds those in slavery who have as good right to be free as he has—He is still for self; and in my opinion, his character has sunk 50 per cent."[46]

As if they did not matter much to their state, neither the three-fifths compromise nor the Fugitive Slave Clause generated much discussion among the Massachusetts delegates. They mostly commented on the three-fifths compromise as a formula for direct taxation, and that seemed fair to many. "Lands cultivated by slaves are not worth as much as lands cultivated by freemen," federalist leader Francis Dana noted, "it would be unjust to tax a slave as much as a freeman."[47] On extending the formula to representation, fellow federalist Thomas Dawes added, "Our *own* State laws and Constitution would lead us to consider those blacks as *free men*, and so indeed would our own ideas of natural justice." Then, they would count as whole persons, and "the Northern States would suffer" in representation.[48] Even though federal laws later passed under the Fugitive Slave Clause would prove especially controversial in Massachusetts a half-century later, no delegate objected to the provision itself.

The only clause in the Constitution relating to slavery that engendered extended debate was the one limiting Congress's otherwise plenary power over foreign imports for twenty years in the case of enslaved Africans or, as that clause put it, "such persons as any of the states . . . shall think proper to admit."[49] It stirred the ire of Shays' Rebellion leader and Revolutionary War officer Thomas Lusk, for example, who otherwise remained silent during the convention. In a long, impassioned speech, he spoke of "the miseries of the poor natives of Africa, who are kidnapped, and sold for slaves," and deplored "their wretched, miserable, and unhappy condition in the state of slavery."[50] He voted against ratification. "How much soever he liked the other parts of the Constitution," James Neal added, his Quaker beliefs "obliged him to bear witness against any thing that should favour the making merchandize of the bodies of men."[51] He too voted no.

Other delegates accepted the clause even if they rejected the Atlantic slave trade. "No man abhors that wicked practice more than I do," Isaac Backus said of the ongoing flow of enslaved Blacks into southern states. "But let us consider where we are, and what we are doing. In the articles of confederation, no provision was made to hinder the importation of slaves into any of those States: but now a door is open."[52] Trying to reason with the dissenters, General Heath asked, "If we ratify the Constitution, shall we do any thing by our act to hold the blacks in slavery—or shall we become partakers of other men's sins? I think neither of them." "The federal Convention went as far as they could" by empowering Congress to end the importation of enslaved Africans in 1808, he maintained.[53] So it went as delegates debated whether twenty years was too long to wait for halting a damnable practice.[54] On balance, the prospect of its ending at some fixed point likely helped federalists win a narrow victory in Massachusetts and, by doing so, carry the battle to other states with rising prospects for ratification.

Maryland and South Carolina loomed next—the first tests of the concessions made at the convention over slavery in states committed to sustaining the institution. Georgia had already ratified the Constitution of course, but Native Americans had reclaimed two-thirds of that thinly populated state's frontier and the white settlers there desperately needed the support of a fortified central government to retake it.[55]

Given its vulnerability to the whims of two big neighbors, Virginia and Pennsylvania, Maryland seemed to federalists as all but certain to ratify the Constitution when its convention met in April. "Maryland, most unquestionably, will adopt it," Washington confidently predicted on January 10.[56] An ardent antifederalist still reeling from her state's vote to ratify, Mercy Otis Warren of Massachusetts still clung to the hope that Maryland would "reject the system." In a nineteen-page panegyric to "the glorious fabric of liberty" under the decentralized confederation published in February, she calculated that Maryland, joined by the Carolinas, Virginia, New York, and Rhode Island, "may yet support the liberties of the Continent" by keeping federalists from gaining the nine states needed for ratification.[57]

Maryland surely disappointed Warren when voters at special elections marked by low turnout chose an overwhelming majority of federalists to the state convention. Those federalists then rammed through ratification with scarcely a nod to either liberty or slavery. It took only a few days, with the last one spent on a failed effort by antifederalists to secure Massachusetts-style recommendatory amendments. The convention ratified the Constitution on April 28, 1788, with eleven antifederalists from three tidewater counties standing against sixty-three members from Baltimore and outer parts of the state. Slaveholding played little if any role in the vote, with delegates from counties with plantation economies supplying most of the votes for each side.

In South Carolina, a state with 43 percent of its population in bondage (compared to 32 percent in Maryland), ratification played out in much the same way. Debate took place first within the state legislature for three days in mid-January over calling a state convention, and then for twelve days in May at the convention itself. Both bodies were grossly malapportioned in a manner that favored ratification. Only adult white males owning at least fifty acres of land or a city lot could vote for members of the legislature or delegates to the convention. Property owners tended to support the federalist cause. The designation of election districts also favored ratification: the federalist-dominated low country with a white population under 30,000 had over 50 percent more representatives than the antifederalist-leaning up-country with over 110,000 white people.

As it turned out, the battle over calling the convention proved more contentious than the convention itself. At the January debate in the legislature, the irascible former governor Rawlins Lowndes, a lawyer and slaveholder, spoke out repeatedly against the Constitution, citing in particular his opposition to any limits on the Atlantic slave trade. "Negroes were our wealth, our only natural resource, yet behold how our kind friends in the north were determined soon to tie up our hands," he roared. "They don't like our slaves, because they have none themselves, and therefore want to exclude us from this great advantage." Dismissing northerners as "governed by prejudices and ideas extremely different from ours," Lowndes called the Atlantic slave trade "justifiable on the principles of religion, humanity and justice, for certainly to translate a set of human beings from a bad country to a better, was fulfilling every part of those principles."[58] This became the core complaint of South Carolina antifederalists. Charleston physician and politician David Ramsey summed it up neatly: "They say that the northern States have no business to interfere with our importation of negroes . . . & that they should be allowed to import them forever."[59]

As much as anything else, Lowndes's rants prompted former Constitutional Convention delegate C. C. Pinckney (who owned 250 enslaved Blacks, more even than Lowndes) to give a broad defense of slaveholders' rights under the Constitution. "I confess," he offered in response to Lowndes, "I did not expect that we should have been told on our return, that we had conceded too much to the [north]eastern states when they allowed us a representation for a species of property which they have not among them." Pinckney then proceeded to give a slaveholder's bullet-point account of slavery under the Constitution. "We have secured an unlimited importation of negroes for twenty years," he said, "we have a security that the general government can never emancipate them, for no such authority is granted, and . . . we have obtained a right to recover our slaves in whatever part of America they may take refuge, which is a right we had not before." On balance, Pinckney concluded, "We have made the best terms for the security of this species it was in our power to make."[60]

On the fundamental importance of slavery for South Carolina, Rawlins and Pinckney agreed. "I am as thoroughly convinced as that gentleman is," Pinckney said, referring to Lowndes, "that the nature of our climate; and the flat, swampy situation of our country oblige us to cultivate our lands with negroes, and that without them S. Carolina would soon be a desert waste."[61] Pinckney simply believed that northerners at the Constitutional Convention had needed some concession on the Atlantic slave trade "to restrain the religious and political prejudices of [their] people on this subject," and felt that South Carolina could secure all the enslaved workers it needed by 1808.[62] A rising star among southern federalists, Pinckney became the Federalist Party's nominee for vice president in 1800 and for president in 1804 and 1808.

Locking arms with Pinckney, on January 19, South Carolina legislators voted to call a state ratifying convention for mid-May and, by a narrow margin, accepted Pinckney's motion for holding it in federalist-friendly Charleston rather than the state's newly designated capital of Columbia. Foreseeing no means to stop the rush to ratify, Lowndes declined his election to the convention, and no antifederalist arose to take his place in speaking out against the Constitution. All the delegates agreed on slavery anyway, with the average federalist delegate owning sixty-six enslaved persons, and the average antifederalist owning thirty-four. Thirty-nine of the 236 delegates, or one in six, owned over one hundred enslaved persons.

Delivering the opening address at the convention, C. C. Pinckney's cousin Charles Pinckney largely avoided the slavery issue. Instead, he painted the Constitution as a bulwark for civil liberty through carefully crafted institutional checks within the general government, and due distributional balances between general and state authority. "When we proceed to review the system by sections," he assured delegates, "it will be found to contain all those necessary provisions and restraints, which while they enable the general government to guard and protect our common rights as a nation . . . will secure to us those rights which, as the citizens of a state, will make us content." With the soaring rhetoric that marked his speech, he boasted of the American people, "It has been fated that we should be the first perfectly free people the world has ever seen."[63] Pinckney did concede the danger of union with the northern states, whose inhabitants he depicted as profoundly different from those of southern states. "The southern citizen beholds with a kind of surprise the simple manners of" New Englanders, he noted. "They in their turn seem concerned at what they term the extravagance and dissipation of their Southern friends, and reprobate as an unpardonable moral and political evil the dominion they hold over a part of the human race."[64] Slavery, Pinckney warned in this opening address, divided America and its people on sectional and religious bases.

Less than two weeks after convening, with much of that time spent on procedural matters, the delegates ratified the federal Constitution by a vote of 149 to 73. Voting en bloc on every matter, federalists accepted five recommendatory amendments, including one further safeguarding state-sanctioned slavery by making explicit that states "retain every power not expressly relinquished by them" in the Constitution.[65] Unlike Hancock's amendments in Massachusetts, however, none of these protected individual rights. C. C. Pinckney's account of why the South Carolina delegation at the Constitutional Convention opposed having a bill of rights could apply to rights-based amendments framed by a Congress dominated by northerners. "Such bills generally begin with declaring, that all men are by nature born free," he explained, "now we should make that declaration with a very bad grace, when a large part of our property consists in men who are actually born slaves."[66] South Carolina's proposed amendments protected states, not people.

Success in South Carolina left federalists only one state shy of the nine needed to secure ratification, with three states—Virginia, New York, and New Hampshire—opening their conventions in June.[67] New Hampshire was widely viewed as the most likely of them to ratify, but few seasoned observers thought that the United States could function without Virginia and New York. That made the outcome in those two big states crucial to the constitution-making process, with voters choosing among candidates committed on the overarching issue: ratify or not. For the first time, factionalism (if not outright partisanship) had taken hold in the United States at a national level.[68] Liberty would take center stage at all three conventions while slavery emerged from the wings to play a leading part only in Virginia.

Of the three overlapping June conventions, the one in Virginia met first, gathering 170 delegates to the State House in Richmond. No one knew which side held the advantage, especially after Washington opted not to stand as a delegate. "His presence alone in the Convention, would have carried twenty votes," St. Jean de Crèvecœur, the French counsel in New York, observed about the Virginia convention. "It is said that he fears that if he appears to be too zealous a federalist, that he would be accused of working for himself, since he cannot ignore the fact that if the new Constitution takes place, he is destined to become the first *great President*."[69] In letter after letter, however, the putative future president voiced his worries about the outcome, and in a particularly gloomy one termed it an "indispensable necessity" for Madison to serve as a delegate and lead the fight for ratification.[70] Once the delegate-election results emerged, Washington concluded that the two sides stood "pretty equally balanced."[71] Jefferson remained in Paris as the American ambassador and Richard Henry Lee declined to serve for health reasons, though Washington attributed Lee's indisposition to the wish of an old-money antifederalist not to play second fiddle at the convention to the demagogic upstart, Patrick Henry.[72]

With the opposition ceded to Henry, already justly famous for his 1775 "Give me liberty or give me death" speech, an over-the-top defense of liberty inevitably became the keynote in the case against the Constitution. "I consider myself as the servant of the people of this Commonwealth, as a centinel over their rights, liberty, and happiness," the silver-tongued Henry said in his opening volley at the convention, leading to his stern warning to Virginians about life under the Constitution: "Instead of securing your rights you may lose them forever."[73] Thus began a sustained barrage of some forty separate long speeches or short remarks by Henry over the course of the four-week convention, with his harshest jabs reserved for making the case for liberty lost and rights at risk. And for Henry, liberty largely meant states' rights because he viewed Virginia as the repository of his freedom. As his remarks became ever more direful, he warned Virginians of the special threat to slavery in a federal union dominated by northerners.

"*They'll free your niggers!*" Henry thundered about Yankees during the convention's final week.[74] "In this State there are 236,000 blacks," he explained, "but there are few or none in the Northern states, and yet if the Northern States shall be of the opinion, that our numbers are [insufficient for defense], may not Congress say, that every black man must fight," with this leading to a general emancipation? Henry offered this as but one example of how a northern-led Congress might destroy slavery under the Constitution. "They will search that paper, and see if they have power of manumission," he warned. "And have they not, Sir? Have they not power to provide for the general defence and welfare? May they not think that these call for the abolition of slavery?"[75] Pointing to the union's geographical scope, he had said from the convention's outset, "There will be no checks, no real balances, in this Government," and asked, "Would this, Sir, constitute happiness, or secure liberty?"[76] By the end, his method became clear. "The majority of Congress is to the North, and the slaves are to the South. In this situation, I see a great deal of the property of the people of Virginia in jeopardy," Henry concluded in his last extended harangue at the convention.[77]

Invoking his authority as a delegate to the Constitutional Convention and "acquaintance with a great many characters who favor this Government," George Mason made an important point that echoed Henry's warning. "There is no clause in the Constitution that will prevent the Northern and Eastern States from meddling with our whole property of that kind," Mason said of slavery. "There ought to be a clause in the Constitution to secure us *that* property, which we have acquired under our former laws, and the loss of which would bring ruin on a great many people."[78] At the convention, Mason had demanded a bill of rights and had voted against the Constitution in part for failing to have one. The lack of explicit protection for the right to maintain state-sanctioned slavery, he now made clear, had numbered among his principal concerns, which he proposed safeguarding by a clause reserving to the states "every Power, Jurisdiction and Right" not "expressly delegated to the Congress."[79]

Virginia federalists who had served at the Philadelphia convention sought to reassure delegates that the Constitution posed no threat to slavery. "I was struck by surprise when I heard him express himself alarmed with respect to the emancipation of slaves," Madison said of Henry. "There is no power to warrant it, in that paper," he commented on the Constitution.[80] Having switched sides on ratification, Edmund Randolph now reasoned from inclusion of the Fugitive Slave Clause, "When authority is given to owners of slaves to vindicate their property, can it be supposed they can be deprived of it?"[81] The presence of such a clause in the Constitution, the future first U.S. attorney general argued, established a federal right for state-sanctioned slavery. Mason disagreed: "No real security could arise from the clause," he declared; it "only meant, that run-away slaves should not be protected in other States." This protection did not extend to assaults on slavery by the general government.[82] Not so, Madison replied with an allusion to the significance attached to the Clause by Constitutional Convention delegates from South Carolina and Georgia, "Even the Southern States, who were most affected, were perfectly satisfied with this provision, and dreaded no danger to the property they now hold."[83] Looking beyond the explicit provisions of the Constitution, Henry snapped of Madison, "He asked me where was the power of emancipating slaves. I say it will be implied, unless implication be prohibited" by a constitutional amendment.[84]

Turning Henry's arguments on their head, federalists asserted that ratification promoted liberty by replacing a feeble confederation with a secure general government. "There is no peace, Sir, in this land: Can peace exist with injustice, licentiousness, insecurity, and oppression?" Randolph asked near the outset of the convention. "These considerations, independent of many others which I have not yet enumerated, would be a sufficient reason for the adoption of this Constitution, because it secures the liberties of the citizen, his person, and property."[85] Turning to those other factors, he raised the specters of invasion and insurrection. "Are we not weakened by the population of those whom we hold in slavery?" Randolph asked. "The number of those people, compared to that of the whites, is an immense proportion: Their number amounts to 236,000—that of whites only to 352,000. Will the American spirit, so much spoken of, repel an invading army" or suppress an insurrection, with so many enslaved Blacks in Virginia?[86] "I see Virginia in such danger," he warned, "if we disunite from the other States."[87] Union, he declared, would protect slavery.

For his part, Madison pointed with pride to the Fugitive Slave Clause as further reason for Virginia slaveholders to embrace the Constitution. "At present, if any slave elopes to any of those States where slaves are free, he becomes emancipated by their laws," in a *Somerset*-like interpretation of the confederation that must have surprised some delegates. The Fugitive Slave Clause "was expressly inserted to enable owners of slaves to reclaim them. This is better security than any that now exists."[88] By answering Henry point by point and painting the Constitution as a shield for slavery, Madison, Randolph, and other federalists defanged their opponents' most potent arguments and, by a slender ten-vote margin, secured ratification of the Constitution in Virginia on June 25. Two days later, in its final act, the convention adopted a series of recommendatory amendments starting with, "Each State of the Union shall respectively retain every power, jurisdiction and right, which is not by this Constitution delegated to the Congress."[89] That amendment, antifederalists hoped, would protect states' rights, including the right to maintain state-sponsored slavery.[90]

With their vote on the 25th, Virginia delegates thought they had delivered the pivotal ninth state to ratify the Constitution. By virtue of a short convention, however, New Hampshire had become that ninth state four days earlier; the news simply had not yet reached Virginia. It arrived at Washington's Mount Vernon on June 27, making the federalist celebration in nearby Alexandria, as Washington observed in a letter on the 28th, "the first public company in America, which had the pleasure of pouring libation to the prosperity of the ten States that had actually adopted the general government."[91]

In their June convention, New Hampshire delegates took only four days to ratify the Constitution. They had met for ten days the previous February, when they had debated the Constitution paragraph by paragraph. After federalists realized that they might fall short of victory, they had secured an adjournment until June, by which time they felt confident of winning over enough delegates to prevail.[92] At that second meeting, the federalist majority voted to dispense with further debate and, after approving recommendatory amendments modeled on those passed by Massachusetts, proceed directly to a vote on ratification, which passed by a margin of 57 to 47.

Years later, the son of one delegate to the New Hampshire convention recalled that the "strongest and leading argument urged against it was derived from the fact that the Constitution sanctioned or tolerated human slavery."[93] Antifederalist leader Joseph Atherton, for example, voiced opposition to the clause protecting the Atlantic slave trade for twenty years. It came down to his understanding of federalism and his moral duty as an American. "The idea that strikes those who are opposed to this clause so disagreeably and forcibly, is, hereby it is conceived (if we ratify the Constitution) that we become *Consenters to* and *Partakers in*, the sin and guilt of this abominable traffic," Atherton explained. While we are not morally obligated to "journey to the Carolinas to abolish the detestable custom of enslaving Africans," he noted, "we will not lend the aid of our ratification to this cruel and inhuman merchandize, even for a day. There is a great distinction in not taking a part in the most barbarous violation of the sacred laws of God and humanity; and our becoming guarantees for its exercise for a term of years."[94] Federalists answered Atherton by pointing to defects in the current system and prospects for enhanced liberty and prosperity under the new one.[95] Those sentiments carried the Constitution to ratification in a decisive ninth state.

Even after Virginia joined New Hampshire in ratifying the Constitution by the end of June 1788, federalists still wanted to secure the assent of New York. The state's large population, central location, and critical port made proceeding without it in the union virtually unthinkable. Led by the state's popular, four-term governor, George Clinton, antifederalists dominated the convention held at Poughkeepsie from June 17 to July 26. But news of ratification by a ninth and tenth state caused Clinton to release his partisans to vote in the best interests of their constituents, producing a 30 to 27 vote for the Constitution. Still, that slim margin required the abstention of six antifederalist delegates from rural districts and votes for ratification by twelve Clintonites from commercial regions. Delegates from the rural upstate, where cries for liberty resonated louder than those for unity, cast every no vote. In fact, throughout the debates leading up to and during the convention, both sides claimed the mantle of liberty, and neither side said much about slavery. New York remained one of the two northern states (along with neighboring New Jersey) not to have either ended slavery or passed a law for its gradual abolition. Although under assault, the institution retained support from federalists and antifederalists alike.[96]

On the federalist side, the emphasis on liberty marked the eighty-five essays authored by Hamilton, Madison, and John Jay and first published in four New York City newspapers under the pseudonym "Publius." Together, they invoke the word 143 times. Using it five times in "Federalist No. 1," Hamilton warned readers, "The vigour of government is essential to the security of liberty" and that ratifying the Constitution "is the safest course for your liberty."[97] In his first essay, Jay wrote of federalists being "enamoured of liberty."[98] Madison, in his initial offering as Publius, hailed liberty as "essential to political life."[99]

Although in his essays Madison stressed the southern conception of states' rights—that the "powers reserved to the several States will extend to all the objects, which, in the ordinary course of affairs, concern the lives, liberties and properties of the people"—the essays expressly mentioned domestic slavery only three times.[100] Twice, in passing references, they boasted of the Constitution's allowing the new government to bar "the importation of slaves" after 1808. "By the old, it is permitted for ever," one essay added.[101] The sole extended discussion of slavery in *The Federalist* appeared in a labored defense of the three-fifths compromise. Much like New York state law, Publius argued, that compromise treated enslaved humans as part property and part person. Akin to how it treated domesticated animals, the author explained, state law treated enslaved humans as property by depriving them of "liberty" and making them "vendible by one master to another." At the same time, by the protection offered under state law to every enslaved human against violence by others, Publius added, "and in being punishable himself for all violence committed against others, the slave is no less evidently regarded by the law as . . . a moral person, not as a mere article of property." In this manner, Publius wrote, existing state law, like the compromise, "regards the *slave* as divested of two fifths of the *man*."[102] Of course, the three-fifths compromise gave that part-person's part-vote to free whites.

At the New York ratifying convention, the lead federalist speaker, Robert R. Livingston (much like his federalist counterpart in South Carolina, Charles Pinckney), opened the case for ratification by asserting that the Constitution centralized only "so much power" as necessary "to ensure our liberties and the blessing of a well ordered government."[103] In their initial replies, the two principal antifederalist speakers, John Lansing Jr. and Melancton Smith, retorted that the union of American states should not come at the cost of liberty.[104] These comments set the stage for much that followed, with Clinton gleefully depicting antifederalists as "the Friends to the Liberties of our Country" and federalists as "the Advocates for Despotism."[105] As in pre-convention commentary, slavery came up only sporadically at the convention. In his opening statement, for example, Smith objected to the three-fifths compromise but subsequently yielded to Hamilton's view of it as a needed concession to southern states.[106] Later, Hamilton listed the power "to prohibit importation of slaves" after 1808 as one of the Constitution's "miscellaneous advantages."[107] Nothing else about slavery appears in the surviving record from the convention.[108]

As a practical matter, the new Constitution took effect after its ratification by New York in July 1788. Federal elections followed in eleven states over the next six months. The new Congress convened in New York City on March 4, 1789. After Congress notified Washington that the electors had unanimously chosen him as president in the first federal election, he took office eight weeks later.

While affirming the unity of the American states and confirming the homage paid by Americans to liberty, the ratification process laid bare deep divisions over slavery between northern and southern states that had not existed before the Revolutionary era. If they believed what they said about slavery under the Constitution at their state conventions, then such key founders as James Wilson of Pennsylvania and C. C. Pinckney of South Carolina gave starkly different meanings to the constitutional clauses relating to slavery. Wilson argued that the clauses undermined it, while Pinckney said they protected it—and both were federalists. Within one state and at the same convention, Henry and Madison expounded those clauses in similarly divergent terms. And whereas southern antifederalists like Henry, Mason, and Lowndes painted the Constitution as a mortal threat to slavery, Gerry, Atherton, and other northern antifederalists portrayed it as a boon to slaveholders.

Liberty united the states; slavery was dividing them into North and South; yet the two emerging national factions, federalism and antifederalism, both bridged sectional divisions by incorporating antislavery partisans from the North and proslavery partisans from the South. Even when those factions hardened into political parties—John Adams's Federalists versus Thomas Jefferson's Democratic-Republicans—both retained their northern antislavery and southern proslavery camps, which would help to hold the nation together for a season.[109]

Yet even as a shared devotion to liberty united Americans during the Revolutionary era, northern federalists increasingly extolled a nationalized, ordered liberty that might or might not include the freedom to enslave others, while southern antifederalists embraced a states'-rights form of liberty that did not extend freedom to Blacks. As the Revolutionary spirit waned, the task of construing the Constitution for liberty and slavery fell to a new general government, states now operating within a federal system, and the people living within the expanding domain of these United States. Provisions in the Constitution not discussed in this context during the drafting or ratification process came into play during the antebellum battles over slavery. These included the Preamble's invocation of "We, the People, . . . to secure the Blessings of Liberty to ourselves," the provision guaranteeing the citizens of each state the privileges and immunities of the citizens of the several states (Article IV, Section 2), and the Habeas Corpus Clause (Article I, Section 9). In the hands of antislavery advocates, such provisions became tools to combat enslavement much as the Northwest Ordinance of 1787, passed by Congress during the Constitutional Convention, became a precedent for outlawing slavery in some federal territories. On liberty and slavery, this Constitution had many uses, and not always a clear meaning. The ambiguities needed to secure ratification by already divided states would in the decades to come sow seeds of disunion as the nation expanded and sectional schisms deepened. In its attempts to mediate liberty and slavery, the founders' compromised Constitution left them on a collision course.

CHAPTER TEN

"I Am Free"

Liberty and Slavery under the Federal Government,
1789–1795

"About ten o'clock I bade adieu to Mount Vernon, to private life, and to domestic felicity," George Washington wrote in his diary for April 16, 1789, "and with a mind oppressed with more anxious and painful sensations than I have words to express, set out for New York in company with Mr. Thompson, and colonel Humphries."[1] Congress had sent its longtime secretary, Charles Thompson, to inform Washington of his election as president. David Humphries of Connecticut had served as the general's aide-de-camp during the American Revolution and as a subordinate at Mount Vernon in the late 1780s. The party also included two enslaved postilions for Washington's carriage, Giles and Paris, and (until left behind in Philadelphia for medical care) the general's enslaved valet, William Lee. These servants wore bright livery emblazoned with the Washington family coat of arms and rode outside the coach. Although needed for the 250-mile-long trip and on display as visible parts of the president-elect's party, Giles, Paris, and Lee went unmentioned in Washington's diary and newspaper accounts of the widely reported journey.[2]

Although not planned as such, Washington's journey through

six states from his home in Virginia to his inauguration in New York became a movable celebration consummating the constitutional union of the states.³ Feted at fourteen stops along the way, with many of those towns and cities reporting larger crowds than had ever assembled in them before, liberty emerged as the unifying theme throughout.⁴

Washington's reception in Baltimore on April 17 was typical. After Philadelphia and New York, Baltimore was the third-largest city on the general's itinerary and, with a population of some 13,500 people (nearly a tenth of them enslaved), the fifth-largest in the union. "We behold," the formal welcome on behalf of the city's residents declared, "an extraordinary thing in the annals of mankind; a *free* and enlightened people, choosing, by a *free* election, without a dissenting vote, the late commander in chief of their armies to watch over and *guard their civil rights* and privileges."⁵ With former Constitutional Convention delegate James McHenry leading the list, most (if not all) of the people signing this proclamation held Blacks in bondage. All of the signers were white.⁶

From Baltimore, after four intermediate stops, Washington reached Philadelphia on April 20, where he received his most enthusiastic reception of the trip. "Who can describe the heartfelt [con]gratulations of more than twenty thousand *free* citizens, who lined every fence, field and avenue," one local newspaper reported. "All classes and descriptions of citizens discovered (and they felt what they discovered) the most undisguised attachment and unbounded zeal for their dear Chief."⁷ The author's use of the word "free" to describe these spectators perhaps reflected the pride Pennsylvanians then took in being the first state (and in 1789, still the only state outside New England) to have abolished slavery—or at least set it on a path toward elimination by passing a gradual abolition statute.

Numbers told the tale. From about 6,000 in 1770, the tally of enslaved persons in Pennsylvania dropped to under 4,000 by Washington's visit, with most residing in rural areas. Slavery had virtually disappeared in Philadelphia—a point of distinction embraced by its citizens.⁸ In contrast, tiny Delaware, the state Washington had just left, with a tenth of

Pennsylvania's total population, had over twice as many enslaved persons, or fifteen percent of its people compared to less than one percent in Pennsylvania. New Jersey, where Washington went next, counted over 11,000 enslaved people, and New York had twice that number but also twice as many people, so that each state held about six percent of its population in bondage.[9] Of course, Washington need not worry about passing through Pennsylvania with Giles, Paris, and Lee. The state's gradual abolition act allowed nonresident slaveholders to retain their human property in Pennsylvania for up to six months, and resident slaveholders to retain indefinitely those born prior to the act's passage and registered within seven months of its effective date.

Perhaps sensitive to the image created by parading through Philadelphia in a carriage attended by enslaved coachmen and footmen, Washington, upon reaching Chester, Pennsylvania (near the Delaware state line), mounted a large white horse to ride the final twenty miles into town. Governor Thomas Mifflin had met Washington at the border along with other dignitaries and four state military units, two mounted and two on foot, complete with fifes and drums. With Washington and Mifflin in front, this entourage, joined by a snowballing number of citizens, processed into Philadelphia with Washington's coach obscurely in the rear. No local newspaper article mentioned the coach or its Black attendants, and none noted any Blacks in the crowd.[10] Crossing the Schuylkill River at Gray's Ferry south of the city, the party passed over a bridge adorned with triumphant arches and a tall pole topped with a liberty cap and flying a blue rattlesnake flag bearing the motto "Don't tread on me."[11] Freedom was on display. Welcoming speeches echoed the theme.

That motif had sounded in Chester, where the mayor hailed Washington as "the public guardian of the liberty."[12] It resounded in Philadelphia, where the public banquet held in Washington's honor raised the federalist toast to "liberty without licentiousness."[13] After Philadelphia and five stops in New Jersey, Washington crossed New York Harbor on a purpose-built barge and glided into the city at the foot of Wall Street, where thousands welcomed him to the new federal capital. Speakers there hailed popular rule and federal union but liberty stood out as the uni-fying theme. The president's own inaugural address, delivered on April 30, 1789, recalled the country's "arduous struggle for its liberties" and spoke of "a reverence for the characteristic rights of *freemen*."[14] He did not elaborate on what this phrase implied for the rights of women and men not free, but notably it did not differentiate among classes of free-men. With this, the first federal administration began.

Martha Washington had remained behind at Mount Vernon for an additional month before starting her trip to New York on May 16 with four more enslaved attendants, including her sixteen-year-old personal maid, Ona Judge.[15] The daughter of Betty, an enslaved mixed-race seam-stress whom Martha Washington had brought to Mount Vernon in 1759 as part of her dower estate, and Andrew Judge, an English-born white indentured servant under contract to George Washington during the mid-1770s, Ona Judge became part of Martha's dower property at her birth in 1773. Later described as having a freckled face, black eyes, and bushy hair, Judge lived at Mount Vernon with her mother in a commu-nal dormitory for enslaved house servants.[16] Washington later called Ona Judge "handy & useful . . . a perfect Mistress of her needle."[17] His indentured servitude having ended, Judge's father departed Mount Ver-non around 1780 for the life of a free white Virginian, leaving Betty and his enslaved daughter behind. Before having Ona, Betty had given birth to at least three other children by two different men, and would later have at least one more by another man, giving Judge four known half-siblings at Mount Vernon. In 1783, Martha Washington selected Judge as her maid and, in 1789, took Judge along with one of Judge's half-broth-ers, Austin (but not Betty), to serve her in New York.

Although urban slavery in the North always differed from planta-tion slavery in the South, New York City remained a comfortable place for slaveholders in 1789. Many wealthy white New Yorkers still held enslaved Black workers and used them openly as domestics at home and as postilions when traveling about town. The Washingtons could do so without exciting comment. In fact, in 1788, New York became the first independent American state to reenact its colonial slave code, ensuring that, despite the change in sovereignty, chattel slavery remained legal.[18]

Three years earlier, however, a small group of prominent New Yorkers under the leadership of John Jay, who then served as the Confederation's secretary of foreign affairs, had formed a state Manumission Society to work for the immediate mitigation and eventual abolition of slavery in New York. Arguing in terms of Revolutionary principles—as he wrote in one typical letter, "To contend for our own liberty, and to deny that blessing to others, involves an inconsistency not to be excused"—Jay had promoted various schemes of gradual abolition for New York since the Revolution began.[19] The state legislature had passed a gradual abolition statute in 1785, only to have it vetoed by Governor George Clinton's Council of Revision purportedly (but disingenuously) because it did not sufficiently protect free Blacks. A fixture in New York politics during the Revolutionary era, Clinton relied on rural Dutch slaveholders in the lower Hudson River valley as part of his political base. No other abolitionist legislation passed in New York so long as Clinton remained governor, and he served until 1795.

Until then, even as the number of both enslaved people and slaveholders in New York City rose, the Manumission Society succeeded mainly in defending the rights of those Blacks already free.[20] Its only legislative victories came in toughening state laws against importing and exporting Africans, securing jury trials for enslaved persons in capital cases, and, most notably, making the voluntary manumission process easier. Prior to the Revolution, every colony discouraged manumission. New York and other northern colonies required that slaveholders, as a prerequisite to freeing anyone, post bonds guaranteeing to pay all costs should the freed person need public assistance.[21] Virginia and many southern colonies barred slaveholders from freeing persons without the express consent of the legislature.[22] These restrictions weighed heavily on Quakers, Methodists, and others compelled to manumit their human property or face religious exclusion. By 1786, New York and other northern states had dropped the bond requirement for manumitting persons certified as capable of supporting themselves.[23] During the same period, Virginia and some other southern states authorized private emancipations for healthy, working-age Blacks. These reforms led to spikes in the number of free Blacks, but births and imports meant that the total count of enslaved persons was not reduced. In every state, only compulsory abolition laws, not voluntary action, reduced the incidence of slavery.

New York did not enact a gradual abolition law until 1799, after Jay became governor. During the seventeen months from March 1789 to August 1790 that it served as the federal capital, New York City remained a friendly seat for slaveholding members of Congress and the administration, including Secretary of State Thomas Jefferson and Attorney General Edmund Randolph. Both of these cabinet officers brought along enslaved servants from Virginia, though Jefferson left his mixed-race mistress Sally Hemings behind.[24] The only New Yorker in Washington's cabinet, Alexander Hamilton, opposed slavery in principle but, having married into a prominent slaveholding family, likely owned some domestic servants as well.

At the time, over 25 percent of the households in New York City contained enslaved workers. That figure rose to about 40 percent in surrounding counties—the highest percentage in the northern states—with most of these households holding only one or two persons in bondage.[25] With so many enslaved workers in the area, more households likely participated in the slaveholding economy by leasing enslaved labor as required for particular tasks. "In the vicinity of New York," an English emigrant commented, "every respectable family had slaves—negroes and negresses who did the drudgery."[26] Typically living apart in the cellars or garrets of the homes of their white owners, these Blacks lacked the often communal culture of plantation life in the South.[27] After his wife arrived with her entourage, the president packed a household staff of about twenty enslaved, indentured, and free servants along with his family and offices into a three-story mansion near the East River. Needing more space, in February 1790 the household moved to a four-story mansion on Broadway near Bowling Green, in a fashionable area of the lower west side recently rebuilt after devastating fires during the Revolutionary War. Described at the time as "the place of residence of the most opulent inhabitants" of New York, the neighborhood had a particularly high number of slaveholding households.[28]

During the Washingtons' stay in New York, Ona Judge and other enslaved servants inevitably worked and mingled with more free Blacks than they had ever known in Virginia. Then America's second-largest urban center after Philadelphia, with some 32,000 people living on the southern end of Manhattan Island, New York City had some 3,000 nonwhite residents—about a third of them free.[29] "Nothing has occurred that should mark this place from one in England except a somewhat greater number of Blacks," a British visitor wrote home from New York City at the time.[30] "Most of the inferior labor of the town is performed by Blacks, some of the petty shops are kept by them and inferior trades carried on," he added in his diary, "many of the Blacks here are not slaves."[31] Judge would have met these free Black shopkeepers, tradesmen, and laborers as she ran errands and did chores for her mistress. Commenting on the skin color of local Blacks, "particularly of women and children in the streets," the traveler noted in a comment that could have included Judge, it "may be seen of all shades." Even the lightest of them, he remarked, who could pass for white "without detection . . . may still be slaves."[32] Judge still was enslaved but, biding her time and her tongue, began entertaining dreams of liberty.

Without acknowledging the ferment over slavery surrounding him in New York, Washington proceeded with the business of forging a nation. For him and other federalists in his circle, that meant building on unifying concepts of liberty and suppressing sectional divisions over slavery. In his dealings with Congress during his first year in office, Washington relied heavily on James Madison who, as a representative from Virginia, served as the president's de facto "prime minister" or effective link with Congress.[33] Indeed, historians generally credit Madison with composing the inaugural address that Washington delivered to Congress in April 1789. In it, Washington depicted "the preservation of the sacred fire of liberty . . . as *deeply*, perhaps as *finally* staked, on the [American] experiment" in government. From this rhetorical high point, he turned to the issue of constitutional amendments, which remained a popular concern as expressed at multiple state ratifying conventions. Using words presumably drafted by Madison, Washington gave his blessing to Congress framing such amendments as would "safely and advantageously" promote the "the characteristic rights of freemen."[34] This passage neatly summarized Madison's evolving vision for a bill of rights.

After opposing the adoption of a bill of rights at the Constitutional Convention in 1787 and dismissing such written provisions as ineffective "parchment barriers" against a popular government during the ratification debates of 1788, Madison switched his stance during his run for Congress.[35] In campaign letters from January 1789, he hailed the addition of a bill of rights to the Constitution as serving "the double purpose of satisfying the minds of well meaning opponents, and of providing additional guards in favour of liberty."[36] In particular, he called for amendments protecting "all those essential rights, which have been thought in danger, such as the rights of conscience, the freedom of the press, trials by jury, exemptions from general warrants, &c."[37] "Such amendments," he asserted, "will render certain vexatious abuses of power impossible."[38]

Jefferson, in a series of private letters from France, had brought Madison around. "A bill of rights is what the people are entitled to against every government on earth, general or particular, & what no just government should refuse or rest on inference," Jefferson wrote in a letter that reached Madison in July 1788, after the Virginia ratifying convention ended.[39] In his reply to Jefferson, Madison explained his change of heart. "In our Government," he wrote in a characteristic manner, "the invasion of private rights is *chiefly* to be apprehended, not from acts of Government contrary to the sense of its constituents, but from acts in which the Government is the mere instrument of the major number of the constituents." Previously, Madison had seen bills of rights (like the Magna Carta) as mainly useful against a government acting contrary to the popular will, but he now realized their value against a tyranny of a majority faction as well. "The political truths declared in that solemn manner," he wrote of formally articulated rights, "acquire by degrees the character of fundamental maxims of free Government, and as they become incorporated with the national sentiment, counteract the impulses of interest and passion."[40] Jefferson, after reading this reply, applauded Madison's reasoning and added a further benefit from a bill of rights: "The legal check which it puts in the hands of the judiciary." Regarding Madison's fear of majoritarian assaults on liberty, such as by legislatively imposed limits on religious freedom, Jefferson warned that under the Constitution, with its strong presidency, "The tyranny of the legislatures is the most formidable dread at present, and will be for long years. That of the executive will come in it's turn." Here too, Jefferson hoped, a bill of rights might help to preserve liberty.[41]

Having campaigned on a pledge to secure a bill of rights, Madison made obtaining one a chief aim of his first term in office. In Congress, with most federalists (still an informal faction and not yet a formal party) more interested in erecting a strong central government than crafting amendments limiting one, Madison had to prod his colleagues incessantly to get anything done. Having Washington endorse the project in his inaugural address helped but, after that, Madison carried on virtually alone. Antifederalists in Congress supported amending the Constitution, of course, but they made up a distinct and isolated minority of the members and, in addition to a bill of rights, they wanted the sort of structural reforms that Washington and Madison deplored. "Avoid every alteration which might endanger the benefits of an United and effective Government," Washington had admonished Congress in his inaugural address.[42] "I should be unwilling to see a door opened for a reconsideration of the whole structure of the Government," Madison added in his June 8, 1789, speech to Congress that launched the amendment process. "But I do wish to see a door opened to consider, so far as to incorporate those provisions for the security of rights, against which I believe no serious objection has been made by any class of our constituents." Such amendments, he said, would "satisfy the public mind that their liberties will be perpetual."[43]

Having surveyed the recommendatory amendments adopted at the various state conventions, Madison offered his draft amendments to Congress on June 8, 1789—four months after its first session began. Nine in number but somewhat different from the twelve that Congress finally passed, Madison's proposals had the hortatory tone of generally accepted political truths declared in a solemn manner that could become fundamental maxims of free government. For example, Madison's fourth declared in part, "The people shall not be deprived or abridged of their right to speak, to write, to publish their sentiments; and the freedom of the press, as one of the great bulwarks of liberty, shall be inviolable."[44] All reasonable Americans accepted these "simple, acknowledged principles" of liberty, Madison reasoned, yet repeating them could help enshrine them.[45]

Crafting amendments to the Constitution without precedent for the process, Madison composed them as alterations integrated to the existing text, with most of those involving individual rights (such as the freedom of religion, speech, and assembly) incorporated into the existing Article I, Section 9, which imposed express limits on the powers of Congress. When Roger Sherman succeeded in getting Congress instead to approve them as appendages to the end of the Constitution, they assumed their distinctive final form, "Congress shall make no law respecting the establishment of religion . . . or abridging the freedom of speech," and the like, rather than as blanket bans against government action or declarations of universal rights.[46] Further, Madison's first proposed amendment, which would have given a Jeffersonian ring to the Constitution's Preamble by stating, "That government is instituted . . . for the benefit of the people; which consists in the enjoyment of life and liberty, with the right of acquiring and using property, and generally of pursuing and obtaining happiness and safety," disappeared in the final iteration.[47] It would have made little sense as an appendage, but as a Preamble it might have carried the weight of similar language in the state constitutions of Massachusetts, Pennsylvania, and New Hampshire, which shook the foundations of slavery there even though they too contained assurances about the rights of acquiring and possessing property.

Faced with a federalist Congress skeptical of revising the Constitution, Madison threaded the needle between putting a meaningless gloss on liberty and proposing basic reforms that could not pass. He may not have wanted to do anything more anyway.[48] In their private letters, many federalist members of Congress expressed relief in the limited nature of Madison's proposals. Some of these federalists depicted them as a sop designed to lure North Carolina and Rhode Island into the union, and a few used the then-popular metaphor, "a tub to the whale," to dismiss them as distractions thrown out to save the ship of state from disaffected antifederalists.[49] Still, the federalist Congress successively trimmed them in committee, the full House of Representatives, the Senate, and a final conference committee before sending a final twelve amendments to the president in September with the request that he forward them to the states for ratification.[50] Many antifederalists deemed these amendments as insufficient to address their concerns for liberty. They did not stand in the way of states ratifying them, however, which the requisite number did by the end of 1791 for the ten amendments that later became known as the Bill of Rights.[51]

Whatever these amendments meant for liberty, given the role played by Madison in their composition and every southern state except Georgia in their ratification, they did not threaten state-sanctioned slavery. They followed the advice given to Madison by North Carolina federalist William Davie regarding the form most likely to win the approval of delegates to his slaveholding state's upcoming ratifying convention. "Instead of a Bill of rights attempting to enumerate the rights of the Indivial," Davie wrote, "they seem to prefer some general negative confining Congress to the exercise of the power particularly granted, with some express negative restrictions in some important cases."[52] By including a provision reserving to the states and individuals those powers not delegated to Congress, South Carolina representative William L. Smith wrote, "If these amendmts. are adopted, they will go a great way in preventing Congress from interfering with our negroes after 20 years or prohibiting the importation of them."[53] No one foresaw abolitionists invoking the Fifth Amendment's Due Process Clause to hobble the utilization of federal fugitive-slave laws.

In her history of the ratification process, Pauline Maier describes Madison's proposed first amendment as "a watered-down, condensed, rearranged version of the first three provisions of the Virginia Declaration of Rights (1776), without its opening assertion that 'all men are by nature equally free and independent.'" Judges in Massachusetts had used a similar phrase in their state constitution to end slavery, she noted, making southern slaveholders uncomfortable with it. Regarding proposals to include a statement regarding "the perfect equality of mankind" in the Bill of Rights, Madison said in his June 8 speech to Congress, "This, to be sure, is an absolute truth, yet it is not absolutely necessary to be inserted at the head of a constitution."[54] Having kept it out of the original Constitution, Madison was not inclined to raise the issue of slavery in the Bill of Rights.

Congressional passage of the Bill of Rights led to ratification of the Constitution by North Carolina in November 1789. Antifederalists had outnumbered federalists by two to one when the North Carolina ratifying convention first met in July 1788, three weeks *after* Virginia ratified the Constitution. These delegates knew that the federal government would go into effect regardless of what they did. This allowed antifederalists to argue that North Carolina should wait to see what amendments passed before ratifying.[55] Their comments highlighted their two principal concerns for North Carolinians (and, by extension, all southerners) under the Constitution: slavery and states' rights.[56]

"The property of the southern states consists principally of slaves,"

one leading antifederalist proclaimed at the July convention. If northerners in Congress "mean to do away [with] slavery altogether, this property will be destroyed."[57] Federalist delegate James Iredell, a future U.S.
Supreme Court justice, replied with a question, "Is there any thing in
this Constitution which says that Congress shall have it in their power
to abolish the slavery of those slaves who are now in the country?"[58]
He went on to present the Fugitive Slave Clause as a safeguard against
northern meddling with southern slavery. "In some of the northern states
they have emancipated all their slaves. If any of our slaves go there and
remain there a certain time, they would by the present laws, be entitled
to their freedom," Iredell said. "This would be extremely prejudicial to
the inhabitants of the southern states, and to prevent it, this clause is
inserted in the Constitution."[59]

With delegates reassured regarding the security of slavery under the
Constitution, antifederalists doubled down on states' rights. "I know it
is said that what is not given up to the United States will be retained by
the individual states. I know it ought to be so, and should be so understood; but, Sir, it is not *declared* to be so," another antifederalist pleaded.
"When there is no rule but a vague doctrine," he warned, Congress
"might exceed the proper boundary without being taken notice of."[60]

Such thinking won over most delegates. "I know the necessity of a
federal government," one delegate explained in a common lament, but "a
bill of rights ought to have been inserted to ascertain our most valuable
and unalienable rights."[61] By a margin of 184 to 84, members of the first
North Carolina convention voted "neither to ratify nor reject the Constitution." After approving thirteen proposed amendments, beginning with
one much like the future Tenth Amendment reserving to the states those
powers not delegated to Congress, they opted to wait and see what Congress did with them.[62]

When Congress then passed twelve amendments, including one
reserving to the states or the people all "powers not delegated to the
United States," North Carolina promptly ratified the Constitution at a
second convention in November 1789.[63] To reach this outcome, it also

mattered that a trusted southern planter had become president, and that North Carolina faced the prospect of Congress imposing foreign tariffs on its trade with other states if it did not join the union. When news of the outcome reached Iredell's home district, the federalist port of Edenton, the town erupted in a celebration of liberty.[64] A federalist poet encapsulated the spirit of the day in the refrain of an ode about North Carolina's ratification titled, "Twelfth Pillar Added to the Grand Federal Temple": "UNION the *Arch* / and LIBERTY the *Base*."[65] Regardless of the state's embrace of slaveholding, this poem presented liberty as the foundation for the new federal union.

With twelve states in the union, Washington in office, and legislation in place establishing the new government, Quakers revived the debate over slavery at the federal level by submitting antislavery petitions to Congress in February 1790. Members of the Society of Friends (or Quakers) had launched the American abolition movement before the Revolution and still supplied much of its energy. Now they had a new tool at their disposal—a general government. "The right of the people . . . to petition the government for a redress of grievances," as the new American Bill of Rights put it, dated back at least as far as Parliament's 1689 Declaration of Rights, which listed it among the "ancient rights of liberties" of English subjects.[66] By 1790, British abolitionists had used this right to flood Parliament with petitions urging an end to the Atlantic slave trade.[67] After having given Congress a year to organize, in a coordinated effort, the Yearly Meetings of New York and Philadelphia Quakers submitted petitions to the House of Representatives on February 11, 1790, urging Congress to do all it could to halt or hinder slavery and the Atlantic slave trade. A day later, a similar plea came from the Pennsylvania Abolition Society signed by its president, Benjamin Franklin, then in the eighty-fourth and final year of his storied life.

"From a persuasion that equal liberty was originally the Portion, and is still the Birthright of all Men," the Society's petition declared, "your Memorialists conceive themselves bound to use all justifiable endeavors to loosen the bands of Slavery and promote a general Enjoyment of the blessings of Freedom. Under these Impressions they earnestly entreat your serious attention to the subject of Slavery; that you will be pleased to countenance the Restoration of liberty to those unhappy Men, who alone in this land of Freedom are degraded into perpetual Bondage." The petition concluded by asking Congress to "step to the very verge of the Powers vested in you, for discouraging every Species of Traffick in the Persons of our fellow Men."[68]

At the time, Congress routinely referred petitions to committee for appropriate action. Viewing the antislavery petitions as plainly inappropriate, several southern members opposed even accepting them, much less referring them to committee. "If I understood it right," Representative Smith of South Carolina said of the Quaker petition from Philadelphia, "it prays that we should take measures for the abolition of the slave trade," which the Constitution protects for twenty years. "If, therefore, it prays for a violation of constitutional rights, it ought to be rejected," he stated.[69] "Referring [them] to committee will be great alarm to the people of the South," Smith added a day later about all three petitions.[70] Other southern members raised the stakes. Referring the petitions to committee, Aedanus Burke of South Carolina warned, would "be blowing the trumpet of sedition."[71] Not just sedition, Georgia's James Jackson thundered, "It would blow the trumpet of civil war."[72] "Do these men expect a general emancipation of slaves by law?" Thomas Tudor Tucker of South Carolina asked about the petitioners. "This would never be submitted to by the southern states without a civil war."[73] "Is clear to me as sun at noonday, if Congress abolishes slavery," Maryland's Michael Stone said of the federal union, "the southern states must give up the confederacy."[74] Burke cautioned, "The rights of the southern states ought not to be threatened."[75]

The irate southern response stirred some northern members to defend the petitioners and their petitions. Connecticut's great compromiser, Roger Sherman, said that he "could see no difficulty" in referring the petitions to committee. "The committee may bring in such a report as may prove satisfactory to gentlemen on all sides."[76] Several members noted that the petitioners only asked Congress to do what the Constitution allowed.[77] The irascible Elbridge Gerry of Massachusetts, who had fought the slavery compromises at the Constitutional Convention, predictably rose to the petitioners' defense. "It was the cause of humanity they had interested themselves in," he declared, "to wipe off the indelible stain which the slave-trade had brought upon all who were concerned with it." For one, he "thought the interference of congress fully compatible with the constitution, and could not help lamenting the miseries to which the natives of Africa were exposed by this inhuman commerce."[78] From this point, the congressional debate over referring the petitions threatened to descend into a sectional brawl over slavery.[79]

A shrewd parliamentarian who wanted nothing more than to have the issue disappear, James Madison knew that, while Congress could not constitutionally bar the importation of enslaved Africans until 1808, it could use its powers over commerce, the military, and federal territories (among others) to weaken slavery. Of these, the only one he mentioned in Congress at this point, perhaps because it carried the most weight, was the presumed power of Congress to limit slavery, as Madison here put it, in "the new States to be formed out of the Western Territory."[80] Madison recognized that he could more effectively forestall any congressional action against slavery by using, rather than resisting, legislative action.

"The best way to proceed in this business is to commit the memorials [to committee] without any debate on the subject," Madison advised his House colleagues. If they did so "as a matter of course," he said, "it could never be blown up into a decision of the question respecting the discouragement of the African slave-trade, nor alarm the owners with an apprehension that the general government were about to abolish slavery in all the states."[81] Northern members wanted to send the petitions to committee anyway and, with Madison supporting that result for his own reasons, they secured it over divided southern opposition on February 12, with all three going to a select committee created to consider them. For the time being, Madison had put off further House debate through a procedural maneuver, and now waited for the committee, which was meeting in private, to report.

The select committee submitted its findings to the full House on March 16. Without making any policy recommendations, it reported seven propositions of what, under the Constitution, Congress could or could not do about slavery. The first three of these stated that Congress could not prohibit the importation of enslaved persons until 1808, could not emancipate "slaves, who already are, or who may, within the period mentioned, be imported into, or born within, any of the said States," and could not interfere with the internal regulation of slavery in the states. The next four said that Congress could impose a ten-dollar tariff on imported slaves, could regulate conditions on slave ships, could bar foreign carriers from the U.S. slave trade, and could exercise these powers humanely. Despite Madison's having flagged the issue, the report said nothing about congressional power over slavery in the territories.[82] Its silence on the point suggested that members wanted to avoid this divisive issue. Although Madison accepted the report as a starting point for quieting the matter, he apparently worried about its oddly worded language regarding emancipation after 1808. Firebrands in Congress from Georgia and South Carolina saw nothing gained from any of the report's concessions. They moved to strike them and substitute a simple resolution rejecting the petitions as "unconstitutional, and tending to injure some of the states."[83] The debate over this motion produced the much strident defense of slavery yet heard in Congress, much of it in one long rant by Georgia representative James Jackson.

Painting a horrific picture of conditions in Africa and a happy one of plantation life, Jackson professed that Africans "would better be imported here by millions than stay in their own country." Rejecting the options of returning Blacks to Africa or freeing them in America, he argued that slavery was the best option for all concerned and perfectly compatible with the commands of "Jesus Christ, who allowed it in his day and his apostles after him." With slavery established in the South and essential to its economy, Jackson concluded, "Congress has no right to interfere."[84] As members rose to refute Jackson's points, the chair ruled the motion to strike the committee's report out of order, and the House settled down to address each proposition separately in deliberate fashion. By this point, Madison apparently hoped that members would put the issue to rest by turning the committee report into a final statement of congressional power over slavery.

The legislative process lasted a week, but one by one, and by narrow margins—some by but a single vote with odd-fellow coalitions of wary southerners and pragmatic northerners—the House pared the committee's seven propositions to three, which then passed. These declared Congress ineligible to ban the importation of slaves until 1808 or to interfere with slavery in the states ever, but free to regulate foreign sales of slaves and conditions on slave ships. The hint that Congress might have the power to emancipate enslaved persons born after 1808 disappeared, replaced by the blanket assertion, "That Congress have no authority to interfere in the emancipation of slaves."[85] With these propositions as precedent, Congress barred further debate on ending the slave trade before 1808 or on ever abolishing slavery. To seal this arrangement, Madison obtained consent to have the propositions printed in the House *Journal*, where they could stand as a guide for future action. Congressional power over slavery "has been so fully discussed," the *Journal* stated, "it cannot be supposed that gentlemen will go over the same ground again."[86] Although this statement did not specifically mention debate over slavery in the territories, Congress would not take it up until 1819, by which time Madison had come to question whether Congress had power to address it.[87] On the most divisive issues in antebellum American politics—free soil and slavery—silence would reign in the halls of Congress for a generation.[88]

Viewing slavery as at odds with democratic ideology but unwilling to abolish it or to free any of his own over 100 enslaved Blacks, Madison shuddered when politicians like Jackson defended slavery as a positive good, or when reformers like the Quakers damned it as an intolerable evil. Either approach invited disunion. Madison simply wanted Congress to ignore the issue and leave it for each state to address, including any newly admitted states in the west. Washington agreed, and said so in private.[89] "The Memorial of the Quakers (& a very mal-apropos one it was) has at length been put to sleep," he wrote in late March, "from which it is not [likely] it will awake before the year 1808."[90]

Even as Congress struggled with the Quaker petitions, Rhode Island battled over ratification. With twelve states having ratified by 1790, tiny Rhode Island could not hold out for long, especially after Congress began the process of imposing foreign trade restrictions on the seafaring state. The independent-minded Rhode Islanders who composed most of the population outside the urban centers of Providence and Newport opposed ratification; the commercial interest demanded it. Both sides saw their liberty at stake.

After having refused to call a state ratifying convention for two years, the lower house of the Rhode Island legislature narrowly passed a bill on January 15, 1790, approving elections for a state convention. With two members absent, the ten-member upper house rejected the measure a day later by a margin of four to five, with one of the negative votes coming from John Williams, a Baptist minister and descendant of the state's Baptist founder, Roger Williams. Governor John Collins then called for the legislature to reconvene the following day, a Sunday, which could not have occurred in any state except Rhode Island with its Baptist-inspired separation of church and state dating from Roger Williams's day. On Sunday, with John Williams absent due to his religious scruples against working on the Sabbath, the call for a convention passed both houses, with Collins breaking a four-to-four tie in the upper house.[91]

The business was not finished, however. With both sides claiming the mantle of liberty, voters outside the state's commercial centers elected a comfortable antifederalist majority to the state convention. That majority opted to meet for a week beginning on March 1, propose changes to the Constitution in the form of a bill of rights and structural amendments designed to secure individual liberty and states' rights, send those proposals to the towns for consideration, and adjourn until May 24.

Rhode Island antifederalists rested their resistance to the Constitution largely on concerns for states' rights, but they did not see this extending to the Constitution's twenty-year exemption for the Atlantic slave trade from the plenary power of Congress over international commerce. Traders themselves, most did not see foreign trade, especially the importation of enslaved persons, as a state matter. No other single issue consumed more time at the six-day session.

Antifederalist Joseph Stanton, who commanded state troops when they included a Black regiment during the Revolution, opened debate on the exemption. After reading aloud from the Constitution's Preamble about securing "the blessings of liberty to ourselves and our posterity," he asked, "Why in the Name of Common [Sense] should not this Liberty be extended to the Africans?"[92] "The southern states must answer for themselves," federalist Joseph Hazard replied. "They can regulate their Trade as they please—We are not interested [on] one Hand nor answerable in our Consciences on the other—They must answer for [their] own Crimes."[93] Antifederalist Job Comstock, whose cousin had led the Black regiment, disagreed. "We ought to address Congress on the subject— to bear Testimony against. Shall the same Community of which [we] are a part Join in Abominations?"[94] Federalist William Barton, who had served with Black soldiers during the war, agreed with Comstock. "We are *all* on board of one ship—The Ship of *Liberty*," Barton said. "If we come into the Compact—we partner with them. As I love the Constitution let us therefore show our Disapprobation of that Trade."[95] Formally decrying the practice as "disgraceful to the cause of liberty," the delegates passed an amendment calling on Congress, "as soon as may be," to end "the importation of slaves."[96]

After three months of public debate over the Constitution and the convention's proposed amendments, much of it bewailing the economic consequences of a trading and maritime state like Rhode Island remaining outside the federal union, delegates reconvened on May 24 in federalist-friendly Newport.[97] With little debate and even less apparent enthusiasm, the delegates ratified the Constitution with their amendments attached. "This day," the federalist *Newport Herald* reported in an article dated May 29, 1790, "exhibits an instance unparalleled in ancient or modern times, of a people rising from a state of anarchy, to liberty and order, without the horrors of a civil war."[98] All the original thirteen states had joined the constitutional union.

News of the Quaker petitions to Congress, and its referral of them to committee, had reached Rhode Island before the first session of its ratifying convention. Indeed, some federalists there unsuccessfully argued that delegates did not need to address the slave trade because Congress was doing so.[99] By the second session, when economic issues eclipsed all else in the delegates' minds, Treasury Secretary Hamilton's plan for the federal government to assume the states' Revolutionary era debts dominated the news from Congress. Rhode Island carried a high percapita war debt, making Hamilton's plan especially welcome.[100] In contrast, the mid-Atlantic states of Pennsylvania, Virginia, and Maryland had largely paid down their war debts. Led by Madison, their members opposed Hamilton's Funding Act in the House, where it failed twice. In June 1790, Secretary of State Jefferson brokered a compromise that gave northern states the Funding Act and the mid-Atlantic states the Residency Act, which moved the federal capital from New York to Philadelphia for ten years, and then to a new federal district on the banks of the Potomac River between Virginia and Maryland. The act removed the capital from a slaveholding city with a growing number of free Blacks to an abolitionist stronghold with a shrinking enslaved population, and then on to a region of entrenched slavery but in a district under federal jurisdiction. The first of these moves had a direct impact on the Washingtons and their enslaved servants, especially Ona Judge.

In 1790, Philadelphia offered a splendid example of a major American city recovering from slavery. For the state of Pennsylvania as a whole, the enslaved population had dropped from nearly 8,000 to under 4,000 over the previous decade. Philadelphia experienced an even steeper decline.[101] Some Pennsylvania farmers and mine owners clung to their enslaved workers, but proper Philadelphians did not. Unlike in New York, the cultural mores of Philadelphia had turned against slavery, and not just among Quakers. By 1783, Philadelphia physician Benjamin Rush—the founder whose public opposition to slavery went back to his 1773 pamphlet assailing it as contrary to Anglo-American principles of liberty— could write that any Philadelphian endorsing slavery "is listened to with horror, and his company avoided by every body."[102]

The 1790 census, conducted before the federal government moved to the city, reported virtually no enslaved persons in households on fashionable Market Street, where Washington lived during his seven years serving as president in Philadelphia, from November 1790 to March 1797. Governor Thomas Mifflin had none. Representative George Clymer, who signed both the Declaration of Independence and the Constitution, had none. U.S. Supreme Court Justice James Wilson, also a signer of both the Declaration and the Constitution, had none. Franklin's grandson Benjamin Bache, who had taken over the family printing business, had none. The wealthy former vice governor Charles Biddle had none. Even Senator and former superintendent of finance Robert Morris, once a major importer and merchant of enslaved Africans, reported none. All lived on Market Street near the president's house, which Morris owned and where Washington stayed during the Constitutional Convention. Yet Washington took eight enslaved domestics with him to Philadelphia and housed them in the official residence. Both Virginians in the cabinet, Randolph and Jefferson, who also lived on Market Street, brought along enslaved servants as well. They could not live without them.

At least initially, Ona Judge slept as a domestic in the room of Martha Washington's eight-year-old grandson, George Washington Parke Custis. The room shared an interior door to the president's bedroom, allowing Martha Washington to summon her maid at any time during the night even as Judge also tended to the boy's needs. These were Judge's duties as Martha Washington's personal attendant.[103] More than in New York, however, Judge met free Blacks while running errands or accompanying her mistress on visits to grand homes staffed by free servants.

On occasion, as a trusted domestic, Judge went to the theater or a visiting circus, or shopped with money given to her by the president. She had never seen a place like Philadelphia where free Blacks, although largely limited to menial jobs and the lowest rungs of the social order, formed their own churches, clubs, and community.[104] "I had many friends among the colored people of Philadelphia," Judge later commented, even as she complained that "she never received the least mental or moral instruction, of any kind, while she remained in Washington's family."[105]

By 1790, Philadelphia had become a magnet for free Blacks. After the exodus that occurred when the British army evacuated Philadelphia in 1778, only a few hundred free Blacks lived in the city by 1780. Hundreds of enslaved Philadelphians gained their freedom through voluntary manumissions during the 1780s, however, and even more arrived from the surrounding countryside and nearby states. Some of these came as fugitives, but many as legally free from places where freed Blacks could not safely remain. The liberalization of manumission laws in Virginia and Delaware during the 1780s led to a rise in free Blacks moving to Philadelphia from those states. Others came from farther afield. In 1795, for example, an English Quaker who received a Jamaican plantation in payment of a debt freed its workers and shipped them to Philadelphia, fearing their reenslavement should they remain in Jamaica. Further, during the 1790s, thousands of white refugees fleeing uprisings by enslaved and free Blacks in the French Caribbean colony of Saint-Domingue (later renamed Haiti) reached Philadelphia and other American cities. Some brought along enslaved Blacks, who, if they settled in Philadelphia, became free under state law—adding some 500 French West Indian Blacks to the local population. All told, the number of free Blacks in Philadelphia more than tripled from under 2,000 to over 6,000 during the 1790s, while the number of enslaved Blacks dropped from 273 to 55.

The proximity of free Blacks did not pose the only problem that Washington and other slaveholders in his administration faced from their move to Philadelphia. Although Pennsylvania's gradual abolition act did not protect runaways from other states or apply to persons owned and registered by state residents when the statute passed, it did stipulate that no one except members of Congress and foreign diplomats could bring enslaved persons into the state for longer than six months. Otherwise, they would become free. This news shocked Washington.

On April 5, 1791, nearly six months after the Washington household settled in Pennsylvania, Attorney General Randolph called on Martha Washington with disturbing news. Randolph had moved to Philadelphia somewhat before the president, and three of his enslaved servants had just claimed their freedom under state law. With the president out of town, Randolph wanted to warn the president's wife what might soon happen within her household. "I have therefore communicated it to you," Washington's personal secretary Tobias Lear wrote urgently to the president that same day, "that you might, if you thought best, give directions in the matter respecting the blacks in this family."[106]

At first, Washington thought that the law might not apply to him because, as he replied to Lear, "my residence is incidental as an Officer of Government only." Nevertheless, he asked Lear to inquire further into the law. If it did apply to the presidential household, which Lear soon found that it did, Washington directed that his enslaved servants rotate out of state every six months to prevent their emancipation. "If upon taking good advise it is found expedient to send them back to Virginia, I wish to have it accomplished under a pretext that may deceive both them and the Public," he wrote. "I request that these Sentiments and this advise may be known to none but *yourself & Mrs. Washington.*"[107]

Washington soon began rotating his enslaved servants back to Mount Vernon, or at least out of Pennsylvania. Indeed, Lear, in his next letter to Washington, reported Randolph's further advice concerning the presidential household's enslaved servants. "If," Lear wrote, "before the expiration of six months, they could, upon any pretence whatever, be carried or sent out of the State, but for a single day, a new era would commence on their return." Accordingly, he added, "Mrs Washington proposes in a short time to make an excursion as far as Trenton, and of course, she will take with her Oney & Christopher, which will carry them out of the State; so that in this way I think the matter may be managed very well."[108] A nephew of William Lee, Christopher Sheels, later replaced Lee as Washington's valet. By the time of this second letter from Lear, Martha Washington had already sent Ona Judge's brother Austin to Mount Vernon, disingenuously writing that she did so "to fulfill my promises to his wife."[109] On a later rotation back to Virginia, Austin drowned crossing the Susquehanna River, leaving Judge with no family members tying her to the presidential household in Philadelphia.

Even though it did not take long for them to understand the true purpose of their regular rotations to Mount Vernon, most of Washington's enslaved servants acquiesced in it. Judge did until May 1796. Her mother had died in 1795, leaving Judge with one less tie to Mount Vernon. Then, early in 1796, news leaked that Washington likely would not accept a third term as president, meaning that Judge would soon leave Philadelphia. Finally, on March 20, 1796, Martha Washington's strong-willed nineteen-year-old granddaughter, Elizabeth Parke Custis, married Thomas Law, a British citizen twice her age who had fathered three sons by an Indian mistress while serving as a British East India Company agent in Calcutta between 1773 and 1791. In 1794, Law moved to Alexandria, Virginia, where Custis lived, to speculate in land set aside for the new capital city. The Washingtons invited the newlyweds to visit them in Philadelphia, where Martha Washington expressed her intention of giving Judge to the bride as a wedding present. As a part of Martha Washington's dower estate, Judge would have gone to one the Custis siblings eventually, but she did not expect it to happen so soon.

"She did not want to be a slave always," a later interviewer reported Judge as saying, "and she supposed if she went back to Virginia, she would never have a chance to escape."[110] Referring to Elizabeth Custis, Judge spoke of a determination "never to be *her* slave."[111] According to her biographer, Erica Armstrong Dunbar, Judge also worried about what might happen to her in a house with Thomas Law, whose children by an Indian mistress had become a topic of gossip in Philadelphia.[112] "Whilst they were packing up to go to Virginia," Judge said in an interview about the Washingtons and their preparations for an extended summer visit to Mount Vernon in 1796, "I was packing to go, I didn't know where; for I knew that if I went back to Virginia, I should never get my liberty." Apparently, her transfer to the Laws would happen during that visit. Having already sent her belongings to friends in Philadelphia's Black community, Judge reported that she "left Washington's house while they were eating dinner."[113] Her escape came on Saturday, May 21, 1796. She never returned.

"ABSCONDED from the household of the President," read an advertisement in the next Monday's edition of the *Philadelphia Gazette*. "ONEY JUDGE, a light Mulatto girl ... of middle stature, slender, and delicately formed, about 20 years of age. She has many changes of good clothes." Her likely destination unknown, the paid notice continued, "As she may attempt to escape by water, all masters of vessels are cautioned against admitting her into them." The ad offered a $10 reward for her return, plus costs if retrieved from out of town.[114]

Judge had escaped by water, taking the commercial sloop *Nancy* to Portsmouth, New Hampshire, in late May. There she supported herself by taking odd jobs, and lived within the port town's small free Black community. The notice of her escape having spread widely, the daughter of New Hampshire senator John Langdon spotted Judge on a Portsmouth street in August and told her father, who informed the president. Known as a slaveholder who doggedly pursued runaways, Washington threw the weight of his office behind catching Judge. Having instigated the enactment of the Fugitive Slave Act of 1793, Washington could have followed its prescribed procedures of using federal courts to recover out-of-state fugitives, but (perhaps to avoid publicity) he tried less public means.[115] So long as he remained president, Washington discreetly enlisted the aid of Treasury Secretary Oliver Wolcott and Wolcott's chief officer in Portsmouth, Collector of Customs Joseph Whipple, to recover Judge.[116] A wealthy merchant who had given up slaveholding, Whipple tried persuasion and deception to gain Judge's return, but declined to employ force.[117] She refused to go.

Continuing the pursuit of Judge after leaving office, Washington dispatched his wife's nephew, Virginia attorney Burwell Bassett Jr., to Portsmouth in 1799.[118] By this time, Judge had married a mixed-race sailor, Jack Staines. She had taken Staines's name, and had given birth to the first of three children. Although Washington had told Bassett that he would *not* free her even if she returned voluntarily, Bassett promised her just the opposite when he first met Ona Staines. "I am free now and choose to remain so," she replied, and sent him away. Bassett then arranged to kidnap her. When Langdon (who, like Whipple, had renounced slavery by this point) learned of this plot, he warned Ona Staines, who fled to the safe house of free Black friends in a nearby village.[119] Bassett returned to Virginia without her.

On December 12, 1799, before he could try again to catch his wife's runaway maid, Washington died, leaving a will that freed his enslaved human property upon his wife's death. He could not reach the dower property of his wife, however. Under Virginia law, when Martha Washington died in 1802, Ona Staines passed with the rest of that dower property to members of the Custis family. They never recovered Staines, who remained a fugitive in New Hampshire, outlived her husband and children, became a devout Christian but increasingly impoverished, and died at age seventy-three on February 25, 1847. Asked if she regretted choosing liberty over slavery, Staines replied to one of her final interviewers, "No, I am free, and have, I trust been made a child of God by the means."[120] No patriot pamphleteer or orator—not Otis, Henry, Paine, nor Jefferson— ever expressed that sentiment with more commitment.

Banneker's Answer

I Am an American

"I am fully sensible of the greatness of that freedom which I take with you on the present occasion," Benjamin Banneker wrote to Thomas Jefferson in August 1791, "when I reflect on that distinguished, and dignified station in which you Stand; and the almost general prejudice and prepossession which is so prevalent in the world against those of my complexion."[1] Jefferson then served as America's first secretary of state with duties that included overseeing a boundary survey for the new federal district in Maryland and Virginia. Earlier in 1791, Banneker, a free Black farmer and almanac maker from rural Maryland, briefly assisted the Quaker land surveyor Andrew Ellicott with the federal-district survey. Banneker lived near the Ellicott family gristmills, and Andrew Ellicott's cousin had encouraged Banneker's talent for computing the local times for future sunrises, sunsets, and other celestial phenomena. When Banneker sent a table of his calculations for 1792 to Andrew Ellicott, who also made such ephemerides, Ellicott forwarded it to Pennsylvania Abolition Society president James Pemberton. He then shared it with Philadelphia astronomers and mathematicians as evidence of the reasoning ability of Black people at a time when comparative anthropology stood at its infancy.

The relative intellectual abilities of Blacks and whites had emerged as an issue in the Revolutionary era debates over slavery. In his 1776 *Dialogue Concerning Slavery*, the abolitionist-minded New England theologian Samuel Hopkins complained that white Americans viewed Blacks as fit for slavery because "we," as whites, "have been used to look on them . . . not as our brethren, or in any degree on a level with us; but as quite another species of animals." Slavery would end, he wrote, "If we could only divest ourselves of these strong prejudices, which have insensible fixed on our minds, and consider [Blacks] as, by nature, and by right, on a level with our brethren."[2]

By this time, some American supporters of slavery had begun to make the case for enslaving Blacks on supposedly scientific grounds, often drawing on the arguments of Scottish philosopher David Hume.[3] "I am apt to suspect the negroes, and in general all other species of men (for there are four or five different kinds) to be naturally inferior to the whites. There never was a civilized nation of any other complexion than white, nor even an individual eminent either in action or speculation," Hume wrote in a comment appended in 1753–54 to his xenophobic essay on nationality traits. "Such a uniform and constant difference could not happen, in so many countries and ages, if nature had not made an *original distinction* betwixt these breeds of men."[4] Such reasoning flew in the face of traditional biblical beliefs of common descent from a divinely created first human pair, but that would not bother a religious skeptic like Hume. His proslavery American disciples embraced the same religious heresy to defend their enslavement of Africans without relinquishing their commitment to liberty for those of their own kind, with some going so far as to lump Blacks with apes and baboons as a single species of Africans.[5]

Following a long but specious recitation of the relative mental, emotional, and physical attributes of whites and Blacks in his 1785 book *Notes on the State of Virginia*, Jefferson gingerly endorsed Hume's implicit polygenism—the belief in the separate creation of the various races or species of people. "Comparing them by their faculties of memory, reason, and imagination, it appears to me that in memory [Blacks] are equal to whites; in reason much inferior, as I think one could scarcely be found capable of tracing and comprehending the investigations of Euclid; and that in imagination they are dull, tasteless, and anomalous," Jefferson wrote. "Never yet could I find that a black had uttered a thought above the level of plain narration; never saw even an elementary trait of painting or sculpture." A litany of such observations led to his stated suspicion that, paraphrasing Hume, "The blacks, whether originally a distinct race, or made distinct by time and circumstances, are inferior to the whites." Slavery could not account for such differences because whites enslaved in ancient Rome, though held in conditions "much more deplorable than that of the blacks on the continent of America," excelled in the arts and sciences, Jefferson noted. Further, he added, some enslaved Blacks "have been liberally educated." This left race as the sole cause of the Black condition.[6]

Coming from a hero of the American Revolution, these widely read comments by Jefferson spurred abolitionists on a search for Black intellectual exceptionalism. They could not leave his views of inborn Black inequality unchallenged if they hoped to end slavery. If they could refute them, however, they felt that the logic of the proclaimed truths of human equality and the right of "all men" to liberty in Jefferson's Declaration of Independence assured their eventual success. "IF these solemn *truths*," New Jersey abolitionist David Cooper wrote in 1783, "are *self-evident*: unless [they] can shew that the African race are not *men*, words can hardly express the amazement which naturally arises on reflecting, that the very people who make these pompous declarations are slave-holders."[7] Abolitionists had Jefferson's polygenism in their crosshairs.

Princeton theologian Samuel Stanhope Smith, a critic of slaveholding, took aim at polygenism in a 1787 address to Philadelphia's American Philosophical Society published under the title *An Essay on the Causes of Variety of Complexion and Figure in the Human Species*. Marshalling far more observations of human types than Jefferson ever mustered, Smith defended the biblical "doctrine of one race" by arguing that skin color and other racial traits derive *solely* from environmental causes, primarily heat and sunlight, with black being "the tropical hue." Moreover, these superficial traits remain mutable. Africans removed to a temperate climate already exhibited some physical transition, Smith claimed, with those fed well and living in humane conditions changing the most. "Mental capacity," he stressed, "which is as various as climate, and as personal appearance, is, equally with the latter, susceptible of improvement, from similar causes."[8] Smith's environmentalism, if accepted, demolished the scientific case for race-based slavery.

Opponents of slavery had long touted the enslaved Boston poet Phillis Wheatley as an example of Black literary ability, but Jefferson, in his *Notes on the State of Virginia*, had preemptively dismissed her from consideration as a counterexample to his argument. "Religion indeed has produced a Phyllis Whately; but it could not produce a poet," he sneered. "The compositions published under her name are below the dignity of criticism."[9] Similarly, in an earlier dismissal of Wheatley's genius, a British West Indian white living in Philadelphia scoffed at abolitionist Benjamin Rush for citing "a single example of a negro girl writing a few silly poems, to prove that the blacks are not deficient to [whites] in understanding."[10] In a seeming response to the 1788 publication of Jefferson's book in Philadelphia, Rush offered two fresh testimonials of Black "mental improvement" at a meeting of the Pennsylvania Abolition Society. One reported on James Derham, a freed Black physician from New Orleans whom Rush hailed as "well acquainted with the healing arts"; another told of Thomas Fuller, an enslaved Black with what Rush called "a talent for mathematical calculation," such as quickly computing in his head "how many seconds there are in a year and a half."[11]

With the first publication of his astronomical calculations in an almanac of 1792, Banneker became the American abolition movement's prime example of native Black intellectual ability. His distinctive attribute involved the skill and inclination to compute the future local time for regular celestial phenomena—that is, those caused by the cyclical motion of the moon and planets as observed from a particular place on Earth, which daily rotated on a tilted axis and annually revolved in an ellipse around the sun. Isaac Newton had established the science of those motions a century earlier, and some people enjoyed making the calculations for various locales.

Like any mathematical computations, making these tables took skill but, at a time when people relied almost exclusively on the sun and moon for light, and farming and fishing remained principal vocations, these specific calculations had practical value. Farmers used them to plant and harvest crops, travelers used them for planning nighttime trips, and (because tides rise and fall with the gravitational pull of the sun and moon) navigators sailing or fishing in oceans and bays relied on them for safety and success. The local time for the rising and setting of the sun and moon, tides, eclipses, and the like varied over the year based on the observer's longitude and latitude, with people typically accessing the information in tables published in annual almanacs keyed to particular locales. Benjamin Franklin had published a widely read annual almanac, *Poor Richard's*, from 1732 until he moved to London in 1757. The immediately popular New England almanac, *Farmer's* (later *Old Farmer's*), first appeared in 1792, with new annual editions ever since.

That same year, with support from local white abolitionists and at the urging of Ellicott, Banneker published his first almanac at age sixty. Ellicott also suggested that Banneker send an advance copy to Jefferson as an example of a Black person's faculty of reason. How much local abolitionists helped with the overall almanac, which included articles and general information, remains unclear, but they gave credit for the calculation of celestial and tidal phenomena to Banneker.[12] In the introduction to the first edition, the editors of *Banneker's Almanack* hailed it as "an extraordinary Effort of Genius . . . by a sable Descendant of Africa, who, by this Specimen of Ingenuity, evinces, to Demonstration, that mental Powers and Endowments are not the exclusive Excellence of white People."[13] This preface carried testimony to the accuracy of Banneker's calculations from Philadelphia scientific instrument maker David Rittenhouse, hailed by Jefferson in his *Notes on the State of Virginia* as a "genius" and "second to no astronomer living."[14] "Every Instance of Genius amongst the Negroes is worthy of attention," Rittenhouse wrote at the time, "because their oppressors seem to lay great stress on their supposed inferior mental abilities."[15]

In a further prefatory endorsement testifying to the ephemeris as "exclusively and peculiarly" the work of Banneker, federalist office-holder and former Constitutional Convention delegate James McHenry addressed the issue of polygenism. "I consider this Negro as fresh proof that the powers of the mind are disconnected to the colour of the skin," he wrote of Banneker. As more such instances of Black attainment emerge, as they must with the amelioration and "final extinction" of slavery, McHenry declared, "The system that would assign to these degraded blacks an origin different from the whites . . . must be relinquished."[16]

The manuscript of his almanac completed by August 1791, Banneker sent a handwritten copy to Jefferson with a cover letter making his case for the right of Blacks to liberty. "We are a race of Beings who have long laboured under the abuse and censure of the world," Banneker wrote, and "have long been considered rather as brutish than human, and Scarcely capable of mental endowments." Having heard "that you are a man far less inflexible in Sentiments of this nature, than many others," he addressed Jefferson with a mix of deference and assertiveness, "I apprehend you will readily embrace every opportunity to eradicate that train of absurd and false oppinions which so generally prevails with respect to us." Banneker offered his almanac as evidence of the reasoning faculty of Blacks. Such work by a member of "the African race," he declared, "and in that colour . . . of the deepest dye," should show "that one universal Father hath given being to us all . . . and endued us all with the same faculties." Noting that his father came to America as "a S[lav]e from Africa," Banneker wrote about Blacks and whites in the United States, "However variable we maybe in Society or religion, however diversifyed in Situation or colour, we are all of the Same Family."[17] We are all Americans, he as much as said, and I am as much an American as you.

In his letter to Jefferson, the sitting secretary of state and esteemed author of the Declaration of Independence, Banneker then made his case for American liberty and against American slavery. "Sir," he began respectfully, "Suffer me to recall to your mind that time in which the Arms and tyranny of the British Crown were exerted with every power-ful effort in order to reduce you to a State of Servitude." Banneker con-tinued, "This Sir, was a time in which you clearly saw into the injustice of a State of Slavery, and ... publickly held forth this true and invalu-able doctrine, which is worthy to be recorded and remember'd in all Suc-ceeding ages. 'We hold these truths to be Self evident, that all men are created equal, and that they are endowed by their creator with certain unalienable rights, that among these are life, liberty, and the pursuit of happyness.' "[18]

"You were then impressed with proper ideas of the great valuation of liberty, and the free possession of those blessings to which you were enti-tled by nature," Banneker went on without any pretext of deference. Yet, "at the Same time," he charged Jefferson, *you* persisted "in detaining by fraud and violence so numerous a part of my brethren under groaning captivity and cruel oppression" and remained "guilty of that most crim-inal act, which you professedly detested in others, with respect to your-selves." Banneker closed this portion of his letter with an admonition drawn from the biblical Job. " 'Put your Souls in their Souls stead,' " he implored Jefferson regarding his enslaved Blacks, "thus shall your heart be enlarged with kindness and benevolence toward them, and thus shall you need neither the direction of myself or others in what manner to pro-ceed herein."[19] Banneker had made his case for liberty to a white Amer-ica still enthralled with Black slavery.

Within ten days of receiving Banneker's letter, Jefferson replied with a courteous four-sentence note. "No body wishes more than I do to see proofs as you exhibit, that nature has given to our black brethren, talents equal to those of the other colours of men," he wrote with measured ambiguity. Jefferson then added with respect to *Banneker's Almanack*, "I consider it as a document to which your whole colour had a right for their justification against the doubts which have been entertained of them."[20] Abolitionists promptly published the exchange but it did not alter Jefferson's behavior.[21] He persisted in holding people in slavery and, as president, defended state-sanctioned slavery. The supposedly scientific debate over monogenism (the common ancestry of all peoples) versus polygenism intensified in antebellum America with the spread of slavery in the South and Southwest and the rise of abolitionism in the North and Midwest.[22] As a rule, antislavery scholars took one side; proslavery scholars took the other. Polarization over the issue reigned in American science as much as it did over slavery in American society.

When the matter of the geographical spread or containment of slavery again reached Congress with the Missouri Compromise of 1820, which admitted Missouri as a slaveholding state but otherwise barred slavery in federal territories north of the new state's southern border, Jefferson called it "a fire bell in the night." He warned, "A geographical line, coinciding with a marked principle, moral and political, once conceived and held up to the angry passions of men, will never be obliterated; and every new irritant will mark it deeper and deeper." With the enslavement of over 1.5 million Blacks in the American South by 1820, Jefferson wrote, "we have the wolf by the ear, and we can neither hold him, nor safely let him go. justice is in one scale, and self-preservation in the other." The maintaining of slavery, Jefferson wrote, "certainly is the exclusive right of every state, which nothing in the constitution has taken from them and given to the general government."[23] Madison too had come around to this viewpoint, questioning in a letter to President James Monroe whether Congress had the authority to limit slavery in the territories, and clearly denying that it had the power to do so in any new state once admitted to the union.[24]

Even as Jefferson and Madison persisted in proclaiming liberty throughout their long lives, their later words demonstrated their continued commitment to state-sanctioned slavery, including in new states carved out of the Louisiana Purchase. As Jefferson put it, the Missouri Compromise sounded "the [death] knell of the Union." After hearing of it, he wrote, "I regret that I am now to die in the belief that the useless sacrifice of themselves, by the generation of '76. to acquire self government and happiness to their country, is to be thrown away by the unwise and unworthy passions of their sons" to bar slavery in future federal territories.[25] Madison expressed much the same sentiment by depicting the object of the Missouri Compromise as "very different from the welfare of the slaves," but rather a partisan effort to divide "republicans of the North from those of the South, and making the former instrumental in giving the opponents of both an ascendency over the whole," where "republicans" referred to members of Madison's splintering Democratic-Republican political party.[26]

Agreeing with Jefferson that a republic based on liberty could not survive a sharp sectional divide over slavery, Abraham Lincoln, a leader among the grandchildren of the generation of '76, and a worthy descendant of that liberty-extolling cohort, saw the prospects for union differently from Jefferson. "A house divided against itself cannot stand," he quoted from scripture in a speech launching his campaign for United States Senate from Illinois in 1858. "I believe this government cannot endure permanently half slave and half free. I do not expect the Union to be dissolved—I do not expect the house to fall—but I do expect it will cease to be divided. It will become all one thing, or all the other."[27]

Lincoln's celebrated House Divided speech was his response to the 1857 U.S. Supreme Court decision in *Dred Scott v. Sandford*, in which Chief Justice Roger Taney asked, "Can a negro, whose ancestors were imported into this country, and sold as slaves, become a member of the political community formed and brought into existence by the Constitution of the United States?" To answer this question, he added, "We must inquire who, at that time, were recognized as the people or citizens of a State." In line with Jefferson's exclusion of Blacks from the protections of American liberty, Taney categorically concluded, "Neither the class or persons who had been imported as slaves, nor their descendants, whether they had become free or not, were then acknowledged as part of the people," and so, he ruled, it remained. Blacks were not American citizens and Congress could not outlaw slavery anywhere.[28] At this point in American history, twenty-five out of thirty-one states, including every state outside the Northeast, barred all Blacks—free and enslaved— from voting.[29]

As Lincoln predicted, the Union did survive the abolition of slavery. It took, however, a civil war to "become all one thing, or all the other." The division echoed the refusal to "confederate" that North Carolina delegate William Davie had warned of in 1787 at the Constitutional Convention, that Patrick Henry had suggested in 1788 at the Virginia ratifying convention, and that South Carolina representative Thomas Tudor Tucker made explicit in his response to Congress receiving antislavery petitions in 1790.[30] Even though Lincoln vowed to respect the constitutional right of states to maintain slavery where it already existed, the threat to slavery and its expansion posed by Lincoln's election as president in 1860 led seven lower southern states to secede from the Union. When Lincoln enforced the principle enunciated at the founding by Madison that state ratification of the Constitution was "*in toto*, and *for ever*" by sending federal troops to stop the insurrection, four more states bolted the Union from April to June 1861.[31]

Following a four-year civil war costing over 600,000 lives, liberty prevailed over slavery and, as Lincoln proclaimed after the Battle of Gettysburg in 1863, "This nation, under God, shall have a new birth of freedom."[32] To abolish slavery officially throughout the Union as urged by such Black abolitionist leaders as Fredrick Douglass, Lincoln pushed the Thirteenth Amendment to the Constitution through Congress early in 1865, shortly before his assassination and the war's end in April. His successor, Andrew Johnson, then helped to secure its ratification by warning of reprisals for former confederate states that failed to join northern and western ones in approving it. The reconstructed Georgia state assembly supplied the final needed vote on December 6, 1865.

Chattel slavery ended everywhere as news spread of the amendment's ratification. The Fourteenth Amendment, ratified three years later, reversed the *Dred Scott* decision by providing that "All persons born or naturalized in the United States, and subject to the jurisdiction thereof, are citizens of the United States and of the state wherein they reside."[33] Then, in 1870, the Fifteenth Amendment barred states and the United States from denying citizens their right to vote "on account of race, color, or previous condition of servitude."[34] In the decades to come these high-sounding guarantees fell victim to low-minded court decisions, domestic terror, scientific racism, and still-strong traditions of states' rights and local authority. The long shadow of slavery continued to undermine declarations of liberty and equality through the twentieth century and into our own. Liberty and slavery remain our conflicted American inheritance.

ACKNOWLEDGMENTS

With my past books, I often found it difficult to know whom to thank first for help with research, writing, and publishing. Because every book is a team effort, there are always many people and institutions deserving mention. This time, however, one person stands out above the rest, my editor at W. W. Norton, Steve Forman.

When I resolved on the topic of liberty and slavery in the Revolutionary era for this book, I sought out Steve to serve as the editor. Not only is he an exceptional technical editor, Steve knows this topic as well as anyone. He pushed me to sort out my thoughts, explicate my meaning, and defend my claims. I came to realize that if Steve questioned my points, I was either wrong or unclear, and he let me figure out which.

The pandemic kept me at home in southern California for most of the research and writing of this book, much more so than for any prior book. Prior fellowships and research trips ended up doing double duty for my work on this one. There were a few exceptions though, and for those I am particularly thankful. A visit to Yale Law School as the Michael A. Doyle '62 and Bunny Winter Distinguished Visiting Professor of Law, which during Covid served primarily as a research visit, proved invaluable. My special thanks for it go to Dean Heather Gerken and Professor Akhil Amar. A second fellowship at the Fred W. Smith National Library for the Study of George Washington at Mount Vernon assisted me as well and allowed for further research at the Virginia Museum of History and Culture in Richmond, the John D. Rockefeller Jr. Library in Williamsburg, Virginia, and Gunston Hall in Fairfax County, Virginia. For this, I thank Keven Butterfield and Stephen McLeod. Online archival resources made available through the library of my former academic home, the University of Georgia, again helped greatly.

Nearer to home, the collections of the Huntington Library and UCLA archives and libraries provided access to needed materials. With closures due to the pandemic, the research and interlibrary loan specialists at the Pepperdine University libraries helped me more than ever before. A grant from Pepperdine enabled me to conduct research at British archives.

While researching and writing a book during a global pandemic poses unusual problems, it also provides unexpected pleasures. More time at home meant more time with family, which allowed for unexpectedly fruitful discussions of liberty and slavery in the Revolutionary era with my spouse and two grown children—more than they likely wanted, but I had a captive audience. Our children have graduated from college but came home, as many adult children did, during Covid. Why pay rent for a small apartment when free rooms with a view stand empty at the family home? I could not have asked for better sounding boards for my thoughts than the pandemic gave me at home. It is with love that I dedicate this book to my spouse Lucy and our children Sarah and Luke.

List of Abbreviations for Frequently Cited Works

AFC: L. H. Butterfield et al., eds., *Adams Family Correspondence*, 15 vols. (Cambridge: Harvard University Press, 1963–). The first 15 volumes in this series, running through October 1804, published as of 2022.

Annals of Congress: *The Debates and Proceedings in the Congress of the United States*, 42 vols. (Washington: Gales and Seaton, 1834).

DAJA: L. H. Butterfield et al., eds., *Diary and Autobiography of John Adams*, 4 vols. (Cambridge: Harvard University Press, 1961).

DGW: Donald Jackson and Dorothy Twohig, eds., *The Diaries of George Washington*, 6 vols. (Charlottesville: University Press of Virginia, 1976–1979).

DHFFC: Linda Grant DePauw et al., eds., *The Documentary History of the First Federal Congress of the United States of America*, 22 vols. (Baltimore: Johns Hopkins University Press, 1972–2017).

DHRC: Merrill Jensen et al., eds., *The Documentary History of the Ratification of the Constitution*, 37 vols. (Madison: State Historical Society of Wisconsin, 1976–). The first 37 volumes published as of 2022.

JCC: Library of Congress, *Journals of the Continental Congress, 1774–1789*, 34 vols. (Washington, DC: Government Printing Office, 1904–1937).

Farrand: Max Farrand et al., eds., *The Records of the Federal Convention of 1787*, 4 vols. (New Haven: Yale University Press, 1937–1966).

LDC: Paul H. Smith et al., eds., *Letters of Delegates to Congress, 1774–1789*, 26 vols. (Washington, DC: Library of Congress, 1976–2000).

LMCC: Edmund C. Burnett, ed., *Letters of Members of the Continental Congress*, 8 vols. (Washington, DC: Carnegie Institute of Washington, 1921–1936).

LPJA: L. Kinvin Wroth and Hiller B. Zobel, eds., *Legal Papers of John Adams*, 3 vols. (Cambridge: Harvard University Press, 1965).

PAH: Harold C. Syrett and Jacob Cooke, eds., *The Papers of Alexander Hamilton*, 27 vols. (New York: Columbia University Press, 1961–1987).

PBF: Leonard W. Labaree et al., eds., *The Papers of Benjamin Franklin*, 43 vols. (New Haven: Yale University Press, 1959–). First 43 volumes in this series, running through March 1785, published as of 2022. Material from forthcoming volumes online at franklinpapers.com.

PFB: Colin Nicolson, ed., *The Papers of Francis Bernard: Governor of Colonial Massachusetts, 1760–69*, 5 vols. (Boston: Colonial Society of Massachusetts, 2007–2015).

PGW-CfS: W. W. Abbot et al., eds., *The Papers of George Washington: Confederation Series*, 6 vols. (Charlottesville: University Press of Virginia, 1992–1997).

PGW-CS: W. W. Abbot et al., eds., *The Papers of George Washington: Colonial Series*, 10 vols. (Charlottesville: University Press of Virginia, 1983–1995).

PGW-PS: W. W. Abbot et al., eds., *The Papers of George Washington: Presidential Series*, 21 vols. (Charlottesville: University Press of Virginia, 1987–2020).

PGW-RS: Dorothy Twohig et al., eds., *The Papers of George Washington: Retirement Series*, 4 vols. (Charlottesville: University Press of Virginia, 1998–1999).

PGW-RWS: W. W. Abbot et al., eds., *The Papers of George Washington: Revolutionary War Series*, 28 vols. (Charlottesville: University Press of Virginia, 1985–). First 28 volumes in this series, running through March 1785, published as of 2022. Material from forthcoming volumes online at franklinpapers.com.

PHL: Philip M. Hamer et al., eds., *Papers of Henry Laurens*, 16 vols. (Columbia: University of South Carolina Press, 1968–2003).

PJA: Robert J. Taylor et al., eds., *Papers of John Adams*, 21 vols. (Cambridge: Harvard University Press, 2003–). First 21 volumes in this series, running through January 1797, published as of 2022. Material from forthcoming volumes online at founders.archives.gov.

PJM: William T. Hutchinson et al., eds., *The Papers of James Madison*, 17 vols. (1st ser., Chicago and Charlottesville: University of Chicago Press and University Press of Virginia, 1962–1991).

PTJ: Julian P. Boyd et al., eds., *The Papers of Thomas Jefferson*, 45 vols. (Princeton: Princeton University Press, 1950–). First 45 volumes in this series, running through March 1805, published as of 2022. Material from forthcoming volumes online at founders.archives.gov.

PTJ-RS: J. Jefferson Looney et al., eds., *The Papers of Thomas Jefferson, Retirement Series*, 17 vols. (Princeton: Princeton University Press, 2005–). First 17 volumes in this series, running through November 1821, published as of 2022. Material from forthcoming volumes online at founders.archives.gov.

Preface

1. Lord Mansfield, "Case of James Sommersett, a Negro, on a Habeas Corpus," in *A Complete Collection of State Trials and Proceedings for High Treason and Other Crimes and Misdemeanors*, ed. T. B. Howell (London: Hansard, 1816), 20:82.

2. [John Adams], "Messieurs Edes & Gill," *Boston-Gazette*, Oct. 21, 1765, 3.

3. [Benjamin Rush], *Vindication of the Address* (Philadelphia: Dunlap, 1773), 30.

Introduction: Crèvecœur's Question

1. John Locke, "The Second Treatise of Government," in John Locke, *Two Treatises of Government* (London: Churchill, [1689] dated 1690), sec. 49.

2. Ibid., sec. 22.

3. The United States Supreme Court adopted a like view of European sovereignty over America in *Johnson v. M'Intosh*, 21 U.S. (8 Wheat.) 54 (1823).

4. Christopher Columbus, Oct. 12, 1492, *Journal of the First Voyage of Columbus* (Madison: Wisconsin Historical Society, 2003), 111 (scholars dispute the authenticity and wording of this document).

5. Locke, "Second Treatise," sec. 142.

6. Ibid., sec. 222.

7. Ibid., sec. 24.

8. John Locke, *The Fundamental Constitutions of Carolina*, Mar. 1, 1669, sec. 110, reprinted in *The Statutes at Large of South Carolina*, ed. Thomas Cooper (Columbia: Johnston, 1836), 1:55.

9. James Thomson, "An Ode," *The Works of James Thomson* (London: A. Millar, 1762), 2:246 (put to music as "Rule, Britannia!").

10. Cecil Jane, ed., *Select Documents Illustrating the Four Voyages of Columbus* (London: Hakluyt, 1930), 1:16.

11. Edmund S. Morgan, *American Slavery, American Freedom: The Ordeal of Colonial Virginia* (New York: W. W. Norton, 1975), 327–37 (quotes from 327–28, 331, 337).

12. Locke, *Fundamental Constitutions*, sec. 110.

13. See Alden T. Vaughn, "The Origins Debate: Slavery and Racism in Seventeenth Century Virginia," *Virginia Magazine of History and Biography* 97 (1989): 340–54; John C. Coombs, "Beyond the 'Origins Debate': Rethinking the Rise of Virginia Slavery," in *Early Modern Virginia: Reconsidering the Old Dominion*, ed. Douglas Bradburn and John C. Coombs (Charlottesville: Univ. of Virginia Press, 2011), 239, 254–58, 268.

14. Morgan Godwin, *The Negro's and Indians advocate, suing for their admission to the church* (London: By Author, 1680), 36.

15. Henry Laurens to Joseph Brown, Oct. 28, 1765, in David Duncan Wallace, *The Life of Henry Laurens* (New York: Putnam, 1915), 218; Henry Laurens to John Lewis Gervais, Jan. 29, 1766, PHL, 5:53–54.

16. Samuel Johnson, *Taxation No Tyranny; an Answer to the Resolutions and Address of the American Congress*, 4th ed. (London: Cadell, 1775), 79. Historian Christopher Brown noted that Johnson's comment reflected wider British establishment thought on the American Revolution. Christopher Leslie Brown, "The Problems of Slavery," in *The Oxford Handbook of the American Revolution*, ed. Edward G. Gary and Jane Kamensky (New York: Oxford Univ. Press, 2012), 439.

17. [Benjamin Rush], *Vindication of the Address* (Philadelphia: Dunlap, 1773), 30.

18. [Richard Wells], "A few POLITICAL REFLECTIONS, submitted to the consideration of the BRITISH COLONIES," *Pennsylvania Packet*, Aug. 8, 1774, 1, reprinted in Richard Wells, *A Few Political Reflections Submitted to the Consideration of the British Colonies* (Philadelphia: Dunlap, 1774), 80.

19. J. Hector St. John de Crèvecœur, *Letters from an American Farmer and Other Essays*, ed. Dennis D. Moore (Cambridge: Harvard Univ. Press, 2013), 31 (letter 3).

20. Ibid., 12 (letter 1 described James's slaves as "fat and well-clad"), 77–82 (letter 5 noting that Native Americans "appear to be a race doomed to recede and disappear before the superior genius of the Europeans").

21. Ibid., 6, 29, 43 (letters 1 and 3).

22. Ibid., 121 (letter 9).

23. Ibid., 123 (letter 9).

24. Ibid., 12 (letter 1).

25. Ibid., 123 (letter 9) (emphasis added).

26. Benjamin Franklin, "Observations Concerning the Increase of Mankind, 1751," PBF, 4:232. For first publication, see [William Clarke], *Observations On the late and present Conduct of the French, with Regard to their Encroachments upon the British Colo-*

nies in North America. . . . To which is added, wrote by another Hand; Observations concerning the Increase of Mankind, Peopling of Countries, &c (Boston: S. Kneeland, 1755).

27. James Otis, *The Rights of the British Colonies Asserted and Proved* (Boston: Edes & Gill, 1764), 24.

28. Ibid., 29.

29. Thomas Jefferson, *Notes on the State of Virginia* (Boston: Lilly & Wait, 1832), 90–91 (query 8).

30. Ibid., 143, 151 (query 14), 170 (query 18).

31. Ibid., 150–51 (query 14).

32. Felix, "The humble Petition of many Slaves, living in the Town of Boston, and other Towns in the Province," *The appendix: Or, Some observations on the expediency of the petition of the Africans, living in Boston, &c. lately presented to the General Assembly of this province* (Boston: E. Russell, [1773]), 10–11.

33. Phillis Wheatley, "An Ode of Verses," in *The Poems of Phillis Wheatley*, ed. Julian D. Mason Jr. (Chapel Hill: Univ. of North Carolina Press, 1987), 125. A later version of this poem included a reference to "we Americans," the only such reference in Wheatley's work. Phillis Wheatley, "On the Death of the Rev. Mr. George Whitefield, 1770," in Mason, *Poems*, 56.

34. Phillis Wheatley, "America," in Mason, *Poems*, 125.

35. Phillis Wheatley, "On Being Brought from Africa to America," in Mason, *Poems*, 533. See also Phillis Wheatley to Samuel Hopkins, Feb. 9, 1774, in Mason, *Poems*, 203 (referring to Africa as "my benighted Country").

36. James Albert Ukawsaw Gronniosaw, "A Narrative of the Most Remarkable Particulars in the Life of James Albert Ukawsaw Gronniosaw," in *Slave Narratives* (New York: Library of America, 2000), 14 ("my country-folks"); Olaudah Equiano, *The Interesting Narrative of the Life of Olaudah Equiano, or Gustavus Vassa, the African* (London: By Author, 1789), 2:247 ("my countrymen").

37. Crèvecœur, *Letters*, 29 (letter 3).

Chapter One: "A Rabble of Negros &c."

1. Robert Goddard deposition, Ch.M.18.184, Boston Public Library (BPL) mss., reprinted in "An Eyewitness Account," *The Boston Massacre: A History with Documents*, ed. Neil L. York (New York: Routledge, 2010), 121–22.

2. Ibid.

3. Goddard gave two depositions in addition to the one quoted here: one for the town's pamphlet about the massacre and one at Preston's trial. Although they differed in

details, all three made the same essential points and none depicted Attucks as an assailant. *A Short Narrative of The horrid Massacre in Boston* (Boston: Edes & Gill, 1770), 87; "Anonymous Summary of Crown Evidence," Oct. 25, 1770, LPJA, 3:57–58.

4. *Boston-Gazette*, March 12, 1770, 2–3.

5. *Boston Chronicle*, March 8, 1770, 79.

6. John Fiske, "Address," in *A Memorial of Crispus Attucks, Samuel Maverick, James Caldwell, Samuel Gray and Patrick Carr* (Boston, 1889), 83.

7. *Boston-Gazette*, March 12, 1770, 3.

8. E.g., Thomas Gage to the Earl of Hillsborough, April 10, 1770, the National Archives of UK (TNA) PRO/CO/5/88, fos. 55–58. Gage served as the commander in chief of British armed forces in North America and Hillsborough was British secretary of state for the colonies.

9. Fisk, "Address," 84.

10. Olaudah Equiano, *The Interesting Narrative of the Life of Olaudah Equiano, or Gustavus Vassa, the African* (London: By Author, 1789), 1:53, 245, 2:17.

11. "Examination before the Committee of the Whole of the House of Commons, 13 February 1766," PBF, 13:124–62.

12. "Adams' Argument for the Defense," *Rex v. Wemms*, 1770, LPJA, 3:266.

13. Thomas Gage to the Earl of Hillsborough. Historian Serena Zabin chronicled various incidents of civilian-military tension in her study of Boston life during this period of British occupation, together with a map of where military families lived. Serena Zabin, *The Boston Massacre: A Family History* (Boston: Houghton Mifflin, 2020), 59–63, 68–74 (map on 68).

14. [John Adams], "Humphrey Ploughjogger to the *Boston Gazette*, 14 October 1765," PJA, 1:147.

15. "Britannus Americanus [Samuel Adams] to the Printers," *Boston-Gazette*, Sept. 7, 1767, 716.

16. E.g., *A Short Narrative of The horrid Massacre in Boston* (Boston: Edes & Gill, 1770), 11; *Boston-Gazette*, Mar. 12, 1770, 2; *Boston Evening-Post*, Mar. 12, 1770, 1.

17. Michael Johnson [Crispus Attucks] inquest, Ch.M.1.8, Boston Public Library (BPL) mss.

18. "Rex v. Preston, Indictment," LPJA, 3:46.

19. *Short Narrative*, 30 (emphasis in original).

20. *A Fair Account of the Late Unhappy Disturbance at Boston in New England* (London: B. White, 1770), 5, 9, 15, 20, 22.

21. See Karsten Fitz, "Commemorating Crispus Attucks: Visual Memory and the Representations of the Boston Massacre, 1770–1857," *Amerikastudien / American*

Studies 50 (2005): 469. One of the surviving original prints has Attucks shaded in as Black, but others, including the one reproduced in this book, show him as white.

22.   Until younger patriots began filling this role, everyone chosen to deliver the Boston Massacre oration through the onset of active warfare in 1775 had attended the 1769 dinner that brought together 350 members of the Sons of Liberty (including Revere, Hancock, and both Adamses) at the Liberty Tree Tavern in Dorchester.

23.   W. C. N., "Communications: The Morning Dawn," *North Star* (Rochester, NY), May 5, 1848, 2.

24.   Mitch Kachun, "From Forgotten Founder to Indispensable Icon: Crispus Attucks, Black Citizenship, and Collective Memory, 1770–1865," *Journal of the Early Republic* 29 (2009): 285; Stephen Kantrowitz, "A Place for 'Colored Patriots': Crispus Attucks among the Abolitionists, 1842–1863," *Massachusetts Historical Review* 11 (2009): 108–9.

25.   Committee of the Town of Boston to Benjamin Franklin, July 13, 1770, PBF, 17:186.

26.   Thomas Gage to William Dalrymple, April 28, 1770, Thomas Gage Papers, William L. Clements Library, University of Michigan ("Gage Papers").

27.   See Eric Hinderaker, *Boston's Massacre* (Cambridge: Harvard Univ. Press, 2017), 193. Even Hutchinson came to believe that town leaders preferred an acquittal to a conviction in Preston's case. Ibid.

28.   Zabin, *Boston Massacre*, 172.

29.   For their part, both Adams and Quincy explained their role as simply doing a lawyer's duty to provide counsel to accused persons—but they had cleared their participation in advance with patriot leaders. "Further," as legal historian Hiller B. Zobel noted, "if sound Whigs occupied defense counsel's table, no one need fear that the hearings would be turned into a trial of Boston's behavior." Hiller B. Zobel, *The Boston Massacre* (New York: W. W. Norton, 1970), 221.

30.   "The Counsel for the Crown or rather the town were but poor and managed badly," Preston later reported about the loyalist-leaning solicitor general Samuel Quincy and the town-appointed Robert Treat Paine, "my Counsel on the contrary were men of parts, & exerted themselves with great spirit & cleverness." Thomas Preston to Thomas Gage, Oct. 31, 1770, Gage Papers. For Preston's trial but not the soldiers' trial, Robert Auchmuty Jr. joined the defense team. For a detailed retelling of both trials, see Zobel, *Boston Massacre*, 240–94.

31.   "Justice Trowbridge's Charge to the Jury," Dec. 5, 1770, LPJA, 3:299.

32.   "Andrew, (Mr. Oliver Wendall's [*sic*] Negro,) sworn," Nov. 30, 1770, LPJA, 3:204.

33.   "Anonymous Minutes of Paine's Argument for the Crown," Oct. 29, 1770, LPJA, 3:92 (from Paine's closing argument in the Preston trial, where Andrew gave similar testimony).

34. "Oliver Wendell, Merchant, sworn," Nov. 30, 1770, LPJA, 3:205 (after noting that Andrew sometimes told amusing stories, Wendell added, "I never knew him to tell a serious lye").

35. For further discussion and documentation of Adams's dual trial strategy, see Hinderaker, *Boston's Massacre*, 202–10.

36. "Adams' Argument for the Defense," Dec. 4, 1770, LPJA, 3:268–69 (italics in original to show oral emphasis); "Adams' Minutes of Crown Evidence," Nov. 28, 1770, LPJA, 3:115.

37. "Adams' Argument," LPJA, 3:262, 266, 269.

38. Ibid., 3:266, 269.

39. In his lengthy argument for the defense, Josiah Quincy quoted an unnamed judge as saying that the jurors had a duty "to cause law and justice IN MERCY to be executed." "Josiah Quincy's Argument for the Defense," Dec. 3, 1770, LPJA, 3:241.

40. In their extraordinarily explicit instructions, the judges told jurors to convict only soldiers proven to have killed someone, and observed that testimony supported such a finding only with respect to Montgomery and Kilroy. In their joint instructions, two of these judges added that if Montgomery was "assaulted with clubs and other weapons, and thereupon fired at the rioters and killed *Attucks*: then you should find him guilty of manslaughter only." "Trowbridge's and Oliver's Charges to the Jury," Dec. 5, 1770, LPJA, 3:299. A third went further to comment, based on the testimony of four witnesses, "we must suppose" that Attucks assaulted Montgomery. "Lynde's Charge to the Jury," Dec. 5, 1770, LPJA, 3:311–12. In fact, only one witness identified Attucks as the assailant, and he simply testified that he "thought" so. "Andrew," LPJA, 3:204.

41. James Lovell, *An Oration Delivered April 2d, 1771* (Boston: Edes & Gill, 1771), 16, 18.

42. Joseph Warren, "Oration, Delivered at Boston, March 5, 1772," in *Orations Delivered at the Request of the Inhabitants of the Town of Boston, to Commemorate the Evening of the Fifth of March, 1770*, 2nd ed. (Boston: Wm. T. Clap, 1807), 45.

43. Joseph Warren, "Oration, Delivered at Boston, March 6, 1775," in ibid., 62–63. Warren delivered this annual address in both 1772 and 1775.

44. Peter Thacher, "Oration, Delivered at Watertown, March 5, 1776," in ibid., 73.

45. John Adams to Matthew Robinson, March 2, 1786, PJA, 18:193.

46. See Zobel, *Boston Massacre*, 220–21; Zabin, *Boston Massacre*, 213–17 (on page 216, quoted Hutchinson as observing at the time that Adams "wishes to black the people [of Boston] as little as may be consistent with his Duty to his Clients").

47. John Adams, *Diary*, Dec. 18, 1765, DAJA, 1:263.

Chapter Two: Imperial Protests and the Metaphor of Slavery

1. "Boston," *Boston-Gazette*, Aug. 19, 1765, 1.

2. A classic historical study of the Stamp Act crisis depicts the Loyal Nine as a precursor group to the Sons of Liberty, with Otis and Adams not part of the initial group but early leaders of the later organization. Edmund M. Morgan and Helen M. Morgan, *The Stamp Act Crisis: Prologue to Revolution* (Chapel Hill: Univ. of North Carolina Press, 1953), 128.

3. Francis Bernard to Board of Trade, Aug. 15, 1765, PFB, 2:301.

4. Ibid.; Francis Bernard, "A Proclamation [Aug. 15, 1765]," *Boston-Gazette*, Sept. 2, 1765, 1.

5. Francis Bernard, "A Proclamation [Aug. 28, 1765]," *Boston-Gazette*, Sept. 2, 1765, 1. See also Francis Bernard to Earl of Halifax, Aug. 31, 1765, PFB, 2:338.

6. The militia had refused to report after the first riot and vowed not to protect the stamps when they arrived, which led Bernard to complain, "In the Case of a Popular Tumult I can't command ten men that can be depended upon; The Militia are worse than no Soldiers at all." Francis Bernard to Richard Jackson, Aug. 24, 1765, PFB, 2:321-22.

7. Ibid., at 321.

8. In September, Bernard reported to London about conditions in Boston, "there is little more of Government left but the form; no Authority remains: Evry thing that is done by the Governor & Council is arraingned in the newspaper & an Account of their Motives is demanded." Francis Bernard to Richard Jackson, Sept. 10, 1765, PFB, 2:356.

9. E.g., "All the power of Great Britain shall not oblige them to submit to the Stamp Act," Bernard reported the protesters saying. "They will die upon the Place first." Francis Bernard to Board of Trade, Aug. 16, 1765, PFB, 2:304.

10. Douglass Adair and John A. Schutz, eds., *Peter Oliver's Origin & Progress of the American Rebellion: A Tory View* (San Marino, CA: Huntington Library, 1961), 54.

11. E.g., [John Adams], "Messieurs Edes & Gill," *Boston-Gazette*, Oct. 21, 1765, 3.

12. Americanus, "A Word of Advice," *Boston-Gazette*, Oct. 21, 1765, 1.

13. "The Pennsylvania Resolves, September 21, 1765," in Edmund S. Morgan, ed., *Prologue to Revolution: Sources and Documents on the Stamp Act Crisis, 1764–1766* (Chapel Hill: Univ. of North Carolina Press, 1959), 51.

14. Americanus, "Advice," 1.

15. In his brief biography of Otis, historian Samuel Eliot Morrison wrote, "Friends and foes alike agreed that from 1761 to 1769, Otis was the political leader of Mas-

sachusetts Bay": Samuel Eliot Morrison, "James Otis," in *Dictionary of American Biography*, ed. Dumas Malone (New York: Scribner's, 1934), 14:102.

16. Adair and Schutz, *Oliver's Origin*, 27.

17. James Otis Jr., in John Adams, "Adams' 'Abstract of the Argument,' Ca. April 1761," LPJA, 2:139.

18. John Adams, *Diary*, ca. Feb. 26, 1770, DAJA, 1:349. Otis's mental condition deteriorated over time after the blow. This observation from Adams's diary dated from over a year later.

19. John Adams to William Tudor, Sr., Mar. 29, 1817, PJA, --: --- (online access at founders.archives.gov).

20. Otis, "Abstract," LPJA, 2:139-44.

21. Only one Boston newspaper criticized the ruling, but even that newspaper emphasized the perfunctory nature of the ruling by noting, "The Judgment of the Court *immediately* given in Favour of the Petition." "Boston, November 23," *Boston-Gazette*, Nov. 23, 1761, 3.

22. Adams later denied that letters ever came back from London and wrongly claimed that "no Judgment was pronounced" in the case. John Adams to William Tudor, Sr., June 1, 1818, PJA, --: --- (online access at founders.archives.gov).

23. John Adams to William Tudor, Mar. 29, 1817.

24. See Akhil Reed Amar, *The Words that Made Us: America's Constitutional Conversation, 1760–1840* (New York: Basic Books, 2021), 18–20; Bernard Bailyn, "Introduction," in *Pamphlets of the American Revolution, 1750–1776*, ed. Bernard Bailyn (Cambridge: Harvard Univ. Press, 1965), 412–14.

25. John Adams to William Tudor, Sr., June 7, 1818, PJA, --: --- (online access at founders.archives.gov).

26. *Journals of the House of Commons*, XXIX, 935.

27. James Otis, "The Rights of the British Colonies Asserted and Proved" (1764), in Bailyn, *Pamphlets*, 443–47 (emphasis added).

28. Ibid., 439–40. Later in the pamphlet, Otis postulated, "That the colonists, black and white, born here are freeborn British subjects, and entitled to all the essential rights of such is a truth not only manifest, from the provincial charters, from the principles of the common law, and acts of Parliament, but from the British constitution." Ibid, 446.

29. Stephen Hopkins, "The Rights of Colonies Examined" (1765), in Bailyn, *Pamphlets*, 507–8.

30. [Christopher Gadsden], "Pro Grege et Rege," June 10, 1769, in *The Writings of Christopher Gadsden, 1746–1805*, ed. Richard Welsh (Columbia: Univ. of South

Carolina Press, 1966), 77–78. Vermont Revolutionary leader Ethan Allen put it even more succinctly when he wrote, "Liberty is agency." Ethan Allen, *Reason: The Only Oracle of Man* (Boston: J.P. Mendum, 1854 repr.), 29.

31. "Within English political thought slavery was a technical term for an ultimate state of dependence and unfreedom . . . but it has particular emotional meaning in the South because of the prevalence there of black chattel slavery." Pauline Maier, "Early Revolutionary Leaders in the South and the Problem of Southern Distinctiveness," in *The Southern Experience in the American Revolution*, ed. Jeffrey J. Crow and Larry E. Tise (Chapel Hill: Univ. of North Carolina Press, 1978), 17.

32. Douglas R. Egerton, *Death or Liberty: African Americans and Revolutionary America* (Oxford: Oxford Univ. Press, 2009), 20–21.

33. In a later analysis of the painting, historian Robert W. Keeny concluded that the second Hopkins in it (along with Esek) might be William rather than Stephen. Robert W. Kenny, "Sea Captains Carousing in Surinam," *Rhode Island History* 36 (1977): 114–15.

34. Daniel Dulany, "Considerations on the Propriety of Imposing Taxes in American Colonies" (1765), in Bailyn, *Pamphlets*, 619.

35. Ibid., 637–38.

36. Ibid., 635.

37. *The Annual Register, or a View of the History, Politics and Literature for the Year 1766* (London: Dodsley, 1773), 194.

38. [John Adams], "Messieurs Edes & Gill," 3.

39. Bernard Bailyn, *Ideological Origins of the American Revolution: Enlarged Edition* (Cambridge: Harvard Univ. Press, 1992), 232–33.

40. F. Nwabueze Okoye, "Chattel Slavery as the Nightmare of the American Revolutionaries," *William and Mary Quarterly* 37 (1980): 28.

41. Jonathan Mayhew, *The Snare Broken: A Thanksgiving Discourse* (London: G. Kearsly, 1766), 3, 8, 14–17, 32–33. Other New England ministers followed Mayhew's lead in characterizing repeal of the Stamp Act as deliverance from "slavery." E.g., Joseph Emerson, *A Thanksgiving Sermon* (Boston: Edes & Gill, 1766), 13; Elisha Fish, *Joy and Gladness: A Thanksgiving Discourse* (Providence: Sarah Goddart, 1786), 16.

42. John Adams, *Diary*, Jan. 16, 1770, DAJA, 1:348.

43. In her study of Revolutionary era rhetoric, Patricia Bradley depicted Samuel Adams as "the single most important individual in establishing the Revolution's public voice." Patricia Bradley, *Slavery, Propaganda, and the American Revolution* (Jackson: Univ. Press of Mississippi, 1998), xv.

44.   [Samuel Adams], "Draft Instructions," MS., Boston Public Library; a text appears in Boston Record Commissioners' Report, vol. 16, 120–22.

45.   [Samuel Adams], "To the Printers," *Boston-Gazette*, Sept. 7, 1767, 3.

46.   [Samuel Adams], "To the Publisher of the Boston-Gazette," *Boston-Gazette*, Oct. 5, 1772, 2.

47.   [Samuel Adams], "Masseurs Edes & Gill," *Boston-Gazette*, Oct. 14, 1771, 2. In a similar vein, Adams later wrote about the American Revolution, "We shall be free if we deserve it." Samuel Adams to James Warren, Sept. 17, 1777, in "Warren-Adams Letters," *Massachusetts Historical Society Collections* 72 (1917): 370.

48.   Based on his analysis of the impact of these letters, historian Zachary McLeod Hutchins concluded, "No North American did more to propagate this tie between slavery and taxation without representation than the only member of the Second Continental Congress to oppose the Declaration of Independence, John Dickinson." Zachary McLeod Hutchins, "The Slave Narrative and the Stamp Act, or Letters from Two American Farmers in Pennsylvania," in *Community without Consent: New Perspectives on the Stamp Act*, ed. Zachary McLeod Hutchins (Hanover, NH: Dartmouth College Press, 2016), 115.

49.   John Dickinson, "The Late Regulations Respecting the British Colonies" (1765), in Bailyn, *Pamphlets*, 679–80; [John Dickinson], *An Address to the Committee of Correspondence in Barbados* (Philadelphia: W. Bradford, 1766), 10.

50.   [John Dickinson], *Letters from a Farmer in Pennsylvania to the Inhabitants of the British Colonies* (London: J. Almon, 1774 repr. of Pennsylvania, 1768, edition], 5.

51.   Ibid., 12, 25.

52.   Ibid., 74–75.

53.   Ibid., 94.

54.   In the most graphic such scene in his *Letters* (although one he likely made up), Crèvecœur described an enslaved person suspended in a cage to die as punishment. "I shudder when I recollect that the birds had already picked out his eyes," Crèvecœur wrote. J. Hector St. John de Crèvecœur, *Letters from an American Farmer and Other Essays*, ed. Dennis D. Moore (Cambridge: Harvard Univ. Press, 2013), 129–30 (letter 9). For a discussion of Crèvecœur's *Letters* as an answer to Dickinson's *Letters*, see McLeod, "Slave Narrative," 133–35.

55.   [Dickinson], *Letters*, 131.

56.   D., "A Song," *Pennsylvania Journal*, June 7, 1768, 2; D., "A Song," *Pennsylvania Gazette*, June 7, 1768, 2.

57.   George Washington to George Mason, Apr. 5, 1769, PGW-CS, 8:178.

58.   Ibid.

59. George Washington to George William Fairfax, June 10, 1774, PGW-CS, 10:97.

60. George Washington to Bryan Fairfax, Aug. 24, 1774, PGW-CS, 10:155. South Carolina slaveholder and merchant Christopher Gadsden similarly personalized the slavery metaphor by writing about the impact by British taxation on Americans, "We are as real SLAVES as those we are permitted to command." Christopher Gadsden, *South Carolina Gazette*, June 22, 1769, quoted in Jack P. Greene, *Imperatives, Behaviors and Identities: Essays in Early American Cultural History* (Charlottesville: Univ. Press of Virginia, 1992), 277.

61. [William Henry Drayton], *A Letter from Freeman of South-Carolina, to the Deputies of North-America, Assembled in the High Court of Congress at Philadelphia* (Charles-Town: n/p, 1774), 29. In a similar vein, an anonymous 1770 essay in the *South Carolina Gazette* advised white readers to "go and entreat some negro to change states with you. Don't fear that you will change for the worse. His situation is greatly superior to yours. He has but one master; you have thousands." *South Carolina Gazette*, Nov. 15, 1770, quoted in Greene, *Imperatives*, 277.

62. [John Adams] to the Inhabitants of the Colony of Massachusetts-Bay, Jan. 30, 1775, PJA, 2:242.

63. Samuel Langdon, "Government Corrupted by Vice, and recovered by Righteousness" (Watertown: Benjamin Edes, 1775), 23.

64. John Adams to Thomas Jefferson, Aug. 24, 1815, PTJ-RS, 8:683 (Adams also listed colonial legislative resolutions as a historical source, but these too used the slavery metaphor).

65. Based on his study of one American colony, historian Jack Greene concluded, "It was precisely their intimate familiarity with chattel slavery that made South Carolinians . . . so sensitive to any challenges to their own liberty as free men." Greene, *Imperatives*, 277–78.

66. [Adams] to Inhabitants, PJA, 2:242.

67. Joseph Warren, "Oration, Delivered at Boston, March 5, 1772," in *Orations Delivered at the Request of the Inhabitants of the Town of Boston, to Commemorate the Evening of the Fifth of March, 1770*, 2nd ed. (Boston: Wm. T. Clap, 1807), 18.

68. Patrick Henry, in *Sketches of the Life and Character of Patrick Henry*, ed. William Wirt (Philadelphia: James Webster, 1817), 120–23. Although everyone there seemed to remember it in some fashion, no contemporary record survives of Henry's speech to the Second Virginia Convention. The first text of it appeared in Wirt's biography of Henry. Wirt interviewed people who had heard it, but they were relying on their memories, not notes.

Chapter Three: A Practice "So Odious"

1. Nathaniel Coffin to Charles Steuart, Oct. 12, 1770, Steuart Papers, Library of Virginia, Richmond, microfilm reel 1, pt. 2, 153, copy of originals in Papers of Charles Steuart, National Library of Scotland, MS. 5026.

2. Olaudah Equiano, *The Interesting Narrative of the Life of Olaudah Equiano, or Gustavus Vassa, the African* (London: By Author, 1789), 1:79.

3. See Mark S. Weiner, *Black Trials: Citizenship from the Beginnings of Slavery to the End of Caste* (New York: Knopf, 2004), 73–76; Steven M. Wise, *Though the Heavens May Fall: The Landmark Trial that Led to the End of Human Slavery* (New York: Da Capo Press, 2005), 2–5.

4. Charles Steuart, "Narrative of the 'Spanish Affair,'" Aug. 16, 1789, Charles Steuart Papers, John D. Rockefeller Jr. Library, Williamsburg, VA, DMS 55.4, folder 2 (also on microfilm M-1130.1).

5. James Parker to Benjamin Franklin, June 11, 1766, PBF, 13:308.

6. Ibid., 13:309.

7. *Pigg v. Caley*, Noy 27 (1618).

8. *Smith v. Brown and Cooper*, 91 Eng. Rep. 566, 566 (K.B. 1701).

9. William Blackstone, *Commentaries on the Laws of England*, 1st ed. (Oxford: Clarendon Press, 1765), 1:123.

10. James Thomson, "An Ode," *The Works of James Thomson* (London: A. Millar, 1762), 2:246.

11. An exchange of this type over when and whether English law recognized a foreign marriage played out in the legal debate over the recognition of Virginia law on slavery in Britain during the *Somerset* case. See "Case of James Sommersett, a Negro, on a Habeas Corpus," in T. B. Howell, ed., *A Complete Collection of State Trials and Proceedings for High Treason and Other Crimes and Misdemeanors* (London: Hansard, 1816), 20:68 (Somerset's counsel speaking of unnatural relations requiring positive law), 71 (Mansfield expanding on issue), 74 (Steuart's counsel countering). Regarding the issue generally, see Wise, *Heavens May Fall*, 160.

12. For this sort of legal debate, see generally David Brion Davis, *The Problem of Slavery in the Age of Revolution, 1770–1823* (Ithaca: Cornell Univ. Press, 1975), 469–71.

13. *Smith v. Gould*, 92 Eng. Rep. 338, 338 (K.B. 1706). The other two cases are *Chamberlain v. Harvey*, 91 Eng. Rep. 994 (K.B. 1697) and *Smith v. Brown and Cooper*, 91 Eng. Rep. 566 (K.B. 1701).

14. *Butts v. Penny*, 83 Eng. Rep. 518, 518 (K.B. 1677). For other decisions from the era finding slaves as property in England, see Helen Tunnicliff Catterall, ed., *Judi-*

cial Cases Concerning American Slavery and the Negro (Washington, DC: Carnegie Institution, 1926), 1:9–10 (e.g., *Noel v. Robinson*, 1 Vernon 459 [1687]; *Gelly v. Cleve*, 1 Ld. Ramy. 147 [1694]).

15. *Cartwright's Case*, cited in Catterall, *Judicial Cases*, 9, as 2 Rushworth 468 (1569).

16. E.g., in *Butts v. Penny*, the Court of King's Bench wrote, "Negros being usually bought and sold among Merchants, so Merchandise, and also being Infidels, there might be a Property in them sufficient to maintain Trover." *Butts v. Penny*, 83 Eng. Rep. 518, 518 (K.B. 1677). Although not ultimately controlling in Holt's ruling, the arguments made on behalf of the slave in *Chamberlain* included that the slave "being baptized according the rite of the Church, he is thereby made a Christian, and Christianity is inconsistent with slavery." *Chamberlain v. Harvey*, 87 Eng. Rep 568, 600–1 (K.B. 1697).

17. "Opinion of Sir Philip York[e], then Attorney-General, and Mr. Talbot, Solicitor-General," in Catterall, *Judicial Cases*, 12.

18. Mark S. Weiner, "New Biographical Evidence on *Somerset's Case*," *Slavery and Abolition* 23 (2002): 124.

19. St. Andrew Holborn records, quoted in Wise, *Heavens May Fall*, 3.

20. "Obituary of remarkable Persons; with Biographical Anecdotes," *Gentleman's Magazine and Historical Chronicle* 68 (1798): 443.

21. E.g., in 1751, when Joe, an enslaved Black that Steuart used as a sailor in his business, ran away, Steuart offered the reward of a pistol in addition to "what the law allows" for anyone capturing and returning him. Paid Advertisement, *Virginia Gazette*, Jan. 10, 1752, 4. See also Paid Advertisement, *Virginia Gazette*, Mar. 12, 1752, 3.

22. For the text of the writ signed by Mansfield ordering Knowles to produce "the body of James Summersett" and show "cause of the taking and detainer of him," see F. O. Shyllon, *Black Slaves in Britain* (London: Oxford Univ. Press, 1974), 77.

23. Steuart had Somerset captured and placed aboard the *Ann and Mary* on November 26, 1771. Mansfield issued the writ on November 28, 1771. Knowles likely produced Somerset by December 10. See Wise, *Heavens May Fall*, 10–11.

24. Sharp's diary entry for January 13, 1772, noted that after Somerset called on him that morning, "I gave him the best advice that I could." Granville Sharp, "Diary," Jan. 13, 1772, in Prince Hoare, *Memoirs of Granville Sharp* (London: Colburn, 1820), 70.

25. Steuart's chief lawyer, John Dunning, representing the side of the enslaved person in the prior case handled by Sharp, had then said about property rights in humans,

"The laws of this Country admit no such property. I know of nothing where this idea exists, I apprehend it only exists in the minds of those who have lived in those countries where it is suffered." "The Case of Lewis (a Negro) v. Stapleton, (1771)" (bound written transcription in Granville Sharp Collection, New-York Historical Society, N-YHS Digital Collections 36291_1.pdf-40). In the *Somerset* case, he argued much the opposite. During the *Somerset* case, Steuart wrote to a friend about trial costs: "The West-India planters and merchants have taken it off my hands; and I shall be entirely directed by them in the further defense of it." Charles Steuart to James Murray, June 15, 1772, in Emory Washburn, "Somerset's Case, and the Extinction of Slavery and Villenage in England," *Proceedings of the Massachusetts Historical Society* 7 (1864): 324. In his *History of English Law*, William Holdsworth names the two chief barristers representing Steuart as two of the three finest barristers of the era. William Holdsworth, *History of English Law* (London: Metheun & Co., 1935), 12:560.

26. "Case of Lewis," 79.

27. During the course of the hearing, Mansfield repeatedly raised the potential cost of the decision to colonial slaveholders in Britain due to the loss of their human property. Mansfield, "Case of Sommersett," 20:70. See generally Shyllon, *Black Slaves in Britain*, 120–21.

28. Lord Mansfield, "Case of Sommersett," 20:81–82 (discussing status of villeinage and slavery in Britain). See generally Paul Finkelman, "'Let Just Be Done, Though the Heavens May Fall': The Law of Freedom," *Chicago-Kent Law Review* 70 (1994): 325–26; Wise, *Heavens May Fall*, 79.

29. See Wise, *Heavens May Fall*, 79; Weiner, *Black Trials*, 80. Among other settlement proposals made from the bench, Mansfield suggested that those who brought the habeas corpus action buy and free Somerset.

30. Steuart to Murray, 7:323 (Mansfield "strongly recommended" settlement and "hinted at emancipating the slave"). Lord Mansfield, "Case of Sommersett," 20:80 ("Mr. Steuart may end the question, by discharging or giving freedom to the negro"). See also Hoare, *Memoirs*, 88; Weiner, *Black Trials*, 81.

31. "Thomas Hutchinson Diary," Aug. 19, 1779, in Peter Orlando Hutchinson, ed., *The Diary and Letters of Thomas Hutchinson* (Boston: Houghton, Mifflin, 1886), 2:276. Steuart also foresaw Somerset prevailing. Steuart to Murray, 7:323.

32. "Thomas Hutchinson Diary," 276 (Hutchinson wrote about Mansfield and the girl, "He calls her Dido, which I suppose is all the name she has"). In his will, Mansfield called this woman by the full name Dido Elizabeth Bell. Wise, *Heavens May Fall*, 183.

33. In his response to the writ, Steuart affirmed that he bought Somerset under Virginia law, did not refer to moving to or residing in Massachusetts, and claimed

that he came with Somerset to Britain to conduct "affairs and business, and with the intention to return to America." "Return to the Habeas Corpus," in "Case of Sommersett," 21.

34. J. Alleyne, "Cause of the Negro Somerset," in Hoare, *Memoirs*, 86. During this course of his argument, Alleyne stressed that "slavery is not a natural, it is a municipal (or statute-made) relation." J. Alleyne, "Case of Sommersett," 20:68. Somerset's lawyers made repeated reference to the famous phrase from the long-lost case of the Russian slave about the air of England being too pure for a slave to breathe.

35. John Dunning, "Case of Sommersett," 20:74.

36. Francis Hargrave, "Case of Sommersett," 20:24. Later, expanding on this train of evils, Somerset's counsel discussed the "horrid cruelties" of American slavery. J. Alleyne, "Case of Sommersett," 20:69.

37. John Dunning, "Case of Sommersett," 20:72.

38. Lord Mansfield, "Case of Sommersett," 20:70–71, 79 ("The setting of 14,000 or 15,000 men at once loose by a solemn opinion, is very disagreeable in the effects it threatens").

39. Lord Mansfield, "Case of Sommersett," 20:79 (the Latin phrase is traditionally translated, "Let justice be done though the heavens may fall").

40. Steuart to Murray, June 15, 1772, 324. For a summary of the criticism of Mansfield in newspapers during the Somerset case, see Shyllon, *Black Slaves in Britain*, 143–48.

41. Lord Mansfield, "Case of Sommersett," 20:82.

42. Ibid., 20:80 ("An application to parliament," Mansfield stated, "is the best, and perhaps the only method of settling the point for the future").

43. "Extract of a Letter from London, dated July 2," *Pennsylvania Packet*, Aug. 24, 1772, 3.

44. "London, June 27," *Boston News-Letter*, Sept. 10, 1772, supp-1 (depicting the number at "near 200 Blacks, with their Ladies").

45. John Riddell to Charles Steuart, July 10, 1772, Steuart Papers, reel 2, pt. 1, 192.

46. "Thomas Hutchinson Diary," 277. For other such comments by Mansfield, see Shyllon, *Black Slaves in Britain*, 165, 168–69; Wise, *Heavens May Fall*, 207–11.

47. Historian F. O. Shyllon discussed the difference between the popular understanding (or "myth") and actual immediate impact (or "reality") of the *Somerset* case in Chapter 10 of his 1974 book, *Black Slaves in Britain*. Shyllon, *Black Slaves in Britain*, 165–76. See also Wise, *Heavens May Fall*, 193–99.

48. See Shyllon, *Black Slaves in Britain*, 157–58.

49. J. Alleyne, "Case of Sommersett," 20:69.

50. Granville Sharp, "Some Remarks on a Late Attempt to Vindicate the Slave Trade by the Laws of God," in Prince Hoare, *Memoirs of Granville Sharp*, 2nd ed. (London: Colburn, 1828), 2:xxxviii.

51. Samuel Johnson, *Taxation No Tyranny; an Answer to the Resolutions and Address of the American Congress*, 4th ed. (London: Cadell, 1775), 89.

52. Samuel Estwick, *Considerations on the Negroe Cause Commonly So Called*, 2nd ed. (London: Dodsley, 1773), 50–51.

53. [Richard Wells], "A few POLITICAL REFLECTIONS, submitted to the consideration of the BRITISH COLONIES," *Pennsylvania Packet*, Aug. 8, 1774, 1 (reprinted in Richard Wells, *A Few Political Reflections Submitted to the Consideration of the British Colonies* [Philadelphia: Dunlap, 1774], 79–80).

54. E.g., "London," *Boston Evening-Post*, July 27, 1772, 1 (no "change in climate [or location] can deprive a person of the property, for which he gave a valuable consideration"); Estwick, *Considerations*, 42–44. See generally David Walderstreicher, *Slavery's Constitution: From Revolution to Ratification* (New York: Hill and Wang, 2009), 40.

55. Lord Mansfield, "Case of Sommersett," 20:79.

56. William Blackstone, *Commentaries on the Laws of England*, 3rd ed. (Oxford: Clarendon Press, 1768), 1:105.

57. "London, June 27," *Boston News-Letter*, Sept. 10, 1772, supp-1.

58. Ben Scotus, "To Lord Mansfield," *Massachusetts Spy*, Sept. 17, 1772, 117.

59. E.g., "Extract of a Letter from London," *Boston Post-Boy*, Sept. 7, 1772, 3 (identified as a loyalist newspaper in Timothy M. Barnes, "Loyalist Newspapers of the American Revolution 1763–1783: A Bibliography," *Proceedings of the American Antiquarian Society* 83 [1973]: 222); "London, May 6," *New-Hampshire Gazette*, Aug. 7, 1772, 2 (identified as a loyalist newspaper in Barnes, "Loyalist Newspapers," 236).

60. [Benjamin Franklin], "The Sommersett Case and the Slave Trade," *London Chronicle*, June 18–20, 1772, in PBF, 19:187–88.

61. Benjamin Franklin to Anthony Benezet, Aug. 22, 1772, PBF, 19:269.

62. John Pendleton Kennedy, ed., *Journal of the House of Burgesses of Virginia*, 1770–72 (Richmond: State Library, 1906), 246 (Mar. 14, 1772, second reading), 263 (Mar. 21, 1772, final passage).

63. See Richard K. MacMaster, "Arthur Lee's 'Address on Slavery': An Aspect of Virginia's Struggle to End the Slave Trade, 1765–1774," *Virginia Magazine of History and Biography* 80 (1972): 148–49.

64. Kennedy, ed., *Journal*, at 284 (Apr. 1, 1772).

65.   [Arthur Lee], *An Essay in Vindication of the Continental Colonies of America, from a Censure of Mr. Adam Smith, in His Theory of Moral Sentiments, with some Reflections on Slavery in General* (London: By Author, 1764), 12, 15, 37–38.

66.   [Thomas Jefferson], *A Summary View of the Rights of British America* (Williamsburg: Clementina Rind, [1774]), 16–17.

67.   John Dunning, "Case of Sommersett," 20:72.

68.   Philip D. Morgan, *Slave-Counterpoint: Black Culture in the Eighteenth-Century Chesapeake and Lowcountry* (Chapel Hill: Univ. of North Carolina Press, 1998), 461 (quoting letter).

69.   "Augusta, June 18, 1774," *Virginia Gazette*, June 30, 1774, 3.

70.   "Augusta, June 18, 1774," *Virginia Gazette*, July 7, 1774, 3; "Augusta, June 18, 1774," *Virginia Gazette*, July 14, 1774, 4.

71.   John Adams, *Diary*, Nov. 5, 1766, DAJA, 1:321.

72.   Joanne Pope Melish, *Disowning Slavery: Gradual Emancipation and "Race" in New England, 1780–1860* (Ithaca: Cornell Univ. Press, 2000), 50, 56 ("slavery had come under fire throughout the colonies, and the onset of the Revolution both intensified the attack and [in New England] weakened the structures and practices that supported the institution").

73.   John Adams to Jeremy Bentham, Mar. 21, 1795, PJA, --: --- (online access at founders.archives.gov).

74.   Thomas Hutchinson to Lord Hillsborough, May 1771, in George Henry Moore, *Notes on the History of Slavery in Massachusetts* (New York: Appleton, 1866), 131 (explaining his veto as in conformity with government policy).

75.   Felix, "The humble Petition of many Slaves, living in the Town of Boston, and other Towns in the Province," *The Appendix; Or, Some Observations on the Expediency of the Petition of the Africans, living in Boston, &c. lately presented to the General Assembly of this Province* (Boston: E. Russell, [1773]), 10–11.

76.   "A Lover of Constitutional Liberty, [Preface]," in ibid., 4.

77.   Hume, "From the Massachusetts Spy of Thursday, January 28, 1773," in ibid., 14.

78.   Peter Bestes et al., "Boston, April 20th, 1773" (Boston: n/p, 1773), in Printed Ephemera Collection, Library of Congress Online Catalog, OCLC Number rbpe03701600 (single page broadsheet).

79.   The *Journal* for the General Court reported the submission of this "Petition of Felix Holbrook, and others, Negros," on June 25, 1773. *Journals of the House of Representatives for Massachusetts, 1773–1774* (Boston: Massachusetts Historical Society, 1981), 50:85.

80.   "Boston, Friday, July 23," *Massachusetts Spy*, July 29, 1773, 1.

81. Ibid.

82. *Journals of the House of Representatives for Massachusetts*, 50:85 (June 25, 1773).

83. John Hancock to Barnards and Harrison, Oct. 21, 1765, reprinted in Abram English Brown, *John Hancock: His Book* (Boston: Lee & Shepard, 1898), 90.

84. *Journals of the House of Representatives for Massachusetts*, 50:94 (June 28, 1773).

85. John Adams, *Diary*, Dec. 17, 1773, DAJA, 2:85–86.

86. "Address of the Africans," January 20, 1774, *Massachusetts Spy*, Sept. 1, 1774, 2.

87. Three weeks after the Boston Tea Party, Adams sent a letter to a fellow committee member noting that "the Negros whose petitions lies on file" were pressing for a response and asking about "the general outlines of your Design" for relief. Samuel Adams to John Pickering Jr., Jan. 8, 1774, reprinted in Moore, *Notes on the History*, 136.

88. "An Act to Prevent the Importation of Negros or other Persons as Slaves into this Province," Mar. 4, 1774, reprinted in Moore, *Notes on the History*, 139.

89. Among the responses to Gage's move, a published address by one local Black apparently associated with the petitions praised the lawmakers, "to their immortal honor be it mentioned," for passing a bill "to put a final stop, to so iniquities a business, as the Slave Trade," and blamed "only" the governor for its defeat. Cæsar Sarter, "Address," *Essex Journal*, Aug. 17, 1774, 1.

90. "Petition of a Grate Number of Blackes," May 25, 1774, reprinted in Herbert Aptheker, ed., *A Documentary History of the Negro People of the United States* (New York: Citadel, 1951), 8–9.

91. "To the . . . General Court assembled, June—Anno Domini 1774," reprinted in Chernoh M. Sesay Jr., "The Revolutionary Black Roots of Slavery's Abolition in Massachusetts," *New England Quarterly* 87 (2014): 124.

92. Even armed troops did not always suffice for the British to venture beyond occupied Boston, as demonstrated by an incident that occurred in February 1775, after Gage heard that patriot forces might have stored eight cannons in Salem. Gage dispatched troops to travel the short distance from Boston to Salem but militia forces blocked their entrance to Salem. Mary Beth Norton, *1774: The Long Year of Revolution* (New York: Knopf, 2020), 330.

93. Stater, "Address," 1.

Chapter Four: The Declaration of Liberty

1. Cæsar Sarter, "Address," *Essex Journal*, Aug. 17, 1774, 1.

2. "The Glorious SEVENTY FOUR," *New-York Journal*, Aug. 18, 1774, 4.

3.   See "Six Dollar Reward," *New-York Journal*, Aug. 18, 1774, S-4 (indentured "Irish servant lad"); "Manor of St. George," Aug. 23, 1774, *New-York Journal*, Aug. 25, 1774, 3 ("a mulatto slave, half Negro and half Indian").

4.   "Boston, Monday, August 15," and "Portsmouth, August 12," *Essex Journal*, Aug. 17, 1774, 2. Similar reports appeared in the same issue of the *New-York Journal* that published "The Glorious Seventy Four." "Boston, August 11," *New-York Journal*, Aug. 18, 1774, 2. For similar articles appearing in later issues, see "New-Jersey," *New-York Journal*, Aug. 25, 1774, 1; "New-York, August 25," *New-York Journal*, Aug. 25, 1774, 3.

5.   Stressing its importance, on the first day of the First Continental Congress, John Adams quoted Patrick Henry as saying, "This was the first general Congress which had ever happened—that no former Congress could be a Precedent." Patrick Henry, quoted in John Adams, *Diary*, Sept. 5, 1774, DAJA, 2:123.

6.   Official credentials for each delegation discussing the source of its appointment appear in the official record for the Congress's opening day. "Monday, September 5, 1774," JCC, 1:15–24. See also Mary Beth Norton, *1774: The Long Year of Revolution* (New York: Knopf, 2020), 148–58.

7.   For example, the public meeting in Charleston, South Carolina, that chose delegates from its colony to the Congress did so by authorizing "every free white person in the province" to cast a ballot in a box set up for that purpose for four hours during the meeting—but as a practical matter only the "gentlemen" present could vote. "CHARLES-TOWN, South-Carolina, July 12," *Boston-Gazette*, Aug. 15, 1774, 1.

8.   Ibid., 1.

9.   See John Andrews to William Barrell, Aug. 10, 1774, in William Sargent, ed., "Letters of John Andrews, Esq., or Boston," *Proceedings of the Massachusetts Historical Society* 8 (1864–65): 339. In his diary, John Adams noted that the delegation departed from Cushing's house. John Adams, *Diary*, Aug. 10, 1774, DAJA, 2:97.

10.   John Adams, *Diary*, Aug. 16, 1774, DAJA, 2:100.

11.   John Adams to Abigail Adams, Sept. 14, 1774, AFC, 1:155.

12.   "Resolutions entered into by the delegates from the several towns and districts in the county of Suffolk," JCC, 1:32–35.

13.   "CHARLES-TOWN," 1.

14.   "NEWBERN (North Carolina)," *Pennsylvania Packet*, Sept. 19, 1774, S-3.

15.   "At a general Meeting of Freeholders," *Boston-Gazette*, Aug. 8, 1774, 2.

16.   "NEWBERN," S-3.

17.   "Meeting of Freeholders," 2.

18. John Adams, *Diary*, Sept. 17, 1774, DAJA, 2:134–35 (Explaining his joy, Adams wrote, "This day convinced me that America will support Massachusetts or perish with her").

19. John Adams, *Diary*, Oct. 24, 1774, DAJA, 2:156 (Adams further observed, "There is no greater Mortification than to sit with a half a dozen Witts, deliberating upon a Petition").

20. "The Association, &c.," Oct. 20, 1774, JCC, 1:76–77.

21. John Adams to William Tudor, Oct. 7, 1774, PJA, 2:188.

22. Patrick Henry, quoted in John Adams, *Diary*, "Notes of Debates in the Continental Congress," Sept. 6, 1774, DAJA, 2:125. To secure proportionate representation for his wealthy, populated colony, Henry offered not to factor in enslaved persons. "If the freemen can be represented according to their Numbers, I am satisfied," he conceded. Ibid.

23. "Resolved," Sept. 6, 1774, JCC, 1:25.

24. Samuel Ward, *Diary*, Sept. 9, 1774, in LMCC, 1:27. For further discussion at the First Continental Congress of these sources of rights, see James Duane, "Address Before the Committee to State the Rights of the Colonists," Sept. 8, 1774, LMCC, 1:23–28 (concluding, "That it is essential to Liberty that the Subject be bound to no Law to which he does not assent by himself or his Representative, a privilege which forms the distinction between Freemen and Slaves per se").

25. "Resolved," Oct. 22, 1774, JCC, 1:102.

26. John Adams, *Diary*, Oct. 28, 1774, DAJA, 2:157.

27. As early as the Congress's opening day, Pennsylvania delegate Joseph Galloway (a closet loyalist) commented privately on the growing alliance between the delegates from Massachusetts and Virginia, both of whom he had characterized as warm for liberty. Joseph Galloway to William Franklin, Sept. 5, 1774, LMCC, 1:9.

28. "To the People of Great-Britain," Oct. 21, 1774, JCC, 1:82.

29. John Dickinson to Arthur Lee, Oct. 24, 1774, LMCC, 1:83.

30. Mercy Warren to Catharine Sawbridge Macaulay, Dec. 29, 1774, in Jeffrey H. Richards and Sharon M. Harris, eds., *Mercy Otis Warren: Selected Letters* (Athens: Univ. of Georgia Press, 2009), 38–39.

31. Abigail Adams to Catharine Sawbridge Macaulay, late 1774, AFC, 1:177–78.

32. Abigail Adams to John Adams, Sept. 22, 1774, AFC, 1:162.

33. Mercy Otis Warren to John Adams, Oct. 1775, PJA 3:268.

34. "The KING's SPEECH, &c.," *Connecticut Courant*, Feb. 6, 1775, 2 (included the replies of the Houses of Commons and Lords).

35. Abigail Adams to John Adams, Feb. 3, 1775, AFC, 1:184 (Adams read the king's speech in the Feb. 2, 1775, issue of the *Massachusetts Spy*).

36. "From the LONDON GAZETTE," *Massachusetts Gazette*, Apr. 10, 1775, 1.

37. James Warren to Mercy Warren, Apr. 6, 1775, *Warren-Adams Letters* (Boston: Massachusetts Historical Society, 1917), 2:45.

38. John Winthrop to Richard Price, Apr. 10, 1775, "The Price Letters," *Proceedings of the Massachusetts Historical Society*, 2nd ser., 17 (1903): 285.

39. Abigail Adams to John Adams, Sept. 22, 1774, 162.

40. E.g., "BOSTON, September 5," *Boston-Gazette*, Sept. 5, 1774, 2.

41. See Benjamin Quarles, *The Negro in the American Revolution* (Chapel Hill: Univ. of North Carolina Press, 1961), vii.

42. "The humble Petition and Memorial of Jamaica," Mar. 2, 1775, *Connecticut Journal*, 1–2.

43. Ibid., 2. The appendix listed the island's productivity—68,160 hogshead of sugar; 5,031 bags of ginger; and the like—and the property generating those products—192,914 "Negroes"; 648 mills; and 647 plantations.

44. [John Allan], *The Watchman Alarm to Lord N---h* (Salem: E. Russell, 1774), 27–28.

45. "Darian (Georgia) Resolutions," Jan. 12, 1775, in Peter Force, ed., *American Archives*, ser. 4 (Washington: Clarke & Force, 1837), 1:1136. In 1739, eighteen of the most prominent members of this coastal community originally founded by the colony's philanthropically motivated founder, James Oglethorpe, had signed the first petition against the introduction of slavery into Georgia. Most signers of the 1775 resolution had Scottish surnames.

46. [Samuel Hopkins], *A Dialogue Concerning the Slavery of the Africans; Shewing it to be the Duty and Interest of the American Colonies to emancipate all their African Slaves* (Norwich, CT: Spooner, 1776), 5, 8–9, 29–30.

47. The Editors, "To the Honorable Members of the Continental Congress," [early 1776], in ibid., iii–iv. Serving as president of his state's Manumission Society, New York delegate John Jay later reprinted and distributed Hopkins's *Dialogue*. See [Hopkins], *Dialogue*, 6–7.

48. R. W. Emerson, "Hymn: Sung at the Completion of the Concord Monument, April 19, 1836," in R. W. Emerson, *Poems* (Boston: Ticknor & Fields, 1846), 250.

49. Quarles, *Negro in American Revolution*, 9–11; Emily Blanck, *Tyrannicide: Forging an American Law of Slavery in Revolutionary South Carolina and Massachusetts* (Athens: Univ. of Georgia Press, 2014), 51–52.

50. George Washington to George William Fairfax, May 31, 1775, PGW-CS, 10:368.

51. John Adams, "Novanglas Papers, 1774–1775," DAJA, 3:314.

52. Annette Gordon-Reed, *Thomas Jefferson and Sally Hemings: An American Controversy* (Charlottesville: Univ. of Virginia Press, 1997), 2, 52.

53. [Thomas Jefferson], *A Summary View of the Rights of British America* (Williamsburg: Clementina Rind, [1774]), 11, 16–17.

54. Ibid., 17.

55. Ibid. Further, in his draft 1776 constitution for Virginia, Jefferson proposed, "No person hereafter coming into this country shall be held in slavery under any pretext whatever." [Thomas Jefferson], "Second Draft by Jefferson," before June 13, 1776, PTJ, 1:353.

56. See, e.g., Thomas Jefferson to Edward Coles, Aug. 25, 1814, PTJ-RS, 7:604; Thomas Jefferson to Thomas Mann Randolph Jr., Feb. 18, 1793, PTJ, 25:230.

57. Jefferson to Coles, PTJ-RS, 7:604; Thomas Jefferson, *Notes on the State of Virginia* (Boston: Lilly & Wait, 1832), 151 (query 14); Thomas Jefferson to Jared Sparks, Feb. 4, 1824, PTJ-RS, --: --- (online access at founders.archives.gov).

58. Jefferson, *Notes on the State of Virginia*, 144, 150–51 (query 14).

59. Benjamin Franklin to John Waring, Dec. 17, 1763, PBF, 10:395. In response to a query from the Enlightenment French philosopher Marquis de Condorcet, Franklin wrote in 1774, "The Negroes who are free live among the White People, but are generally improvident and poor. I think they are not deficient in natural Understanding, but they have not the Advantage of Education. They make good Musicians." Benjamin Franklin to Marquis de Condorcet, Mar. 20, 1774, PBF, 21:151.

60. [Benjamin Rush], *An Address to the Inhabitants of the British Settlements in America, upon Slave-Keeping* (Boston: Boyles, 1773), 1–4.

61. Ibid., 28.

62. Quarles, *Negro in American Revolution*, 10–11.

63. George Washington to [John Hancock], July 10, 1775, PGW-RWS, 1:90.

64. "Council of War," Oct. 8, 1775, PGW-RWS, 1:125.

65. "Minutes of the Conference Between a Committee of Congress, Washington, and Representatives of the New England Colonies," Oct. 23, 1775, PBF, 22:237 (only members of Congress and Washington attended this day).

66. George Washington to John Hancock, Dec. 31, 1775, PGW-RWS, 2:623. With this order, Washington biographer Henry Wiencek noted, "for the first time in his life Washington had responded in a fair way to an appeal from free blacks." Henry Wiencek, *An Imperfect God: George Washington, His Slaves, and the Creation of America* (New York: Farrar, Straus, 2003), 204.

67. "Tuesday, January 16, 1776," JCC, 4:60 (Congress resolved, "That the free negroes who have served faithfully in the army at Cambridge, may be re-inlisted therein, but no others").

68. John Adams to William Heath, Oct. 5, 1775, PJA, 3:183.

69. William Heath to John Adams, Oct. 23, 1775, PJA, 3:230.

70. See Quarles, *Negro in American Revolution*, 16–17 (noted official restrictions, which had limited practical effect); Blanck, *Tyrannicide*, 52 (Massachusetts); Douglas R. Egerton, *Death or Liberty: African Americans and Revolutionary America* (Oxford: Oxford Univ. Press, 2009), 76 (Connecticut).

71. Quarles, *Negro in American Revolution*, 17.

72. Ibid., vii.

73. See Gary B. Nash, *The Forgotten Fifth: African Americans in the Age of Revolution* (Cambridge: Harvard Univ. Press, 2006), 24–30; Egerton, *Death or Liberty*, 68–70; Alan Taylor, *American Revolutions: A Continental History, 1750–1804* (New York: W. W. Norton, 2016), 146–51.

74. Egerton, *Death or Liberty*, 68–70; Taylor, *American Revolutions*, 148–49.

75. William Lyttelton, "Debate in the Commons on the Address of Thanks," Oct. 26, 1775, *The Parliamentary History of England from the Earliest Period to the Year 1803* (London: T. C. Hansard, 1813), 18:733.

76. James Johnstone, "Debate in the Commons on the Address of Thanks," Oct. 26, 1775, ibid., 18:747 (Johnstone derisively depicted Lyttelton's suggestion as a "scheme").

77. [Lord Dunmore], "A Proclamation," *Pennsylvania Journal*, Dec. 6, 1775, 2.

78. For a graphic depiction of the episode, including the estimate that the enslaved Blacks joining Dunmore's camps "died by the hundreds" from smallpox, see Cassandra Pybus, *Epic Journeys of Freedom: Runaway Slaves of the American Revolution and Their Global Quest for Liberty* (Boston: Beacon Press, 2006), 17–19.

79. Richard Henry Lee to Catherine Macaulay, Nov. 29, 1775, *Papers of the Lee Family*, Lee Family Digital Archives, Stratford Hall, Stratford, VA.

80. Edward Rutledge to Ralph Izard, Dec. 8, 1775, *Correspondence of Mr. Ralph Izard of South Carolina* (New York: Francis & Co., 1844), 165.

81. See generally Woody Holton, *Forced Founders: Indians, Debtors, Slaves, and the Making of the American Revolution in Virginia* (Chapel Hill: Univ. of North Carolina Press, 1999), 158–60; Woody Holton, *Liberty Is Sweet: The Hidden History of the American Revolution* (New York: Simon & Schuster, 2021), 204 (writing of the reaction in Virginia, Holton concluded, "No other document—not even Thomas Paine's *Common Sense* or the Declaration of Independence—did more than Dunmore's proclamation to convert white residents of Britain's most populous American colony to the cause of independence"). Countless patriots denounced the proclamation in the harshest tones, with Washington calling it

"diabolical." George Washington to Richard Henry Lee, Dec. 26, 1775, PGW-RWS, 2:610. The *Pennsylvania Journal* published the proclamation under a caption about Dunmore, "Not in the legions Of horrid Hell, can come a devil more damn'd." "Williamsburg, (in Virginia) November 24," *Pennsylvania Journal*, Dec. 6, 1775, 2.

82. In his analysis of the proclamation's impact, historian Sean Wilentz concluded, "Dunmore's gambit, instead of breaking the patriots' will, reinforced their allegiance to the independence cause, based on their conviction, built up for a decade, that British authorities would use any tactic to enforce their iron rule." Sean Wilentz, "The Paradox of the American Revolution," *New York Review of Books* 69 (Jan. 13, 2022): 27. Given how Britain had protected and profited from slavery in its American colonies, colonists could not rationally fear that Britain would abolish slavery in those colonies. Although it readily repeated virtually every plausible charge against the British, for example, Thomas Paine's *Common Sense* never suggested that the British might end slavery in the colonies. [Thomas Paine], *Common Sense* (Philadelphia: R. Bell, 1776), 59.

83. George III, "A Proclamation for Suppressing Rebellion and Sedition," Aug. 23, 1775 (London: Eyre & Strahan, 1775) (one page broadside).

84. [Paine], *Common Sense*, 58. Regarding Dunmore's proclamation and its impact on both American colonists (which he referred to as "us") and enslaved Blacks (referred to as "them"), Paine wrote, "The cruelty hath a double guilt, it is dealing brutally by us, and treacherously by them." Ibid., 59.

85. George Washington to Joseph Reed, Apr. 1, 1776, PGW-RWS, 4:11 (for clarity, initial capitalization and italic of "common sense" follows Taylor, *American Revolutions*, 159). As Washington's letters about it indicate, Washington considered Dunmore's proclamation one such "persecution."

86. [Paine], *Common Sense*, 59.

87. Ibid., 28.

88. Thomas Jefferson, "III. Jefferson's 'original Rough draught' of the Declaration of Independence, 11 June–4 July 1776," PTJ, 1:426.

89. Paul Leicester Ford, ed., *The Autobiography of Thomas Jefferson, 1743–1790* (Philadelphia: Univ. of Pennsylvania Press, 1914), 33, 39–40.

90. "The unanimous Declaration of the thirteen United States of America," July 4, 1776, JCC, 5:510 (this version in the official journal used the word "unalienable" rather than "inalienable," but later printings restored to Jefferson's word). Franklin substituted "self-evident" for Jefferson's "sacred & undeniable," and Congress replaced Jefferson's "inherent and" with "certain."

Chapter Five: "Liberty Is Sweet"

1. See Henry Wiencek, *An Imperfect God: George Washington, His Slaves, and the Creation of America* (New York: Farrar, Straus, 2003), 208 ("At the time Phillis Wheatley was the most famous black person in America; indeed she was the *only* famous black person in America").

2. Margaretta Matilda Odell, *Memoir and Poems of Phillis Wheatley: A Native African and a Slave* (Boston: Geo. W. Light, 1834), 9–10.

3. Phillis Wheatley, "On Messrs hussy and Coffin," *Newport Mercury*, Dec. 21, 1767, 3.

4. "To be sold by *Elizabeth Aborn*" and "Ran-away from the Subscribers," *Newport Mercury*, Dec. 21, 1767, 4.

5. Phillis Wheatley, "To the University of Cambridge, In New England," in *The Poems of Phillis Wheatley*, ed. Julian D. Mason Jr., rev. ed. (Chapel Hill: Univ. of North Carolina Press, 1989), 52.

6. Phillis Wheatley, "America," in Mason, *Poems*, 125; Phillis Wheatley, "On Being Brought from Africa to America," in Mason, *Poems*, 53.

7. Wheatley, "America," 125 (emphasis added).

8. Phillis Wheatley, "An Elegiac Poem," in Mason, *Poems*, 134.

9. An admirer of his paintings, Wheatley wrote a poem in praise of Moorhead's work. Phillis Wheatley, "To S. M. A young *African* Painter, on Seeing His Work," in Mason, *Poems*, 104–5.

10. Phillis Wheatley, "To the Right Honorable William, Earl of Dartmouth, His Majesty's Principal Secretary of State for North-America," in Mason, *Poems*, 83.

11. "Poems on various Subjects, religious and moral," *Monthly Review* 49 (1773): 458–59.

12. Phillis Wheatley to David Worcester, Oct. 18, 1773, in Mason, *Poems*, 197.

13. Phillis Wheatley to Samson Occom, Feb. 11, 1774, in ibid., 204.

14. Phillis Wheatley to George Washington, Oct. 28, 1775, PGW-RWS, 2:242.

15. Phillis Wheatley, "To His Excellency General Washington," in Mason, *Poems*, 167.

16. George Washington to Phillis [Wheatley], Feb. 28, 1776, PGW-RWS, 3:387.

17. Susan P. Schoelwer, executive director of historic preservation and collections at George Washington's Mount Vernon, "Life Portraits of George Washington—Draft," 2021.

18. As explained more fully in Chapter 6, Mount Vernon archivist Susan P. Schoelwer doubts both attributions.

19. "Advertisement, May 23," *Philadelphia Gazette*, May 24, 1796, 1 (depicted Judge as "ABSCONDED from the household of the President of the United States").

20. George Washington, *Diary*, Aug. 2, 1771, DGW, 3:45; Cassandra Pybus, *Epic Journeys of Freedom: Runaway Slaves of the American Revolution and Their Global Quest for Liberty* (Boston: Beacon Press, 2006), 4.

21. Lund Washington to George Washington, Dec. 3, 1775, PGW-RWS, 2:480. Lund Washington was George's distant cousin, and his letter did not distinguish clearly between enslaved and indentured servants.

22. "Book of Negroes," from Guy Carleton, 1st Baron Dorchester, *Papers*, National Archives, Kew (PRO 30/55/100) 10427, 90–91.

23. Pybus, *Epic Journeys*, 19–20. According to a copy found in the Toner Transcripts in the Library of Congress, taken from a manuscript memorandum made by Lund Washington in April 1781, and enclosed in his letter of April 18, 1781, to George Washington, the loss suffered by Mount Vernon to the British warship *Savage* was principally in slaves including "Harry. a man about 40 years old, valuable, a Horsier." George Washington Papers, ser. 3, subser. 3H, Varick Transcripts, Letterbook 2, http://www.loc.gov/resource/mgw3h.002.

24. For the advertisement by his former owner, John Corlies, offering a reward for the return of Titus, see "THREE POUNDS, Reward," *Pennsylvania Gazette*, Nov. 22, 1775, 1.

25. Benjamin Quarles, *The Negro in the American Revolution* (Chapel Hill: Univ. of North Carolina Press, 1961), 28.

26. See Philip D. Morgan and Andrew J. O'Shaughnessy, "Arming Slaves in the American Revolution," in *Arming Slaves from Classical Times to the Modern Age*, ed. Christopher Leslie Brown and Philip D. Morgan (New Haven: Yale Univ. Press, 2006), 189 ("At best, about eight hundred slaves escaped to Dunmore").

27. Lord Dunmore to Secretary of State, Mar. 30, 1776, in Peter Force, ed., *American Archives*, ser. 5 (Washington: Clarke & Force, 1851), 2:160.

28. Lord Dunmore to Secretary of State, June 26, 1776, in ibid., 2:162.

29. A muster of the Black Guides and Pioneers taken in September 1777, as the company participated in the British march on Philadelphia, listed 172 members. A muster in December 1777, after the British occupied Philadelphia, reported 208 members. Gary Nash, *Forging Freedom: The Formation of Philadelphia's Black Community, 1720–1840* (Cambridge: Harvard Univ. Press, 1988), 49.

30. Thomas Jones, *History of New York during the Revolutionary War* (New York: New-York Historical Society, 1879 repr.), 2:76; Prybus, *Epic Journeys*, 24–32.

31. Prybus, *Epic Journeys*, 27–29.

NOTES TO PAGES 112–117

32. Wheatley, "Washington," in Mason, *Poems*, 167.

33. George Washington to John Augustine Washington, May 31–June 4, 1776, PGW-RWS, 4:413.

34. Portions of this paragraph and some ensuing ones are drawn from or based on the author's earlier book, *Franklin & Washington: The Founding Partnership* (New York: HarperCollins, 2020), 121, 128–32.

35. Jonathan Dickinson Sergeant to John Adams, Aug. 13, 1776, PJA, 4:453–54.

36. John Adams to Jonathan Dickinson Sergeant, Aug. 17, 1776, PJA, 4:469.

37. George Washington to John Hancock, Dec. 9, 1776, PGW-RWS, 7:284.

38. George Washington to Samuel Washington, Dec. 18, 1776, PGW-RWS, 7:370.

39. Thomas Paine, *The American Crisis, Number I* (Norwich: Trumbull, [1776]), 1–2.

40. George Washington to John Parke Custis, Jan. 22, 1777, PGW-RWS, 8:123.

41. J. M. Varnum to George Washington, Jan. 2, 1778, PGW-RWS, 13:125.

42. George Washington to Nicholas Cooke, Jan. 2, 1778, PGW-RWS, 13:114.

43. "The Rhode Island Slave Enlistment Act," Feb. 14, 1778, in Michael Lee Lanning, *Defenders of Liberty: African Americans in the Revolutionary War* (New York: Citadel Press, 2000), 205.

44. Nicholas Cooke to George Washington, Feb. 23, 1778, PGW-RWS, 13:646. The case of Thomas Nichols offers an example of how the program worked. He signed up for the regiment in May 1778 with the required approval of his owners, Benjamin and Phoebe Nichols, who received 120 pounds from the state. Under his service agreement, he would retain his freedom by serving through the end of the war. By January 1781, however, Thomas was so sick and worn out that he wrote his former owners about returning to their service. Thomas Nichols to Benjamin and Phoebe Nichols, Jan. 18, 1781, in Christian M. McBurney, "The Discovery of an Important Letter from a Soldier of the 1st Rhode Island Regiment," *Journal of the American Revolution*, Apr. 14, 2021 (online resource at allthingsliberty.com).

45. "Rhode Island Slave Enlistment Act," 205.

46. Lanning, *Defenders of Liberty*, 75–78.

47. In August 1777, shortly after completing the constitution, several delegates rejoined Vermont's small "Green Mountain" militia that, combined with troops from New Hampshire, routed a large foraging party sent by Burgoyne to commandeer supplies from the New Hampshire Grants at Bennington. With those much-needed supplies, Burgoyne's main army might have withstood the American forces at Saratoga.

48. "Constitution of Vermont—1777," ch. I, art. I, in Francis Newton Thorpe, ed., *The Federal and State Constitutions, Colonial Charters, and Other Organic Laws of the*

States, Territories, and Colonies Now or Heretofore Forming the United States of America (Washington, DC: Government Printing Office, 1909), 6:3739–40.

49. "Resolved," May 10, 1776, JCC, 4:342. Founded by colonists from Massachusetts under their own charters, Rhode Island and Connecticut did not need to revise their founding documents. Other than those two states, only Massachusetts had not adopted a new state constitution by July 1777.

50. Constitution of Pennsylvania—1776," Declaration of Rights, art. I, in Thorpe, *Federal and State Constitutions*, 5:3082.

51. Harvey Amani Whitfield, *The Problem of Slavery in Early Vermont, 1777–1810* (Montpelier: Vermont Historical Society, 2014).

52. The rugged terrain and short growing season in Vermont could not sustain the sort of plantation agriculture suited to slavery, and few Vermonters could afford to purchase or keep enslaved household workers. Still, the absence of many enslaved persons and conditions conducive to slavery could just as easily cause Vermonters to ignore the issue as to act on it.

53. "The Rejected Constitution of 1778," art. V, in Oscar Handlin and Mary Handlin, eds., *The Popular Sources of Political Authority: Documents on the Massachusetts Constitution of 1780* (Cambridge: Harvard Univ. Press, 1966), 192–93.

54. John Adams to James Warren, July 7, 1777, PJA, 5:242–43. For racial, property-ownership, and tax-payment restrictions on voting in 1778, see Alexander Keyssar, *The Right to Vote: The Contested History of Democracy in the United States* (New York: Basic Books, 2000), 340–41 (table of suffrage requirements, 1776–1790).

55. "The petition of A Great Number of Blackes," Jan. 13, 1777, reprinted in Herbert Aptheker, ed., *A Documentary History of the Negro People of the United States* (New York: Citadel, 1951), 10.

56. Lemuel Haynes, "Liberty Further Extended," in Ruth Bogin, "'Liberty Further Extended': A 1776 Antislavery Manuscript by Lemuel Haynes," *William and Mary Quarterly* 40 (1983): 94–104 (emphasis added). Various sermons and writings by so-called New England or Edwardsian theologians and their offshoot New Divinity or Hopkinsian disciples, presented selflessly striving for the liberty of others (whether from slavery or British oppression), as examples of the disinterested benevolence that constituted evidence of salvation.

57. "Hardwick," May 20, 1778, in Handlin and Handlin, *Popular Sources*, 216.

58. "Boothbay," May 20, 1778, in ibid., 248.

59. E.g., "Upton," May 20, 1778, in ibid., 263 ("colour"); "Georgetown," May 25, 1778, in ibid., 177 (objecting to the article disenfranchising persons for "being

born in Africa, India or ancient America or even being much Sun burnt"); "Blanford," May 27, 1778, in ibid., 282 ("Differences in Complexion"); "Westminster," June 9, 1778, in ibid., 312 ("couler").

60. "The Essex Result, 1778," in ibid., 329.

61. "Sutton," May 18, 1778, in ibid., 231.

Chapter Six: "Contending for the Sweets of Freedom"

1. "THREE POUNDS, Reward," *Pennsylvania Gazette*, Nov. 22, 1775, 1.

2. See Gary Nash, *Forging Freedom: The Formation of Philadelphia's Black Community, 1720–1840* (Cambridge: Harvard Univ. Press, 1988), 49, 56.

3. "Cash Accounts," May 1768, PGW-CS, 8:84 n. 2 (In the same transaction, Washington paid over three times as much for "Mulatto Will" as for a "Negro boy" named Adam).

4. G. W. Parke Custis, *Recollections and Private Memories of Washington* (Washington: William H. Moore, 1859), 28–29.

5. See, e.g., G. W. Parke Custis, *Recollections and Private Memories of Washington* (Philadelphia: J. W. Bradley, 1861), 1 (the 1859 edition of this book [cited above] identifies the reflections as first appearing in the pages of Washington DC's *National Intelligencer*; the title page of the 1861 edition depicts the author as Washington's "adopted son").

6. George Washington to David Stuart, Aug. 13, 1798, PGW-RS, 2:525 (Stuart married the widow of Custis's father in 1783).

7. See Henry Wiencek, *An Imperfect God: George Washington, His Slaves, and the Creation of America* (New York: Farrar, Straus, 2003), 308–10.

8. For example, one published account from a patriot source reported on a raiding "party of the enemy, consisting of Tye with thirty blacks, thirty-six [loyalist] Queen's Rangers, and thirty refugee Tories" plundering property in Monmouth County, taking ten patriot militia members prisoners, and killing or wounding five more. "TRENTON, June 28," *Pennsylvania Evening Post*, June 30, 1780, 71–72. See also "TRENTON, April 12," *Pennsylvania Evening Post*, April 15, 1780, 40 (reporting on a raid by "a party of Negros and Refugees").

9. Judith Van Buskirk, "Crossing the Lines: African-Americans in New York City Region During the British Occupation, 1776–1783," *Pennsylvania History* 65 (1998): 88 ("One quarter of Ward's four-hundred-man force was black").

10. Douglas R. Egerton, *Death or Liberty: African Americans and Revolutionary America* (Oxford: Oxford Univ. Press, 2009), 65–67; Graham Russell Hodges, *Slavery*

and Freedom in the Rural North: African Americans in Monmouth County, New Jersey, 1665–1865 (Lanham, MD: Roman & Littlefield, 1997), 97–104.

11.   "TRENTON, April 24," *New Jersey Gazette*, Apr. 24, 1782, 2.

12.   Mount Vernon archivist Susan P. Schoelwer doubts both attributions. As explained by Schoelwer, Jonathan Trumbull painted a 1780 portrait of Washington with a Black aide from memory five years after the military scene it depicts, suggesting that the artist would have painted Lee either from memory or by using an unknown model. Although this picture now bears the title "George Washington and William Lee," it formerly bore the title "George Washington" without any mention of Lee. A later Washington family portrait with an unidentified Black servant in the background dates from after Lee's active service and likely depicts a butler or waiter rather than a valet. Further, the pictured servant stands erect at a time when Lee could no longer stand erect due to crippling workplace injuries to both knees.

13.   Benjamin Quarles, *The Negro in the American Revolution* (Chapel Hill: Univ. of North Carolina Press, 1961), 78–79.

14.   Ibid., ix (uses the term "patriot forces" and "American armies" here interchangeably but does not appear to include militia forces in this total). Compiled in 1961 as part of Quarles's groundbreaking study, the figure remains widely accepted by leading historians in the field. See, e.g., Philip D. Morgan and Andrew J. O'Shaughnessy, "Arming Slaves in the American Revolution," in *Arming Slaves from Classical Times to the Modern Age*, ed. Christopher Leslie Brown and Philip D. Morgan (New Haven: Yale Univ. Press, 2006), 198 ("about five thousand black Americans served in the Continental Army"); Egerton, *Death or Liberty*, 64 (up to 5,000 in "the Continental Army").

15.   Evelyn M. Acomb, ed., *The Revolutionary Journal of Baron Ludwig von Closen, 1780–1783* (Chapel Hill: Univ. of North Carolina Press, 1958), 89.

16.   Morgan and O'Shaughnessy, "Arming Slaves," 198.

17.   Quarles, *Negro in American Revolution*, 77.

18.   *Lists and Returns of Connecticut Men in the Revolution, 1775–1783* (Hartford: Connecticut Historical Society, 1909), 80–81.

19.   Ibid., 445–46 (index listing of 120 soldiers with only a first name followed by the word "Negro" and many others with only a first name and no added descriptor, which likely also designated Blacks).

20.   Ibid., 365–68.

21.   In his chapter on the subject, military writer Michael Lee Lanning quotes a 1775 navy recruiting broadside from Rhode Island as stating, "Ye able backed sail-

ors, men white or black, to volunteer for navy service in ye interest of freedom." Michael Lee Lanning, *Defenders of Liberty: African Americans in the Revolutionary War* (New York: Citadel, 2000), 88.

22. Ibid., 87–96; Quarles, *Negro in American Revolution*, 83–93. Quarles estimated that nine out of ten "sailors of African dissent in the Virginia navy . . . were slaves, many of whom were enlisted in the guise of free men as substitutes for their masters." Ibid., at 89. Regarding numbers, Lanning warns, "Almost nothing exists in the official archives in the way of reliable statistical information. Crew lists for naval and merchant vessels, if they exist at all, rarely note the race of crewmen." Lanning, *Defenders of Liberty*, 88–89.

23. E.g., ibid., 198 ("about" 5,000 Black Americans in the Continental Army versus "perhaps" 12,000 on the British side); Egerton, *Death or Liberty*, 64 ("up to" 5,000 Blacks in the Continental Army versus "nearly" 15,000 on the other side).

24. Buskirk, "Crossing the Lines," 76–82.

25. Thomas Jones, *History of New York during the Revolutionary War* (New York: New-York Historical Society, 1879 repr.), 2:76. Another count estimated the total of recently arrived Blacks for Manhattan in 1779 at 1,200. Egerton, *Death or Liberty*, 89.

26. Cassandra Pybus, *Epic Journeys of Freedom: Runaway Slaves of the American Revolution and Their Global Quest for Liberty* (Boston: Beacon Press, 2006), 26–27.

27. For example, in 1779, the British commandant of New York ordered, "All Negroes that fly from the Enemy's Country are Free—No person whatever can claim a Right to them—Whoever sells them shall be prosecuted." Daniel Jones, "Order relative to Refugee Negroes," June 7, 1779, quoted in Buskirk, "Crossing the Lines," 84.

28. Henry Clinton, "Proclamation," *Royal Gazette* [New York], July 3, 1779, 3.

29. Quarles, *Negro in American Revolution*, 142–46. In the assault on Savannah, for example, a local Black guide named Quamino Dolly conducted British troops through a wooded swamp to a position behind the patriot lines. Silvia R. Frey, *Water from the Rock: Black Resistance in a Revolutionary Age* (Princeton: Princeton Univ. Press, 1991), 84.

30. Henry Clinton to Lord Cornwallis, May 20, 1789, quoted in Quarles, *Negro in American Revolution*, 138.

31. Henry Clinton, "Memorandum for the Commandant at Charlestown and General Earl Cornwallis," June 3, 1789, quoted in ibid., 138.

32. John André, "Suggestions for gaining dominion over the American Colonies," [1780], quoted in Pybus, *Epic Journeys*, 40.

33. Quarles, *Negro in American Revolution*, 138 (report of John Cruden, commissioner for the seizure, care, and management of all estates and property sequestered by the British in South Carolina).

34. E.g., Alexander Hamilton to Elias Dayton, July 7, 1777, PAH, 1:283–84 (ordering a recaptured enslaved Black serving with the British returned to his patriot owner).

35. Quarles, *Negro in American Revolution*, 106–10, 185.

36. John Laurens to Henry Laurens, Jan. 14, 1778, PHL, 12:305.

37. Henry Laurens to John Laurens, Jan. 28, 1778, PHL, 12:368. Six days earlier, when first reading his son's letter of January 14, the elder Laurens replied, "More time will be required for me to consider the propriety of your scheme for raising a black Regiment, than you seem to have taken for concerting the project— there is nothing reasonable, which you can ask & I refuse— I will not refuse this, if after mature deliberation you will say it reasonable." Henry Laurens to John Laurens, Jan. 22, 1778, PHL, 12:328.

38. George Washington to John Rutledge, Mar. 15, 1779, PGW-RWS, 19:493.

39. John Laurens to Henry Laurens, Feb. 17, 1779, PHL, 15:60.

40. Alexander Hamilton to John Jay, Mar. 14, 1779, PAH, 2:18. Although his father was one of the largest slaveholders in New York and he owned some enslaved servants himself, John Jay had favored adding a provision to the 1777 state constitution for gradually abolished slavery in New York and later cofounded the New York State Society for Promoting the Manumission of Slaves. John Jay to Robert R. Livingston and Gouverneur Morris, Apr. 29, 1777, in Elizabeth M. Nuxoll, ed., *The Selected Papers of John Jay, 1760–1779* (Charlottesville: Univ. of Virginia Press, 2010), 1:412.

41. "Thursday, March 18, 1779," JCC, 13:336.

42. Henry Laurens, "Draft Committee Report," Mar. 25, 1779, LDC, 12:247.

43. "Report of the Committee on the Circumstances of the Southern States, and the Ways and Means for their Safety and Defense," JCC, 13:386.

44. "Resolved," Mar. 29, 1779, JCC, 13:387–88. Under its proposal, Congress would pay the expense of clothing and feeding the Black troops.

45. George Washington to Henry Laurens, Mar. 20, 1779, PGW-RWS, 19:542.

46. See John Collins to William Greene, Mar. 30, 1779, LDC, 12:263 (placing date of passage on the previous Saturday, March 27, 1779).

47. William Whipple to Josiah Bartlett, Mar. 28, 1779, LDC, 12:258. As fellow delegates from New Hampshire in 1776, Whipple and Bartlett voted for American independence and signed the Declaration of Independence.

48. Among the ten others in Washington's small boat, Leutze portrays the Quaker general Nathanial Greene, the future president James Monroe, two persons dressed as farmers, and a solder in Scottish apparel. It was a historical painting meant to represent symbolically rather than to depict accurately a turning point in the American Revolution.

49. John Laurens later expressed his belief about Georgia that the proposal would "be outvoted there with as much disparity as" in South Carolina. John Laurens to George Washington, May 19, 1782, PGW-RWS, --: --- (online access at founders. archives.gov).

50. John Laurens to South Carolina Council, [May 1779], *Catalogue of Autograph Letters and Manuscripts* (New York: Dodd, Mead, 1905), 33.

51. The proposal "was heard in anger and rejected" by the Privy Council. See *Catalogue of Autograph Letters and Manuscripts*, 33. One legislator present reported that the proposal received "about twelve votes" out of about seventy-two in the South Carolina House of Representatives and "was received with horror by the planters." David Ramsey to William Henry Drayton, Sept. 1, 1779, in R. W. Gibbes, ed., *Documentary History of the American Revolution* (New York: Appleton, 1857), 121.

52. Christopher Gadsden to Samuel Adams, July 6, 1779, in Richard Welsh, ed., *The Writings of Christopher Gadsden, 1746-1805* (Columbia: Univ. of South Carolina Press, 1966), 166.

53. Laurens to Washington, May 19, 1782, PGW-RWS, --: --- (online access at founders.archives.gov).

54. "Tuesday the 5th," Feb. 5, 1782, A. S. Salley Jr., ed., *Journal of the House of Representatives of South Carolina: January 8, 1782-February 26, 1782* (Columbia: State Company, 1916), 56.

55. Nathanial Greene to George Washington, Mar. 9, 1782, PGW-RWS, --: --- (online access at founders.archives.gov).

56. Nero Brewster et al., "State of New Hampshire," Nov. 12, 1779, in Isaac W. Hammond, "Slavery in New Hampshire," *Magazine of American History with Notes and Queries* 21 (1889): 63-64.

57. New Hampshire House of Representatives, "Daily Journal," June 9, 1780, in ibid., 21:64.

58. Compare "Constitution of New Hampshire—1776," in Francis Newton Thorpe, ed., *The Federal and State Constitutions, Colonial Charters, and Other Organic Laws of the States, Territories, and Colonies Now or Heretofore Forming the United States of America* (Washington, DC: Government Printing Office, 1909), 4:2451-53, with

"Constitution of New Hampshire—1784," pt. I, art. I, in ibid., 4:2453 ("All men are born equally free and independent").

59.   Prime and Prince, "To the Honbl General assembly of the State of Connecticut," May 11, 1779.

60.   "The petition of Pomp," Oct. 20, 1779, reprinted in Herbert Aptheker, ed., *A Documentary History of the Negro People of the United States* (New York: Citadel, 1951), 13.

61.   Charles J. Hoardly, ed., *The Public Records of the State of Connecticut* (Hartford: Case, Lockwood, 1785), 2:427–28. The Connecticut legislature likely received other freedom petitions in 1779. See Quarles, *Negro in American Revolution*, 44. One such petition apparently submitted to the governor in 1780 may have never reached the legislature. See Vincent J. Rosivach, "Three Petitions by Connecticut Negroes for the Abolition of Slavery in Connecticut," *Connecticut Review* 17 (1995): 79–92.

62.   Compare "The Rejected Constitution of 1778," art. V, in Oscar Handlin and Mary Handlin, eds., *The Popular Sources of Political Authority: Documents on the Massachusetts Constitution of 1780* (Cambridge: Harvard Univ. Press, 1966), 192–93, with "The Constitution of 1780," pt. 2, ch. I, sec. III, art. IV, in ibid., 445 ("Every male person, being twenty-one years of age . . .").

63.   "Constitution of 1780," pt. 1, art. 1, in ibid., 442.

64.   All the returns, including votes and comments on various articles, appear in ibid., 475–930. The town of Hardwick, for example, approved the Declaration of Rights but proposed amending the opening affirmation to read, "All men, whites and blacks, are born free and equal." "Hardwick," in ibid., 830. The 1780 constitution received enough votes in the first returns for ratification without amendment.

65.   "Constitution of Pennsylvania—1776," Declaration of Rights, art. I, in Thorpe, *Federal and State Constitutions*, 5:3082 ("all men are born equally free and independent").

66.   E.g., "Constitution of North Carolina—1776," Declaration of Rights, arts. VIII–XIII, in ibid., 5:2787–88 (for example, Article XIII provides that "every freeman, restrained of his liberty, is entitled to a remedy").

67.   Edmund Randolph, *History of Virginia* (Charlottesville: Univ. of Virginia Press, 1970), 252. "The Constitution of Virginia—1776," Bill of Rights, sec. 1, in Thorpe, *Federal and State Constitutions*, 7:3613 (as adopted, the opening section asserted, "That all men are by nature equally free and independent, and have certain inherent rights, of which, when they enter into a state of society, they cannot, by any compact, deprive or divest their posterity . . .").

68. At the time, commentators tied the legislation to the constitutional provision. E.g., "PHILADELPHIA in General Assembly, Feb. 10, 1780," *Pennsylvania Packet*, Feb. 17, 1780, 3 ("This act . . . flowing from the Constitution of Pennsylvania, which declares, 'that all men are born equally free' . . .").

69. "Council to Assembly," Nov. 7, 1778, in Samuel Hazard, ed., *Pennsylvania Archives*, ser. 1 (Philadelphia: Joseph Severns & Co., 1853), 7:79.

70. Ibid.

71. Joseph Reed, "In Council, February 5, 1779," *Journals of the House of Representatives of the Commonwealth of Pennsylvania* (Philadelphia: Dunlap, 1782), 1:307. On the history of this legislation, see Nash, *Forging Freedom*, 59–63.

72. "Friday, February 5, 1779, P.M.," *Journals of the House*, 1:304.

73. "PHILADELPHIA," *Pennsylvania Packet*, Mar. 4, 1779, 1 (text of Bryan's bill). For Bryan's central role in this process, see Gary B. Nash and Jean R. Soderlund, *Freedom by Degrees: Emancipation in Pennsylvania and Its Aftermath* (New York: Oxford Univ. Press, 1991), 100–105. For the legal restrictions on Blacks lifted by the legislation, see Edmund Raymond Turner, "The Abolition of Slavery in Pennsylvania," *Pennsylvania Journal of History and Biography* 38 (1912): 137.

74. "PHILADELPHIA," 1. In this version but not the final statute, the bill banned marriage or cohabitation "between a negro and a white," with the cohabitating white subject to a 100-pound fine and the Black subject to seven years servitude.

75. Compare "*A supposed* Preamble *of the proposed* Act *for the gradual* ABOLITION *of* SLAVERY," *Pennsylvania Journal*, Mar. 3, 1779, 3, with "Pennsylvania—An Act for the Gradual Abolition of Slavery, 1780," sec. 1, available online at avalon .law.yale.edu.

76. "PHILADELPHIA," *Pennsylvania Packet*, Dec. 23, 1779 (text of bill "Printed for consideration").

77. See "Wednesday, March 1, 1780, P.M.," *Journals of the House*, 1:435 (reporting on the House voting to dismiss a petition from Lancaster County "on account of its indecency").

78. "Tuesday, February 15, 1780, P.M.," *Journals of the House*, 1:424–25 (roll call vote 40 ayes to 18 nays for passage); "Wednesday, March 1, 1780, P.M.," ibid., 435 (roll call vote 34 ayes to 21 nays for engrossed bill). For a list of the counties each member represented, see "List of Members," Oct. 25, 1779, ibid., 390–91. Comparative census data does not exist for 1780 to show if slavery was more present in these rural counties than in other Pennsylvania counties, but the 1790 census shows little relative difference.

79. See Nash and Soderlund, *Freedom by Degrees*, 105–10.

80. "PHILADELPHIA in General Assembly, Feb. 10, 1780" and "TO BE SOLD," *Pennsylvania Packet*, Feb. 17, 1780, 3.

81. "TO BE SOLD," *Pennsylvania Packet*, Feb. 17, 1780, 4.

82. "To be sold," *Pennsylvania Evening Post*, Mar. 3, 1980, 26.

83. "Dissentient," Mar. 1, 1780, *Journals of the House*, 436.

84. Nash and Soderlund, *Freedom by Degrees*, 112–13. On petitions submitted by free Blacks opposing the extension, including one freed by his former owner's failure to register him, see Nash, *Forging Freedom*, 63–64.

85. John André, "Suggestions for gaining dominion over the American Colonies," [1780], Henry Clinton Papers, University of Michigan, quoted in Pybus, *Epic Journeys*, 40.

86. The law authorized distributions of "a healthy found negro, between the ages of ten and thirty years, or sixty pounds in gold or silver, at the option of the soldier," at the end of military service. *Acts Passed at a General Assembly Begun and Held in the Town of Richmond, on Monday the Sixteenth Day of October, in the Year of Our Lord, One Thousand Seven Hundred and Eighty* (Richmond: Dixon & Nicolson, [1781]), 8.

87. Pybus, *Epic Journeys*, 45–47.

88. Reverend James Madison to James Madison, Jan. 18, 1781, PJM, 2:293.

89. Joseph Jones to James Madison, Jan. 17, 1781, PJM, 2:289.

90. Thomas Jefferson to William Gordon, July 16, 1788, PTJ, 13:363–64. In his recent history of the war, Alan Taylor estimated the total for 1781 in Virginia at "4,000 runaways." Alan Taylor, *American Revolutions: A Continental History* (New York: W. W. Norton, 2016), 241.

91. Johann Ewald, *Diary of the American War: A Hessian Journal* (New Haven: Yale Univ. Press, 1979), 305.

92. Jefferson to Gordon, PTJ, 13:364 ("This I knew afterwards to have been the fate of 27. of them. I never had news of the remaining three, but presume they shared the same fate"). For the accurate count, see Pybus, *Epic Journeys*, 48.

93. Pybus, *Epic Journeys*, 53–54.

Chapter Seven: A House Dividing

1.   Nathaniel Wraxall, quoting Lord North, in Alan Taylor, *American Revolutions: A Continental History, 1750–1804* (New York: W. W. Norton, 2016), 296 (Wraxall was a Tory member of Parliament serving under North).

2.   William Bacon Stevens, *History of Georgia* (New York: Appleton, 1847), 2:289.
     See also Silvia R. Frey, *Water from the Rock: Black Resistance in a Revolutionary Age*
     (Princeton: Princeton Univ. Press, 1991), 174 (estimating the number of enslaved
     Blacks removed from Georgia at "four to six thousand").

3.   For various accounts of this evacuation, see Benjamin Quarles, *The Negro in
     the American Revolution* (Chapel Hill: Univ. of North Carolina Press, 1961), 163
     (incomplete British embarkation returns from Savannah list 1,568 Blacks to
     Jamaica and 1,956 Blacks to East Florida); Cassandra Pybus, *Epic Journeys of
     Freedom: Runaway Slaves of the American Revolution and Their Global Quest for Liberty* (Boston: Beacon, 2006), 58, 233–34 n. 4 (cites East Florida governor Patrick Tonyn as claiming that some 5,000 enslaved people went from Savannah to
     East Florida, but this seems too high); Gary B. Nash, *The Forgotten Fifth: African
     Americans in the Age of Revolution* (Cambridge: Harvard Univ. Press, 2006), 40
     ("about four thousand African Americans sailed away"). To little effect, the Georgia Assembly had petitioned the departing British commandant not to transport
     or carry off any "Negroes or other Property belonging" to American subjects and
     warned that doing so would "inflame, and irritate the good people of this State"
     against loyalists. *Journal of the House of Assembly*, "Resolved," July 4, 1782, in Allen
     D. Candler, *The Revolutionary Records of the State of Georgia* (Atlanta: Franklin-Turner, 1908), 3:121–22.

4.   *Journal of the House of Assembly*, "Resolved," July 15, 1782, in Candler, *Records of
     Georgia*, 3:127.

5.   Douglas R. Egerton, *Death or Liberty: African Americans and Revolutionary America* (Oxford: Oxford Univ. Press, 2009), 151; Darold D. Wax, "'New Negroes Are
     Always in Demand': The Slave Trade in Eighteenth-Century Georgia," *Georgia
     Historical Quarterly* 68 (1984): 215–16. Antebellum historian William Bacon Stevens estimated that "from three-fourths to seven-eighths" of the surviving Blacks
     "were carried off in the general embarkation." Stevens, *History of Georgia*, 2:289.

6.   "Evacuation of Charlestown," *Pennsylvania Packet*, Jan. 9, 1783, 3 (firsthand
     account from the loyalist *New-York Gazette*). The official return of people embarking during the final two days, after most ships had sailed for New York, recorded
     5,333 Blacks and 3,794 whites departing Charleston, with roughly nine out of ten in
     both groups destined for East Florida or Jamaica and all the Blacks likely enslaved.
     "The Centennial Address," in City of Charleston, *Yearbook—1883* (Charleston:
     News & Courier, 1883), 416.

7.   American general Nathanial Greene reported to Congress on the peaceful transfer
     of control. Nathanial Greene, "Evacuation of Charlestown," *[Boston] Independent*

Ledger, Jan. 27, 1783, 3 (noting the threat by British general Alexander Leslie that "an attack from us might lay the town in ashes, and that if they were permitted to embark without interruption, every care should be taken for its preservation").

8.　Loyalist judge Thomas Jones provided a lurid and likely exaggerated description of the plight of loyalists left behind in Charleston in his later published manuscript about the Revolutionary War. "No sooner had the evacuation taken place in Charlestown," he wrote, "than the rebels, like so many furies, or rather devils, entered the town, and a scene ensued, the very repetition of which is shocking to the ears of humanity." Thomas Jones, *History of New York during the Revolutionary War, and of the Leading Events in the Other Colonies at that Period* (New York: New-York Historical Society, 1879), 2:236.

9.　"Extract of a letter, dated Uxbridge, near Charlestown," *New-Jersey Gazette*, Dec. 18, 1782, 3.

10.　Greene, "Evacuation of Charlestown," 3.

11.　Alexander Leslie, quoted in Quarles, *Negro in American Revolution*, 165.

12.　"South Carolina Delegates Petition," quoted in Pybus, *Epic Journeys*, 59.

13.　Ibid., 58–60 (estimates evacuation at 7,000 to 8,000 Blacks with 15 percent going as free); Nash, *Forgotten Fifth*, 43 (estimates number of departing Blacks as "at least 10,000 and perhaps even 12,000"); Frey, *Water from the Rock*, 174–79 (while concluding that the actual count of enslaved Blacks leaving Charleston "lies beyond historical recovery," Frey gives "a reasoned guess of about ten thousand"); Quarles, *Negro in American Revolution*, 164–67 (reports only the official figure of 5,327).

14.　"Preliminary Articles of Peace," art. 7, in Hunter Miller, ed., *Treaties and Other International Acts of the United States of America* (Washington, DC: Government Printing Office, 1931), 2:99.

15.　Henry Laurens to S. C. Delegates, Dec. 16, 1782, PHL, 16:79–80 ("I urged and [sic] addition of the latter part of Article 7th prohibiting the carrying away Negroes"); Henry Laurens to Lewis Gervais, Dec. 14, 1782, PHL, 16:73–74 (suggesting the role played by "our dear friend Mr Oswald").

16.　Boston King, "Memoirs of the Life of Boston King, a Black Preacher," in *Unchained Voices: An Anthology of Black Authors in the English Speaking World of the Eighteenth Century*, ed. Vincent Carretta (Lexington: Univ. of Kentucky Press, 1996), 356.

17.　Guy Carleton, "Account of a Conference between Washington and Sir Guy Carleton," May 6, 1783, PGW-RWS, --: --- (online access at founders.archives. gov).

18. George Washington to Guy Carleton, May 6, 1783, PGW-RWS, --: --- (online access at founders.archives.gov). In a similar vein, Virginia congressional delegate James Madison complained to American ambassador in Paris Thomas Jefferson that Carleton's reading was "a palpable and scandalous misconstruction of the Treaty." James Madison to Thomas Jefferson, May 13, 1783, PTJ, 6:269.

19. George Washington to Daniel Parker, Apr. 28, 1783, PGW-RWS, --: --- (online access at founders.archives.gov).

20. Guy Carleton to George Washington, May 12, 1783, PGW-RWS, --: --- (online access at founders.archives.gov).

21. George Washington to Benjamin Harrison, May 7, 1783, PGW-RWS, --: --- (online access at founders.archives.gov).

22. "HARTFORD, *September* 15," *New-York Gazetteer*, Sept. 22, 1783, 3.

23. Brutus, "Messieurs TORIES," *New-York Gazetteer*, Oct. 27, 1783, 1.

24. Quarles estimated the total number of Blacks leaving New York at over 4,000 but his estimates are typically conservative. Quarles, *Negro in American Revolution*, 172.

25. King, "Memoirs," 356.

26. E.g., at one point, the Virginia slaveholder and patriot leader Richard Henry Lee complained to Washington about the British that, to get enslaved Blacks to follow them, "force, fraud, intrigue, theft, have all in turn been employed to delude these unhappy people, and to defraud their masters!" Richard Henry Lee to George Washington, Sept. 17, 1781, PGW-RWS, --: --- (online access at founders.archives. gov).

27. Ibid.

28. George Washington to Elias Boudinot, June 23, 1783, PGW-RWS, --: --- (online access at founders.archives.gov). For the commissioners' complaint to Washington about the process, see Egbert Benson et al. to Washington, Jan. 18, 1784, PGW-CfS, 1:50–52.

29. George Washington to John Jay, Sept. 27, 1785, PGW-RS, 3:285.

30. Judith Jackson Petition to Lord Dunmore, Sept. 18, 1783, Domestic Papers of the National Archives, United Kingdom, 30/55/81.

31. The other two were Harry Washington and a twenty-year-old woman named Deborah, all bound for resettlement in Nova Scotia.

32. Cassandra Pybus, "Jefferson's Faulty Math: The Question of Slave Defections in the American Revolution," *William and Mary Quarterly*, 3rd ser., 62 (2005): 264.

33. Tho. Randall et al., "To His Excellency GEORGE WASHINGTON," *Rivington's New-York Gazette*, Nov. 29, 1783, 2.

34. Among the best accounts of this effort, see Pybus, *Epic Journeys*, 139–55, 169–202; Frey, *Water from the Rock*, 194–98.

35. Zachary Macaulay, Jan. 5, 1797, Zachary Macaulay Papers, Huntington Library, San Marino, CA. A subsequent white governor of the Sierra Leone colony complained about the "republican frenzy" of the freed Black settlers from America and declared that they exhibited all that was "vile in the American." Thomas Perronet Thompson, quoted in Pybus, *Epic Journeys*, 205.

36. The timing of Sharp's honorary degree suggests that the college awarded it mainly for Sharp's role in sending freed Blacks back to Africa—an effort many white Virginians then supported. In his letter transmitting the honorary doctor of law degree to Sharp, William and Mary college president James Madison (a cousin of then member of Congress James Madison Jr.), mentions only Sharp's work to end the Atlantic slave trade and books about the slave trade that Sharp donated to the college. James Madison to Granville Sharp, June 21, 1791, ABOLITION AND EMANCIPATION PART 4: Granville Sharp Papers from Gloucestershire Record Office, reel 57, item 13/1/M2, Sterling Library, Yale University, New Haven, CT. Based on no historical evidence except inference, one article asserted that the college awarded this degree to Sharp because of his work as an abolitionist, but the author was not a historian and her article did not appear in a peer-reviewed journal. Terry L. Meyers, "Thinking about Slavery at the College of William and Mary," *William & Mary Bill Rights Journal* 21 (2013): 1215.

37. Compare Egerton, *Death or Liberty*, 220, with Pybus, *Epic Journeys*, 218.

38. John Neilson to George Washington, Dec. 6, 1783, PGW-RWS --: --- (online access at founders.archives.gov).

39. "In GENERAL ASSEMBLY, December 9, 1783," *Pennsylvania Packet*, Dec. 12, 1783, 3.

40. Wilmington Delaware Officials to George Washington, Dec. 16, 1783, George Washington Papers, ser. 3, Varick Transcripts, 1775–1785, subser. 3C, Civil Officials and Private Citizens, Letterbook 5: Jan. 12, 1783–April 10, 1785, MSS 44693: reel 005, Manuscripts Division, Library of Congress, Washington, DC.

41. "ANNAPOLIS (Maryland) Dec. 25," *Pennsylvania Journal*, Jan. 3, 1784, 2.

42. Ninety years later, the Confederate States of America, a racist union formed to preserve and protect Black chattel slavery, would put that same face at the center of its official seal.

43. Thomas Mifflin, ["Answer of the President"], Dec. 23, 1783, JCC, 25:838.

44. George Washington to the States, June 8, 1783, PGW-RWS, --: --- (online access at founders.archives.gov).

45. Ibid.

46. E.g., "George Washington to the Merchants of the City of Philadelphia, Dec. 9, 1783," *Pennsylvania Packet*, Dec. 12, 1783, 3 (repeating many of the main themes of his circular letter).

47. James Madison, June 30, 1787, Farrand, 1:486.

48. Responding to an abolitionist in 1795, Adams depicted slavery as "a subject to which I have never given any very particular attention." John Adams to Jeremy Belknap, Mar. 21, 1795, in PJA, --: --- (online access at founders.archives.gov).

49. James Otis, "The Rights of the British Colonies Asserted and Proved" (1764), in *Pamphlets of the American Revolution, 1750–1776*, ed. Bernard Bailyn (Cambridge: Harvard Univ. Press, 1965), 436.

50. John Adams to Jeremy Bentham, Mar. 21, 1795, PJA, --: --- (online access at founders.archives.gov). Of the thirty known freedom suits brought in Massachusetts by this time, the plaintiffs won twenty-nine of them. Emily Blanck, "Seventeen Eighty-Three: The Turning Point in the Law of Slavery and Freedom in Massachusetts," *New England Quarterly* 75 (2002): 27.

51. "The Body of Liberties, 1641," sec. 91, in William Whitmore, ed., *A Biographical Sketch of the Laws of the Massachusetts Colony from 1630 to 1686* (Boston: Rockwell and Churchill, 1890), 53.

52. "Constitution of 1780," pt. 1, art. 1, in Oscar Handlin and Mary Handlin, eds., *The Popular Sources of Political Authority: Documents on the Massachusetts Constitution of 1780* (Cambridge: Harvard Univ. Press, 1966), 442.

53. During the ratification process for the 1780 constitution, for example, the return for the town of Hardwick approved the Declaration of Rights but, by a vote of 68 ayes to 10 nays, proposed an amendment to make sure that it would not "be misconstrued hereafter, in a manner to exclude blacks" from the promise of being born free and equal. "Hardwick," in Handlin and Handlin, *Popular Sources*, 830.

54. Catharine Sedgwick, "Slavery in New England," *Bentley's Miscellany* 34 (1853): 421.

55. Blanck, "Seventeen Eighty-Three," 75:39 (discussing Sedgwick defense of the slaveholder in the similarly signal 1782 freedom suit of *Jennison v. Caldwell*).

56. William Cushing Papers, "Notes on Law Cases, 1783," Massachusetts Historical Society, microfilm reel 1, 98–99. Regarding the role of public opinion in effecting this change, Cushing told the jurors, "Whatever sentiments have formerly prevailed in this particular ... a different idea has taken place with the people of America, more favorable to the natural rights of mankind ... without regard to color, com-

plexion, or shape of noses." In his private notes, Cushing commented about his jury instructions, "By the foregoing Charge, Slavery in Massachusetts was forever abolished." For a published excerpt from Cushing's instructions, see "[Charge of the Chief Justice]," *Proceedings of the Massachusetts Historical Society* 13 (1874): 294.

57. George H. Moore, *Notes on the History of Slavery in Massachusetts* (New York: Appleton, 1866), 203, 215.

58. "Queries Respecting the Slavery and Emancipation of Negroes in Massachusetts, Proposed by the Hon. Judge Tucker of Virginia, and Answered by the Rev. Dr. Belknap," *Collections of the Massachusetts Historical Society*, ser. 1, 4:201, 203 (1835 reprint of 1795 publication). On the role of public opinion in ending slavery in Massachusetts, and a balanced assessment of other factors, see A. Leon Higginbotham, *In the Matter of Color: The Colonial Period* (New York: Oxford Univ. Press, 1978), 96–99; John Cushing, "The Cushing Court and the Abolition of Slavery in Massachusetts: More Notes on the 'Quork Walker Case,'" *American Journal of Legal History* 5 (1961): 474–75 ("when public opinion would no longer tolerate slavery it disappeared, and not before").

59. "Free Colored and Slave Population," in U.S. Bureau of the Census, *Negro Population, 1790–1915* (Washington, DC: Government Printing Office, 1918), 57.

60. Articles of Confederation, art. IV.

61. For a detailed analysis of this complex episode, see Blanck, "Seventeen Eighty-Three," 75:32–38.

62. William Cushing to John Hancock, Dec. 20, 1783, p. 2, The Morgan Library & Museum, MA 1235.

63. Ibid., p. 3; "In Council," Oct. 1, 1783, in Adele Stanton Edwards, ed., *Journals of the Privy Council, 1783–1789* (Columbia: Univ. of South Carolina Press, 1971), 82.

64. Emily Blanck, *Tyrannicide: Forging an American Law of Slavery in Revolutionary South Carolina and Massachusetts* (Athens: Univ. of Georgia Press, 2014), 145.

65. Michael J. Klarman, *The Framers' Coup: The Making of the United States Constitution* (New York: Oxford Univ. Press, 2016), 261. In 1783, Virginia also enacted a statute freeing those reenslaved by their masters after those masters presented them as *free persons* to serve in their place as part of the state militia during the war. The Virginia militia did not accept enslaved Blacks. Laws of Virginia, Oct. 1783 sess., chap. III, in William Waller Hening, ed., *The Statutes at Large* (Richmond: George Cochran, 1783), 11:308–9.

66. South Carolina's Privy Council declared that the failure of Massachusetts to restore "said Negroes" to their owners in South Carolina was "contrary to the Articles of Confederation." "In Council," 82.

67. Articles of Confederation, art. III.

68. Articles of Confederation, art. II.

69. Articles of Confederation, art. VIII.

70. "Art. III," Draft Articles of Confederation, July 12, 1776, JCC, 5:547.

71. Edward Rutledge to John Jay, June 29, 1776, LDC, 4:338.

72. Thomas Burke to Richard Caswell, Apr. 29, 1777, LDC, 6:672.

73. "AN ACT for reviving and amending several Acts and Ordinances of the General Assembly," 1783, reprinted in Thomas Cooper, ed., *The Statutes at Large of South Carolina* (Columbia: A.S. Johnston, 1838), 4:540.

74. "Art. XI," Draft Articles of Confederation, July 12, 1776, JCC, 5:548.

75. "Notes of Debates," July 30, 1776, JCC, 6:1079, 1099.

76. Samuel Chase, in ibid., 6:1099.

77. John Adams, in ibid.

78. James Wilson, in ibid., 6:1080, 1100–1101.

79. Thomas Lynch, in ibid., 6:1080.

80. Benjamin Franklin, in ibid.

81. Benjamin Harrison V, in ibid., 6:1100.

82. John Witherspoon, in ibid., 6:1101.

83. U.S. Congress, "Address to the States," Apr. 26, 1783, JCC, 24:281–82 ("On whatever side indeed this rule be surveyed, the execution of it must be attended with the most serious difficulties"): "Committee consisting of Mr. Dane, et al., report," Mar. 8, 1786, JCC, 30:102.

84. "Friday, March 28, 1783," JCC, 24:215 n. 1.

85. James Madison, "Notes on Debates," Mar. 29, 1783, PJM, 6:406–8; "Friday, March 28," JCC, 24:215.

86. "Resolved," Apr. 1, 1783, JCC, 24:223–24; "Resolved, by nine states," Apr. 18, 1783, JCC, 24:260–61; "Committee consisting of Dane report," JCC, 30:103, 107.

87. Commenting on states with large numbers of enslaved persons paying less per person to Congress than states with small numbers of enslaved persons, Jefferson commented in 1786, "slaves being of less value in a state than freemen, Congress made abatements." Thomas Jefferson, "Observations on Démeunier's Manuscript," June 22, 1786, PTJ, 10:35.

88. Articles of Confederation, art. V.

89. Compare "Art. XVIII," Draft Articles of Confederation, July 12, 1776, JCC, 5:551, with Articles of Confederation, art. IX (emphasis added). Dickinson had originally based quotas on the number of inhabitants "who are not slaves" but altered

this to "white Inhabitants" before submitting it to Congress, making this distinction purely racial rather than strictly about slavery. "Art. XVIII," JCC, 5:551.

90. "Resolved," Sept. 29, 1786, JCC, 31:703.

91. Michael J. Klarman, *The Framers' Coup: The Making of the United States Constitution* (New York: Oxford Univ. Press, 2016), 263.

92. "An Act to authorize," Mar. 1, 1784, JCC, 26:114 ("that the states so formed . . . having the same rights of sovereignty, freedom and independence, as the other states"). The "equal footing" language appeared in Jefferson's draft legislation implementing the cession. Thomas Jefferson, "Report of the Committee, 1 March 1784," PTJ, 6:603–5.

93. On Jefferson's beliefs regarding slavery harming enslavers and the enslaved, see Thomas Jefferson, *Notes on the State of Virginia* (Boston: Lilly & Wait, 1832), 169–70 (query 18).

94. For Jefferson's proposal, see Jefferson, "Report," PTJ: 6:603–4.

95. As contained in the final committee report, the provision stated, "5. That after the year 1800, of the Christian æra, there shall be neither slavery nor involuntary servitude in any of the said states, otherwise than in punishment of crimes whereof the party shall have been convicted to have been personally guilty." Thomas Jefferson, "IV. Revised Report of the Committee, 22 March 1784," PTJ, 6:609.

96. "Motion made by Spaight," Apr. 19, 1784, JCC, 26:247.

97. "On the question to agree," Apr. 22, 1784, JCC, 26:279.

98. "The report as amended," Apr. 22, 1784, JCC, 26:275 (emphasis added).

99. As it turned out, the Carolinas and Georgia ceded their western land to Congress, from which Congress carved the states of Tennessee, Alabama, and Mississippi. Virginia never ceded its western lands south of the Ohio River to Congress but permitted that region to apply directly to Congress for admission as the state of Kentucky. All four of these new states allowed slavery.

100. Thomas Pickering to Rufus King, Mar. 8, 1785, Rufus King Papers, New-York Historical Society.

101. "The Committee Resolve," Apr. 6, 1785, JCC, 28:239. Rufus's original proposal did not include the fugitive-slave provision. "Motion made by King," Mar. 16, 1785, JCC, 28:164.

102. "Motion made by King," Mar. 16, 1785, JCC, 28:165 (Virginia and the Carolinas opposed even considering King's measure, as did the lone delegate from Georgia; the Maryland delegation split 2–1 while all delegates from northern states supported considering it). For a discussion of this episode and the antislavery sentiments of both Pickering and King, see Robert Ernst, *Rufus King: American Federalist* (Chapel Hill: Univ. of North Carolina Press, 1968), 54–55.

103. "The Committee," Sept. 19, 1789, JCC, 31:669–73 (text of committee proposal); "Ordinance for the government of the Western Territory," May 10, 1787, JCC, 32:281–83 (text as submitted).

104. "An Ordinance for the government of the United States North West of the river Ohio," July 12, 1787, JCC, 32:343. Except for its Fugitive Slave Clause, this language (with its controversial exception for enslaving convicted criminals) became the model for the Thirteenth Amendment to the U.S. Constitution.

105. Nathan Dane to Rufus King, July 16, 1787, LDC, 24:358.

106. See, e.g., Peter S. Onuf, *The Origins of the Federal Republic: Jurisdictional Controversies in the United States, 1775–1787* (Philadelphia: Univ. of Pennsylvania Press, 1783), 169–71.

107. William Grayson to James Madison, Aug. 8, 1787, LDC, 24:393–94.

108. For more on this sale as reason for supporting the antislavery provision, see Paul Finkelman, "Slavery and the Northwest Ordinance: A Study in Ambiguity," *Journal of the Early Republic* 6 (1986): 351–53.

109. See, e.g., Staughton Lynd, "The Compromise of 1787," *Political Science Quarterly* 81 (1966): 225–50; Alfred W. Blumrosen et al., *Slave Nation: How Slavery United the Colonies & Sparked the American Revolution* (Naperville, IL: Sourcebooks, 2005), 188–92. For the case against this supposition, see Richard Beeman, *Plain, Honest Men: The Making of the American Constitution* (New York: Random House, 2009), 215–18.

110. Salmon P. Chase, *The Statutes of Ohio and of the Northwestern Territory* (Cincinnati: Corey & Fairbank, 1833), 1:18.

111. Ulrich Bonnell Phillips, *American Negro Slavery: A Survey of the Supply, Employment and Control of Negro Labor as Determined by the Plantation Regime* (New York: Appleton, 1918), 128.

112. The phrase comes from former president Thomas Jefferson, who used it in predicting that Congress excluding slavery in the territories as executed by the Missouri Compromise would become the death "knell of the Union." Thomas Jefferson to John Holmes, Apr. 22, 1820, PTJ-RS, 15:550.

Chapter Eight: The Compromised Convention

1. Benjamin Franklin to James Parker, Mar. 20, 1751, PBF, 4:119.

2. [Benjamin Franklin], "Philadelphia, May 9," *Pennsylvania Gazette*, May 9, 1754, 2.

3. "Albany Plan of Union," in Charles C. Tansill, ed., *Documents Illustrative of the Formation of the Union of the American States* (Washington, DC: Government Printing Office, 1927), House Document No. 398.

4. Believing that the British could only be defeated and liberty secured by a "united" effort, Franklin by this time consistently spoke in terms of "America" rather than of individual colonies. E.g., Benjamin Franklin to Thomas Life, June 5, 1775, PBF, 22:59 (regarding British military actions strictly against Massachusetts in 1775, Franklin wrote of "hostilities being commenced by General Gage against America").

5. Edward J. Larson, *Franklin & Washington: The Founding Partnership* (New York: HarperCollins, 2020), 39–42, 52–57.

6. "Minutes of the Conference between a Committee of Congress, Washington, and Representatives of the New England Colonies," Oct. 23, 1775, PBF, 22:237.

7. Benjamin Franklin, "Proposed Articles of Confederation," on or before July 21, 1775, art. III, PBF, 22:122–23.

8. Ibid., art. II, PBF, 22:122 (emphasis added).

9. Ibid., arts. VI, VII, PBF, 22:124.

10. Congress established both committees on the same day, June 11, 1776, with the membership of the committee charged with preparing the Articles of Confederation named on June 12. See "Resolved," June 11, 1776, JCC, 5:431; "Resolved," June 12, 1776, JCC, 5:433.

11. "Articles of confederation and perpetual union," art. III, July 12, 1776, JCC, 5:547 (Dickinson draft).

12. Ibid., art. XVII, JCC, 5:550.

13. John Adams, "Notes of Debates," July 30, 1776, JCC, 6:1079 (quotes Franklin as observing about giving one vote to each state in Congress, "a confederation upon such iniquitous principles will never last long"). See also Thomas Jefferson, "Notes of Debates," Aug. 1, 1776, JCC, 6:1102 ("Dr Franklin thought that the votes should be so proportionated [to the number of inhabitants] in all cases").

14. On Madison, e.g., see James Madison to Thomas Jefferson, Aug. 12, 1786, PTJ, 10:233. On Hamilton, e.g., see Alexander Hamilton to James Duane, Sept. 3, 1780, PAH, 2:401–6.

15. Annapolis Convention, "Address of the Annapolis Convention," Sept. 14, 1786, PAH, 3:689.

16. During the 1780s, the estimated number of enslaved Blacks in Pennsylvania fell by half from over 7,000 to under 4,000 while the number in Virginia rose by about 70,000 from roughly 220,000 to nearly 290,000.

17. James Madison made this point at the convention when he observed, "The States were divided into different interests . . . the most material of which resulted . . . principally from the effects of their having or not having slaves." Notes of James Madison (hereinafter "Madison"), June 30, 1787, Farrand, 1:486.

18. Among the early Philadelphia-area Quaker abolitionists that Franklin published were four of the most influential: Ralph Sandiford, Benjamin Lay, John Woolman, and Anthony Benezet. In 1772, speaking about their shared opposition to the slave trade, Benezet called Franklin "a real friend and fellow traveller on a dangerous and heavy road." Anthony Benezet to Benjamin Franklin, Apr. 27, 1772, PBF, 19:113.

19. E.g., Benjamin Franklin to Anthony Benezet, Feb. 10, 1773, PBF, 20:40–41 (expression of friendship and vow to "act in concert"); Benjamin Franklin to Deborah Franklin, June 10, 1758, PBF, 8:92 (discussing Lay's portrait, which Franklin's wife Deborah had acquired).

20. Benjamin Lay, *ALL SLAVE-KEEPERS That keep the Innocent in Bondage, APOS-TATES* (Philadelphia: B. Franklin, 1727), 40.

21. Benjamin Franklin, "A Conversation on Slavery," Jan. 26, 1770, PBF, 17:39.

22. Benjamin Franklin, "Thoughts on Privateering and the Sugar Islands: Two Essays," after July 1782, PBF, 37:619–20.

23. On the evolution of Franklin's views of slavery, see Gary B. Nash, "Franklin and Slavery," *Proceedings of the American Philosophical Society* 150 (2006): 618–35.

24. Tench Coxe to James Madison's notes, Mar. 31, 1790, PJM, 13:132 (in this letter, Coxe characterized the petition as "very strong" and the request to submit it "as an overzealous act of honest men").

25. Benjamin Franklin to Thomas Jefferson, Apr. 19, 1787, PTJ, 11:302.

26. E.g., George Washington to John Jay, Aug. 15, 1786, PGW-CfS, 4:213.

27. As the delegates assembled in May, Franklin called their work "A most important business" and expressed his "hope" that it "will be attended with Success." Benjamin Franklin to Richard Price, May 18, 1787, PBF, 45: --- (online access at franklinpapers.org).

28. Erasmus Darwin to Benjamin Franklin, May 29, 1787, PBF, 45: --- (online access at franklinpapers.org).

29. E.g., George Washington to James Madison, Nov. 5, 1786, PJM, 9:162; James Madison to George Washington, PJM, 9:382.

30. For the representation on May 25, 1787, see Journal, May 25, 1787, Farrand, 1:1–2. No more than eleven states were represented at the convention at any one time and sometimes as few as nine.

31. Journal, May 29, 1787, Farrand, 1:15.

32. Ibid., 1:16 (emphasis added), with text of the Virginia Plan following in Madison's notes, "Resolutions proposed by Mr Randolph," May 29, 1787, 1:20–22, and "The Virginia Plan or Randolph Resolutions," Farrand, 3:593–94 (noting correction).

33.   Journal, May 29, 1787, Farrand, 1:16, with text of Pinckney's Plan at Charles Pinckney, "The Draught of a Federal Government," Farrand, 3:604–9.

34.   James Madison to George Washington, Apr. 16, 1787, PJM, 9:383.

35.   James Madison made this point again at the convention when he observed, "The great division of interests in the U. States . . . lay between the Northern & Southern," which he tied "principally from the effects of their having or not having slaves." Madison's notes, June 30, 1787, Farrand, 1:486.

36.   Madison's notes, "Resolutions proposed by Mr. Randolph," res. 2, May 29, 1787, Farrand, 1:20 (emphasis added). For "quotas of contribution" as euphemism, see Sean Wilentz, *No Property in Man: Slavery and Antislavery at the Nation's Founding* (Cambridge: Harvard Univ. Press, 2018), 61.

37.   Madison's notes, "Resolutions," res. 5, 7, Farrand, 1:20–21; Pinckney, "Draught," arts. II, III, Farrand, 3:605–6 (Pinckney introduced the title of "President" for the chief executive).

38.   William Pierce, "Character Sketches of Delegates to the Federal Convention," Farrand, 3:96.

39.   Pinckney, "Draught," art. II, Farrand, 3:605.

40.   E.g., Richard Beeman, *Plain, Honest Men: The Making of the American Constitution* (New York: Random House, 2009), 154; Wilentz, *No Property*, 67–68. See also Michael J. Klarman, *The Framers' Coup: The Making of the United States Constitution* (New York: Oxford Univ. Press, 2016), 270 ("The proffered reason for counting only three-fifths of the slave for purposes of apportioning financial requisitions was that slave labor was less efficient than free labor . . . because slaves had 'no interest in their labor'").

41.   On Franklin, see Benjamin Franklin, *Observations concerning the Increase of Mankind*, [4th ed.], in Benjamin Franklin, *The Interest of Great Britain Considered* (London: William Bradford, 1760), 41 (by writing that "almost every slave being *from the nature of slavery* a thief," Franklin suggested that an enslaved worker was not as productive as a free one). Explaining why the Confederation Congress asked less of states with many enslaved persons than those with few, Jefferson noted in 1786, "slaves being of less value in a state than freemen, Congress made abatements." Thomas Jefferson, "Observations on Démeunier's Manuscript," June 22, 1786, PTJ, 10:35.

42.   Making the point that even according a fractional share of a free agent to an enslaved person lessened the status of free persons, the antislavery Massachusetts delegate Elbridge Gerry complained at the convention, "Freemen of Massts. not to be put upon a Footing with the Slaves of other States." William Paterson, June 11, 1787, Farrand, 1:208. Similarly, the Pennsylvania critic of slavery Gouverneur

Morris lectured the convention, "The people of Pena. would revolt at the idea of being put on a footing with slaves." Madison's notes, July 11, 1787, Farrand, 1:583.

43.   Madison's notes, May 30, 1787, Farrand, 1:36–38.

44.   Madison's notes, June 11, 1787, Farrand, 1:196.

45.   Journal, June 11, 1787, Farrand, 1:193.

46.   Ibid.

47.   Notes of Robert Yates, June 11, 1787, Farrand, 1:206.

48.   Ibid., at 1:205.

49.   See Beeman, *Honest Men*, 155; Wilentz, *No Property*, 291 n. 16.

50.   Madison's notes, June 11, 1787, Farrand, 1:201.

51.   At one point in these heated exchanges, Delaware's Gunning Bedford Jr. shot back against such threats, "The Large States dare not dissolve the confederation. If they do the small ones will find some foreign ally of more honor and good faith, who will take them by the hand and do them justice." Madison's notes, June 30, 1787, Farrand, 1:492.

52.   Madison's notes, July 28, 1787, Farrand, 1:452 (Franklin); Yates, June 18, 1787, Farrand, 1:580 (Hamilton).

53.   Madison's notes, June 30, 1787, Farrand, 1:486–87. Similarly, at the convention, South Carolina delegate Pierce Butler depicted the interests of northern and southern states "to be as different as the interests of Russia and Turkey." Ibid., Aug. 29, 1787, 2:451.

54.   Christopher Leslie Brown, "The Problems of Slavery," in *The Oxford Handbook of the American Revolution*, ed. Edward G. Gray and Jane Kamensky (New York: Oxford Univ. Press, 2013), 428.

55.   Madison's notes, July 2, 1787, Farrand, 1:511.

56.   Madison's notes, June 30, 1787, Farrand, 1:488.

57.   Benjamin Franklin to Pierre-Samuel du Pont de Nemours, June 9, 1788, PBF 45: --- (online access at franklinpapers.org). Regarding Franklin as a chess player, Jefferson recalled a time during a game Franklin played with the Duchess of Bourbon in France during the American Revolution, "Happening once to put her king into prise, the Doctr took it. 'ah, says she, we do not take kings so.' 'we do in America,' says the Doctor." Thomas Jefferson, "Anecdotes of Benjamin Franklin," Dec. 4, 1818, PTJ-RS, 13:463.

58.   Madison's notes, July 6, 1787, Farrand, 1:542.

59.   Madison's notes, July 11, 1787, Farrand, 1:580.

60.   Ibid., at 1:580.

61.   Ibid., at 1:581.

62. Ibid.

63. Madison's notes, July 9, 1787, Farrand, 1:561. Peterson added here that, through the three-fifths compromise, the Constitution should not give "an indirect encouragemt. of the slave trade." Ibid.

64. Madison's notes, July 11, 1787, Farrand, 1:587.

65. U.S. Constitution, Article I, Section 2.

66. Madison's notes, July 11, 1787, Farrand, 1:588.

67. Among those delegates piling on, Rufus King of Massachusetts noted about including Blacks in the rule of representation, "The admission of them along with Whites at all, would excite great discontents among the States having no slaves." Madison's notes, July 11, 1787, Farrand, 1:586. With only ten states represented at this point, six states voted against the three-fifths compromise including, along with most northern states, South Carolina, which still favored counting enslaved and free people equally. Journal, July 11, 1787, Farrand, 1:577.

68. Madison's notes, July 12, 1787, Farrand, 1:593. Remarkably, the actual language of the original census proposal then under consideration stated, "A census shall be taken of the free white inhabitants and 3/5ths of those of other descriptions," which on its face would lump free Blacks with enslaved ones. Madison's notes, July 11, 1787, Farrand, 1:579.

69. Ibid., 1:594.

70. Report of the Committee of Detail, art. VII, sec. 4, in Madison's notes, Aug. 6, 1787, Farrand, 2:183 (emphasis added).

71. Ibid., art. VII, sec. 6.

72. E.g., as approved the congressional committee charged with composing it, Jefferson's draft Declaration of Independence (like Jefferson's 1774 pamphlet, *A Summary View of the Rights of British America*) leveled this charge against the king. "III. Jefferson's "original Rough draught" of the Declaration of Independence, 11 June–4 July 1776," PTJ, 1:426.

73. Madison's notes, Aug. 21, 1787, Farrand, 2:364.

74. Ibid.

75. Brown, "Problems of Slavery," 431.

76. Madison's notes, Aug. 22, 1787, Farrand, 2:271 (Charles and C. C. Pinckney of South Carolina), 372 (Abraham Baldwin of Georgia), 373 (Rutledge of South Carolina and Hugh Williamson of North Carolina).

77. Madison's notes, Aug. 21, 1787, Farrand, 2:364.

78. Madison's notes, Aug. 22, 1787, Farrand, 2:372 (quoted passage by Wilson echoed by Dickinson).

79. Ibid., 2:370.

80. Madison's notes, Aug. 8, 1787, Farrand, 2:222 (spoken when the Committee of Detail released its draft).

81. Madison's notes, Aug. 21, 1787, Farrand, 2:364.

82. Madison's notes, Aug. 8, 1787, Farrand, 2:220.

83. Madison's notes, Aug. 21, 1787, Farrand, 2:364.

84. Madison's notes, Aug. 22, 1787, Farrand, 2:371.

85. Madison thought the two delegations had that "understanding." Madison's notes, Aug. 29, 1787, Farrand, 2:449 n. By this deal, delegates from Connecticut (and perhaps other northeastern states) did not vote to extend the Atlantic slave trade simply to keep states of the lower South in the union but also to gain support of those states on striking the two-thirds requirement for passing trade legislation. Paul Finkelman, "Slavery and the Constitution: Making a Covenant with Death," in *Beyond Confederation: Origins of the Constitution and American National Identity*, ed. Richard Beeman et al. (Chapel Hill: Univ. of North Carolina Press, 1987), 221. Some historians posit that this deal included New England and lower South delegates more broadly but even these historians typically see it starting with delegates from Connecticut and South Carolina or, more particularly, with Ellsworth and Rutledge. E.g., Wilentz, *No Property*, 74–75; Douglas R. Egerton, *Death or Liberty: African Americans and Revolutionary America* (Oxford: Oxford Univ. Press, 2009), 244. See also C. C. Pinckney, "The South Carolina General Assembly," Jan. 17, 1788, DHRC, 27:123 (discussing aspects of such an arrangement with delegates from New England).

86. Madison's notes, Aug. 22, 1787, Farrand, 2:371.

87. Ibid., 2:374.

88. Richard Dobbs Spaight, July 26, 1788, *Proceedings and Debates of the Convention of North-Carolina, Convened at Hillsborough* (Edenton, NC: Hodge & Wills, 1789), 122. See also James Iredell, July 26, 1788, ibid., 123–24 ("the states of Georgia and South-Carolina, had lost a great many slaves during the war, and they wished to supply the loss").

89. Madison's notes, Aug. 22, 1787, Farrand, 2:372. South Carolina's Rutledge promptly seconded Baldwin's point by saying that South Carolinians would never ratify the Constitution unless "their right to import slave be untouched," even though his colleague C. C. Pinckney later proposed and he accepted a twenty-year limit on that right. Ibid., 2:373.

90. Ibid., 2:371.

91. Ibid., 2:374.

92.   Madison's notes, Aug. 25, 1787, Farrand, 2:417. About this deadline, Madison predicted at the convention, "Twenty years will produce all the mischief that can be apprehended from the liberty to import slaves." Ibid., 2:415.

93.   Madison's notes, Aug. 22, 1787, Farrand, 2:373 (emphasis added).

94.   Beeman, *Honest Men*, 333.

95.   Madison's notes, Aug. 29, 1787, Farrand, 2:453–54.

96.   When the Privileges and Immunities Clause came up for a final vote at the convention, South Carolina's C. C. Pinckney objected that "some provision should be included in favor of property in slaves." Madison's notes, Aug. 28, 1787, Farrand, 2:443.

97.   Madison's notes, Aug. 28, 1787, Farrand, 2:443.

98.   See Wilentz, *No Property*, 103.

99.   See Beeman, *Honest Men*, 215–18. Further, coordination between the two bodies would have involved too many players for none of them to have claimed credit or left a paper trail.

100. In 1857, ruling the 1820 Missouri Compromise unconstitutional, the Supreme Court would hold that the federal government did not have the power to limit slavery in federal territories and, consequently, citizens could bring, keep, or sell enslaved people there. *Dred Scott v. Sandford*, 60 U.S. 373 (1857).

101. James Oakes, "Was Emancipation Constitutional?" *New York Review of Books* 64 (May 12, 2022): 533; Beeman, *Honest Men*, 330 ("The fugitive slave clause of the United States Constitution was not merely a provision that passively countenanced slavery").

102. C. C. Pinckney, "The South Carolina General Assembly," Jan. 17, 1788, DHRC 27:124.

103. "The Meeting in Framingham," *The Liberator*, July 7, 1854, 106 (first publication of Garrison's speech).

104. Madison's notes, June 27, 1787, Farrand, 1:441.

105. At the convention, two Connecticut delegates, Sherman and Ellsworth, suggested that slavery was dying out in America but both did so in the course of defending a constitutional provision extending the Atlantic slave trade, which they supported as part of a deal on trade matters with delegates from South Carolina. Hence, these comments can be discounted as self-serving. Historian Douglas Egerton called them "a rhetorical ploy." Egerton, *Death or Liberty*, 245. In any event, C. C. Pinckney promptly dismissed them by saying that he "did not think S. Carolina would stop her importations of slaves in any short time." Madison's notes, Aug.

22, 1787, Farrand, 2:373. In fact, the first ten years following the American Revolution brought the largest influx of Africans to the Americas of any decade in
history. Brown, "Problems of Slavery," 431.

106. U.S. Constitution, Preamble (quote).

107. E.g., in the 1856 *Dred Scott* decision, Chief Justice Roger Taney wrote for the court
that "the people of the United States," as used in the Constitution, did not include
American Blacks, "whether emancipated or not." *Dred Scott v. Sandford*, 60 U.S.
(19 How.) 393, 404–5 (1857).

108. Madison's notes, Aug. 22, 1787, Farrand, 2:374.

109. Pinckney, DHRC 27:124. Historian Don Fehrenbacher called this clause, "The
one unambiguously proslavery provision of the Constitution." Don E. Fehre-
bacher, *The Slaveholding Republic: An Account of the United States Government's
Relations to Slavery* (New York: Oxford Univ. Press, 2001), 44.

110. Madison's notes, July 9, 1787, Farrand, 1:561.

111. Madison's notes, Aug. 25, 1787, Farrand, 2:415 (emphasis added).

112. Ibid. In 1788, at the first North Carolina ratifying convention, slaveholding fed-
eralist and later U.S. Supreme Court Justice James Iredell commented about the
Constitution, "Though the word *slave* be not mentioned, this is the meaning of it.
The northern Delegates, owing to their particular scruples on the subject of slav-
ery, did not choose the word *slave* to be mentioned." James Iredell, July 29, 1788,
Convention of North-Carolina, 201. See also James Iredell, July 26, 1788, ibid., 124.
For an example of old Congresses not using the word "slave" in formal documents,
see "Resolved," Mar. 5, 1783, JCC, 24:173.

113. Luther Martin, "Genuine Information," Nov. 29, 1787, Farrand, 3:210. In a similarly blunt albeit less confrontational manner, Dickinson lectured the delegates
about not using the word "slaves" in the Constitution: "The omitting the Word
will be regarded as an Endeavour to conceal a principle of which we are ashamed."
John Dickinson, "Notes for a Speech," July 9, 1787, in *Supplement to Max Farrand's
The Records of the Federal Constitution of 1787*, ed. James H. Huston (New Haven:
Yale Univ. Press, 1987), 158.

114. Abraham Lincoln, Seventh Debate, Oct. 15, 1858, transcript available online from
the Lincoln Home National Historic Site website of the National Park Service
(noting "enthusiastic applause" for the statement).

115. For a wide-ranging discussion of this issue, see Sean Wilentz, *No Property in Man:
Slavery and Antislavery at the Nation's Founding* (Cambridge: Harvard Univ. Press,
2018).

116. Madison's notes, Sept. 17, 1787, Farrand, 2:642. Regarding the new government having power to do more than the prior one to advance or to retard slavery, see Fehrenbacher, *Slaveholding Republic*, 47.

117. U.S. Constitution, Preamble (quote).

Chapter Nine: "We, the States"

1. U. S. Constitution, Preamble.

2. Patrick Henry, "Virginia Convention Debates," June 4, 1788, DHRC, 9:930.

3. "In Convention," Sept. 7, 1787, Farrand, 2:665 (emphasis added).

4. U. S. Constitution, Article 7.

5. The 1790 census reported that 55 percent of the American people lived in just four states: Virginia, Massachusetts, Pennsylvania, and North Carolina. Either one of two other states, New York or Maryland, could replace North Carolina or Pennsylvania in this list and the combined population of the other nine would remain below 50 percent.

6. James Madison to Alexander Hamilton, [July 20, 1788], PJM, 11:189.

7. In 1776, New Jersey's first state constitution extended voting rights to "all inhabitants of this Colony, of full age, who are worth fifty pounds," which included women and Blacks so long as they owned sufficient property. "Constitution of New Jersey—1776," article IV, in Francis Newton Thorpe, ed., *The Federal and State Constitutions, Colonial Charters, and Other Organic Laws of the States, Territories, and Colonies Now or Heretofore Forming the United States of America* (Washington, DC: Government Printing Office, 1909), 5:2596. No married women could vote, however, because, under coverture laws, the husband owned all the property of a married couple. Blacks and all women lost the right to vote in New Jersey by 1807 state statute.

8. "In Convention," Farrand, 2:665.

9. "Assembly Proceedings," Sept. 17, 1787, DHRC, 2:58.

10. William Findley and Robert Whitehill, "Pennsylvania Assembly Debates," Sept. 28, 1787, DHRC, 2:71, 75.

11. Daniel Clymer, "Pennsylvania Assembly Debates," Sept. 28, 1787, DHRC, 2:76–77.

12. Ibid., in DHRC, 2:78.

13. George Clymer, "Pennsylvania Assembly Debates," DHRC, 2:73.

14. "Address of the Seceding Assemblymen," Sept. 29, 1787, DHRC, 2:116 (raising the lack of "any declaration of rights").

15. Daniel Clymer, "Pennsylvania Assembly Debates," DHRC, 2:78.

16. "Centinel I," *Independent Gazetteer*, Oct. 5, 1787, DHRC, 2:158–67 (quotes at 158–59, 162, 164).

17. Historian Pauline Maier called Wilson's speech "a landmark in the ratification debates." Pauline Maier, *Ratification: The People Debate the Constitution, 1787–1788* (New York: Simon & Schuster, 2010), 80. By the end of 1787, Wilson's speech appeared in thirty-four newspapers. "James Wilson: Speech at a Public Meeting in Philadelphia, 6 October," DHRC, 13:337–38, 344 n. 1.

18. E.g., William Findley, "Pennsylvania Convention Debates," Dec. 3, 1787, DHRC, 2:462.

19. E.g., "An Officer of the Late Continental Army," *Independent Gazetteer*, Nov. 6, 1787, DHRC, 2:212. At the state convention, James Wilson accused Findley and Whitehill of leveling this charge. James Wilson, "Pennsylvania Convention Debates," Dec. 4, 1787, DHRC, 2:499.

20. James Wilson, "Pennsylvania Convention Debates," Dec. 4, 1787, DHRC, 2:499. For a similar claim by Wilson from the prior day, see James Wilson, "Pennsylvania Convention Debates," Dec. 3, 1787, DHRC, 2:463.

21. Robert Whitehill, "Pennsylvania Convention Debates," Nov. 28, 1787, DHRC, 2:393.

22. James Wilson, "Pennsylvania Convention Debates," Nov. 26, 1787, DHRC, 2:365.

23. The Delaware convention ratified by a vote of 30 to 0 on December 7, 1787; the New Jersey convention ratified 38 to 0 on December 18, 1787; the Georgia convention ratified 26 to 0 on December 31, 1787. DHRC, 3:48, 130, 216.

24. McIntosh opened this paragraph of his letter by observing, "It is known to have been the intention of the Eastern and Northern States to abolish slavery altogether when in their power." Lachlan McIntosh to John Wereat, Dec. 17, 1787, DHRC, 3:260.

25. Elbridge Gerry to Massachusetts General Court, Oct. 18, 1787, DHRC, 4:98.

26. Significant opposition to ratification existed in Rhode Island, North Carolina, and New Hampshire as well but the union could go into effect without them—in fact, it did without Rhode Island and North Carolina.

27. "To the Honorable Richer Henry Lee, Esquire," *Connecticut Courant*, Dec. 24, 1787, DHRC, 3:508. Rather than also condemn him as a slaveholder, this essayist praised George Washington for his "brilliant virtues." Ibid.

28. "A Landholder VIII," *Connecticut Courant*, Dec. 10, 1787, DHRC, 3:506.

29. "A Landholder VI," *Connecticut Courant*, Dec. 10, 1787, DHRC, 3:490.

30. A Freeman, "To the People of Connecticut," *Connecticut Courant*, Dec. 31, 1787, DHRC, 3:519. The notably comprehensive DHRC project reported finding no

antifederalist writing containing such a statement. Ibid., 3:519 n. 1. Project editors attribute later essays by "A Freeman" in Pennsylvania to Tench Coxe, but not this one. Ibid., 15:453–54. For similar federalist arguments, see "A Landowner II," *Connecticut Courant*, Nov. 12, 1787, DHRC, 3:401; The Republican, "To the People," *Connecticut Courant*, Jan. 7, 1788, DHRC, 3:528.

31. Reflecting its standing in the corpus of American writing, this definition appeared in John Winthrop, "Speech to the General Court," in *The Norton Anthology of American Literature*, ed. Nina Baym, 5th ed. (New York: W. W. Norton, 1979), 2:233. Here, Winthrop contrasted "civil or federal liberty" with "natural liberty," which he defined as "a liberty to evil as well as to good." Ibid.

32. Samuel Huntington, "The Connecticut Convention," Jan. 9, 1788, DHRC, 3:555.

33. Oliver Wolcott, "The Connecticut Convention," Jan. 9, 1788, DHRC, 3:557. Both Huntington and Wolcott signed the Declaration of Independence, as did Gerry and Lee.

34. "The Connecticut Form of Ratification," Jan. 9, 1788, DHRC, 3:562.

35. Christopher Gore to Rufus King, Dec. 23, 1788, DHRC, 5:507; Christopher Gore to George Thatcher, Jan. 9, 1788, DHRC, 5:656.

36. E.g., the printed record has Abraham White, one of the convention's most vocal antifederalist members, stating at the end, "He had opposed the adoption of the Constitution, upon the idea that it would endanger the liberties of his country." Abraham White, "Massachusetts Convention Debates," Feb. 6, 1788, DHRC, 6:1487. Historian Pauline Maier concluded about the Massachusetts convention, "The opposition was based less on specific provisions in the Constitution than on a deep fear for the liberties of the people and a distrust of the men of property or education who supported ratification." Maier, *Ratification*, 187.

37. Amos Singletary, "Massachusetts Convention Debates," Jan. 21, 1788, DHRC, 6:1296. After the convention ratified the Constitution, Singletary stood out as one of the principal opponents not pledging to support the new government. Maier, *Ratification*, 211.

38. Amos Singletary, "Massachusetts Convention Debates," Jan. 25, 1788, DHRC, 6:1345–46.

39. Jonathan Smith, "Massachusetts Convention Debates," Jan. 25, 1788, DHRC, 6:1346–47.

40. Thomas Thatcher, "Massachusetts Convention Debates," Feb. 4, 1788, DHRC, 6:1418–19.

41. Isaac Backus, "Massachusetts Convention Debates," Feb. 4, 1788, DHRC, 6:1422. Several federalist delegates with religious credentials made similar

arguments. Daniel Shute, "Massachusetts Convention Debates," Jan. 31, 1788, DHRC, 6:1375; Phillips Payson, "Massachusetts Convention Debates," Jan. 31, 1788, DHRC, 6:1377.

42. Tristram Dalton to Stephen Harper, Jan. 31, 1788, DHRC, 7:1563.

43. Nathaniel Barrell, "Massachusetts Convention Debates," Feb. 5, 1788, DHRC, 6:1449.

44. John Hancock, "Massachusetts Convention Debates," Feb. 6, 1788, DHRC, 6:1475.

45. William Heath, "Massachusetts Convention Debates," Jan. 30, 1788, DHRC, 6:1371.

46. Samuel Thompson, "Massachusetts Convention Debates," Jan. 25, 1788, DHRC, 6:1354. A less authoritative account has Thompson saying, "If the southern States would not give up the right of slavery, we should not join with them." Samuel Thompson, in Theophilus Parsons, "Notes of the Convention Debates," Jan. 25, 1788, DHRC, 6:1356.

47. Francis Dana, "Massachusetts Convention Debates," Jan. 18, 1788, DHRC, 6:1242.

48. Thomas Dawes Jr., "Massachusetts Convention Debates," Jan. 18, 1788, DHRC, 6:1244.

49. U.S. Constitution, Article 1, Section 9, Clause 1.

50. William Lusk, "Massachusetts Convention Debates," Feb. 4, 1788, DHRC, 6:1421.

51. James Neal, "Massachusetts Convention Debates," Jan. 25, 1788, DHRC, 6:1354; James Neal, "Massachusetts Convention Debates," Jan. 31, 1788, DHRC, 6:1377.

52. Isaac Backus, "Massachusetts Convention Debates," Feb. 4, 1788, DHRC, 6:1422.

53. William Heath, "Massachusetts Convention Debates," Jan. 30, 1788, DHRC, 6:1371.

54. Listing the names of multiple speakers on each side, the convention's printed record noted, "Both sides depicted the slave-trade in the most pointed terms," and even those defending the twenty-year delay sought "the annihilation of this odious, abhorrent practice." "Massachusetts Convention Debates," Jan. 26, 1788, DHRC, 6:1358.

55. In December 1787, before he knew the official outcome from Georgia, Washington noted that the situation on the state's frontier "will, or at least ought to shew the people of it, the propriety of a strict union, and the necessity there is for a general government." George Washington to James Madison, Dec. 7, 1787, PGW-CfS, 5:478.

56.   George Washington to Henry Knox, Jan. 10, 1788, PGW-CfS, 6:28.

57.   Mercy Otis Warren, "Observations on the Constitution," Feb. 1788, DHRC, 16:287–88. In this pamphlet, Warren (like Washington) commented, "Georgia apprehensive of a war with the Savages, has acceded in order to insure protection." Ibid.

58.   Rawlins Lowndes, "South Carolina General Assembly," Jan. 16, 1788, DHRC, 27:108–9.

59.   David Ramsay to Benjamin Rush, Apr. 21, 1788, DHRC, 27:261.

60.   Charles Cotesworth Pinckney, "South Carolina General Assembly," Jan. 17, 1788, DHRC, 27:121, 124. The speaking notes for Pinckney's address contained bullet points about the Constitution: the more enslaved people "we import . . . the greater is our influence in *their* government by representation of 3/5ths"; "Security that our Slaves shall not be free"; and "Whenever our Slaves are found to be delivered up." Charles Cotesworth Pinckney, "Notes on Debates," Jan. 17, 1788, DHRC, 27:141 (emphasis added). On interpreting the three-fifths compromise as a victory for the South, see also Charles Cotesworth Pinckney, "South Carolina Convention Debates," May 14, 1788, DHRC, 27:337.

61.   Ibid., DHRC, 27:123. Similarly, Lowndes said, "Without negroes this state would degenerate into one of the most contemptible in the union." Rawlins Lowndes, "South Carolina General Assembly," Jan. 16, 1788, DHRC, 27:108.

62.   Charles Cotesworth Pinckney, "South Carolina General Assembly," Jan. 17, 1788, DHRC, 27:123. Expressing his view that twenty years supplied enough time for South Carolina to import its needed enslaved workers, Pinckney assured legislators, "While there remained one acre of swamp land uncleared in South Carolina, I would raise my voice against restricting the importation of negroes." Ibid. Regarding "the importations of the ensuing 20 years, added to the natural increase of those we already have" supplying "a sufficient number for cultivating all the lands in this state," see an essay published during the legislative debate by Pinckney ally David Ramsey. Civic, "To the Citizens of South Carolina," Feb. 4, 1788, DHRC, 27:217.

63.   Charles Pinckney, "South Carolina Convention Debates," May 14, 1788, DHRC, 27:324, 334–35.

64.   Charles Pinckney, "South Carolina Convention Debates," May 14, 1788, DHRC, 27:329.

65.   "South Carolina Form of Ratification," May 23, 1788, DHRC, 27:400.

66.   Charles Cotesworth Pinckney, "South Carolina General Assembly," Jan. 18, 1788, DHRC, 27:158.

67. The New Hampshire convention first met in February 1788, but subsequently adjourned until June. It reconvened after both the Virginia and the New York conventions began but concluded before either of them.

68. E.g., in a dispatch to Paris, St. Jean de Crèvecœur, then serving as the French counsel in New York, reported on this phenomenon in all three states, "Federalists & Antis (as they are called here) spare no means to have the choice of the people fall on the persons whose principles are similar to those of their parties." St. Jean de Crèvecœur to Comte de la Luzerne, May 16, 1788, DHRC, 9:585.

69. Ibid.

70. George Washington to James Madison, Feb. 9, 1788, PGW-CfS, 6:89 (Washington here added about ratification, "It is scarcely possible to form any decided opinion of the *general* sentiment of the people of this State, on this important subject").

71. George Washington to Thomas Johnson, Apr. 20, 1788, PGW-CfS, 6:218.

72. George Washington to James Madison, Jan. 10, 1788, PGW-CfS, 6:32.

73. Patrick Henry, "Virginia Convention Debates," June 4, 1788, DHRC, 9:929–30.

74. Hugh Blair Grigsby, *The History of the Virginia Federal Convention of 1788* (Richmond: Virginia Historical Society, 1890), 1:157, n. 142. Even in 1788, using the "n word" in a formal setting was shocking enough that contemporary publishers and printers of the debates did not report it. Delegates there did, and it appeared in this well-documented nineteenth-century account based on their recollections.

75. Patrick Henry, "Virginia Convention Debates," June 24, 1788, DHRC, 10:1476.

76. Patrick Henry, "Virginia Convention Debates," June 5, 1788, DHRC, 9:959.

77. Patrick Henry, "Virginia Convention Debates," June 24, 1788, DHRC, 10:1477. On this speech generally, see Robin L. Einhorn, "Patrick Henry's Case against the Constitution: The Structural Problem with Slavery," *Journal of the Early Republic* 22 (2002): 549–73.

78. George Mason, "Virginia Convention Debates," June 11, 1788, DHRC, 9:1161 (emphasis added).

79. For the amendments that Mason proposed at the Virginia convention and promoted for the New York convention, see George Mason to John Lamb, June 9, 1788, DHRC, 9:821. See generally Madison's Notes, Sept. 12, 1787, Farrand, 2:587–88.

80. James Madison, "Virginia Convention Debates," June 24, 1788, DHRC, 10:1503. At another point in the convention debates, Madison affirmed, "No power is given to the General Government to interpose with respect to the property in slaves

now held by the States." James Madison, "Virginia Convention Debates," June 17, 1788, DHRC, 10:1339.

81. Edmond Randolph, "Virginia Convention Debates," June 24, 1788, DHRC, 10:1484.

82. George Mason, "Virginia Convention Debates," June 17, 1788, DHRC, 10:1343.

83. James Madison, "Virginia Convention Debates," June 17, 1788, DHRC, 10:1343.

84. Patrick Henry, "Virginia Convention Debates," June 24, 1788, DHRC, 10:1504.

85. Edmund Randolph, "Virginia Convention Debates," June 6, 1788, DHRC, 9:973.

86. Ibid., 9:977–78.

87. Ibid., June 9, 1788, DHRC, 9:1085. To this, Randolph added the warning, "Our negroes are numerous, and daily becoming more so. When I reflect on their comparative number, and comparative condition, I am the more persuaded of the great fitness of becoming more formidable than ever" through union. Ibid., 9:1086.

88. James Madison, "Virginia Convention Debates," June 17, 1788, DHRC, 10:1339.

89. "Amendments to the Constitution," "Virginia Convention Debates," June 27, 1788, DHRC, 10:1553.

90. Madison and other federalists deplored these "recommendatory alterations," as Madison termed them in a letter reporting on them to Hamilton. James Madison to Alexander Hamilton, June 27, 1788, PJM, 11:181.

91. George Washington to Charles Cotesworth Pinckney, June 28, 1788, PGW-CS, 6:364.

92. At the time, the federalist chair of the state convention, Governor John Langdon, explained these maneuvers (and expressed his confidence in the outcome) in a letter to Massachusetts federalist Rufus King. John Langdon to Rufus King, Feb. 23, 1788, DHRC, 28:234. Both Langdon and King had served as delegates from their states to the Constitutional Convention.

93. George W. Nesmith to Joseph B. Walker, Aug. 25, 1888, DHRC, 28:193.

94. Joshua Atherton, "Convention Speech," ca. Feb. 18, 1788, DHRC, 28:208–9. See also "Anti-Federalist, No. I," *Exeter Freeman's Oracle*, Feb. 8, 1788, DHRC, 28:116.

95. See, e.g., Samuel Livermore and Samuel Langdon in *New Hampshire Spy*, June 21, 1788, DHRC, 28:371.

96. For a discussion of the politics of slavery and abolition in New York during the confederation period, see Arthur Zilversmit, *The First Emancipation: The Abolition of Slavery in the North* (Chicago: Univ. of Chicago Press, 1967), 146–52.

97. [Alexander Hamilton], "The Federalist. No. 1," *New York Independent Journal*, Oct. 27, 1787, DHRC, 19:145–46 (emphasis added).

98. [John Jay], "The Federalist 2," *New York Independent Journal*, Oct. 31, 1787, DHRC, 13:519 (emphasis added).

99. [James Madison], "The Federalist. No. 10," *New York Daily Advertiser*, Nov. 22, 1787, DHRC, 14:176.

100. [James Madison], "The Federalist. No. XLIV," *New York Independent Journal*, Jan. 26, 1788, DHRC, 15:479 (later renumbered 45) (emphasis added). See also [James Madison], "The Federalist. No. XXXVIII," *New York Independent Journal*, Jan. 16, 1788, DHRC, 15:484 (later renumbered 39) ("the proposed Government cannot be deemed a national one; since its jurisdiction extends to certain enumerated objects only, and leaves to the several States a residuary and inviolable sovereignty over all other objects").

101. [James Madison], "The Federalist 38," *New York Independent Journal*, Jan. 12, 1788, DHRC, 15:358; [James Madison], "The Federalist 42," *New York Packet*, Jan. 22, 1788, DHRC, 15:427 (first quote in both essays 38 and 42, second quote from essay 38).

102. Publius, "The Federalist 54," *New York Packet*, Feb. 12, 1788, DHRC, 16:108–9 (probably by Hamilton because he used this argument at the convention and it relied on New York state law of slavery). The author did not reference constitutional provisions for habeas corpus protection, which could have bolstered his argument.

103. Robert R. Livingston, "New York Convention Debates," June 19, 1788, DHRC, 22:1688.

104. John Lansing Jr., "New York Convention Debates," June 20, 1788, DHRC, 22:1709 (fear of "dissolution ought not to induce us to submit to any measure, which may involve in its consequences the loss of civil liberty"); Melancton Smith, "New York Convention Debates," June 20, 1788, DHRC, 22:1712 (objects to "sacrificing or even endangering our liberties to preserve the Union").

105. George Clinton to John Lamb, June 21, 1788, DHRC, 22:1798 (quote from a letter written at the outset of the state convention).

106. Melancton Smith, "New York Convention Debates," June 20, 1788, DHRC, 22:1715; "Extract of a letter," *New York Packet*, June 24, 1788, DHRC, 22:1742.

107. Alexander Hamilton, "New York Convention Debates," July 12, 1788, DHRC, 22:2195. Observers noted that here as elsewhere at the convention, Hamilton often repeated arguments from "The Federalist" essays. E.g., George Clinton to John Lamb, June 28, 1788, DHRC, 23:2357 ("the little Great Man employed in repeating over Parts of Publius to us").

108. See entries for "Fugitive Slave Clause," "Slave Trade," "Slavery," and "Three-Fifths Compromise" in "Cumulative Index," DHRC, 23:2644, 2775, 2790.

109. As the two-party national political structure emerged over the first quarter century under the Constitution, the Federalist Party twice nominated the proslavery southerner C. C. Pinckney for president, twice nominated the non-slaveholding

northerner John Adams for president, and once nominated the two of them on one ticket for president and vice president. During the same period, the Democratic-Republican Party consistently nominated non-slaveholding northerners for vice president (included the antislavery Elbridge Gerry in 1812) to run alongside the Virginia slaveholders Jefferson, Madison, and James Monroe for president.

Chapter Ten: "I Am Free"

1. "Diary entry," Apr. 16, 1789, DGW, 5:445.

2. For a representative newspaper account listing Thompson and Humphreys traveling with Washington without any mention of enslaved attendants, see "PHILADELPHIA, APRIL 29," *Freeman's Journal*, Apr. 29, 1787, 3.

3. Noting that "Washington's journey to his inauguration resembled a triumphal procession of royalty," biographer James Thomas Flexner commented, "the explosion of enthusiastic strangers into his presence seemed all that the most ardent Federalist could have desired." James Thomas Flexner, "The President's Progress," *American Heritage* 20 (June 1969): 73, 75.

4. For Philadelphia, see William Spohn Baker, *Washington After the Revolution* (Philadelphia: Lippincott, 1898), 124 (quoting from an account in the *Pennsylvania Gazette*, "The number of spectators who filled the doors, windows and streets, which he passed, was greater than on any other occasion we ever remember").

5. James McHenry et al., "ADDRESS to the PRESIDENT," *Pennsylvania Packet*, Apr. 28, 1789, 3 (emphasis added).

6. Further stressing the emphasis on liberty in a slaveholding state, an ode to Washington in the *Maryland Journal* hailed him as "sacred Freedom's delegated voice, / Thy grateful country's uncorrupted choice." "From the Maryland Journal, An Ode," *Pennsylvania Packet*, May 1, 1789, 3.

7. "Philadelphia, 22 April," *Federal Gazette*, Apr. 22, 1789, 2 (emphasis added).

8. From about 1,400 in 1767, the number of enslaved people in Philadelphia had dropped to under 700 in 1775 and about 200 in 1790. See Gary B. Nash, *Forging Freedom: The Formation of Philadelphia's Black Community, 1720–1840* (Cambridge: Harvard Univ. Press, 1988), 33; U.S. Bureau of the Census, *Heads of Families at the First Census of the United States Taken in the Year 1790: Pennsylvania* (Washington, DC: Government Printing Office, 1907), 10.

9. U.S. Bureau of the Census, *A Century of Population Growth from the First Census of the United States to the Twelfth, 1790–1900* (Washington, DC: Government Printing Office, 1909), 133 (population figures for free and enslaved population by state).

10. E.g., "Philadelphia, 22 April," 2 (describing Washington's horse as "elegant" while commenting about the carriage only that Washington ordered it "into the rear of the whole line").

11. "Philadelphia, 24 April," *Federal Gazette*, Apr. 24, 1789, 2.

12. William Martin, "To his Excellency, George Washington, Esq." Apr. 20, 1789, in Frank Monaghan, *Notes on the Inaugural Journey and Inaugural Ceremonies of George Washington* (New York: New York World's Fair, 1939), 25.

13. "Philadelphia, 21 April," *Federal Gazette*, Apr. 21, 1789, 3.

14. George Washington, "First Inaugural Address: Final Version," Apr. 30, 1789, PGW-PS, 2:176 (emphasis added).

15. Please "hasten her advancing towards New York," George Washington's secretary Tobias Lear had written about Martha Washington to George Augustine Washington at Mount Vernon on May 3. Tobias Lear to George Augustine Washington, May 3, 1789, PGW-PS, 2:248.

16. "Advertisement," *Philadelphia Gazette*, May 23, 1796, 3 (description of Judge in the advertisement offering a reward for her recapture; this newspaper was different from Benjamin Franklin's *Pennsylvania Gazette*, which no longer printed such notices).

17. George Washington to Oliver Wolcott Jr., Sept. 1, 1796, PGW-PS, 20:639.

18. For a discussion of this "cruel blow" for abolitionists, see Arthur Zilversmit, *The First Emancipation: The Abolition of Slavery in the North* (Chicago: Univ. of Chicago Press, 1967), 151.

19. In 1777 at New York's first constitutional convention, Jay supported a motion by Gouverneur Morris to add a provision providing for the eventual abolition of slavery in the state. See John Jay to Robert R. Livingston and Gouverneur Morris, Apr. 29, 1777, Elizabeth M. Nuxoll et al., eds., *The Selected Papers of John Jay, 1760–1779* (Charlottesville: Univ. of Virginia Press, 2010), 1:411. Quote from undated letter by John Jay in William Jay, *The Life of John Jay with Selections from his Correspondence* (New York: J & J Harper, 1833), 1:231.

20. National Museum of American History director Roger G. Kennedy calculated that "there was a 23 percent increase in the number of slaves and a 33 percent increase in slaveholding in New York City during the 1790s." Roger G. Kennedy, *Burr, Hamilton, and Jefferson: A Study in Character* (New York: Oxford Univ. Press, 2000), 92. New York County records report only 76 manumissions between the Society's founding and the passage of New York's gradual abolition bill in 1799—hardly an impressive number given the roughly 2,500 enslaved persons then living in the county. Indeed, many of the Society's members (including Jay, Robert Troup, Aaron Burr, and Alexander Hamilton)

owned enslaved domestic servants. The Society's most notable efforts included a school for free Black children and defending kidnapped free Blacks from reenslavement. Shane White, *Somewhat More Independent: The End of Slavery in New York City, 1770–1810* (Athens: Univ. of Georgia Press, 1991), 9–10, 28, 81–86.

21.   Benjamin Joseph Klebarner, "American Manumission Law and the Responsibility for Supporting Slaves," *Virginia Magazine of History and Biography* 63 (1955): 445 (partial list).

22.   North Carolina lodged this authority with county courts, but Virginia, Maryland, South Carolina, and Georgia required a special act of the legislature typically conditioned on a showing of meritorious service by those granted their freedom. See Klebarner, "Manumission Law," 443 (partial list).

23.   See ibid., 444 (partial list); Zilversmit, *First Emancipation*, 121–23, 150–53 (many of these laws excluded enslaved older persons and children presumably because of their inability to care for themselves).

24.   Annette Gordon-Reed, *Thomas Jefferson and Sally Hemings: An American Controversy* (Charlottesville: Univ. of Virginia Press, 1997), 195.

25.   U.S. Bureau of the Census, *Heads of Families at the First Census: New York* (Washington, DC: Government Printing Office, 1908), 9, 116–37. See also Shane White, "Slavery in New York State in the Early Republic," *Australasian Journal of American Studies* 14 (1995): 2–3.

26.   Alexander Coventry, quoted in White, "Slavery," 2.

27.   See White, *Somewhat More Independent*, 88.

28.   Ibid., 41–43 (quoting the visiting French noble, duc de La Rochefoucauld-Liancourt).

29.   U.S. Bureau of the Census, *Heads of Families: New York*, 9.

30.   William Strickland to John Robinson, Sept. 21, 1795, in William Strickland, *Journal of a Tour in the United States of America, 1794–1795* (New York: New-York Historical Society, 1971), 229.

31.   William Strickland, "A Journal and Notes," Sept. 25, 1794, in ibid., 63–64.

32.   Ibid., 65.

33.   See "Editorial Note," PJM, 12:121 ("Thus J[ames] M[adison] was in effect the 'prime minister,' the bridge between the executive and legislative, during this critical formative period of the federal government").

34.   "Address of the President to Congress," Apr. 30, 1789, PJM, 12:123 (with an editorial note stating, "There is good reason to believe that J[ames] M[adison] composed Washington's first inaugural address").

35.   At the Constitutional Convention, Madison joined two other Virginia delegates (Washington and John Blair) in voting against fellow Virginia delegates George

Mason and Edmund Randolph on a motion to add a bill of rights. See Madison's Notes, Sept. 12, 1787, Farrand, 2:588. In "The Federalist 48," Madison argued that bills of rights in state constitutions did little to restrain popular governments. [James Madison], "The Federalist, No. 47," *New-York Packet*, Feb. 1, 1788, DHRC, 16:4 ("parchment barriers against the encroaching spirit of power") (later renumbered as 48). At the Virginia ratifying convention, Madison added that governments with enumerated powers do not need bills of rights and any attempt to list rights might call into question those not listed. James Madison, "Virginia Convention Debates," June 24, 1788, DHRC, 10:1502.

36. E.g., James Madison to George Eve, Jan. 2, 1789, PJM, 11:404 (campaign letter for public distribution).

37. James Madison to Thomas Mann Randolph, Jan. 13, 1789, PJM, 11:416 (campaign letter for public distribution).

38. James Madison to A Resident of Spotsylvania County, [Jan. 27, 1789], PJM, 11:428 (campaign letter for public distribution).

39. Thomas Jefferson to James Madison, Dec. 20, 1787, PTJ, 12:440.

40. James Madison to Thomas Jefferson, Oct. 17, 1788, PTJ, 12:20.

41. Thomas Jefferson to James Madison, Mar. 15, 1789, PTJ, 14:661.

42. "Address of the President," PJM, 12:123.

43. James Madison, June 8, 1789, *Annals of Congress*, 1:450.

44. Ibid., 1:451.

45. During the congressional debate over the amendments, Madison stated, "I venture to say, that if we confine ourselves to an enumeration of simple, acknowledged principles, the ratification will meet with but little difficulty." Madison, Aug. 15, 1789, *Annals of Congress*, 1:766.

46. U.S. Constitution, Amendment I.

47. Madison, June 8, 1789, *Annals of Congress*, 1:451.

48. During the congressional debates over the amendments, Madison stated, "While I approve of these amendments, I should oppose the consideration at this time, of those that are likely to change the principles of the Government." Madison, Aug. 15, 1789, *Annals of Congress*, 1:775.

49. E.g., Pennsylvania federalist representative Lambert Cadwalader commented on Madison's proposal, "Tho of little or no Consequences it will calm the Turbulence of the Opposition, in Virga, & some of the other States, and certainly bring N. Carolina into the Union." Lambert Cadwalader to George Mitchell, in Helen E. Veit et al., eds., *Creating the Bill of Rights: The Documentary Record from the First Federal Congress* (Baltimore: Johns Hopkins Univ. Press, 1991), 268. Federalist representative George Clymer used the "tub to the whale" metaphor for the amendments in

one private letter and called them "bread pills power of paste & neutral mixtures" for imaginary illness in another. George Clymer to Richard Peters, June 8, 1789, and George Clymer to Tench Coxe, June 28, 1789, in ibid., 245, 255.

50. "Amendments to the Constitution," Sept. 24, 1789, *Annals of Congress*, 1:948. The Constitution does not give the president any official role in the amendment process and Congress never again sent proposed amendments to the president for forwarding to the states.

51. E.g., after the Senate passed the amendments, antifederalist senator Richard Henry Lee of Virginia wrote to Virginia antifederalist Patrick Henry about them, "As they came from the H. of R. they were very far short of the wishes of our Convention, but as they returned by the Senate they were certainly much weakened. . . . I am grieved to see that too many look at the Rights of the people as a Miser examines a Security to find a flaw in it!" Richard Henry Lee to Patrick Henry, Sept. 14, 1789, in Veit et al., *Creating the Bill of Rights*, 295. Nevertheless, Lee and Henry did not stand in the way of Virginia ratifying the amendments as the critical eleventh and final state in 1791.

52. William R. Davie to James Madison, June 10, 1789, PJM, 12:211.

53. William L. Smith to Edward Rutledge, Aug. 10, 1789, in Veit et al., *Creating the Bill of Rights*, 273.

54. Madison, June 8, 1789, *Annals of Congress*, 1:454.

55. E.g., Samuel Spencer, a leading spokesperson for antifederalists at the North Carolina convention, declared, "He expected the amendments would be adopted, and when they were, this state was ready to embrace it." Samuel Spencer, July 31, 1788, *Proceedings and Debates of the Convention of North-Carolina, Convened at Hillsborough* (Edenton, NC: Hodge & Wills, 1789), 256.

56. E.g., "We see plainly that men who come from New-England, are different from us," one delegate warned about government under the Constitution. "They do not know the state of our country: They cannot with safety legislate for us." Joseph Taylor, July 24, 1788, ibid., 44–45.

57. James Galloway, July 26, 1788, ibid., 124.

58. James Iredell, July 26, 1788, ibid., 124.

59. James Iredell, July 29, 1788, ibid., 201.

60. Samuel Spencer, July 28, 1788, ibid., 161; Samuel Spencer, July 29, 1788, ibid., 193. See also Timothy Bloodworth, July 29, 1788, ibid., 192–93 ("Without the most express restrictions, Congress may trample on your rights. Every possible precaution should be taken when we grant powers. Rulers are always disposed to abuse them").

61. James M'Dowall, July 30, 1788, ibid., 237.

62. Willie Jones, "Motion," Aug. 2, 1788, ibid., 279.

63. At the second convention, a failed motion for further amendments made by anti-federalist delegates conceded regarding the proposed amendments passed by Congress, "Said amendments embrace in some measure, when adopted, the object that this State had in view by a Bill of Rights, and many of the amendments proposed by the last Convention." "Journal of the Convention of N.C., 1789," Nov. 22, 1789, in Walter Clark, ed., *The State Records of North Carolina* (Goldsboro, NC: Nash Brothers, 1907), 22:45.

64. "LAUS DEO," *State Gazette of North Carolina*, Dec. 3, 1789, DHRC, 31:789.

65. "TWELFTH *PILLAR ADDED TO THE GRAND* FEDERAL TEMPLE," *Boston Independent Chronicle*, Dec. 17, 1789, DHRC, 31:799.

66. U.S. Constitution, Amendment I; An Act Declaring the Rights and Liberties of the Subject, 1698, 3 Wil. 3, sec. 1 (Eng.).

67. Granville Sharp to Pennsylvania Abolition Society, July 30, 1788, PBF, 47: --- (online access at franklinpapers.org) ("Upwards of an hundred petitions have been presented to Parliament, some soliciting, in unqualified terms, the Abolition of a traffic so disgraceful to humanity").

68. Pennsylvania Abolition Society to United States Congress, Feb. 3, 1789, PBF, 48: --- (online access at franklinpapers.org).

69. William Smith, Feb. 11, 1790, DHFFC, 12:288.

70. William Smith, Feb. 12, 1790, DHFFC, 12:297.

71. Aedanus Burke, Feb. 12, 1790, DHFFC, 12:296.

72. James Jackson, Feb. 12, 1790, DHFFC, 12:296. The following day, after declaring "that religion is not against" slavery, Jackson added that acting on the petitions was "likely to light up the flames of civil discord, for the people of the southern states will resist one tyranny as soon as another." James Jackson, Feb. 13, 1790, DHFFC, 12:308.

73. Thomas Tudor Tucker, Feb. 12, 1790, DHFFC, 12:306.

74. Michael Stone, Feb. 12, 1790, DHFFC, 12:300–301.

75. Aedanus Burke, Feb. 11, 1790, DHFFC, 12:286.

76. Roger Sherman, Feb. 12, 1790, DHFFC, 12:303.

77. E.g., Theodore Sedgwick, Feb. 11, 1790, DHFFC, 12:288; Joseph Parker, Feb. 11, 1790, DHFFC, 12:284; Joshua Seney, Feb. 12, 1790, DHFFC, 12:302.

78. Elbridge Gerry, Feb. 11–12, 1790, DHFFC, 12:289, 312.

79. E.g., on the second day of debate, Pennsylvania representative Thomas Scott deplored "this monstrous principle, that the conqueror is absolute master of his

conquest; that he may dispose of his property, and treat it as he pleases." Georgia's James Jackson immediately replied, "There never was a government on the face of the earth, but what permitted slavery: The purest sons of freedom in the Grecian republics, the citizens of Athens and Lacedaemon, all held slaves." Thomas Scott and James Jackson, Feb. 12, 1790, DHFFC, 12:307–8.

80. *Annals of Congress*, Feb. 12, 1790, 1:1246 (in particular, Madison said with respect to enslaved persons, that Congress might restrict "the introduction of them into the new States to be formed out of the Western Territory").

81. James Madison, Feb. 11–12, 1790, DHFFC, 12:289, 304.

82. "Report of the Special Committee," *Annals of Congress*, Mar. 23, 1790, 2:1524.

83. Thomas Tudor Tucker, "Motion," Mar. 16, 1790, DHFFC, 12:723.

84. James Jackson, Mar. 16, 1790, DHFFC, 12:719, 721, 732.

85. "Report of the Committee of the whole House," *Annals of Congress*, Mar. 23, 1790, 2:1524–25.

86. Ibid., 2:1523.

87. James Madison to James Monroe, Feb. 10, 1820, PJM-RS, 2:6–7 (called it "a very doubtful policy" and not clearly implied by the Ordinance of 1787).

88. This and the following paragraph borrow from Edward J. Larson, *Franklin & Washington: The Founding Partnership* (New York: HarperCollins, 2020), 256–57.

89. "The final decision" on the petitions, Washington wrote in a letter to his in-law and confidant David Stuart, "was as favourable as the proprietors of that species of property could well have expected considering the great dereliction to Slavery in a large part of this Union." George Washington to David Stuart, June 15, 1790, PGW-PS, 5:525.

90. George Washington to David Stuart, Mar. 28, 1790, PGW-PS, 5:286–88 (the bracketed word is unintelligible in the original—"likely" fits in context).

91. For an account of this episode, see "Extract of a Letter," *Providence Gazette*, Feb. 6, 1790, DHRC, 26:719.

92. Joseph Stanton Jr., "Rhode Island Convention (First Session) Debates," Mar. 3, 1790, DHRC, 26:923, 926 (quote).

93. Joseph Hazard, "Rhode Island Convention (First Session) Debates," Mar. 3, 1790, DHRC, 26:923.

94. Job Comstock, "Rhode Island Convention (First Session) Debates," Mar. 3, 1790, DHRC, 26:924.

95. William Barton, "Rhode Island Convention (First Session) Debates," Mar. 3, 1790, DHRC, 26:924–25 (emphasis added).

96. Rhode Island Convention (First Session), "Amendments to the Constitution of the United States," Mar. 6, 1790, DHRC, 26:981.

97. For examples of that intervening public debate, compare Spectator's federalist essay in the *Newport Herald* promising, "We may yet be respectable," with an antifederalist essay, No. III, in the same newspaper, warning that with ratification, "This flourishing country must dwindle to servitude." "Spectator," *Newport Herald*, Mar. 25, 1790, DHRC, 26:799; "No. III," *Newport Herald*, Apr. 1, 1790, DHRC, 26:803.

98. "Newport, May 29, 1790," *Newport Herald*, June 3, 1790, DHRC, 26:1028.

99. See George Hazard, "Rhode Island Convention (First Session) Debates," Mar. 3, 1790, DHRC, 26:926.

100. In its petition to Congress respecting the assumption of its war debts following ratification, the Rhode Island Assembly noted, "This State incurred a much larger debt than perhaps any of her sister states, in proportion to her estimated rate in the valuation of the United States." Rhode Island Assembly, "Memorial to Congress," in John W. Richmond, *Rhode Island Repudiation: or the History of the Revolutionary Debt of Rhode Island*, 2nd ed. (Providence: Sayles et al., 1855), 30.

101. The 1790 federal census reported 210 enslaved persons in Philadelphia, down from 442 listed in a 1779 census conducted by the city's constables. U.S. Bureau of the Census, *First Census: Pennsylvania*, 10; Nash, *Forging Freedom*, 58.

102. Benjamin Rush to Granville Sharp, Nov. 28, 1783, in John A. Woods, ed., "The Correspondence of Benjamin Rush and Granville Sharp, 1773–1809," *Journal of American Studies* 1 (1967): 20. Following his comment, Rush noted that the sentiment was peculiar to the local region, adding, "In South Carolina the *negromania* (for it is certainly a species of madness) still prevails."

103. Erica Armstrong Dunbar, *Never Caught: The Washingtons' Relentless Pursuit of Their Runaway Slave, Ona Judge* (New York: Atria, 2017), 57–58.

104. E.g., the first two independent Black churches in the United States—the African Church of Philadelphia (later named St. Thomas's African Episcopal Church) and Bethel Church (later Mother Bethel African Methodist Episcopal Church)—opened in Philadelphia during 1794. Seven years earlier, local free Blacks led by free Black ministers Richard Allen and Absalom Jones had formed Philadelphia's Free African Society, a quasi-religious benevolent mutual-aid organization—the first of its kind in America. Nash, *Forging Freedom*, 98, 112–33.

105. "Washington's Runaway Slave," *Liberator*, Aug. 22, 1845, 1 (first quote from an 1845 interview that initially appeared in the May 22, 1845, issue of the *Granite Freeman*); Benjamin Chase, "A Slave of George Washington," *Liberator*, Jan. 1, 1847, 3 (second quote, probably paraphrased from an 1847 interview of Judge).

106. Tobias Lear to George Washington, Apr. 5, 1791, PGW-PS, 8:67. Later commu-
    nications with Randolph clarified that the six-month rule applied to any nonres-
    ident, including the president, not exempted by law. Having become a citizen of
    Pennsylvania upon moving there so that he could practice law, Randolph did not
    enjoy the six-month grace period: his enslaved servants became free the moment
    he became a citizen of Pennsylvania. Tobias Lear to George Washington, Apr. 24,
    1791, PGW-PS, 8:131.

107. George Washington to Tobias Lear, Apr. 12, 1791, PGW-PS, 8:85.

108. Tobias Lear to George Washington, Apr. 24, 1791, PGW-PS, 8:131–32.

109. Martha Washington to Fanny Bassett Washington, Apr. 19, 1791, in Joseph E.
    Fields, ed., "Worthy Partner": The Papers of Martha Washington (Westport, CT:
    Greenwood, 1994), 230.

110. Chase, "Slave of Washington," 3.

111. "Runaway Slave," 1 (emphasis added).

112. Dunbar, Never Caught, 97.

113. "Runaway Slave," 1.

114. "Advertisement," 3.

115. "An act respecting fugitives from justice, and persons escaping from the service
    of their masters," Feb. 12, 1793, Annals of Congress, 3:1414–15 (text of statute). For
    an alleged abuse of these procedures, see the earliest known petition by Blacks to
    Congress. Jacob Nicholson et al., "To the President, Senate, and House of Repre-
    sentatives," Jan. 30, 1797, Annals of Congress, 6:2015–18.

116. George Washington to Oliver Wolcott Jr., PGW-PS, 20:639–40 (directing Wol-
    cott to have the customs collector "seize [Judge], and put her on board a Vessel
    bound immediately to [Philadelphia], or to Alexandria"). George Washington
    to Joseph Whipple, Nov. 28, 1796, PGW-PS, 21: --- (online access at founders.
    archives.gov) (asking that, if Judge will not return without "compulsory means to
    effect it, . . . you would oblige me, by pursuing such means as are proper, to put her
    on board a Vessel bound either to Alexandria or the Federal City"). Washington
    makes no mention in either letter of using the formal judicial processes prescribed
    by the Fugitive Slave Act and, in his letter to Whipple, wrote about the capture,
    "The less is said before hand, and the more celerity is used in the act of Shipping
    her, when an opportunity arises, the better. . . ." Ibid.

117. Joseph Whipple to George Washington, Dec. 22, 1796, PGW-PS, 21: --- (online
    access at founders.archives.gov) ("My mode of proceeding then, was adapted to
    my feelings . . . that a Servant . . . returning voluntarily of infinitely more value . . .
    than one taken forceably like a felon to punishment").

118. George Washington to Burwell Bassett Jr., Aug. 11, 1799, PGW-RS, 4:237–38.

119. "Runaway Slave," 1 (quote); Chase, "Slave of Washington," 3.

120. "Runaway Slave," 1.

Epilogue: Banneker's Answer

1.   Benjamin Banneker to Thomas Jefferson, Aug. 19, 1791, PTJ, 22:49.

2.   [Samuel Hopkins], *A Dialogue Concerning the Slavery of the Africans; Shewing it to be the Duty and Interest of the American Colonies to emancipate all their African Slaves* (Norwich, CT: Spooner, 1776), 34.

3.   E.g., *Personal Slavery Established, by the Suffrages of Custom and Right Reason* (Philadelphia: Dunlap, 1773), 19 (borrowing from Hume, this pamphlet stated, "There never was a civilized nation of any other complexion than *white*; nor ever any individual eminent either in action or speculation that was not rather inclining to the *fair*"). See also [Richard Nisbet], *Slavery Not Forbidden by Scripture* (Philadelphia: [John Sparhawk], 1773), 21–22 (quoting Hume).

4.   David Hume, "Of National Characters," in *Essays: Moral, Political and Literary,* ed. T. H. Greene and T. H. Grose (London: Longmans, 1889), 1:252 n. 1 (emphasis added).

5.   Commenting on a visit in 1773 to the Carolinas, Josiah Quincy II of Massachusetts noted in his diary, "The Africans are said to be inferior in point of sense and understanding, sentiment and feeling to Europeans and other white nations. Hence the one infer a right to enslave the other." "Journal of Josiah Quincy, Junior, 1773," in *Proceedings of the Massachusetts Historical Society*, 3rd ser., 49 (1916): 463. For an example of lumping Blacks with various primates as a single "species" of "Africans," see *Personal Slavery Established*, 19 ("I would yet subdivide the Africans into five *classes*, aranging them in the order as they approach nearest to reason, as 1st, Negroes, 2d, Ourang Outangs, 3d, Apes, 4th, Baboons, and 5th, Monkeys").

6.   Thomas Jefferson, *Notes on the State of Virginia* (Boston: Lilly & Wait, 1832), 146–50 (query 14). In a private letter to Jefferson, the Philadelphia-born South Carolina physician David Ramsay, who questioned slavery even as he kept enslaved servants, commented about this passage from *Notes on Virginia*, "You have depressed the negroes too low. I believe all mankind to be originally the same and only diversified by accidental circumstances." David Ramsay to Thomas Jefferson, May 3, 1786, PTJ, 9:441.

7.   [David Cooper], *A SERIOUS ADDRESS TO THE RULERS OF AMERICA, On the Inconsistency of their Conduct respecting SLAVERY* (Trenton: Isaac Collins, 1783), 12.

8.   Samuel Stanhope Smith, *Essay on the Causes of the Variety of Complexion and Figure in the Human Species, To Which Are Added Strictures* (Philadelphia: Robert Aitken,

1787), 12, 58, 74–75, 87, S-30. For more on Smith's essay, see Mark A. Noll, *Princeton and the Republic, 1768–1822* (Princeton: Princeton Univ. Press, 1989), 116–22; John C. Greene, *American Science in the Age of Jefferson* (Ames: Iowa State Univ. Press, 1984), 322–27; Nicholas Guyatt, "Samuel Stanhope Smith," *Princeton Alumni Review*, May 2016.

9. Jefferson, *Notes on the State of Virginia*, 147 (query 14). Jefferson had more regard for the published letters of the freed Black British shopkeeper Ignatius Sancho but still wrote, "His letters do more honor to the heart than the head." Ibid. For examples of abolitionist literature touting Wheatley, see [Benjamin Rush], *An Address to the Inhabitants of the British Settlements in America, upon Slave-Keeping* (Boston: Boyles, 1773), 2 n.; Thomas Cooper, *Letters on the Slave Trade* (Manchester: C. Wheeler, 1787), 30.

10. [Nisbet], *Slavery Not Forbidden*, 23 n.

11. Benjamin Rush, "At a meeting of the Pennsylvania Society for the abolition of slavery," Nov. 14, 1788, *American Museum* 5 (1789): 61–63.

12. Jefferson later expressed his private suspicions that Ellicott helped Banneker even with his calculations. Thomas Jefferson to Joel Barlow, Oct. 8, 1809, PTJ-RS, 1:588. Banneker's chief biographer concluded that, while Banneker received support from the Ellicotts in developing his mathematical skills, he personally prepared the ephemeris and initiated the idea of publishing it in an almanac while white abolitionists supplied the articles, introduction, and other materials in the published almanac. Silvio A. Bedini, *The Life of Benjamin Banneker* (Rancho Cordova, CA: Landmark, 1972), 144 (quote), 168–74.

13. [Editors' Introduction], *Benjamin Banneker's Pennsylvania, Delaware, Maryland, and Virginia Almanack and Ephemeris, For the Year of our Lord, 1792* (Baltimore: Goddard & Angell, [1791]), 2.

14. Jefferson, *Notes on the State of Virginia*, 68–69 (query 6).

15. David Rittenhouse to James Pemberton, Aug. 6, 1791, in the Library Company of Philadelphia, *Negro History, 1553–1903* (Philadelphia: Winchell, 1969), 70–71 (Pemberton then served as president of the Pennsylvania Abolition Society).

16. James McHenry to Messrs. Goddard and Angell, Aug. 20, 1791, in *Banneker's Almanack*, 3–4.

17. Benjamin Banneker to Thomas Jefferson, Aug. 19, 1791, PTJ, 22:49–50.

18. Ibid., PTJ, 22:50–51.

19. Ibid., PTJ, 22:51.

20. Thomas Jefferson to Benjamin Banneker, Aug. 30, 1791, PTJ, 22:98. Jefferson later commented privately about Banneker and his almanac as evidence of "the

grade of understanding of the negroes": "We know he had spherical trigonometry enough to make almanacs, but not without the suspicion of aid from Ellicot, who was his neighbor & friend." Thomas Jefferson to Joel Barlow, PTJ-RS, 1:588.

21. *Copy of a Letter from Benjamin Banneker to the Secretary of State, with his Answer* (Philadelphia: Daniel Lawrence, 1792).

22. For an antebellum restatement of the so-called scientific case for polygenism that included Jefferson's contributions but also that of over two dozen other authorities, see John Campbell, *Negro-mania: being an Examination of the Falsely Assumed Equality of the Races of Man* (Philadelphia: Campbell & Power, 1851).

23. Thomas Jefferson to John Holmes, Apr. 22, 1820, PTJ-RS, 15:550.

24. James Madison to James Monroe, Feb. 10, 1820, PJM-RS, 2:6–7.

25. Thomas Jefferson to John Holmes, PTJ-RS, 15:551.

26. James Madison to James Monroe, PJM-RS, 2:6.

27. "Speech of Hon. Abraham Lincoln, June 17, 1758," *Chicago Tribune*, June 19, 1758, 2.

28. *Dred Scott v. Sandford*, 60 U.S. (19 Howard) 393, 403, 407 (1857).

29. Alesander Keyssar, *The Right to Vote: The Contested History of Democracy in the United States* (New York: Basic Books, 2000), 349–54.

30. See Madison's notes, July 12, 1787, Farrand, 1:593 (Davie); Patrick Henry, "Virginia Convention Debates," June 24, 1788, DHRC, 10:1476–77; Thomas Tudor Tucker, Feb. 12, 1790, DHFFC, 12:306.

31. James Madison to Alexander Hamilton, [July 20, 1788], PJM, 11:189.

32. Abraham Lincoln, "Address at Gettysburg, Pennsylvania," Nov. 19, 1863, in *Lincoln's Selected Writings*, ed. David S. Reynolds (New York: W. W. Norton, 2015), 328 (phrasing from preferred Bliss copy of the address, one of five manuscript versions).

33. U.S. Constitution, Amendment 14, Section 1.

34. U.S. Constitution, Amendment 15, Section 1.

INDEX